MW00804764

Political Party Financing and Electoral Politics in Nigeria's Fourth Republic

African Governance, Development, and Leadership

Series Editor: Sabella O. Abidde, Alabama State University

Advisory Board: Getachew Metaferia, Georges Nzongola-Ntalaja, Adebayo Oyebade, Gloria Chuku, Gorden Moyo, and Olubukola Stella Adesina

The African Governance, Development, and Leadership series identifies and elaborates on the strategic place of governance, development, and leadership within African studies. Reflecting the fact that life in Africa continues to change; particularly in political, development, and socio-economic arenas; this series explores issues focusing on the ongoing mobilization for good governance, viable and impartial institutions, and the search for sustainable and economic development. Addressing gaps and larger needs in the developing scholarship on Africa and the African diaspora, this series publishes scholarly monographs and edited collections in the humanities, social science, and social scientific traditions.

Recent Titles

Political Party Financing and Electoral Politics in Nigeria's Fourth Republic

By Babayo Sule

LEXINGTON BOOKS
Lanham • Boulder • New York • London

Published by Lexington Books
An imprint of The Rowman & Littlefield Publishing Group, Inc.
4501 Forbes Boulevard, Suite 200, Lanham, Maryland 20706
www.rowman.com

86-90 Paul Street, London EC2A 4NE

British Library Cataloguing in Publication Information Available

Library of Congress Cataloging-in-Publication Data

Names: Sule, Babayo, author.
Title: Political party financing and electoral politics in Nigeria's Fourth Republic / by Babayo Sule.
Other titles: African governance, development, and leadership.
Description: Lanham : The Rowman & Littlefield Publishing Group, Inc., 2023. | Series: African governance, development, and leadership | Includes bibliographical references and index. | Summary: "This book provides a detailed analysis of the process of political party financing in Nigeria from 1999 to the present. Babayo Sule links the party financing process with the electoral process and explores issues of democratic accountability, transparency, and corruption in Nigeria under democratic rule"— Provided by publisher.
Identifiers: LCCN 2022054680 (print) | LCCN 2022054681 (ebook) | ISBN 9781666919219 (cloth) | ISBN 9781666919226 (epub)
Subjects: LCSH: Campaign funds—Nigeria. | Democracy—Nigeria. | Nigeria—Politics and government—1993-2007. | Nigeria—Politics and government—2007-
Classification: LCC JQ3099.A3 S85 2023 (print) | LCC JQ3099.A3 (ebook) | DDC 324.7809669—dc23/eng/20221110
LC record available at https://lccn.loc.gov/2022054680
LC ebook record available at https://lccn.loc.gov/2022054681

Contents

Acknowledgements

All praise and authority belong to Almighty Allah (SWT) for granting me the health, wisdom, time and the rare opportunity to write this little book as part of my contribution to the global community as a dedication to resolving one of the major tenets of global good governance and leadership of mankind for better. May His blessings and praises be upon His Messenger and his slave, Muhammad (PBUH).

My exceptional gratitude, appreciation, indebtedness and respect go to Professor Sabella Abidde of the Department of History and Political Science, Alabama State University, the Series Editor for this book. His resilience, guidance, support and critical evaluation of my proposal resulted in this work. My kind appreciation, regards, appreciation and loyalty go to Sydney Wedbush, my editing consultant whose timely response, kind observations, guidance, support and motivation propelled me to work tirelessly. He constantly keeps me on my toes with updates and incessant reminders amid his tight schedule without minding my sluggishness. But for his efforts, this work may not see the light of day. My appreciation goes to the reviewers whose critical and valuable inputs shaped and consolidated the work and the entire editorial and production team who worked indefatigably to make this book a reality. Special gratitude to Lexington, an imprint of Rowman & Littlefield, for honouring my work with acceptance and publication. The time, finance and all logistics expended in actualising this book are highly appreciated.

My unreserved gratitude and appreciation to my father Dr Hamza Sule Wurobokki, who has been constantly and tirelessly supporting me morally, financially and with everything that a superb father provides for his loyal son. I remain indebted, loyal and obedient. The same goes for my uncle, Alhaji Aminu Suleiman Wurobokki. I must express my indebted gratitude to my fathers Alhaji Ibrahim Zamfara and Dr Usman Sambo who stood by my side with their moral, financial and all kinds of support continuously. The entire Modibbo Wurobokki family is acknowledged and appreciated for cooperation, support and prayers.

My regards and exceptional appreciation, prayers, commitment and appreciation to my wives, Fatima Ibrahim Zamfara and Maryam Usman Sambo, who stood by my side in all circumstances and for their patience, perseverance, kind understanding and their support during my academic life journey and their sacrifices, especially, during the writing of this manuscript. I pray and seek for Almighty Allah (SWT)'s favour, guidance, blessings and protection for my beloved children Fatima Musa Ibrahim, Khadijatu Babayo Sule, Maimuna Musa Ibrahim, Rukayyatu Babayo Sule, Sulaiman Babayo Sule, Hamza Babayo Sule, Rumaisa'u (Ummu Sulaimin) Babayo Sule, Usman Babayo Sule and Aishatu Babayo Sule. May Allah bless, guide, protect, shower mercy and elevate you for the best of usefulness to mankind.

I must acknowledge and appreciate as well as extend my appreciation to my academic mentor Professor Habu Mohammed of the Department of Political Science, Bayero University Kano, my MSc supervisor who exposed me to the rigours of scientific research in Political Science and whose continuous advices are valuable in my entire life. And to Professor Dr Mohd Azizuddin Mohd Sani and Professor Madya Dr Bakri Bin Mat both of the School of International Studies, College of Law, Government and International Studies, Universiti Utara Malaysia who thoroughly and benignly exhibited patience in the painstaking process of guiding my PhD work. And for all those friends, families, teachers, mentors and guardians that space will not allow to be fully enlisted. I am grateful for your support and prayers. Stay blessed.

Figures and Tables

FIGURES

TABLES

Chapter 1

Introduction

Democracy is continuously being presented on a global platform as the best form of political organisation because it allows the people to have their will in determining who governs them. The principles of democracy in promoting individual liberty, economic freedom and political choice convinced most of the states globally to adopt it and it is the most popular governmental system in operation and practice worldwide (Dhal, 2019). The apologies of democracy agreed that despite its shortcomings and some tendencies for abusing peoples' mandate, it remains the best choice far from being challenged by other political systems because it is the only platform that promotes liberty, freedom and active participation in the governance process and it is in democratic practice that some guardrails including civil societies, media freedom, freedom of association and criticisms and vibrant opposition are supported and encouraged to enhance good governance (Diamond, 2019; Litt, 2020).

One of the fundamental tenets and processes of democracy is an election. An election is the only legitimate process of acquiring power in a democratic system. An election holds periodically with the primary goal of providing a mandate of legitimacy to the winner (Buttorff, 2019). An election enables the electorates or the governed to determine decisively who rules them, who shall continue to rule, the need and aspirations for change or continuation of an existing political leadership based on performance, failure or other influential reasons (Fredrickson, 2019). An election is a set of activities and processes in a cycle of repetitive rituals where especially in liberal democracies are operated. In an election, irrespective of the system of voting adopted be it secret ballot, direct open voting, delegated representation or Electoral College, voters are willingly and freely motivated to vote for candidates of their choice. The outcome of a legal electoral process determines who controls power (Aspinall & Berenschot, 2019). An election is associated and heralded with fanfares of campaign jamboree, manifesto and wooing voters to support candidates. This set of activities is carried out by political parties.

Political parties are the machinery for partisan contests and access to power in an electoral process. In essence, sound and ideological parties are considered major characteristics of a healthy democratic process (Woolley & Howard, 2018). Parties play vital roles in democratisation and electioneering process involving political mobilisation, leadership recruitment, ideological alternatives, capture and control of power, safeguarding the governed from excess and abuse of power through a constructive opposition engagement, political socialisation and community services (Gerbaudo, 2019). There is no room for securing legitimate power in a democracy without parties. Even the communist states that practise a one-party system still have a party platform to mobilise and contest (Scarrow & Webb, 2017; Poguntke, 2017). Parties compete in an election through a convincing manifesto and campaign promises that easily market the parties and their candidates. In the case of older parties, they rely on their legacies, performances and ideology to secure power (Webb & White, 2007) but this is different in the case of emerging democracies like Nigeria and other African countries where the parties are still fragile, devoid of ideological principles and seek power more than leadership and good governance (Abba & Babalola, 2017).

Political parties are vehicles for the electoral contests in any democracy which means all activities of the conduct of an election revolve around what parties decided to do or not to do (Sartori, 2005). Democracy is a political system that is expensive since financial backup is necessary. Candidates aspiring for elective political offices must cater for expenses that accrue in the process of the campaign (Gunther et al., 2002). However, democracies differ in this perspective. In some cases, parties and candidates are sponsored through public funding, particularly those that performed in general elections in form of a grant which is distributable by electoral management bodies of respective countries that practise public funding (Dalton et al., 2011). But most liberal democracies in the twenty-first century prefer and operate private funding. Irrespective of the type of funding process adopted, financing of parties and candidates in democracies is a requirement. This is because campaign expenditures in media adverts, logistics, transportation and accommodation and other related expenses are obligatory for any contender for a political office (Diamond & Gunther, 2001; Richard & Peter, 2018).

Political party financing is a subject of concern for policymakers and other stakeholders in elections and democracy because it reawakens the question of accountability and transparency. Rules and regulations are designed differently by various countries and regions to that effect but compelling compliance is proving to be difficult. Even the advanced democracies of the West such as America and England are not spared from money politics and excess spending in the party financing process (Piccio & Van Biezen, 2018). In the process of party financing, bribery, corruption, lack of full disclosure, excess spending and violation of regulations are obtainable across democracies worldwide as reported in a comprehensive study (Falguera et al., 2014). The phenomenon of corrupt practices in party financing and subversion of the democratic process through excessive money spending and other unethical practices such as rigging and authoritarian democracies led some scholars (Spengler, 2015; Brennan, 2016; Levitsky & Ziblatt, 2018; Runciman, 2018; Dhal, 2019; Diamond, 2019, Levitsky & Way, 2019; Lu & Chu, 2022) to postulate that democracy is dying, ending, in recession and retreat. This was earlier sensed by Plato (2005) and Aristotle (2015), the great Greek philosophers who believed that democracy, despite originating from the Greek city-states, might not be good as a political organisation because the few oligarchs may buy and bribe their way to power at the detriment of better qualified and competent candidates. This notwithstanding does not discourage the likes of Dhal (2019) and Diamond (2019) from arguing that democracy is still the best even with its shortcomings. The continuous changes and regulations may cater for the mistakes in their views.

Party financing is not conducted in a vacuum. There are regulations and guiding principles for spending during the electoral contests. But there is no universal law for countries or regions to adhere to. States establish their laws based on their unique environment, political culture and political system and changing pattern of the game. For instance, in Africa, it was reported (Smilow, 2014; Sule, 2021) that over-reliance on public funding, abuse of state resources, bribery and corruption, vote-buying, violence, excessive spending and violation of regulations are the major issues in party financing. In the case of Asia, funding shifted wholly to private funding and that becomes a source of worry because of corporate private funding and corruption in the process (Piccio & Ohman, 2014). In Latin America and the Caribbean, party financing is associated with corruption, money politics, scandals, criminal activities, irregularities and violation and subversion of the electoral process (Londono & Zovatto, 2014). In Europe, sound regulations exist but they are ineffective in enforcement. Excessive spending, corruption, the influence of money politics and irregularities marred the process in most European countries. America is not an exception when it comes to party financing in terms of corruption, influence of money politics and excessive spending (Howell, 2017). The process of party funding, therefore, calls for urgent policymaking at the individual state level and through regional cooperation to address the menace before democracy is fully surrendered to the highest bidder.

The emerging democracies are affected more by issues of party financing because they are trying to settle and establish new laws that will address the problem in an incremental process. One of the states that are suffering from this menace is Nigeria. Nigeria is an interesting area of study in the subject matter of party financing for many reasons. A study (Sule, 2021) of party financing in African states revealed that Nigeria has the most comprehensive and detailed laws on party financing in the continent but ineffective and weak monitoring and compliance remain the issue. The country adopted full private funding (Electoral Act as Amended 2022) while foreign donations are prohibited (Nigerian 1999 Constitution as Amended). The ban on foreign donation and private funding made the Nigerian party financing process in outlook advanced and similar to many European and American regulations. However, the failure of the electoral body, the Independent National Electoral Commission (INEC) to monitor and ensure compliance renders the laws weak and non-operative (Sule et al., 2017). Excessive spending, violation of regulations, bribery and corruption, vote-buying and money politics and lack of sanction are reported (Sule et al., 2022) as the major issues associated with regulations in party financing in Nigeria.

Nigeria attracts interest because of its pivotal position globally on many fronts. The territory known as Nigeria today emerged from the antecedents and vicissitudes of historical epochs in three stages: the pre-colonial, colonial and post-colonial periods. Before the advent of British colonialism, there was no single entity called Nigeria but rather a plethora of kingdoms, comity of chiefdoms, scattered societies in spatial geographical settings and migrants or wanderers, especially herders (Falola & Genova, 2009). These various independent but interdependent political bodies were neighbours. There was substantial evidence of intermarriage, trade, wars of rivalry and alliance among them (Campbell & Page, 2018). By the mid-nineteenth century, particularly in 1856, the British started to annex the Nigerian territory beginning with Lagos, a lagoon with direct access to the Atlantic Sea. This was not the first contact of the Nigerian territory with the West. Rodney (1972) and Ake (1981) posited that the British explorers and missionaries were in contact with the Nigerian territory as early as the fourteenth century through imperialism, slave trade, evangelism and tourism. However, the formal colonisation took over four centuries after the first contact. Nigeria's vast and diverse mineral resources and potential for market and labour attracted Britain (Campbell & Page, 2018).

The British colonial rule created Nigeria or rather, the current Nigerian state was the arbitrary and artificial creation of the British during colonialism. By 1890, the British succeeded in conquering the southern part of today's Nigeria and in 1902, the northern region was subdued. In 1914, the British colonial governor Sir Frederick Lord Lugard amalgamated the southern and northern protectorates and declared them Nigeria. From 1914, the Nigerian colony underwent several structural and physical political, economic and social changes later culminating in the formation of a federal state with three regions and the Colony of Lagos. Nigeria secured political independence peacefully from Britain in 1960 under the federal structure and a Westminster parliamentary system (Siollun, 2021).

Nigeria is one of the countries in the world that underwent deep waters of political and economic crises. Not long after winning the political independence, a bloody military coup smeared the political environment in the country. The three major ethnic groups of Igbo, Hausa/Fulani and Yoruba struggled for political freedom amid mutual hostility and politics of regionalism, ethnicity and religion (Agbu, 2016a). In post-independence, forging an acceptable political order and power-sharing formula became difficult with each of the major ethnic groups having the political identity of its region and ethnic group than national cohesion. The other ethnic groups (more than 400 in number) were not left behind in their quest for access to power and national resources. The 1966 bloody military coup by the Igbo army officers was instantly countered by the Hausa military officers causing a serious political turmoil that ended in civil war (1967–1970). In the aftermath of the civil war, states were created and later Local Government Reform took place in 1984. The state creation continued to give local autonomy to the voice of the minority and to devolve and decentralise power resulting in the thirty-six states in the Nigerian federation with the Federal Capital Territory Abuja (FCTA) as the administrative headquarters of the country (Siollun, 2021).

The attempts to restructure the Nigerian political system could not yield the desired and satisfactory results for the competing regions and ethnic groups. Military coups and counter-coups decimated the political system and stagnated the democratisation process. In less than forty years of political independence, Nigeria recorded three failed Republics or setbacks to democratisation (Falola & Genova, 2009). The elite's reckless attitude towards power and the fragile nature of the Nigerian political economy were attributed to the causes of these dilemmas. Nigeria is an interesting area of study in politics because it holds some strategic ranking in the global context of nation-states. The country is the sixth populous in the world with a population of an estimated 208 million based on the 2006 census and is projected by 2050 to be the third populous country in the world with a projected population of 500 million (Statista, 2022). Nigeria is the tenth largest oil-producing country in the world, the biggest Black nation on earth in which it is postulated that one out of every four Black people on earth is a Nigerian. The country is politically divided into seven geopolitical zones of Northeast, Northcentral, Northwest, Southeast, South-South and Southwest and FCTA with thirty-six states. There are 774 local government areas distributed across the states. Oil remains the main source of foreign exchange and source of foreign revenue (Campbell & Page, 2018).

Nigerian politics is characterised by primordial sentiments and primitive accumulation. The organised ruling elites utilised Nigeria's fragile social coexistence in consolidating themselves into power. They employ religion, ethnic and regional sentiments to secure support and votes to win elections. On assumption of power, the ruling elites concentrated on self-enrichment and personal accumulation to the detriment of the anticipated social services and infrastructure delivery. This made the Nigerian elections violent, irregular, war-like and far from a fair exercise (Collier, 2007). Political parties since the First Republic were formed on the platform of ethnic and regional affiliation (Diamond, 1995a). However, the Fourth Republic made an exceptional difference in the history of Nigerian democracy. Democracy is now enjoying twenty-three uninterrupted years of operation since 1999 and the parties in the Fourth Republic shifted gradually from ethnic and regional to the elites' version of power consolidation and control (Le Van, 2015). The Fourth Republic made an interesting period of study because the cumulative years of democratic experiment surpassed the entire experience of Nigerian democratic practice in the last forty years. The First Republic (1960–1966) lasted for only six years, the Second Republic (1979–1984) lasted for four years and the Aborted Third Republic (1990–1991) was abandoned as the process was ongoing after the Social Democratic Party (SDP) candidate, Chief MKO Abiola led the 12 June 1991 election that was annulled before the declaration of the winner (Usuanlele & Ibhawoh, 2017). But the Fourth Republic (1999–2022) remains steady for over twenty years which is unprecedented in Nigerian political history and democratic experience. The Fourth Republic has its hiccups and challenges that sometimes threatened to collapse it yet it surmounts the obstacles so far and it may be Nigeria's final strive for democratisation if the elite succeeded in careful guarding of their nonchalant attitude towards governance which is gradually collapsing democratic values and pushing people to despair.

The party politics and contests of Nigeria's Fourth Republic are constitutionally a multi-party system allowing for many parties to be registered from 1999 starting with Alliance for Democracy (AD), All Peoples Party (APP) and Peoples Democratic Party (PDP). Although more than 100 parties were registered officially by the INEC since 1999, the PDP went ahead to capture the power and consolidate itself in total control of almost all the elective positions in the country from the presidential to the gubernatorial, National Assembly and even local council elections (Agbu, 2016a). This dominance continued for sixteen years unchallenged until 2015 when the newly formed opposition All Progressives Congress (APC), a merger of mega opposition parties including Action Congress of Nigeria (ACN), All Nigeria Peoples Party (ANPP), a faction of All Progressives Grand Alliance (APGA), Congress for Progressive Change (CPC) later joined by newPDP that broke away from the ruling PDP in 2014 after a crisis in their national convention, defeated the incumbent PDP in the 2015 presidential election setting a historical record of the incumbent president unseated by an opposition party (Lukman, 2021).

Elections in Nigeria's Fourth Republic have always been accompanied by challenges that ridicule their credibility, integrity and acceptability. Although there are significant improvements in the process of electoral conduct, specifically from 2011, the 2015 and 2019 general elections are far from being fair or credible in the fullest sense of the terms (Burchard & Simati, 2019). The 2003 and 2007 general elections were rated by international observers as anything but war (Bratton, 2008; Onapajo, 2014). Political violence characterised the elections, godfathers sponsored thugs to terrorise and intimidate perceived opposition and threats against the victory of their anointed godsons. In some cases, political assassination resulted from the violence as in the case of Bola Ige and Harry Marshal, as well as other important political figures in the opposition and even the ruling party (Birch, 2020). Vote-buying, ballot snatching, ballot box stealing, ballot stuffing, inflation of results, altering of results and declaration of winners as losers and losers as winners were the main attributes of the 2003 and 2007 general elections (Delay, 2019; Demarest & Langer, 2019). The introduction of the accreditation process in 2011 and card readers in the 2015 general elections succeeded in drastically curbing rigging and irregularities in the Nigerian electoral process. One major issue with Nigeria's election in the Fourth Republic is that ethnic and religious voting dominate the pattern of choice. Electorates are being manipulated by the elites against their opponents based on primitive sentiments. This perceived ethnic and religious as well as regional voting sometimes ended in inimical violence as in the case of the 2011 post-election violence. The campaign for political office is undertaken based on people's sentiments instead of issue-based and performance indicators (Igwe & Amadi, 2021).

Money is excessively used in Nigerian elections in the Fourth Republic illegally. Even with the existence of the Electoral Act 2006 later amended as Electoral Act 2010 and now passed as a new law Electoral Act 2022 and Sections 225 and 226 and their sub-sections in the 1999 Constitution as amended provide unequivocal regulations on party financing, campaign expenditure, disclosure, monitoring and transparency, political parties and politicians continued to spend lavishly and extravagantly in arresting their campaign activities. The most annoying aspect is that many studies (Anyadike & Eme, 2014; Lawal, 2015; Onyekpere, 2015; Nwangwu & Ononogbu, 2016; Olorunmola, 2016; Sule et al., 2017a; Sule et al., 2017b; Sule et al., 2018a; Okeke & Nwali, 2020; Sule et al., 2022) on Nigerian party financing and electoral process in the Fourth Republic identified a connection between political corruption, abuse of public resources and violation of regulations in party financing. These studies reported all sorts of irregularities in financing including looting of public funds for the campaign expenditure. For instance, Sule et al. (2017a) reported that a sum of $2.1 billion earmarked for the procurement of weapons to fight the Boko Haram insurgency was diverted for the PDP campaign in the 2015 general election. In another study, Sule et al. (2018c) reported bribing of electoral officials and vote-buying while Onyekpere (2015) presented the case of overspending and violation of laws of campaign financing which Sule et al. (2017b) stressed that impunity deprived the process of being investigated.

The Nigerian democratic experiment is gradually stabilising and that is interpreted as continuous conduct of electoral cycles, enactment of regulations, party activities and electoral politics. Party financing is a headache to advanced democracies and this is severe in states like Nigeria. The existence of regulations is not enough to convince stakeholders that electoral processes in Nigeria are fair, accountable, transparent and can claim integrity. Party financing laws are being reformed in the country in 2006, 2010 and 2022. New ideas and strategies of compelling compliance and transparency are being enshrined in the laws. However, many issues surround the existence of the regulations and their operations. Investigation as revealed in subsequent chapters disclosed that the level of awareness of laws on party financing, ethical practices, violations and sanctions is infinitesimal among the Nigerian electorates. This high level of ignorance leverages parties and politicians to violate the laws with impunity and to develop recalcitrant strategies for evading compliance and transparency. Perhaps, one expensive pre-requisite of democratic governance that Nigeria is battling with is civic education. Citizens are dormant and docile in following keenly what is transpiring in the political arena to censor and hold accountable their elected leaders while the guardrails such as civil societies, opposition and the media are either complicit or are manoeuvered to remain inactive.

The general elections conducted in Nigeria from 1999 to 2019 continue to portray the unregulated and unpunished violation of electoral rules, specifically, party financing regulations. This is in spite of the unequivocal and comprehensive provisions in the 1999 Constitution and the Electoral Act 2006 that underwent reform twice in 2010 and 2022. Parties and candidates recklessly spent above the set ceiling, received donations above the maximum donation ban, trampled on the contribution ban and in some reported cases (Sule, 2018; Sule et al., 2022) used public treasury to sponsor their campaign expenditures. In the process, prohibited activities were overtly carried out by parties, candidates and their frontmen such as vote-buying, bribing electoral officials, subversion of process, sponsoring violence and other dubious illegal means to win at all costs. A cycle of electoral corruption emerges in the system. Politicians used excessive money beyond the limit to win, engage in contract inflation, looting, awarding contracts to themselves and their cronies in proxies, and favouring their ethnic, religious and regional affiliations instead of the distribution of development projects and programmes evenly. Thus, political corruption begets a kind of clientelism where the Nigerian election is turned into a lucrative investment that led to the scramble for control of power by any means that will aid power brokers and their cohorts.

The problem of corruption in party financing affects the integrity of elections, impairs the credibility of the elections, damages the reputation of Nigeria among the comity of nationhood globally and deprives the citizens of good governance and dividends of democratic rule. The issue extends beyond individuals. The country continues to groan in misrule by incapable, incompetent, greedy, selfish leaders who find solace in raping the public treasury because they believe that the electoral process is the function of their money influence and expenditure incurred to secure victory. And the biggest challenge is the inability of the electoral body, the INEC, to monitor and sanction the defaulters. INEC is bestowed constitutionally with powers to monitor, audit and sanction erring parties and candidates, but it has not been doing that due to scarcity of manpower, paucity of funds for execution, logistics problem, politics, lack of cooperation of parties and politicians, low level of awareness from the public and selfish motive of some officials who are bribed by politicians to cover offences. Since the INEC could not monitor effectively the expenditures and financial activities of parties and candidates, it is only feasible to achieve an accountable and transparent party financing process if reforms are designed that can carry all stakeholders and ensure the caveat for severe punishment and deterrence to mitigate the phenomenon.

It is within the context of the aforementioned background that this study presents a new dimension in the study of Nigerian democracy and politics in the Fourth Republic, an effort to examine the level of accountability, transparency, integrity and credibility of the electoral process with regard to party financing and campaign regulations. The study is relevant and necessary emanating from inadequate attention given to the subject of study. It is discovered that few scholars have studied the phenomenon. But the area deserves a comprehensive and deeper investigation into the issue, specifically that new development unfolds in the field in terms of reformed financing laws, new electoral laws and the development in the reckless display of money politics with impunity (Sule, 2022). The excessive spending is beyond the threshold in the regulations and the new law, the Electoral Act 2022, which is now in operation in the build-up to the 2023 general election needs to be studied for future reforms.

The book intends to achieve three main objectives. The first is to fill the gap of knowledge by presenting new fresh knowledge in a field that is rare in democratic and electoral studies. Worldwide, scholars pay less attention to issues of democratic accountability and transparency. Even in advanced democracies, few studies (Alexander, 1989; Ferguson, 1995; Gomez, 2000; Williams, 2000; Walecki, 2003; Roniger, 2004; Bryan & Baer, 2005; Samples, 2005; La Raja, 2008; Doublet, 2010; Yadav, 2011; Gans Morse et al., 2014; Mcmenamin, 2013; Schweizer, 2013; Piccio et al., 2014; Walecki, 2015; February, 2016; Nwangwu & Ononogbu, 2016; Ohman, 2016; Walecki, 2017; Piccio & Van Biezen, 2018; Fiorelli, 2021) across the world paid attention to the subject matter. Thus, there is a need to expand the frontiers of knowledge from this perspective, particularly in a country like Nigeria which has the potential of becoming one of the world powers in the future. As an emerging democracy, understanding how and why Nigerian elections and party financing are conducted is vital in the study of global political corruption and democracy.

Second, the study intends to open an opportunity for comparative studies in the field to advance the discourse of knowledge from the perspective of election and party studies in developing countries or emerging democracies. The study will motivate other similar democracies like Nigeria such as Indonesia, India, Brazil, Mexico, South Africa, Tanzania and Ethiopia to adopt and develop the same epistemological rigours to compare or present individual studies with that of Nigeria which in return will provide the chance to scrutinise various cases either individually but comparatively or directly compared to make cases (Collier, 1993).

The third objective is to present practical policy implications for the legal framework and applicable measures that will address the identified problems. Models, policy frameworks and practical guidelines are provided in the end for the policymakers and the electorates to adopt and remedy the situation. The models and frameworks carefully integrate both policymakers and the electorates because, in the Nigerian political context, policies are not readily accepted and implemented by those in power, especially those coming from academic studies, because the status quo is romanced by the ruling class as the plausible alternative of perpetuating themselves into power. Thus, any policy alternative or framework towards good governance must be dual in nature and the electorates must be sensitised to participate in the process since democracy enables for that otherwise it may be archived deliberately no matter how efficacious it may be in addressing a problem. The models and framework presented in the last part of this work are expected to go a long way in addressing the menace of electoral misconduct, irregularities and corruption in the party financing process in Nigeria's Fourth Republic and beyond.

The methodology of the study is a qualitative research design where data were generated from numerous sources including in-depth interviews with informants in the field of study (Creswell, 2014; Creswell, 2015). The data were utilised from information derived from a PhD study. The interviews

were conducted in 2017 in various parts of the country but most of the interviews were conducted in Abuja. The study is a qualitative case study (George
& Bennett 2005), a particularistic qualitative case study in essence because a
special case within a specific period is studied (Gerring, 2007; Yin, 2018) in
a particular area which is party financing and electoral process in Nigeria's
Fourth Republic. The primary source or in-depth interviews were supported
with documented sources, the existing resources on the subject matter and
other relevant materials (Scott, 2006; Simmons, 2014) that support or dispute
a proposition. Informants were identified and consulted based on certain
considerations including proximity, accessibility, quality of information
required or delivered and the role played in the subject of study (Bogden &
Biklen, 2007; Sharan, 2009). The interviews were conducted and informants
were consulted for data gathering using semi-structured questions to allow
for flexibility of responses and the attainment of saturation points (Braun &
Clarke, 2013).

The informants were drawn from six categories. The first category is the
national executive/senior officials of four main parties chosen based on their
participation in general elections at the national level and their presence in
state and local council elections for at least ten years and above, specifically
from 2011 to 2019 general elections. The parties consisted of APC, PDP,
SDP and Democratic People's Party (DPP). The second category is the politicians both serving and contestants during the time of the interview who were
carefully selected from all the four elective offices of the Senate, House of
Representatives, governors and State House of Assembly. The president or
presidential aspirant was not accessed because of lack of accessibility while
the chairman of the local council and councillors were skipped because at
the time of the conduct of the interview they were not on the ground because
all the states did not conduct the LG polls. The third category is the academics where four of them were identified and selected from various Nigerian
universities but all of them were in the Department of Political Science for
expert interviews. The fourth category is the senior INEC officials whom
three of them were consulted. The fifth category is the senior officials of the
Economic and Financial Crimes Commission (EFCC) because issues of corruption were involved in the study and the last category was the members
of civil societies selected and interviewed in Abuja based on geopolitical
representation.

The method used in the analysis is content analysis and thematic analytical interpretations. Themes and sub-themes were extracted and analysed as
presented in the preceding chapters (Lune & Berg, 2017). In cases where the
arguments of the informants are strong and represent factual commentaries,
references were made to that but where the submissions are common and can
be complemented with documented sources in consensus, the views were

presented without necessarily referring to the source which is direct informants' interview (Scott, 2006). This process enabled for arrival of findings
and practical policy implications. It is anticipated that the study will attract
the interest of policymakers; academics; civil societies; the electoral body
INEC, the EFCC and international institutions and organisations like the
Institute for Democracy and Electoral Assistance (IDEA), International Federation for Electoral Systems (IFES), International Republican Institute (IRI),
National Democratic Institute (NDI), Organisation for Economic Cooperation and Development (OECD), the African Union (AU), the European Union
(EU) and the Economic Community of West African States (ECOWAS); and
many other agencies, institutions and individual researchers.

The book is organised into eleven chapters. The current chapter is the overview of the problem identified in the study by way of introducing the subject
of study, the problem that motivates the study, the objectives of the book, the
methodology used and the anticipated benefits or policy implications and the
contribution of the book. In chapter 2, some relevant terms are conceptualised
because of their recurring appearance in the work and the critical pivot of the
terms including political parties, party systems, elections, electoral politics
and political party financing. All these concepts are explained explicitly,
briefly but in a technique that will guide the reader on the usability of the
terms within the contexts of the work. Chapter 3 examines the overview of an
election, electoral conduct and general elections in Nigeria's Fourth Republic
consisting of 1999, 2003, 2007, 2011, 2015 and 2019 elections. The pattern,
dimension, changes, character and factors that determined the outcome and
voting trends were extensively discussed. In chapter 4, a broader view of
political parties including their character, origin, organisation, institutionalisation and systems are explored comprehensively followed by the examination of the Nigerian political parties in the Fourth Republic and their character
and activities.

In chapter 5, the nature of political party financing is discussed from a
global perspective to a regional and national views. This includes the regulations across world countries, types of funding, the structure of funding,
legal sources, contributions limit, disclosure, auditing, sanction of offenders
and the need for reforms. Chapter 6 made an effort in linking the body of
literature with some theoretical postulations on party financing and electoral
politics. Three theories or frameworks of clientelism, rational choice theory
and game theory were adopted and applied within the context of the literature and the body of the work to strengthen the propositions and various
views of scholars on the problematique of political party financing, political
corruption and the integrity, accountability and transparency of electoral
process in Nigeria. Chapter 7 analyses critically the regulations and issues
of laws of party financing in Nigeria. The chapter, specifically, exposes the

insufficiency and loopholes in party financing regulations in Nigeria and the need for reforms that are plausible and practicable. Chapter 8 discusses the Electoral Management Body in Nigeria (EMB), the INEC which has the constitutional mandate of monitoring party financing, holding parties and candidates accountable and sanctions. The chapter answers why INEC failed to monitor parties' expenditure and sanction the defaulters as empowered by law.

In chapter 9, the influence of money politics is revisited in the process of party financing in Nigeria, especially, excessive spending, monetisation of the electoral process, violation of regulations and other offences. Chapter 10 built on chapter 9 and continued with the discussion of the effects of electoral corruption on the Nigerian electoral process and its integrity. Issues such as vote-buying, bribing electoral officials, the use of public treasury and violation of regulations were examined. Chapter 11 concludes the discussion with policy implications by suggesting some practical measures of effective monitoring and reforms in future. The chapter presents the limit of the study and suggestions for further inquiry in the field in addition to explaining the role played by the book in providing the targetted audience with a valuable contribution on the subject of election, political parties and African democracy.

Chapter 2

Conceptualising Operational Terms

This chapter conceptualises major operational terms and keywords that constantly repeat themselves in the book. It is expedient to acknowledge and exponentially evaluate the valuable terms to save the book from an overload of repetition and redefining issues and terms while they appear throughout. This will save the reader the trouble of verbosity and overstretched discussion that can be succinctly addressed. Some key operational terms including political parties, party systems, elections, electoral politics and the Nigerian Fourth Republic are briefly but extensively examined in the chapter.

POLITICAL PARTIES

It is not an easy task to conceptualise political parties in a precise term that will save the trouble of a belaboured discourse. Some analysts prefer to draw back on history and trace the roots of the term and its establishment but others feel that limiting the efforts at conceptualisation may not necessarily drag to the background (Kam & Newson, 2020; Hudson, 2021). It suffices to look at the real and contemporary development to explain the meaning. Political parties are considered pillars of democracy and a fundamental requirement that must be minimally satisfied for democracies to thrive and flourish. In essence, parties build democracy while democracy sustains, changes and shapes parties. It is common knowledge that parties are the instruments that offer the opportunity for representation and election. Hence, any meaning of parties should not deviate from this logic and perception (Maisel, 2022).

Parties are seen from different perspectives depending on the circumstances that motivate studying them. One vital element that continuously resurfaces when parties are mentioned is the issue of interest and mobilisation. People who share a common interest and the need to advance this interest in society found the machinery of parties convenient and explicit to achieve that goal (Kernalegenn & Van Haute, 2020). Parties are perceived as the umbrella that unifies diverse individual interests and subordinates them to a common superficial ideology through mobilisation, recruitment and contest for power control. From this assertion, parties may not necessarily be a platform that attracts only a homogenous interest. Heterogeneous interests are sometimes welcome and lured into party membership but they are harmonised and reinvigorated into a common goal that is bigger, pressing and convincing to secure power (Sandri & Seddone, 2021).

Parties are ideological tenets for the promotion of members' interests and the desire to influence public policy through a process of competing for power in an election that is legally upheld by law in society. Ideology matters most in political parties because it is the future grease that wheels the rail of parties when the going is tough, especially, during internal schism and contradicting personal interest of members (Bale et al., 2020). This vital element is what divides the well-established parties in advanced democracies from parties that are emerging and trying to democratise or organise and institutionalise. Most of the parties in advanced European democracies and America succeeded in inculcating ideology that permanently absorbed shocks and steer their affairs progressively (Haider & Wauters, 2019). But the emerging democracies in Africa, Asia and East Europe are struggling with ideological formation making the parties and electoral process ethnic, regional, religious and less issue-based (Kelly, 2020). This is not to exonerate the American and European parties from the same alibi of the emerging parties and this does not translate into a unilinear categorisation because some parties as in China, India and Russia are emerging ones but they have their ideology well-established from the inception of their formation, communist or religious in approach (Dickson, 2021; Mehta, 2022).

Parties represent many things to many groups. It is an assembly of political interest groups. Parties are the ideological umbrella for collating a common goal and a common interest of homogenous members (Cesari, 2020). Parties are platforms for power competition and power control in democratic systems. Yet, parties can be regional, ethnic or presentation of a coalition of pressure groups. Others are theological parties, particularly, Christian and Islamic parties across Europe and Muslim countries (Haynes, 2020; Mantilla, 2021). Other parties represent class formation and ethnic outlook while some are authoritarian and are established to fulfil the desire of meeting the qualification of nomenclature of the term 'democracy' in modern times. Parties are thus categories of various individual interests but one common uniting factor of all parties in the contemporary political system is the desire to capture power in a state through the instrumentality of election or referendum (Smith, 2021).

The pattern in which parties emerged and are formed varies according to period, state, democratic system and political actors. In Europe and America, the oldest democracies and ancient political parties, parties pre-dated electoral democracy and are mainly engineered by civil societies, pressure groups, interest groups and suppressed bodies (Basile, 2019; Jones, 2020). They were resisted and countered by state authorities until societies succumbed to democratisation pressure (Langguth, 2019). Even in this case, the earlier version of electoral democracy favoured a kind of caste system in Europe and America with a specific category earmarked to vote while others were disenfranchised. Thus, early parties and their formation were elitist (Brewer & Maisel, 2021). In authoritarian societies, elites or power brokers formed structures that will answer the title of parties to ward off the pressure from the international movement for universal democratisation (Sandri & Seddone, 2021). In some of these authoritarian societies, opposition parties were suppressed or blocked, membership is restricted while internal politics is emasculated (Golosov, 2022). In emerging democracies like Africa, Asia, East Europe, Latin America and the Caribbean, parties with religious, ethnic, regional, family and other cleavages affiliations appeared and influenced membership and voting based on these cleavages even in non-performance mood (Hinnebusch et al., 2021). Other parties are populist parties with populist leaders who exploit societal divisions and sentiments including racism, religion, ethnicity and nativism to secure the popular support of the voters (Schwörer, 2021).

Yet, parties are organised and institutionalised in stages and sequences. The period of existence, operation, active participation in electoral politics, ruling or opposition role, grassroots engagements and other considerations determine how parties are organised and institutionalise (Hiskey & Moseley, 2020). To organise, parties require a loyal membership, fellowship, deep-rooted connectivity with grassroots members, an established linkage between the parliament members of parties that are elected under its platform and the represented and the ability to influence national policies and politics (Pettitt, 2020). Party organisation is not an easy task. In advanced democracies, it took many decades and they are currently undergoing reshaping. In some instances, populist leaders overturn the party organisation to their charismatic ideals while in others the organisation continues as it is with some adjustments that may frequently occur to accommodate diversities and challenges encountered in its way to political activities and electoral participation (Wagner, 2020).

Party institutionalisation on the other hand is the ability of the members to penetrate society and become a political instrument that consolidates democracy. Institutionalisation requires members' cooperation, will, commitment and subordination of individual interests to collective interests (Harmel et al.,

2019). Party institutionalisation requires some paramount elements including a sound ideology, principles, internal democratic fair play, philosophy and mechanisms for dispute settlement and leadership recruitment and training in values that are appreciated by the members (Aylott & Bolin, 2021). To actualise this, advanced political parties sacrificed the personal interests of members in their heydays but these principles and ideologies are increasingly diminishing even in American and European parties. Personal interest, money politics and internal chaos are taking a toll on the affairs of these parties. Developing democracies in Africa, Asia and East Europe are facing a great hurdle in institutionalisation challenged by ethnic loyalty, regional affiliation, religious sentiments and political division accentuated by the selfish and reckless actions and inactions of elites in their insatiable quest for personal power (Smith, 2020).

Parties are positioned as the most valuable component and pillar of democracy because an election is the only legal method approved to secure and authoritatively control power in democracies and elections are only possible beneath the platform of parties. This is due to the crucial role they play in election, democratisation and governance process. Fundamentally, parties recruit and train leaders through a chain of mobilisation and political activities. These trained leaders succeed in becoming either party leaders and continue to organise and operate parties' cells and caucuses or advance to become national political leaders who use the process to advance the interest of their respective parties (Pettitt, 2020). On assuming power, parties endeavour to install their ideologies. The left, right and centre, the conservatives, the liberalists and the progressives all compete for power to permeate national politics with their ideological persuasion. Parties influence policymaking and decision-making through struggles to capture the power and dominate the political process. They intensify their grip on the control of parliament to have a smooth sail of their policy documents and plan of action (Ceron, 2019).

Parties are instrumental in playing the role of opposition. Not all parties control or capture power. In multi-party systems, competition becomes usually intense and in most cases, elections produced coalition governments and alliances because of the lack of a clear winner. Some parties accepted the role of opposition and checkmate the excesses of ruling parties to block despotism (Singh, 2021). Apart from the opposition role, parties administer community services to the environs. During the period of urgent needs or acute shortages, they intervene and provide for the poor and the needy. They play the role of first aid, awareness creation, scholarship, sensitisation and mobilisation to swing voting or block swing voting. Some parties are determinants of winners even when they are not winning. The significant votes that they are controlling are instrumental in direct winning for any major party that gets their nod. In this regard, parties bargain for what they feel is a win-win after the election (Evans, 2020).

Parties have other duties that they performed which consist of organisation, party selection and conducting party primaries. All these are internal affairs that are freely executed by parties within themselves based on their respective constitutions as supervised and regulated by election Management Body (EMB) in a state. Some of the activities of parties are carried out digitally including recruitment and organisation (Barbera et al., 2021). Parties propel the electoral process and democratic governance. All struggles to contest elections and control power rest on the shoulders of parties.

PARTY SYSTEMS

Political parties take different shapes, natures, backgrounds, settings and operational techniques. The classification of parties consists of both the traditional pattern and changing models as advanced by scholars. The common party system that dominates the discourses of traditional classification is based on number systems: one-party, two-party and multi-party systems. In a one-party system, the state officially recognises only one party by law, and in some instances, opposition and disregard for this type of party are handled with stiff responses as national treason and deviation (Evans, 2020). Most of the communist states of China, Russia and Cuba operate one-party system. In Russia, the Russian Workers Party offers a platform for representation of workers' unions for collective decision-making (Golosov, 2022). The party is recognised as the only means of attaining power. In China, the Chinese Communist Party (CCP) represents the replica of Russia's Workers Party (Dickson, 2021).

One of the characteristics of a one-party system is resentment of opposition. All politicians, party members, interest groups and civil societies unite under the umbrella of the state official party. This, however, does not mean that there was no competition for power or electoral contest but all these political activities are carried out under the official party's platform. Various groups express their interests and struggle to capture power (Singh, 2021). This simply represents a typical internal party primary in other party systems where two or many parties are constitutionally allowed to field candidates that will compete in final elections. In a one-party system, political unity is easily achieved while diversities are managed comfortably but containing heterogeneous groups in plural societies is unsuitable in a one-party system (Smith, 2021).

In a two-party system, two strong contending parties compete for power but the number of parties is not usually limited to two parties. In some cases of two-party systems like the United States, United Kingdom, Germany and other world democracies, two parties interchangeably compete for power control and they provide an alternative choice platforms for the citizens. The Democrats and the Republicans in the United States have been in charge of political control for more than a century despite the existence of other parties such as the Green Party, Libertarian and other smaller ones. However, the United States is considered a two-party system because of the dominance of the two major parties (Maisel, 2022). The same scenario is obtainable in the United Kingdom and many other European countries. The identification of a system as two-party does not entail the presence of only two parties but rather the dominance and control of two parties (Kernalegenn & Van Haute, 2020). Nigeria is experiencing its longest democratic practice in the Fourth Republic (1999–2022) with a similar trend in the United States and the United Kingdom. Constitutionally, Nigeria is a multi-party system but in practice, two parties All Progressives Congress (APC) and Peoples Democratic Party (PDP) dominate the twenty-three years of democratic experiment (Sule, 2022).

The two-party system is characterised by power changing hands between two major dominant parties. Other smaller parties that may exist can grab a few seats or hold a position of influence in coalition and alliance. But this phenomenon will never uproot the dominant parties from their main role of major parties and power control interchangeably. In a two-party system, an alternative platform of choice is enabled unlike the one-party politics, opposition is tolerated, encouraged and supported by civil societies and other pressure groups. Additionally, in a two-party system, opposing views and ideologies allow voters to determine where to pledge their allegiance (Kam & Newson, 2020).

The last type of the traditional classification of the party system is the multi-party system. In a multi-party system, the state laws recognise multiple parties and allow for registration of countless parties that fulfil the minimum criteria for the registration by regulations. This type of party system takes different forms. In the case of India, the parties are registered in stratification based on geography. Some are local parties, some state, some regional and others national. Each party is lawfully allowed presenting candidates based on its area of jurisdiction. For instance, the BJP party is national and can present candidates at all levels during national elections in India but parties that are registered at regional, state and local levels are only allowed to field candidates in their respective regions, states and local councils (Mehta, 2022). In some states like Nigeria, more than one hundred parties are registered from 1999 to 2022 (Sule, 2022). This is possible because the constitution has not set any limit to a number of parties and the procedure of registration is simplified. During general elections, as many as seventy parties joined the race, but only the APC and the PDP exhibit serious contests. In some circumstances, many parties are deregistered after general elections, particularly, the 2019 general election, after they failed to meet the minimum requirements for continued existence as registered parties (Sule, 2020).

A multi-party system is flexible in offering the opportunity for choice among the competing parties. The system is, however, expensive, cumbersome and difficult for electorates to choose while overtasking the electoral bodies in the management and conduct of elections. The ballot papers and other election materials are bulky and difficult to convey and operate (Sule, 2020). Oftentimes, mistakes in choice occur when numerous parties appear on ballot papers. The cost of administering elections in multi-party systems is high and only the rich countries can afford it even though, middle-income countries and poor countries such as India, Nigeria and Brazil operate them. In a multi-party system, alliances and coalitions are likely to occur in many elections to determine the parties that win. Some parties forfeit their candidature and support a party with a better chance in return for a bargain (Bale et al., 2020).

The above party classification is portrayed as traditional. Modern classification recognises changes and new dimensions including several factors. One of them is a classification based on ideologies. The ideological leaning of parties determines their classification. Most of the ideologies swing in between liberal and conservative or capitalist and communist (Haider & Wauters, 2019). But the ideological classification of parties goes beyond this categorisation. Some parties are theological promoting religious values and laws, specifically, Islamic parties (Cesari, 2020). Yet, others hold a national creed that borders between philosophy and religion including the BJP in India and CCP in China (Dickson, 2021). Ideology is a distinguishing factor that establishes a clear-cut difference between advanced parties and emerging parties, particularly, in African democracies (Kelly, 2020).

Parties in modern days are classified based on periodisation. Some parties are considered old and advanced due to the period that they have spent in active politics and by extension, power control and other roles of opposition, leadership recruitment and community services (Mantilla, 2021). Others are tagged as new or emerging depending on the period that they are formed. Most parties in Africa, Asia, Latin America and the Caribbean are the offshoot of colonial legacies of imposition of the Western democratic system and are finding it difficult to operate in the same way that their counterparts in Western democracies are operating (Kernalegenn & Van Haute, 2020). In essence, some parties in developing democracies are just emerging amid many decades of political independence. Nigeria, one of the biggest emerging democracies, has its ruling party and main opposition all formed in less than three decades (Sule, 2022).

Circumstances and environment of the processes and antecedents in which the parties emerged is another factor in classifying parties (Kam & Newson, 2020). In Europe, for example, parties were established before full democratisation as pressure groups and ideological bodies for fostering a common interest of members (Aylott & Bolin, 2021). Yet, in other states in Europe and America, parties spearheaded and pressed for democratic arrangement (Brewer & Maisel, 2021). In other societies, parties were formed as reactions against colonial oppression and as an opportunity to participate in self-governance and struggles for political freedom and national liberation (Hinnebusch et al., 2021). In other cases, parties were formed by the military clandestinely to pave the way for the military transformation into civilian rulers and these parties usually remain authoritarian and brutal in their leadership style (Schwörer, 2021). In other cases, parties were formed as a reaction against pressure to democratise. These parties are often fragile and are bound to collapse in the long run because of challenges to ideology, organisation and institutionalisation (Langguth, 2019).

In another segment, parties can be classified based on their affiliations and sentiments. Such parties are found in plural societies. Some parties look ethnic, others regional and others religious while others are clannish in outlook. These types of parties sought votes within the enclave of their influence and they hardly make any effort in attracting support beyond their affiliation. Yet, some parties are elitist and are restricted in membership to the elite class but they often seek support from all groups even if their policies and programmes favour elitist orientation. They gain support through clientelism, patrimonialism and prebendel political arrangement (Singh, 2021).

ELECTION

An election is a phenomenon that legitimises power holding and authoritative control of state apparatus and machinery of government in democratic regimes. It is perceived that an election is a process of establishing a mutual contract between the voters and policymakers where the popular support of the former is sought by the latter in return for favourable policies and development projects (Schultz & Toplak, 2023). In a democracy, irrespective of the nature be it liberal or social or any form, an election is a pillar that qualifies a leader to have a constitutional mandate from mundane public support to initiate and execute policies. Unlike in tyrannical systems, in democracies, elections offer the opportunity for peaceful choice and change of leadership in tranquillity without resorting to violence (Rush, 2023).

An election is an old system of choosing leaders. The idea of election dates back to many communities thousands or millions of years ago. How societies organise and choose leaders and decision-making significantly varies from one society to another and from one period to another (Chasman & Cohen, 2020). Precisely, democratic elections are preferably linked to Greek city-states some 4,000 years ago when the people in the city-states assembled in market squares to elect their leaders but not only election, they voted for policies and decisions and the majority is regarded as the largest voice. The election continues in ancient Rome during the period of the caesars to medieval Europe and modern Europe. The idea of an election is representation. During the Greek city-states, people represent themselves because of the sizeable nature of the inhabitants who were easily and conveniently contained in the market square (Dimova, 2020). This pattern of choosing leaders and voting in decision-making and policy choice is absolutely impracticable in the medieval and ancient periods because of the increasing population explosion and sophistication in policymaking and diplomacy. Thus, a strategy of determining who leads was devised in the medieval period through contests, competition for power and representation of constituents. This process is gradually taken over by media, digital spaces and technological giants (Hemmingway, 2021).

An election offers an opportunity for policy choice, ideological underpinnings, protests of policies and misgovernance and changing misrepresentation (Rosanvallon, 2018). Political office seekers are provided with the platform to express and display their manifestoes and policies while the electorates are allowed to choose from among the contenders based on who convinces them or who performs better (Shaw, 2018). If a party or a candidate is given an opportunity and falters, voters have the absolute choice of replacing him in another electoral cycle. Likewise, if the mandate offered to a party or a candidate is handled with fulfilment and performance, the electorates may give such a party or a candidate the chance to continue for a maximum period of legal stay in office where a fixed period is stipulated and where this limit does not exist, electorates can vote such a candidate or a party for as much as they wish continuously (Orr, 2023).

Elections are conducted periodically. The set period for conducting elections differs from one democracy to another and from one political system to another. Various elective offices exist to compete for power control (Walter, 2021). Central among them are the executive offices of presidents and prime ministers and parliaments either a single chamber or upper and lower depending on the laws of a state. In some states like the United States and Nigeria, a period of four years is earmarked for electing the executives and lawmakers. In other systems such as France, Germany and Russia, the constitutional period is six years. In the case of the United States and Nigeria, the limited term for the executive elective offices is two terms of four years, but there is no limit to the terms of members of parliament or congress. Many lawmakers in Nigerian and US chambers spent more than twenty years (Forsberg, 2021). In the case of Israel and Malaysia and many democracies, prime ministers can spend four years of non-fixed limited term continuously until they abdicate personally or they are defeated (Coleman & Brogden, 2020).

An election is undertaken in various patterns. In some democracies, a simple majority is a process of determining the winner. A candidate in such democracies may win the election once he secures a simple majority even if the margin of win between the leading candidate and the runner-up is just 1 percent of the total votes. This is mostly operated in presidential systems like Nigeria, Brazil, Mexico, Kenya, South Africa and most presidential styles (Miezah, 2018). In other cases, a winner is only determined if their party secures the majority seats in the parliament which enables for forming a government as in the case of India, Malaysia, the United Kingdom and New Zealand (Mulroy, 2023). In other systems such as the United States, getting the majority of votes is not enough to secure victory. A presidential candidate requires two-thirds of the Electoral College even if they lost the popular votes (Foley, 2020). In other electoral systems, apart from securing a simple majority, one needs to fulfil some criteria such as securing 25 percent of two-thirds of states in the federation in Nigeria for a presidential candidate to win (Forsberg, 2021).

There are other systems of electing leaders in democracies. Apart from a simple majority strategy, an alternative voting system is operated in some democracies where the electorates are provided with the opportunity to vote for all the contestants in an alternative form where the preferred candidates are chosen first, followed by the next option and the next sequentially. The candidate that gets the highest first option is elected. In other cases, proportional representation is adopted where voters are offered the chance of voting their candidates of choice based on preference and the percentage of votes allocated (Gardasevik & Toplak, 2023).

Elections are conducted in democracies by Electoral Management Bodies (EMBs). These EMBs are structured based on the culture, population, geography and political system of a state. Some electoral bodies are state-controlled and are influenced by state policies and politicians. In most democracies nowadays, EMBs are made independent and are given full autonomy to operate in the process of conducting elections (King et al., 2020). For instance, the Nigerian EMB is called the Independent National Electoral Commission (INEC) to showcase and emphasise their freedom from political interference. EMBs are becoming liberal and independent with an active partnership of international observers and other agencies that monitor elections globally. Additionally, EMBs are adopting useful reforms that are increasingly making elections transparent and credible. These measures include a digital electoral process and party financing reforms (James & Garnett, 2023).

Elections are monitored and watched closely to ensure accountability, transparency, credibility and integrity. This is because global democracies are increasingly witnessing contested elections where rigging, manipulation, irregularities and malpractice as well as the use of excessive money are reported. To mitigate these inconsistencies, EMBs are migrating to digital electoral conduct (Roberts, 2023). Digital elections are executed through computer gadgets and other digital equipment that accredit and conduct elections and then transmit the results electronically (Krimmer & Esteve, 2023). This process is considered a giant leap in electoral integrity albeit a critical reservation of unwanted interference and the effects of cyberwarfare among the giant tech nations. The Russian case of alleged meddling in the process of the 2016 presidential election in America is still fresh in the minds of those who are cynical about digital elections (Aral, 2020; Payton, 2020).

It is observed that elections present liberty and the opportunity for the electorates to choose their leaders independently and willingly. However, in many instances, this liberty is not guaranteed and is curtailed or truncated by selfish politicians who invoked a zero-sum game to win elections at all costs (Miller, 2021). Violence, manipulation and intimidation are often reported in elections, particularly, in Africa, Asia and Latin America in the electoral process. In some cases, winners are denied their victory and the mandate is stolen by the incumbent (Waxman & McCullough, 2022). This raises a critical question of whether elections change leadership or enables voters to have their will and choice prevail in many democracies. In some circumstances, violence erupted on the announcement of electoral results while some studies (Birch, 2020; Ezeh, 2023) established the occurrence of violence before, during and after the elections due to perceived or recorded subversion of the process.

Contemporarily, elections are conducted periodically in more than 170 countries of the world and there is increasing pressure for the non-democratic state to embrace electoral democracy. Except for a few Gulf States, Morocco in Africa and a few others including Brunei Darussalam in Asia (Torres-Van Antwerp, 2022), most countries of the world operate electoral democracy either under a liberal process or a socialist/communist system (Timmerman, 2020). Even the volatile African elections that are often characterised by violence and subversion of the process are gradually meeting up with the basic standard of preparing and delivering a credible election with some considerable element of integrity and acceptability (Cheeseman et al., 2020; Fombad & Steytler, 2021; Norris, 2023). Elections for now remain the key means of acquiring constitutional mandate, peaceful change of leadership, democratic representation and the process of displaying support or resistance to public policies and choice of programmes and projects (Brewer & Maisel, 2021). Elections are regarded as tranquilisers that allocate constitutional power to the preferred individuals while at the same the means of ousting those who violate their terms of the contract with the electorates after a period of trial that may be satisfactory or dismal depending on how the voters decided to judge (Madsen, 2019).

ELECTORAL POLITICS

The term 'electoral politics' denotes the vicissitudes and permutations that herald the conduct of elections. Politicians and parties compete to win elections and this competition involves various strategies, persuasions, promises, blackmail, manipulation and all techniques that will dislocate opponents and give an edge to the contenders (Johnson, 2020). It is observed that elections are the only legitimate means of capturing power and designing policy programmes in democratic states. It is also noted that while politicians and parties may have overall national interest and the development of individuals in their hearts, they may have their ambition, selfish motives and clandestine projects that they strive to achieve when elected to office. These motives can be financial gain, power prestige, favouring stooges and cronies, influencing the flow of economic activities and social settings and other related cleavages. This is easily achievable when a party or a group of politicians are in control of power (Prabhu, 2020).

Politics and elections are considered games. Typical of a football competition, two or more teams compete to cruise to victory using all strategies that will pay but within the stipulated regulations of the game. The teams are quite aware of the strengths and weaknesses of their rivals, the nature of the competition and the rules. Hence, players adopt varieties of tactics to outsmart their rivals. Politics and electoral politics resemble football competitions (Hechter, 2019). In their desire to get elected, politicians make all promises, adopt strategies that will expose the weaknesses of their opponents and exhibit their strengths. Just like game theory, electoral politics is identified as a rational choice process where politicians and parties engage the electorates and play on their psyche to win in a chain of relationships that look a win-win for both the politicians and the voters (Weirich, 2021). In some context, voters are rewarded with money, cash, kind, offer of appointments, contracts and other related opportunities while the politicians use money, religion, ethnic affiliation, regional sentiments, socio-economic issues, national security matters, foreign policy and diplomacy and policy orientation to woo votes and supports (Frahm, 2019). To actualise this, clientelism emerges where a patron–broker relationship occurs between parties, politicians, their messengers and the voters. Most cases involve reward, promises or threats and coercion (Aspinall & Berenschot, 2019).

Electoral politics is occupied with several issues. One of them is ideological contests. Parties and politicians are actively engaged, particularly, in political debates and communications on the ideology that they stand to present when elected to offices. Political parties are constantly attached to ideological leanings because they must have a philosophy that they are standing to promote and protect (Moody, 2022). This might not be true in all cases because sometimes national interests, changing circumstances, political interests and the desire to win elections may obscure the genuine intention and ideology of politicians. However, ideology is vital in electoral politics because some parties were permanently perceived with a specific principle and interest and voters are supporting these parties based on that perception. The Democrat in the United States is seen as liberal while the Republican as conservative in the same way the Conservative party in the United Kingdom is seen as pro–status quo and the Labour party as progressive or liberal. Most parties in European and American democracies are seen as such. The campaign strategies of these parties are persuasive of the ideologies and the benefits that accrue with these ideologies and they gain support from this lineage (Moody, 2022).

Electoral politics is anchored around socio-economic issues in many democracies. Politicians and parties divest contending issues of economy, social security, security, inflation, unemployment rate, rate of school enrolment, nutrition levels and education to attract voters. Some promise to increase budgetary allocations to critical sectors like health while others pledge to cut and replace them with other stipends of welfare (Önnudóttir et al., 2022). The performance of ruling parties is attacked while the ruling parties strive and present data to convince that they have fulfilled their manifestoes and campaign promises and as such, they deserve to be given additional opportunity to do more good. Campaign issues dominate electoral politics in democracies, especially, where the parties are solid and well-organised and institutionalised. Major issues of poverty, income level, job creation, freedom and liberty, human rights, accessibility to potable drinking water, food security and other related issues are prioritised in electoral politics. The issue-based campaign is part of electoral politics but not only the determinants of how parties and their candidates managed to secure victory (Önnudóttir et al., 2022).

Foreign policy, diplomacy and international politics play vital roles in electoral politics, especially, in advanced countries that successfully overcome the basic needs of infrastructures and survival. In developing economies, issues of infrastructure dominate the scene. In advanced countries, how states relate, their prime policy direction in international relations, issues of global migration, climate change, global warming, national and international security, terrorism, health pandemics and several other pressing global issues pre-occupy parties and their manifestoes (Kane, 2019). In

2019, the issue of the COVID-19 pandemic played a decisive role in the victory and defeat of many parties and politicians. Opinion polls and surveys on election predictions always consider public perception and responses to COVID-19 and the efforts of policymakers in responding to countermeasures in preventing the virus (Önnudóttir et al., 2022). The famous agenda that earned President Donald Trump the White House seat borders around nativism, populism and conservative white supremacist stances. The same conservative promise and return to ancient Britain culture and values earned the Conservative party a decisive victory in the 2020 election. Thus, in developed democracies, foreign policy objectives and the international political economy are essential in electoral politics (Brewer & Maisel, 2021).

However, other elements play a prominent role in electoral politics in both developed and developing democracies. Religion, geography, ethnic group and financial gain are explicitly exploited by parties and their candidates during their campaigns, particularly, in plural societies of Africa and Asia and Europe (Szakonyi, 2020). Plurality is not an exclusive attribute of African and Asian states. Many European states are as plural as African countries and indeed, America is more plural than most African states. Some European countries succeeded in building a stable democracy only after forging Consciosationalism (Foblets et al., 2019). The elements of ethnicity, race, religion and regional politics always hold a strong determinant in American politics as in other European democracies (Richey & Taylor, 2021). However, in the context of African democracies, particularly, these elements are prioritised ahead of issues and performance in office. A party or politician that performs abysmally may easily secure victory in the next election because his religion, ethnicity or geographical background controls a majority of the population and that alone fetches more votes for him than other candidates.

Electoral politics do not rely on campaign issues alone to fetch victory for parties and candidates. The politicians adopt other strategies such as money politics. They violate party financing regulations and electoral laws to circumvent their way into victory. Clientelism, vote-buying, bribery, corruption and other manipulative techniques are employed by politicians to win. In the process, gradually, democracy is turned into a bazaar for the highest bidder (Schnurr, 2023). Due to the influence of moneybags in arresting electoral ambition, credible candidates with low financial strength are automatically screened out from the race. Excessive spending determines the victory of contestants in the aftermath of patrimonialism, Prebendelism and clientelism where public goods are awarded based on whims and personal gain of the ruling class. Money politics is quite threatening and subversive to democracies contemporarily and are constantly occupying a strategic position in electoral politics (Stonestreet, 2023).

More so, it should be noted that not only money politics and electoral corruption help draw electoral victory during the process of electoral politics. Politicians employ dirtier ways of achieving victory including threats, intimidation, coercion and violence. Most of the current elections conducted in Africa are, for example, enmeshed in one form of violence or the other (Themner, 2017). This is not a unique case, however, with Africa alone. The 2020 US presidential election recorded some share of violence and allegations of disenfranchisement. Many European elections are involved in controversies about disenfranchising many voters, particularly, in areas of strong opposition holding. All these according to Birch et al. (2020) are forms of electoral violence. In places where the brutal act transgressed beyond civility, innocent voters are injured, prevented from voting, maimed, inflicted with psychological injuries and killed in some instances. Some post-election violence in states like Kenya in 2007 and Nigeria in 2011 costs more than 1,000 lives each separately (Maoz & Henderson, 2020).

Electoral politics are better accepted as whatever politicians do to win an election both legal and illegal, moral and amoral, acceptable and unacceptable, if they believe it will lead to success. It can involve even fake and practically unimplementable promises deliberately to influence the psychology of voters to support them. The electorates are promised heaven and honey but end up in some instances swallowing the bitter pill of reckless, irresponsible and anti-masses policies (Dervin & Simpson, 2021). A good example is the APC in Nigeria formed in 2013 and which became the main opposition that challenged the ruling PDP in the 2015 general election (Folarin, 2021). The opposition APC won but the major campaign promises of revamping the economy, addressing security and anti-corruption crusades are carried to the worse level unprecedented in the country's history. People never had it that bad and suffered before like under the APC that promised to be pro-masses and progressives (Sule, 2022). Thus, electoral politics can take any dimension that will lead to victory irrespective of the outcome after the election.

POLITICAL PARTY FINANCING

Political party financing is the entire process involved in sponsoring and undertaking campaign expenditures of political parties and candidates. Party funding is fundraising for executing the campaign and all the expenses incurred in the process including the raised revenue (Uberoi, 2016). The process of party financing is structured into individual campaign expenses and political parties' expenditures. All these processes and activities are not carried out freely or based on the volition of the parties or the candidates. There are set regulations that guide how parties and candidates can operate and behave in party financing including the legal sources of funds and the maximum limit for regulated expenditure. Regulations in party funding vary from one state to another and from one region to another. There is a move currently to foster regional cooperation at continental levels (Sakyi, 2015).

Party financing involves the use of money for media advertisements, transportation, logistics, cost of acquiring forms, both expression of interest and nomination and responsibilities of party delegates and party loyalists and supporters. In essence, a total of all that a party or a candidate can spend from his declaration of the contest to the final election is the term 'party funding' (Van Biezen et al., 2017). Various democracies are increasingly coming under the cross fire of censure for corruption allegations involved in violation of regulations and excessive spending. Responding to these allegations and sensing the damages that party financing is causing to the integrity of democracies globally, reforms are quickly initiated by states individually, regionally and by international organisations. To safeguard the accountability, transparency and integrity of democracies, regulations are enacted by states to curb illicit financing and counter corrupt practices in the process (Yli-Viikari & Krokfors, 2018).

Party financing is regulated by the laws of respective states. In some states, public funding is constitutionally enabled where the government finances the parties based on performance, size and other logical considerations. This is offered in form of grants to parties and the parties distribute to their flagbearers to arrest their campaign expenditure. In other democracies, full private funding is enshrined in the laws but some regulations are provided to monitor and control how private donations and personal savings are utilised in campaign expenditure by setting a limit to donation and expenditure. In other states, a combination of both public and private funding is constitutionally provided (Reed et al., 2021). The international organisations and institutions of research are mounting pressure on states to introduce regulations on party financing and to adopt reforms that will enhance accountability and transparency. This effort is yielding fruitful results as new laws are being introduced while the existing ones are undergoing reforms across states that operate as democracies (European Union, 2018). The logic of party financing regulations is to enable a fair playground for all contestants to eschew taking advantage of financial leverage by the wealthy to buy their way into elective offices against the financially weak candidates. It is also aimed at extricating the monetisation of democracy where leadership will turn into a bargain like a market commodity to deter misgovernance and misrepresentation. Party financing emphasises consolidating transparent and fair elections (Mendilow & Phélippeau, 2018).

In most states, the EMBs are saddled with the task of regulating and monitoring party financing of political parties. Some major themes are earmarked for censorship including foreign donations. Some democracies allow it but many prohibit any assistance from abroad. Other items that regulations in party financing pay attention to include a maximum donation from individuals and organisations, sources of funds, maximum spending limit, scrutinising and auditing parties' statement of accounts, disclosure principles and several other laws that deal with violations and sanctions (Schnurr, 2023). Additionally, the type of media campaign, period of the campaign and issues bordering on illegality such as vote-buying, bribery, influencing electoral officials and other offences are all regulated and frowned upon by regulations to ensure accountability and transparency. All democracies both advanced and emerging are guilty of violating the process through excessive spending, vote-buying, bribery and other related offences. Indeed, party financing is a big headache for democratic integrity and transparency. The use and abuse of state resources are reported across the globe, which is alarming (Stonestreet, 2023).

Party financing is problematic because of the tendency for corrupt practices and violations which eventually affect the integrity and transparency of the electoral process. Money politics is a major cause. The process of party financing is bedevilled with what is termed 'political corruption' (February, 2016). Political corruption is bigger than corrupt practices in the process of party funding, but party financing is a big part of political corruption. Politicians, particularly in democracies where private funding is encouraged, find it beneficial to spend lavishly on electioneering campaigns (Fiorelli, 2021). During party primaries, the richest manipulate the process through bribing the delegates, vote-buying, buying party officials and anyone that cares to be bribed has affected the chances of many candidates (Sule, 2022). Money politics corrupt electoral process and electoral corruption affects the outcome, performance and output of elections and policymaking. Politicians that buy their way into power eventually indulge in recouping the huge expenditure incurred, loot to cover future election expenses and accumulate to secure their future financially and to continue to be influential even after their tenure in political offices. They convert themselves into godfathers who continue to play politics from the background (Johnstone & Pattie, 2014).

Godfatherism is a major factor that corrupts the party financing process. Godfathers are financial sponsors of elections who emerged from all facets of politics including business tycoons, investment moguls, politicians, retired and serving military generals, royal leaders and other stakeholders that possess financial power to anoint and sponsor candidates into political offices. Godfatherism causes clientelism because they are the patrons who employ brokers that mediate between them and the clients. The brokers acquire resources from the godfathers and disburse them to clients in return for a promise of voting for their anointed candidates (Fiorelli, 2021). This political relationship is detrimental to democracy, good governance, transparency and credible elections. This is because the godfathers spend excessively, violating regulations, they sponsor violence and use coercion to cruise their godsons to victory and when their anointed godsons emerge victorious from the elections, they hijack government machinery and control state resources personally, thereby depriving the electorates of the dividends of the contract of delivery between them and the elected. Democracy and elections are bastardised by godfatherism, and this scenario is possible in all democracies worldwide (Ohman, 2018).

Political parties have different sources of income and expenditure than individual candidates. Parties raised their income through members' donations, contributions, fundraising, fees, administrative charges, selling of forms, fines and grants from governments. By extension, some parties that control power sourced their funding from the public treasury (Sule et al., 2019). Candidates on the other hand source their funds through personal contributions, grants from parties, donations, fundraising, sponsorship of wealthy individuals and godfathers and other sources that may not be disclosed. The laws are unequivocal concerning illegal sources. Several democracies such as the United States, the United Kingdom and Nigeria state in their regulations that any foreign source is banned and receiving donations from this source is the contradiction of laws and violation. The remedy or sanction is forfeiting the received funds by surrendering them to the EMBs (Power, 2018).

Chapter 3

Elections and the Electoral Process in Nigeria

An election is the lubricant of a democratic journey in the contemporary world. A periodic election is a necessary ingredient of liberal democracy and indeed, all forms of democratic rule. An election is the main principle that distinguishes democracy from autocratic and absolute monarchical regimes. An election is a rare opportunity for the citizens to exercise their franchise, make policy choice preferences by voting for a particular party or candidate to assume power and continue or discontinue if they are dissatisfied. Similarly, an election offers a platform for parties to represent their ideology and interests if they succeed in securing victory. For a democratic regime to be identified as credible and good, a healthy election with a transparent process is a requirement. A transparent electoral process requires fair play for all the parties and the contenders, freedom and liberty of the electorates to vote for candidates of their choice without intimidation or subversion, a willing and a standard process that enables a satisfactory outcome and competing mechanisms that allow the citizens to choose from among many alternatives.

An election performs many functions, and it has processes. There must be Electoral Management Bodies (EMBs) that preferably should be independent and neutral to evade unnecessary interruption of politicians and the ruling class. There must be rules and guidelines provided constitutionally or enacted temporarily by the authorities concerned for the conduct of the election. The election that is qualified to be considered an election must fulfill the minimum aforementioned criteria in addition to other factors such as level playing ground, freedom of choice without harassment, the ability to vote and have the votes count and to allow for civil societies and observers to participate in the process to have their input in checking and improving the process.

With the majority of world countries today operating democracies, elections are taking place periodically globally, and that has drawn the attention of policymakers and the international community to the need to strengthen democratic practices and values to safeguard people's liberty and preferences. It is a credible election that distinguishes democracy from authoritarian and other despotic regimes notwithstanding other factors and qualities. Without a sound and credible election that meets the minimum integrity, democracy becomes ridiculed. The intervention of so many variables such as rigging, money politics, elites' manipulation of the process via the media, declining liberty of the people and the neglect of the people-oriented policies is culminated in what many scholars (Spengler, 2016; Levitsky & Ziblatt, 2018; Dahl, 2019, Diamond, 2019 and Lu & Chu, 2022) argue that democracy is in recession, declining and battling with its soul contemporarily.

Nigeria returned to the democratic path on 29 May 1999 after more than two decades of military rule. The transition process was not a preferred one but it was immediately accepted by the civil society and the international community as a stepping stone towards complete democratisation. The Fourth Republic proved to be promising and enduring surmounting several hurdles and stringent obstacles to sustain Nigeria's democratisation for more than two consecutive decades. In sequence, six successful elections were carried out in the Fourth Republic in 1999, 2003, 2007, 2011, 2015 and 2019 and the seventh one is coming in 2023. There are indicators that Nigeria's democracy may be sustained considering the dark tunnel of subterfuge and crises that the country faced since 1999. Anytime an election approaches, the Nigerian environment becomes tense, anxiety heralds the process, and ethnic, religious and regional colouration adulterates and pollutes the political arena while security threats and challenges threaten always to halt the process. Fortunately, the six elections were handled amid the daunting challenges.

The Nigerian election is impeded by myriads of challenges just like the other African democracies as observed by Salih (2001), Lindberg (2006) and Collier (2009). In essence, Collier (2009) likened the Nigerian elections and their kind to wars of guns and other lethal weapons. Politicians that dominate the political space are never ready to relinquish power irrespective of the election outcome. All forms of prevarications are employed to subvert the process to the advantage of the ruling class and the ruling party. Besides, money politics has contaminated the political process to the extent that votes are traded like merchandise properties in the bazaar. All those who are perceived as a threat to the electoral victory of the powerful groups and their supporting godfathers are subdued with multi-level inducements in some stages and later life-threatening cautions if they refuse to cooperate. In this process, the Nigerian elite form a conglomeration of a political cartel that distributes power and allocates political seats and resources to themselves and to those they want to curry favour to them.

Nevertheless, those who studied the Nigerian election and politics in the Fourth Republic including Adejumobi (2010), Agbu (2016b) and Hamalai et al. (2017) believed that significant progress is being made gradually. For example, the 2015 general election was adjudged as the most credible and progressive election in Nigeria's Fourth Republic (Sule et al., 2018f) despite the retrogression that was sadly witnessed in the credibility of 2019 (Sule et al., 2019). Elections will continue to take place in Nigeria if the democratic dispensation continues to operate. This chapter examined the broader perspective of election from the global viewpoints and its role in democratic sustainability and, specifically, the Nigerian election and its background in the Fourth Republic analytically. Various issues, dimensions, changes, factors and challenges that precipitate the successes recorded were explored while the challenges were identified and presented to suggest policy practice and reform that will remarkably improve the process to make Nigeria's democracy an African model that will lead and guide the African continent towards democratisation as the biggest country in the region.

MEANING AND NATURE OF ELECTION

We determine who rules us in the modern governance system through an election. Representation is made permissible and legitimate to only those who earned their power through elections in democratic settings. Parties present their manifestoes, ideologies and interests and persuade voters to support them. The voters on the other hand continue to support or oppose parties through the instrumentality of the electoral process and the technicality of a periodic choice. Although the election was practised in ancient times and medieval Europe, it was in the 1800s that popular elections gained solid ground and spread. By the 1840s, several countries across the world, including the United States, many European states, and countries in Latin America, the Caribbean and Africa have experienced one form of election or the other. By 1850, about thirty-one independent states carried out elections and in 1900, specifically after the end of the First World War, more than forty-three independent states had carried out legislative elections at least once (Przeworski, 2018). Elections are simply a channel of messaging which reminds the elected to do the citizens' bidding which ordinarily, the citizens if given an opportunity, would have done by themselves yet, the interests and the need to compromise some issues by the representatives are necessary sometimes (Przeworski, 2018). Precisely, elections gained wider practice in the third wave of democratisation when the countries of Africa and Asia joined the democratic race in the twentieth century (Baldini & Papallardo, 2009).

Elections are procedures of choosing governments through vote counting. These procedures differ from one system to another as the pattern of elections in the presidential system cannot be the same in the parliamentary system and a mixed presidential–parliamentary system. The number of elective offices and the process differ. In the presidential system, voters directly elect their executive removable only by a fixed tenure or other constitutional matters but in a parliamentary system, the election of executives takes place in two steps, the electorates elect the legislators who in turn elect the prime minister from among them. Even within the presidential system, the mode of electing the executives differs. In some cases, a simple majority suffices but in other cases, some technicalities exist such as the security of the majority added with some proportion in certain districts or provinces or securing two-thirds of the Electoral College votes in the case of the American presidential election (Przeworski, 2018).

Elections are the most attractive event of democracy to the citizens, media, politicians and scholars. Election simply means turning votes into seats and contests into power control and authority (Herron et al., 2018). Hall (2018) conceives an election as the biggest national event where a tranquil mobilisation of the national citizens takes place peacefully and wilfully. An election is the process of compulsory voting in a periodic ritual involving several contestants and political positions where the voters are required to cast their votes for the party and candidates of their choice in a free and fair process. Many democracies today made elections mandatory for all eligible voters determined by the criteria set by individual respective laws of independent states (Singh, 2021). However, in spite of the mandatory status of election constitutionally in many democracies, not all citizens vote even in advanced democracies like America. A study (Bolger, 2019) reports that only some categories voted in recent American elections and the voters' turnout is steadily declining because of the perception of the public that the policymakers neglect their priorities in policymaking. This recent development made Sautter (2019) conclude that the US election is on the brink.

Election does not concern voters only as it concerns the governments too. Elections are about freedom, liberty and choice. They are also about control and constraint (Harrop & Miller, 1987). Elections are regarded as the ways of choosing new leaders and discarding the old ones in political systems. Elections are ways of deciding who holds executive and legislative powers in a state (Lindberg, 2006). Elections are won with all sorts of tricks and deception. A fifth-century Roman politician, Marcus Tillus Cicero, summed it up that if you want to win an election, prepare the following strategies in your favour which include having the backing of family and friends, surrounding oneself with the right people, calling in all favours, build a wide base of support, promise everything to everybody, sound communications skills, stay with the locals, know the weakness of the opponents and exploit them, flatter voters shamelessly and give people hope (Freeman, 2012). This view implies that politicians may deceive the voters to gain victory in an election and that is what urges Achen and Bartels (2016) to conclude that the current electoral systems and democracy may not produce responsible and responsive leaders. Through this process, voters elected narcissists and sociopaths who introduced controversial policies and programmes which throw the society into chaos (Eddy, 2019).

A new dimension emerged in theorising election and its meaning through the lens of voting behaviour. One of them is the rational choice theory of election. Developed with some predictions and assumptions, the theory is premised on the context of portraying an election as a decision-making process which involves rationality by both the voters and the politicians (Bendor et al., 2011). The theory was postulated by Downs (1957) and Arrows (1951), Olson (1961) and Arrows (1986) and it is still being given attention by scholars (Kuhn, 1983; Elster, 1986; Coleman & Fararo, 1992; Green & Shapiro, 1994; Grafstein, 1999; Archer & Tritter, 2001; Lichbach, 2003; Guzman, 2008 and Oppenheimer, 2012) and there are many academic efforts that apply the theory to elections. One of them is the study on Nigeria's 2015 general election by Sule (2018). The theory assumes that an election is a process of decision-making with rationality where the politicians seek a political position to satisfy their rational needs and where the voters choose from among the alternatives based on the best outcome that they are anticipating from a party or a candidate.

Another theory of election developed is the games of an election. With its root in Von Neumann and Morgenstern (1957), game theory emerged as the matrixes of mathematical explanations of complex decision-making in an intensely competitive environment (Wallis, 2014). Smith (2015) argues that elections and games share similar characteristics. This is because each game or election determines a decisive result obtained according to established rules with aftermath or an outcome. In mathematics, the rules for arriving at a final decision are based on logic and the formalisation of common sense. Similarly, games and elections are decisions based on logic and anticipated favourable results by the players (Hodge & Klima, 2000). Three major elements affect the success of players in a game just like in an election. The elements are chance, strategy and choice. The chance that a party or a candidate has, the strategy the candidate adopts in playing the game and the choices they makes all combine to determine his victory or failure (Smith, 2015). Votes are games played by politicians and voters in choosing preferred alternatives that appeal to them (Khan, 2019). In this regard, Khan (2019) argues that the game of voting is gradually and systematically eroding the value of ideologies in voting. The theory is further consolidated in the applicability for the study of elections when Schofield (2015) argues that vying for political control by parties is a political game competition that involves players who want to attract spectators (voters) to support their cause.

An election is linked as the clientele process that turns democracy into a commodity for sale. Clientelism has dominated contemporary elections across the world. The process of a bargain for power by national elites on the threshold of give and take is bastardising democratic accountability and electoral transparency. Patrons, brokers and clients are engaged in a cycle of material relationships during an electoral cycle. Parties woo voters' support with cash and kinds in many democracies. Vote-buying, campaign financing, bribery, corruption and other financial irregularities or illicit transactions affect the electoral process in almost all world democracies today. In some cases, corporate bodies donate beyond the limit and sponsor parties or candidates with the expectation of a reward. In other instances, voters are paid in cash and kind or are promised rewards of contract, appointment, project allocation and other benefits for supporting a party or a candidate. In this regard, democracy is swayed by trading, and elections are converted into a lucrative business venture for the voters and the politicians. The politicians that emerged through this process mismanage public resources, enrich themselves, violate laws and due process and engage in patronage, renting and patrimonial activities (Aspinall & Berenschot, 2019). Clientelism has assumed a new dimension in contemporary democracies where the patrons and their brokers engage in the process of violating the maximum spending limit and denying disclosure undetected by concealing donations, electoral bribery, adopting violence in a divide-and-rule strategy, use of fake news and digital frontiers to sway voters' opinions by using the last resort, rigging (Cheeseman & Klaas, 2018).

Elections have some grotesque features or dilemmas that are raising more questions than answers. For instance, one person represents a whole constituency or even the nation. How often he represents them really and how he compromises the representation with his personal representation is an issue on one hand and how he represents his party and party's interest is another. Emerson (2012) concludes that elected officials will definitely do more for their parties in their tenure of office than their electorates. Achen and Bartels (2016) also believed that elections, the kind of current representative will not produce a responsive government. Ordinarily, voting is the pillar of democracy and elected representatives should do what people want. Hence, what the majority wants to become policies which make democracy portray the people as the rulers but what the rulers are doing entirely negates the free will of the voters and this changed the popular view that elections are a democracy. The conduct of periodic and popular elections may not necessarily translate into good governance in the modern political system (Achen & Bartels, 2016). In essence, the policy-based choice is only determined by the type of democracy operated within a state. It is only obtained in advanced democratic systems to a certain extent (Burlacu & Toka, 2014).

In some situations, strategic voting shapes the outcome and the relevance of the election. Strategic voting occurs when the voters perceived the need to vote in a particular way originally, against their preferred choice but a strategic alternative and a favourable decision that will avoid the waste of votes (Aldrich et al., 2018). For instance, if candidates are faced with multiple choices, say three candidates for the post of a president or a prime minister, two of the candidates are seen as the frontrunners ahead of the third and many voters prefer the third one, they may avoid wasting their votes by voting for the third candidate since he may not win based on pro- jection. They may instead align with either the first or the second candidate. If they choose the second one based on polls opinion, he may overtake the first one and if they choose the first, he will proceed to win comfortably with an overwhelming majority. In this case of strategic voting, candidates are vital, the choice is important and votes are strategic. The third candidate may withdraw for the second and form a coalition or an alliance that will lead to victory.

Elections play many roles in democracy. One of them is the smooth transi- tion and continuous consolidation of democratic values and practices, par- ticularly in African countries where the presence of elections does not signify full democratisation but a transitional liberalisation that promotes increased democratic governance. Elections provide an opportunity for policy choice to the electorates who often vote based on promises, manifestoes or practi- cal performances of the elected either to offer them the chance to continue with the preferred policy choice or to change the elected if the policy is not favourable. Election enables power to change hands smoothly without war or violence if incumbents are defeated. Elections signify civil duties, political participation, responsibilities and freedom. Elections further consolidate civil liberty and citizens' power to alternate policy and determine the direction of decision-making (Lindberg, 2006). Elections shape the future in democra- cies because the choice made by voters will determine the future of policy, decisions, well-being and development of the society or the other way round (Fowler & Smirnov, 2007). Democratic elections enabled the voters to choose political leaders from among the varieties of choices that they faced. What impresses the voters in the choice of leadership is the policies, promises and the desire for a party ideology or apology (Blais, 2011). The provision of universal public goods such as electricity is shaped by the outcome of elec- toral choices, particularly in developing countries (Min, 2015).

There are various structures of electoral systems, and no one is said to be better than the other because each is appealing to representation (Norris, 2004). Lijphart (1994) argues that for a better understanding of electoral systems, the dimensions of the systems should be observed and critically analysed. McLean (2018) presents three systems of the electoral process in which one of them is May's theorem of simple majority where a candidate who secures a simple majority even if the difference is one is the winner. The second is the median voter theorem posited by Black and Downs, in which an average voter can determine who wins by the median score based on the uniform decision of the average voters who collapsed into one unique decision. The third is the Arrows theorem where the position of the person preferred by the median voter will win. This process is structured in a way that an average voter can vote using an alternative system where if there are three candidates A, B and C, he will elect all three based on a scale of preference and the candidate with the highest alternative of the preferred votes wins.

McLean (2018) further presents the families of the typologies of the electoral systems based on the mode of the choice pattern. The first is interest aggregation which is used for electing one person. For instance, in the presidential system, voters vote for only one candidate of their choice and if he secures the majority from 50 percent and above, he wins, if there is no clear winner, the two highest scorers are bid for a rerun while the low performers are eliminated. In this case, second-round occurs. The principal–agent system is used for electing many people as in the case of the parliament election where multiple members are to be elected. A proportional system is the one in that the voters elect many people through some processes which one of them is listing. A voter is expected to choose only one party and the parties are listed alphabetically or on other considerations. The choice of a candidate and a party is influenced by the environment and the nature of the political contests including the electoral systems, types of parties and the citizens' context of political participation (Dalton & Anderson, 2011). Parties do not only influence the environment of elections but they give directions and guidance to the elections. Before any election proper, parties practise a rehearsal known as party primaries to present their best options for the final election. Party primaries are handled by parties internally with the supervision of EMBs. Party primaries enhance transparency, representation and competition. Party primaries are carried out by voters, party supporters, party members, party delegates, party elite and a single leader in some cases (Cross et al., 2016).

Electoral systems matter because they are the foundation that displays the citizens' preferences and alternatives to the policy choice and responses to the government (Gallagher & Mitchell, 2018). Herron et al. (2018) believed that electoral systems are influenced by the party system in a democratic environment. This is because electoral systems have effects on the party systems in terms of their chances and competing for victory (Shugart & Taagepera, 2018) in the same way that the electoral systems affect the voters' turnout (Smith, 2018) just as reported by Norris (2018a) that electoral systems influence electoral integrity. Succinctly, these scholars in their variant views are trying to justify and convince the interesting parties in the election and electoral systems that the success of the election, voters' turnout, integrity, credibility and other determinants of election success are affected by the electoral system adopted or applied in a given area or a state. Baldini and Papallardo (2009) argue that electoral systems are products of circumstances of the political history of a given area which are measured by six dimensions as the following: the right to vote, the right to be a candidate, the electoral register, the agency in charge of the election, the procedure for casting votes and the procedure to sort out the winners and losers. In essence, elections are conditioned, controlled and constrained by governments on the level of the electoral systems allowed to operate (Harrop & Miller, 1987).

An election requires integrity because of the importance of its impacts. People's trust, liberty, freedom, security, resources and vital decisions that will influence their lives positively or negatively are all products of who they elect to lead them. Therefore this process needs to have the integrity to safeguard and protect the citizens. Electoral integrity, according to Norris (2018b), can be understood positively or negatively. On the negative aspects, scholars are concerned with whether the contests are manipulated, fraudulent and characterised by malpractice. On the positive side, the measure of electoral integrity is determined by whether elections can be considered free and fair, genuine and credible and competitive and democratic. An election is said to have integrity when it meets the agreed international conventions and global norms covering the entire election cycle from the pre-election, during the conduct of the election and in the post-election period. The internationally agreed conventions are found in written declarations, treaties, protocols, case law and guidelines issued by international organisations and international election monitors and endorsed by member-states (Norris, 2018b). Norris (2018b) further presents the electoral integrity cycle which consists of election laws, electoral procedures, boundaries, voter registration, party and candidate registration, campaign media, campaign finance, the voting process, vote count, results and finally, EMBs.

Conducting an election periodically is a Herculean task that many states can face. Elections are difficult to execute because multiple choices are sometimes carried out simultaneously, huge resources are disbursed, a large crowd is managed and attended to, and the process is tedious and painstaking. The process is difficult because it is expected to be carried out by electoral workers who are trained to carry an array of activities in the pre-electoral, the electoral and the post-electoral period. The management of elections is risky because it is sensitive to even negligible errors in the whole process. Election administration according to Hall (2018) is the administrative process used for the preparation of casting of ballots, compiling the electoral results and determining the winner from the outcome of what the people expressed in their choice without any interference. Election administration is undertaken in an election cycle. The election cycle has three periods. The first is the pre-election period which consists of voter registration, training of electoral staff, recruitment of ad hoc staff where applicable, voter education and planning of the voting proper. The second is the election period where voting occurs, ballots are counted and official results are announced. The final stage is the process of auditing the election, the future preparation and observed anomalies are rectified for future smooth conduct of the election (Hall, 2018).

In essence, election administration is rule-making, rule-application and rule-implementation. Election administration encounters several challenges that affect its success when the process is bedevilled with voter-fraud, vote-buying, intimidation, ballot-box stealing, ballot-box stuffing, manipulation of results and other malpractice (Norris, 2018a). Election administration is carried by EMBs. EMB is the body that plans the elections and provides overall administrative and technical support for all aspects of the electoral conduct in a given country. The EMBs are found to be effective if they are permanent and independent of the executive or any other arm of government in a state. This is followed if they have the full constitutional mandate of the responsibility for the direction and management of the state (Hall, 2018). In most democracies like the US and the UK, election administration is the responsibility of the local governments except for some cases (Hale et al., 2015). This system is also operated in some African countries like Nigeria where the national elections are managed by the Independent National Electoral Commission (INEC) but the local council polls are the responsibility of the State Independent Electoral Commissions (SIECs) (Deribe et al., 2020). Elections are failing the voters because the management bodies are often facing problems that are avoidable but they are affecting the electoral process such as discarded ballots, poll workers being poorly trained, the registration lists sometimes cumbersome and works with much delay, machines malfunction and partisan electoral officials changed the rules of the game to support themselves and cheat the opposition (Gerken, 2009).

Elections are strengthened with some activities and institutions. One of them is election observation. The essence of election observation and monitoring is to enhance democracy and rule of law across nation-states. The international donors and agencies of international organisations such as the United Nations, European Union, the African Union (AU) and other related umbrella bodies carried out the task of election observations. In the twenty-first century, donors and international organisations are empowering domestic observers and civil societies within states to develop the capacity and technical procedure for the observation and reporting. Election observation is Western intervention in the post–Second World War period (Hesseling, 2000). However, election observation has controversies regarding its objective and consequences. Observation in countries that are recalcitrant and have undemocratic political systems is much more difficult. Identifying and defining what exactly the observers are doing is difficult. Despotic governments like the African democracies sometimes manipulate the observation process to favour the report in their way. Besides, the motive of the observers and donors is questionable. The observers may have an obscured motive that will make them careless about the outcome of the elections or the democratisation process (Abbink, 2000).

Election monitoring is meant to foster transparency in the electoral process. For example, the Open Election Data Initiative by the National Democracy Institute strives to facilitate transparency in making some electoral process information open and public including the list of polling units, voters' register, voting laws and rights, regulations on party financing and other procedures. Since the end of the Cold War era, electoral observation become a widely used tool in ensuring electoral integrity. This activity involves many intergovernmental regional organisations including the Organisation of American States (OAS), the Organisation for Economic Cooperation and Development (OECD), the Council of Europe, the AU, the Electoral Institute of South Africa (EISA), the Asian Network for Free Elections (ANFREL). The bilateral development agencies too are not left behind in the monitoring of elections including the National Democracy Institute, the International Republican Institute (IRI), the International Foundation for Electoral Systems (IFES) and the Carter Centre (Norris, 2017). The intergovernmental monitoring organisations published regularly reports evaluating the quality, credibility and integrity of the monitored elections over a period of time. Since 1962 the OAS has monitored over 200 elections in more than 30 countries, deploying more than 5,000 international observers (Norris, 2017).

The main issue with monitoring of elections by international groups is the personalisation and politicisation of the reports and the process in many cases. Arceneaux and Leithner (2017) argue that the politicisation of monitoring has causes and consequences which is being affected by the foreign policy interest of bilateral donors and the method used by each organisation. The degree of the professionalisation of the observers and how they arrive at their reports is questioned in some cases. It should be noted that over forty donors or observers endorsed a common code of conduct but still, the observation lacks a common standardisation (Arceneaux & Leithner, 2017). The donors often adopt a common stand in enforcing compliance when diplomacy failed by using pressure on states to implement electoral reforms, protect the opposition and the use of conditionality and diplomatic engagement which succeeded in operation by 15 governmental and intergovernmental actors after they applied in 668 elections in 119 countries (Donno, 2017). Coma (2017) supports the aforementioned submission that international monitors can improve electoral transparency and integrity through the use of deterrence and enhancing reform implementation.

The role of election or its status in contemporary democracy is eroding. Some decades back, it was adjudged that elections produced democracy while democracy is the product of elections. The notion that election is a legitimate means of free choice is being overturned by the recent developments in authoritarian democracies. At the turn of the twenty-first century, a paradox of electoral viability is being reversed. The view that elections are the distinguishing dividing lines between dictatorships and non-dictatorships is being demystified by the actions of some democrats. For instance, in the twentieth century, dictators are known to have suspended all electoral processes and even the constitutions themselves on the assumption of power while all democracies maintained their periodic elections. Contemporarily, dictators hold elections too. Many dictatorial regimes today hold regular elections and allow multi-party competition. The strategy adopted by dictatorial regimes is suppressing the opposition's participation and roles in the democratic process. An election that is ridiculed and subverted is organised to secure legitimacy and to claim democracy. In most cases, parties boycott elections because of perceived injustice and an unfair process that is not free (Buttorff, 2019). Such boycotts of elections and the conduct of authoritarian elections according to Buttorff (2019) are found in the Arab world. But there are other studies (Lindberg, 2006 and Collier, 2009) that identified the African, Asian and Latin American regions as authoritarian elections and regimes. In essence, Birch (2020) argues that developing democracies undertake periodic elections only to claim democratic legitimacy but the level of fraud and malpractice are far from allowing the process to be democratic.

The authoritarian elections often resulted in contentious elections. Contentious elections are increasing after the Cold War with the proliferation of more democracies across the globe. Contentious elections are elections that are conducted full of fraud, mistrust and intolerance and often trigger mass protests and violence (Norris et al., 2015). Contentious elections undermine democratisation in emerging countries that are shaking off the yoke of dictatorship from their political system, increasing societal destabilisation and social uprisings in vulnerable states, and overall, affecting the socioeconomic development of the developing economies (Norris et al., 2015). Apart from the aforementioned consequences of contentious elections, voters' turnout is decreased (Nikolayenko, 2015), mass protests with national security implications are catalysed (Sedziaka & Rose, 2015), leaders are overthrown in the process (Higashijima, 2015) in developing democracies with the military likely to intervene and capitalise on the created instability and chaos as their justification, mass violence is triggered (Kuhn, 2015) and people's choice is impeded. Collier (2009) likened some elections in authoritarian democracies and contentious elections to wars with lethal weapons such as guns by the politicians to secure victory at all costs. But it is not only in the developing countries that elections are subverted. It is observed (Fredrickson, 2019) that American elections in recent years are manipulated, fraudulent and involved irregularities of defying the standard norms and rules that previously allow the citizens to have a freedom of choice.

But it is not only the internal subjugation of elections that harmfully threatens democracy alone. Foreign interference in the electoral process is now an albatross on the neck of global democratisation. Foreign powers have been meddling in the elections of world countries either directly or through proxies. Throughout the Cold War, foreign intervention in elections had become a feature of national elections. Blum (2002) showcased unnecessary US intervention in foreign elections including the overthrow of democratically elected regimes in more than fifty countries, especially, in Africa, Asia, and Latin America and the Caribbean. In essence, Blum (2013) argues that democracy is the deadliest export commodity that America is imposing on other countries because they are being forced to implement a system that may not likely be relevant to their culture and where the implementation is made according to the whims of America but the leaders exhibited some degrees of independence and freedom from America, the democracy is thwarted. Kovalik (2018) justifies that America spent billions to change the outcome of elections around the world to control the global democracy not based on integrity but on its national interest or elite politics. Again, nearly fifty cases in Africa, Asia, East Europe and Latin America and the Caribbean are presented by Blum (2013). In modern times, the explosion of the internet and digital elections are the main problems that is affecting elections and enabling foreign intervention in elections (Alvarez & Hall, 2008). The Russian intervention in the US 2016 presidential election, the 2017 French Presidential Elections, the 2019 EU parliamentary elections and the Brexit question are all examples of how the foreign interventions in elections are threatening to erode electoral integrity and sovereignty worldwide (Hollis & Ohlin, 2021).

In the case of Africa, it is observed (Fombad & Steytler, 2021) that democratisation and elections are steadily declining in Africa over the last thirty years. It should be understood that elections have been taking place in Africa from the colonial period to the early period of political independence in the 1960s. The idea of election in Africa is not an alien or foreign introduction of the colonial powers. Many pre-colonial states chose their leaders through a fair electoral process (Nohlen et al., 1999). In the third wave of democratisation after the Cold War, Africa made a significant breakthrough in reversing dictatorship and authoritarian regimes with increased regular elections. However, after thirty years of practice, the trend declined tremendously which made Fombad and Steytler (2021) declare that democracy is declining in Africa. The justification of this position is the weakness of constitutional democracy in Africa with authoritarian leaders concealing themselves under the umbrella of an election. Such leaders refused to enable a healthy environment for competition and opposition (Hesseling, 2000). The Cameroon president Paul Biya is at the stage for more than four decades in the same way the Ugandan president Yoweri Museveni is heading to the same decades. Many cases of such authoritarian disguise in democracy exist all over Africa in one form or the other (Fombad & Steytler, 2021). Most African states are today a one-party system in practice, the opposition is emasculated and respect for rule of law and human rights are suppressed. Earlier, Lindberg (2006) observed the same phenomenon with the African democracy and elections but he is soft in his approach giving the continent the benefit of time since he recognises that the presence of elections does not necessarily interpret into democracy. Violence is the common norm in African elections aided by the nature of the electoral institutions (Fjelde & Hoglund, 2014 and Sigman & Lindberg, 2020). The moral question of election in Africa anchors around the role of the electoral bodies and the policymakers to be sincere in delivering acceptable elections (Cheeseman et al., 2020).

RULES OF ELECTION CONDUCT IN NIGERIA

The constitution of the Federal Republic of Nigeria provides that INEC is the legal body with the powers to conduct elections into the office of the president and his deputy, governors and their deputies, National Assembly and State Houses of Assemblies and FCT Abuja local council polls. The SIECs are responsible for the LG polls across the 36 states of the federation in all the 770 local governments exempting the 6 local councils in FCT Abuja which is directly conducted by the INEC (Global Legal Research Centre, 2011). The elections into the these offices are constitutionally undertaken every four years except for the local council polls conducted by SIECs under states' supervision which has no specific term. It is bastardised and manipulated by the state governors to the extent that they are conducted differently across the thirty-six states as per the wish and desire of the respective governors (Deribe et al., 2020).

Elections are carried out with the active participation of political parties. The Nigerian 1999 Constitution provides a clause on freedom of association in Section 40 which extends to the interpretation of the formation of parties and belonging to them as members by interested individuals. For an individual to participate in an election in Nigeria, he must attain a specified age which is eighteen years and above as provided in Section 65 while Section 79 and its sub-sections provide mandatory requirements for electing an officer into the National Assembly including the time limit. Section 106 reveals those who are eligible to contest for a seat in the National Assembly while Section 107 indicates those who are disqualified. Section 132 to Section 139 provide conditions for contest and election into the Office of the President, disqualification, tenure, illness that can incapacitate a president or an aspirant or a candidate into the office and matters related to resignation (Policy and Legal Advocacy Centre, 2019).

The election into the Office of the Vice President as provided in Section 142 including other related matters like those of the president. Sections 176 to 184 provides for the establishment of the Office of the Governor, qualification for election, disqualification, death, incapability and the process for the conduct of the election. Section 187 provides the same regulations for the Office of the Deputy Governor. Section 225 and Section 226 and their sub-sections provide the legal provisions and regulations of financing of political parties, sources of income and expenditure, campaign spending limit and auditing of parties' finances. Sanctions and other related matters are provided in the same sections and their sub-sections against those who violate the regulations. In addition, powers are conferred by some sub-sections of the INEC to monitor and regulate parties and their activities (Policy and Legal Advocacy Centre, 2019).

The second legal document that is operated in Nigeria for the conduct of elections is Electoral Act 2022. For the sake of clarity, it should be understood that all the previous elections conducted in Nigeria were operated with Electoral Act 2006 for the 1999, 2003 and 2007 elections, and the Electoral Act 2010 was used for the conduct of 2011, 2015 and the 2019 general elections. Henceforth, the 2023 general election and beyond would be conducted using the Electoral Act 2022. Section 1 of the Electoral Act 2022 provides that INEC is an independent body established to conduct elections and other matters related to elections. Section 2 provides the functions of INEC covering all aspects from election to party monitoring and registration of voters as well as delineation of constituencies. Section 3 explains the provision of the body's sources of funds. Section 4 provides for the expenditure of the Commission. Section 9 and Section 10 with their sub-sections provides for voters' registration and continuous registration exercise. Section 13 provides for the transfer of registration of voters from one unit or constituency to another. Section 14 to Section 22 provide additional explanations on other issues related to voters' cards such as issuance, replacement, distribution and usage. Section 23 and Section 24 provide laws relating to offences on voters' registration and selling of voters' cards.

Section 25 up to Section 78 and their sub-sections provide all the rules relating to election conduct involving party primaries, submission of candidates' list, replacement of candidates, nomination, contest, delineation of polling units, provision of election materials, the appointment of election officials, custody of election materials, the voting proper, collation of results, announcing of results, declaration of winners, election petition tribunals and other matters arising. It should be understood that the Electoral Act 2022 is not in practice yet. It will come into play in the 2023 general election but the law was already passed into an act on 25 February 2022. The previous elections have their respective separate guidelines for the conduct of the specific elections. For instance, the 2015 general election had in its guidelines the use of voter accreditation and the use of Smart Card Readers (SMCs).

The latest election conducted was the 2019 general election. The guidelines for the conduct of the 2019 general election provided that SCRs must be used for accreditation and voting while inconclusive was affirmed. An inconclusive election means a situation whereby the total number of votes cancelled is more than the margin of a win among the contestants. This implies that even if the total accredited votes in the ward or wards or constituencies that the votes are cancelled are less than the total number of registered voters in the area, still the election remains inconclusive. For example, if a ward has 50,000 registered voters, 20,000 are accredited for the voting on the election day, the margin of winning is 5,000 but 2,000 votes are cancelled apart from the total valid votes, the calculation of inconclusive will take into consideration all the total registered votes of 50,000 even if only 20,000 is accredited. This scenario resulted in serious malpractice in and rigging of the 2019 general election, particularly in the gubernatorial elections where in some states like Kano, Benue, Plateau, Sokoto and some others elections were overstretched intentionally to the inconclusive status when the incumbent sensed defeats. Violence erupted in the process with massive vote-buying and rigging as reported by Sule and Sambo (2021). Other guidelines in the 2019 general election are discussed further.

The regulations in Section 1 affect the president and vice president, governors and deputy governors, National Assembly (Senate and House of Representatives, Chairmen and Vice Chairmen FCT Abuja and Councillors FCT Abuja). Regulation numbers 2, 3, 4, 5, 6 and 7 provide for who can vote, where to vote, when to vote, and appointment of polling unit officers and APOs. Regulations 8 to 26 stipulated the process of accreditation and voting process which include accreditation of voters by 7:30 a.m., opening of poll, method of voting, mandatory use of SCRs for accreditation and voting, issues of missing name in voting register, card failure, taking care of a person with a disability, accidental destruction of ballot paper, use of electronic devices in the polling units, close of voting, sorting and counting, recounting pasting of results, transmission and reporting of cases of over-voting or cancellation which declare those affected units' results as null and void (INEC, 2019).

Regulations 27 to 32 present the criteria for the collation of results, from the registration area, local government area, state constituency and federal constituency, senatorial constituency, governorship and presidential election. Phone calls were prohibited during the collation process by officers. Various respective forms called forms ECs are filled up each in its designated area and pasted up to the final collation centre by the electoral workers. Section 33 and its subsections make provision that supplementary elections can occur where the election is declared null and void in an area and it is believed that the result will affect the overall outcome. Where the total number of cancelled votes is less than the margin of lead between the leading candidate and contending candidates, the officer shall declare the results. Where the margin of lead between the two leading candidates is not more than the total number of voters registered in polling units where elections are not held or voided in line with Sections 2 and 53 of the Electoral Act, the election is declared inconclusive and a new date is fixed for holding the supplementary election (INEC, 2019).

The aforementioned regulations may have some roots in the statutory laws of election conduct but they are not in the 1999 Constitution and the Electoral Act 2022 as amended. By the 2023 general election, new regulations may emerge different from the previously discussed ones. A study (Sule & Sambo, 2021) suggests that the inconclusive aspect should be jettisoned as part of the guidelines for the conduct of elections in the future to avoid the terrible events that unfolded from the findings of the study in the inconclusive elections of violence including killings, vote-buying, rigging and malpractice and other irregularities that touched the integrity of the elections. However, some guidelines may change such as the enactment of the use of SCRs as a mandatory part of accreditation and voting. In the 2015 and the 2019 general elections, they were part of the guidelines but not a mandatory provision in the law. The cases of over-voting in some states and other elective positions that were taken to the court such as Kano could not be reversed because the judges argued among other factors that the use of SCRs was not a mandatory law that could affect elections outcome in Nigeria. In the 2023 general election, apart from the mandatory use of SCRs, the collation of results directly through an e-voting process may form part of the guidelines. It may definitely do so in the future even if it is not considered in 2023 because of some challenges. The INEC deployed the use of Biometric Verification Accreditation

System (BVAS) in the Ekiti and Osun 2022 Governorship elections in May and July respectively and the success recorded is encouraging and signifying additional measures of counter-rigging and transparency (Sule, 2022).

CHALLENGES OF ELECTORAL PROCESS
IN NIGERIA'S FOURTH REPUBLIC

Nigeria has conducted more elections in the Fourth Republic than the aggregate elections held from 1960 to 1999. As observed in the aforementioned scholarly views, elections in Africa are not smooth and are not even expected to be perfect or fair because they are elections in a transitory democratic process. Several issues bedevilled the credibility and integrity of the elections throughout their cycles (Nwankwo, 2020). Despite the challenges, significant improvements are being recorded and as the elections are being conducted, the process is continuously witnessing some reforms, measures and other mechanisms that are enhancing fairness, transparency and credibility. Nevertheless, there are recurring challenges that must be attended to improve the credibility and integrity of the electoral process in Nigeria. Some of the challenges are identified and observed here.

Funding or cost of elections in Nigeria is expensive and is gulping huge sums of money since 1999. As the democratic rule is shooting forward in Nigeria taking a lasting process and steady periodic elections, the cost of elections in Nigeria is alarming. In essence, Nigeria is one of the most expensive elections in the world. In the 2007 general election, INEC spent N45.5 billion ($108,462,454.10 million). The 2011 general election gulped over N111 billion ($264, 600, 712.20 million), the 2015 general election N125 billion ($297, 973, 775.00 million) and the 2019 general election cost about N240 billion ($572,109,648.00 million) (Sambo & Sule, 2021). This implies that Nigeria spent more than Canada in the 2007 general election, more than the UK in the 2011 general election and more than Australia in the 2015 general election (Abdallah, 2018). Nigeria is one of the few African countries that constitutionally forbids foreign donation and sponsorship of elections. The fact that Nigeria spent more than advanced old democracies such as Canada, the UK and Australia indicates that Nigeria is running an expensive election. Several factors aided this scenario. One is population. Nigeria has a total population and number of voters more than the three countries combined together. Second is the failure to preserve election materials such as computers and other gadgets after an election cycle against future elections. With each election period, INEC has to procure new equipment. Besides, the politics of the funding is another issue (Okolie et al., 2019). Sometimes the executive releases the funds to conduct the election, which often affects the electoral calendar leading to postponement and other logistic issues. In the build-up to the 2019 general election, the executive-legislative feud led to an incessant delay in the passage of the appropriation budget for the election conduct coupled with the lack of proactive measures of the executive in preparing the budget earlier (Sambo & Sule, 2021).

One of the major problems that elections conduct faced in Nigeria is logistics. Related to the above, Nigeria is a large contiguous geographical area with many terrains and land features that vary from one region to another. The conveyance of election materials and other sensitive documents sometimes encountered hurdles and challenges that delayed the elections or even postponement. The procurement of the election materials themselves is done dubiously by contracting some companies that supply materials from abroad (Onapajo, 2019). Sensitive materials and other electoral documents should be produced in Nigeria for national security reasons. But it is suspected that indigenous companies may connive with either the ruling party or any interesting party including the opposition to have access to them which will compromise the process (Sule et al., 2021). Some areas, such as the Niger Delta, are swampy with mangroves and creeks where transportation is through the means of water by boats and canoes. In some northern areas, the Sahara makes transportation of election materials challenging and delaying. All these logistics issues are compounded by the shortage of materials and failure of electricity which led computers and other gadgets to shutdown, failure of card readers to accredit in many places all coupled to make the electoral process and its logistics difficult. In many instances, elections commenced late in the evening hours when other places are rounding up while in many instances, elections are shifted to the next day. This logistics problem delayed election results and overburdened the electoral officials and the voters making it frustrating and in some cases, low voter turnout and disenfranchisement of many electorates (Sule et al., 2019b).

Nigerian elections are discredited and diverted by ethnic, religious and regional voting patterns. The elite inculcates into the minds of voters the political culture of sentiments and emotions. This has become more pronounced in the Fourth Republic. However, the roots of ethnoreligious and regional politics and voting were sown during colonialism. Parties that emerged were ethnic, religious and regional in outlook while the nationalists that fought for political independence did so in fragmented and disjointed national cohesion (Nnoli, 1988). The elites that assumed power control after political independence turned political power into economic investment and since they have nothing to show as performances that will qualify them to earn a second chance from voters, they resorted to the exploitation of the vulnerable points of the Nigerian electorates and infused into their psyche regional politics, infiltrated the voting influence of the electorates with religion and ethnic politics (Joseph, 1991). This development is considered the bane of democratic good governance in Nigeria. In essence, some scholars (Diamond, 1995b and Adejumobi, 2010) argued that the previous republics in Nigeria collapsed because of the intensity of the ethno-religious and regional politics. Instead of campaigning based on issues, politicians manipulated voters to support them based on the above-identified identities and clan affiliation.

Ethnic and religious politics are not unique to the Nigerian democratic system. These elements play vital roles in securing support and victory for the contestants even in advanced democracies. For instance, Lijphart (1979) argues that power-sharing among the various heterogeneous components in states like Austria, Switzerland, Sweden, Netherlands and Portugal sustained and consolidated democracy. Democracy in plural societies is characterised by ethnic and religious voting and the desire for minority autonomy. However, the Nigerian case becomes annoying considering that the elites are using the identity elements to secure power only and enrich themselves. In other plural societies, regional, ethnic and religious leaders bargain for positions to draw benefit to their minority groups to avoid marginalisation and deprivation (Nwankwo, 2019). In Nigeria, the goal is to get access to power and enrich self. Besides, the ethnic and religious voting identity is causing violent elections in Nigeria and is denying the country the opportunity to be led by credible and competent leaders with integrity and determination for genuine societal building (Mbah et al., 2019). The implications are misgovernance occurs while resource allocation is misplaced by the policymakers to favour their ethnic and religious groups. In most cases, even appointments into sensitive offices with national security architecture and other areas that require strict merit and qualification are sacrificed on the altar of favouritism and nepotism. The usual outcome of election results in Nigeria justifies ethnic voting considering where the candidates and their bloc votes emerged from (Onapajo & Babalola, 2019).

Violence characterised elections in Nigeria's Fourth Republic. The former president Olusegun Obasanjo himself described the 2003 general election as a war (Human Rights Watch, 2007). Electoral violence is seen as a process which is perpetrated by coercion, aggression, irregularities and targeted destruction against lives, properties and social amenities (Birch et al., 2020). The reports by Human Rights revealed massive intimidation, political assassination, political thuggery, banditry, stealing of ballot boxes, terrorising voters and ostracising them from the polling units to enable ballot thumping and ballot stuffing and killings and injuries perpetrated by sponsored political errand boys distributed across the country in various names such as Area Boys in Lagos, OPC and Egbesu in the Southwest, Bakassi in the Niger Delta Yan Jagaliya in Kano, Sara Suka in Bauchi, Yan Kalare in Gombe and ECOMOG in Maiduguri and other places with various nomenclatures. These violent groups were armed with lethal weapons such as machetes, clubs, spears, knives, horns and guns in some places to terrorise perceived threats and opposition. Political violence in Nigeria's Fourth Republic affects seriously the credibility and fairness of the elections because, in many instances, results were manufactured and declared where the actual voters were disenfranchised by violence (Onuoha et al., 2019).

In essence, African elections are embedded in the controversies of election violence not only in Nigeria. About 60 percent of the elections conducted in Africa in the 2000s are heralded with violence and the outcomes are accompanied by post-election violence (Burchard & Simati, 2019). Electoral violence in Nigeria takes three stages: pre-election violence, election violence and post-election violence (Shenga & Pereira, 2019). The National Democratic Institute (NDI) reported on Nigeria's 2007 general election about 280 election-related deaths before the conduct of the election. The NDI further reported that the Nigerian electoral body, the INEC, reported 50 deaths, and 1,093 electoral offenders after the first round of the election but the Transition Monitoring Group (TMG) reported the figure of deaths to 80 (Onapajo, 2014). Violence continues to erupt during Nigerian elections unabated. The post-election violence in the 2011 presidential election claimed 2,000 lives in Jos, Plateau State, alone, and the Kaduna State case became gruesome which led to the death of over 700 people. Similar violence was recorded in Kano, and several other northern states with churches, mosques, police stations, shops and businesses set ablaze totalling 1,000 reported deaths (Igwe & Amadi, 2021). The US International Centre for Electoral Support (USICES) reported that over 1,000 lives were lost in Nigeria to electoral violence during the 2011 post-election violence (USICES, 2018). In 2015, about 100 were killed in electoral violence across the country (Kwarkye, 2019). According to SBM Intelligence, as reported by Human Rights Watch, which monitors political and socioeconomic development in the country, 626 people were killed during the election cycle in Nigeria in 2019 starting with violent campaigns in 2018 (Delay, 2019).

Money politics is a big problem in the Nigerian elections since 1999. Vote-buying as reported by many studies (Adeyi, 2008; Ayoade, 2008; Walecki, 2008; Smah, 2008 and Sule et al., 2018d) has become a great obstacle on the path to a credible election in Nigeria. Money politics is transacted at different levels. The party primaries turned out to be a bazaar where the highest bidder always has his way. The 2019 party primaries of the All Progressives Congress (APC) and the People's Democratic Party (PDP) were bedevilled with outrageous vote-buying of the delegates to the extent that each delegate is bought at the cost of $5,000 (N2,074,950.00 million) in the PDP presidential primaries (Sule, 2019 and Sule, 2022). In the build-up to the 2023 general election, the scenario worsened where the presidential candidates of the APC and the PDP were allegedly reported to have bought each vote of the delegates at the cost of $25,000 (N10,374,750.00 million) (Sule, 2022). The cost of obtaining party nomination forms themselves systematically eliminated all poor and average Nigerians. The ruling APC fixed the cost of nomination forms for president at N100 million ($240,884), governorship at N50 million ($85,470), Senate at N20 million ($34,188), House of Representatives at N10 million ($17,094) and State Assembly at N2 million ($3,418). The leading opposition party, the PDP, pegged N40 million ($68,376) as the cost for presidential nomination forms, N21 million ($35,897) for governorship, N3.5 million ($5,982) for Senate, N2.5 million ($4,273) for House of Representatives and N1.5 million ($2,564) for State House of Assembly (Itodo, 2022).

The ruling and major opposition parties were rebuked for this high monetisation of politics but the ruling APC responded that they will provide a discount of 50 percent for women and youth but how could the disadvantaged afford the 50 percent of the amount from where? As if it is not enough, the party leaders of the APC arrogantly replied to the critics that their party nomination forms are not meant for the poor or sugarcane sellers. This is the party that its Presidential flagbearer in the 2015 presidential election could not afford the cost of nomination form and campaign finances until the poor supporters donated about N186 million ($448,203.57 thousand) (Sule, 2022). Money politics takes the second aspect of excessive spending, donating above the contribution ban and abuse of public resources and violation of campaign finance regulations. In the field, the general elections are enshrouded with vote-buying, bribery and abuse of the process. The state governorship election in 2016, 2019 and beyond was reported to have been engaged in vote-buying worth N15,000 thousand ($36.15) (Sule & Sambo, 2021). Godfathers are responsible for the highly monetised politics in Nigeria as reported by Olarinmoye (2008), Ogundiya (2009) and Sule et al. (2018c). They are the moneybags behind some contestants and spent lavishly to climb them onto power using all means of bribery and corruption. Money politics transformed Nigerian politics into a business venture where the investors (politicians) buy votes to gain victory to recoup their money and generate profit at the expense of the negligence of public priority of common infrastructure and deliverable necessary services.

One of the unique phenomena of the Nigerian elections that continues to repeat itself is the postponement of elections from their initial scheduled timetable due to failure of logistics, ill-preparations and other obstacles that appeared on the way of the electoral body. The phenomenon occurred in 2007, 2011, 2015 and the 2019 general elections. This means the electoral body is not learning or reforming adequately if a single problem will continue to repeat itself for more than a decade and in four consecutive elections (Thurston, 2018). The 2019 general election, the recent one, was postponed from 16 February to 23 February 2019, for the presidential and National Assembly elections and from 28 February to 9 March 2019, for the governor-ship and State House of Assembly and that had affected the election process. This problem has several implications for Nigerian elections. One of them is voter apathy because only 34.76 percent turned out in the election. Many voters traversed the country from one region to another to their hometowns to cast their votes but when the election was postponed they decided to go back to their businesses and forfeit the election. Economically, the cost of the election went higher from the approved N189 billion to at least N240 billion due to the postponement because some of the logistics must be restrategise and the cost implications (Sambo & Sule, 2021).

Another big problem of Nigerian elections in the Fourth Republic is wide massive malpractice and irregularities. Onapajo (2014) emphasises the fraud that interrupted Nigerian elections as the subversion of the process, violence, and rigging, inflation of voting figures, ballot snatching, ballot thumping, and ballot-box stealing and spoiling of the votes of opposition. Various scholars (Tar & Zak-Williams, 2007; Human Rights Watch, 2007; Casimir et al., 2013; Bariledum et al., 2016; Isma'ila & Othman, 2016; Ozoemena & Evan-gelina, 2019; Dada, 2021) believed that electoral fraud is committed in Nige-ria through multiple stages and processes leading to challenges of legitimacy and good governance. Apart from challenges of good governance, electoral fraud in Nigeria is accompanied by protests in disagreement and legitimacy questions (Daxecker et al., 2019). Nigeria has a history of tumultuous and controversial elections in the past with the five elections in 1999, 2003, 2007, 2011 and 2015 all full of allegations of fraud and irregularities (Dele-Adedeji, 2019). Hakeem and Okeke (2014) see the electoral umpire and courts as col-laborators for electoral fraud since manipulated elections could not be handled fairly by the courts of law in the country. Varella (2021) identified that one of the popular ways of electoral fraud in Nigeria is vote-buying. She added that statistics in the 2019 general election revealed that about 25 percent of voters were wooed with monetary incentives to vote for some candidates. However, Nwangwu et al. (2018), presented a positive view of electoral fraud in Nigeria where they concluded that the adoption and implementation of digital tech-nology via SCRs is an elixir to Nigeria's battling electoral system.

Bribery and corruption are another epics of the challenges of the Nigerian elections. Politicians buy their way into power through dubious games and means that involved illegal bargains through bribery and corruption (Igiebor, 2019). Reports indicate a situation whereby electoral officials are bribed to favour the results of the election to the bidding parties. This scenario is evi-dent in Nigeria as in the case of a professor who was jailed for three years with a fine of N100,000 for collecting bribes and electoral fraud in the con-duct of the 2019 general election in Calabar (Imukodo, 2021). The famous

Dasukigate is an example here where \$2.1 billion (N817,479,000,000.00 billion) earmarked for the procurement of weapons to fight the Boko Haram insurgency was diverted to the sponsorship of the PDP campaign in the 2015 general election. Another case is the bribing of the INEC officials by the former minister of petroleum Diezani Alison Maduekwe of N23 billion (\$55,423,021.80 million) believed to have been looted from the public treasury through the Ministry of Petroleum Resources (Sule et al., 2017a). This is one aspect of the bribe. Security agencies are also found to have been bribed in several elections and are sometimes actively involved in the process of rigging the election as reported in states like Ekiti in 2014 and several others before and beyond. Bribing voters with fake promises is another angle of bribery and corruption in the electoral process in Nigeria's Fourth Republic. Politicians promised eloquent and good policies while intentionally being deceitful to win elections. On assumptions of power, they will feign ignorance and cite unforeseen circumstances as the reasons for reneging against their promises (Sule et al., 2017a).

Clientelism and godfatherism dominate the electoral process in Nigeria's Fourth Republic. As discussed in chapter three 3, clientelism is never an exclusive practice in the Fourth Republic only because it has historical antecedents from the vicissitudes of colonial history to post-colonial Nigeria. Votes are traded and bargained based on patron-broker-client relationships. Godfathers emerged in the 1960s and are identified as financiers of elections and controllers of politics (Demarest, 2020). Money is supplied by the godfathers to bribe and sponsor godsons who will represent them in the corridors of power to serve their interest in most cases, the political economy of state power and control. Buy-off and pay-off are negotiated in the process. Voters are promised rewards in cash or kind by patrons and brokers and in some cases, as stressed by Lindberg and Morrison (2010) and Lindberg and Weghorst (2010), swing-voting occurred where the voters are influenced by ethnic, religious and regional considerations as the consolation of the support in voting a particular candidate. In other cases, Antunnes (2010) argues that coercion is used not necessarily as a bargain for reward or promises.

One important ethics and quality of a good election is the enabling of laws and regulations that guide the process. Not only the availability of the laws and regulations but also the audacity to implement them and monitor them. The Nigerian elections in the Fourth Republic falter from such privileges because while well-articulated regulations were constitutionally enacted, violating them with impunity is the challenge here. Several cases were presented in this study. An example is a report by Onyekpere (2015) of violation of the maximum spending limit where a presidential candidate that is stipulated by law to spend no more than N1 billion for his entire campaign expenditure spent about N7 billion for his media expenses only and the same is reported with the other who spent about N3 billion. A clear violation yet, no action is taken or any sanction. Another case is the donation limit. A campaign donation of N250 million was given by Alhaji Abdussamad Rabiu (BUA) against the maximum contribution ban of N1 million in 2010 (Ohman, 2014). Additionally, the fundraising dinner of former president Goodluck Jonathan in his bid to seek for the second term saw about N22 billion raised above the ceiling with impunity (Nwangwu & Ononogbu, 2016). Violations of regulations are not as much problems by themselves as the failure to hold to account the violators. This serious lapse is affecting elections in Nigeria and their integrity.

OVERVIEW OF ELECTIONS IN NIGERIA'S FOURTH REPUBLIC

Democracy stimulates elections while elections emulsify democracy. In this regard, examining the analysis of the voting pattern and results of elections in Nigeria's Fourth Republic will guide in understanding the nature, pattern and evolution of political parties including their characteristics and how people respond to them. This includes the illustration of party systems, party institutionalisation and organisations and electoral process and electoral systems. All these can be seen visibly if the results of the elections are elaborated in figures. As mentioned earlier, elections in the Fourth Republic took place six times and the seventh is on its way a few months to 2023. Elections in the Fourth Republic started in 1999 when the military promised willingly to return Nigeria on the track to democracy after the Abdulsalami Abubakar Military Administration announced a one-year transition in 1998 when he succeeded General Abacha after his eventual death.

A number of 57,369,560 million were registered as voters by the INEC. Political parties are mandatorily required to open and maintain offices at least, and membership in two-thirds of the states in Nigeria which is twenty-four states out of thirty-six and the Federal Capital Territory (FCT) Abuja. As a result of such stringent conditions, only three political parties fulfilled the criteria and got registered. They are PDP, APP and AD (National Democratic Institute, 1999). The results of the 1999 general election showed national domination of the elective seats by the PDP as shown in table 3.1.

The results displayed the character of ethnic and regional politics on one hand and the emergence of a national party for the first time. All the six governorship seats won by AD were from the Southwest states while all the nine governorship seats won by APP were from northern states and the same applies to the seats won by both the parties in the National Assembly. The presidential contest was purposely made a pure Yoruba affair to pacify them on the inflicted injury of the cancellation of the 12 June 1991 presidential

Table 3.1   Analysis of the 1999 general election in Nigeria

Presidential Election			
Party	Candidate	Results	Percentage
A D	Olu Falae	11,110,287	36.69
APP	Did not field a candidate	–	–
PDP	Olusegun Obasanjo	18,738,14	61.88
Other	Invalid	431,611	1.43
Total		**30,280,043**	**100**

Governorship Election		
Party	Seats	Percentage
AD	6	16.67
APP	9	25
PDP	21	58.33
Total	**36**	**100**

National Assembly Election The Senate		
Party	Seats	Percentage
AD	19	17.43
APP	23	21.10
PDP	66	60. 5
Undecided	1	0.92
Total	**109**	**100**

House of Representatives		
Party	Seats	Percentage
AD	44	12.22
APP	110	30.56
PDP	206	57.22
Total	**360**	**100**

Source: INEC 2000 (the tabulation and computation into percentage was made by the author in 2022).

election by the Babangida Military Administration. The AD and APP wanted to maintain the culture of regional and ethnic parties of the previous republics. However, the PDP looked national in orientation as it won all elective seats in all the geopolitical zones except for the governorship seats in the Southwest which were all taken by the AD. This was the foundation behind the consolidation and expansion of the ruling PDP sixteen years later. The 1999 results revealed ethnic and regional voting in Nigeria while the weak institutionalisation and lack of ideology of parties manifested. Votes were bought too. The PDP consolidated itself in power and swept the 2003 general election in a landslide victory.

The 2003 general election indicated the tradition of the maintenance of the national outlook and dominance by the ruling PDP. Practically, the PDP converted the Nigerian party system into an unofficial one-party system. It

Table 3.2 An Analysis of the Voting Pattern and Results in the 2003 general election

Presidential Election

Party	Candidate	Results	Percentage
PDP	Olusegun Obasanjo	24,456,140	58.20
ANPP	Muhammadu Buhari	12,710,022	30.25
APGA	Chukwuemeka Odumegwu Ojukwu	1,297,445	3.09
UNPP	Jim Nwobodo	169,609	0.40
NCP	Gani Fawehinmi	161,333	0.38
PAC	Sarah Jubril	157,560	0.37
NDP	Ike Nwachukwu	132,997	0.32
JP	Chris Okotie	119,547	0.28
PRP	Balarabe Musa	100,765	0.24
PMP	Arthur Nwankwo	57,720	0.14
APLP	Emmanuel Okereke	26,921	0.06
NNPP	Kalu Idika Kalu	23,830	0.05
MDJ	Muhammadu Dikko Yusuf	21,403	0.05
ARP	Yahaya Ndu	11,565	0.03
DA	Abayomi Ferreira	6,727	0.02
BNPP	Iheanyichukwu Godswill Nnaji	5,987	0.01
NAC	Olapade Agoro	5,756	0.01
LDPN	Pere Ajuwa	4,473	0.01
MMN	Mojisola Adekunle Obasanjo	3,757	0.01
19	**Total**	**42,018,73**	**100**

Governorship Election

Party	Seats	Percentage
AD	1	2.78
ANPP	7	19.44
PDP	28	77.78
Total	**36**	**100**

National Assembly Election
The Senate

Party	Seats	Percentage
AD	6	5.50
ANPP	27	24.77
PDP	76	69.72
Total	**109**	**100**

House of Representatives

Party	Seats	Percentage
AD	34	9.44
ANPP	96	26.67
APGA	2	0.56
NDP	1	0.28
PDP	223	61.94
PRP	1	0.28
UNPP	2	0.6
Vacant	1	0.28
Total	**360**	**100**

Source: INEC 2003 (the tabulation and computation into percentage was made by the author in 2022).

seized the five AD states in the Southwest and four ANPP states in 2003. More National Assembly seats in the upper and the lower chambers were won by the PDP. The results also showed more voters turnout than in later elections in 2011, 2015 and 2019 general elections. More regional and ethnic parties surfaced such as the APGA represented by Odumegwu Ojukwu from the Southeast and the PRP by Alhaji Balarabe Musa from the North. The 2003 general election was observed as fraudulent, faulty, incredible and subversive. The beneficiary of the election, former president Olusegun Obasanjo was mentioned to have called the election a 'do or die' meaning a war (Human Rights Watch, 2007). Massive rigging, disenfranchisement of voters, changing of results, and manufacture of results, money politics and violence characterised the election. The domestic civil societies and international observers chastised the election and demanded immediate reform in the process. However, PDP expressed its decisiveness and the determination to dominate the Nigerian elections and politics by winning all elective seats in all the six geopolitical zones and FCT Abuja amid the lamentations of massive malpractice and irregularities. Nevertheless, the ruling PDP ignored all the ominous signs and continued with the same style as shown in table 3.3 from the 2007 general election.

The 2007 general election maintained the tradition of the 2003 general election. The PDP continued to assert its unparalleled dominance unchallenged. A significant development worthy of mentioning here is how some smaller parties secured national seats in governorship and National Assembly elections. This indicated that the voters are gradually becoming politically socialised and the increasing intra-party conflicts within the ruling PDP forced some good candidates out of the party to secure victory on other platforms. Politics of massive intra-party and inter-party switching emerged including the vice president himself Alhaji Atiku Abubakar who switched to Action Congress (AC) to contest the post of the President when he was edged out by his party the PDP. The violence and rigging and other irregularities manifested more than in the 2003 general election. In essence, the beneficiary of the process, late president Umaru Musa Yar'adua himself confessed that the 2007 general election that brought him to the seat of the president was flawed and affected by malpractice, irregularities and other challenges but he promised Nigerians that a better and credible election will be delivered in 2011. To stick to his words, he inaugurated the Justice Uwais Electoral Reform Committee which made sound recommendations that finally made the procedure and the guidelines of the 2011 general elections and beyond even though not all of them (Adeniyi, 2010).

In a study, Mohammed and Aluigba (2013) disclosed that the majority of the respondents that were consulted, 60 percent of them, agreed that the 2007 election and indeed other previous elections in the country were rigged. They

Table 3.3   Analysis of the 2007 general election in Nigeria

Presidential Election			
Party	Candidate	Results	Percentage
PDP	Umaru Musa Yar'adua	24,638,063	69.82
ANPP	Muhammadu Buhari	6,605,299	18.72
AC	Atiku Abubakar	2, 637,848	7.47
PPA	Orji Uzor Kalu	608,803	1.73
DPP	Attahiru Bafarawa	289,324	0.84
APGA	Chukwuemeka Odumegu Ojukwu	155,947	0.44
AD	Pere Ajuwa	89,247	0.25
FDP	Chris Okotie	74,049	0.21
ADC	Patrick Utomi	50,849	0.14
HDP	Ambrose Owuru	28,519	0.08
ALP	Emmanuel Okereke	22,677	0.06
APS	Lawrence Adedoyin	22,409	0.06
NDP	Habu Fari	21,934	0.06
CPP	Maxi Okwu	14,027	0.04
BNP	Bartholomew Nnaji	11,705	0.03
NCP	Emmanuel Obayuwana	8,229	0.02
NAC	Olapade Agoro	5,752	0.02
NMM	Mojisola Obasanjo	4,309	0.01
18 Parties	**Total**	**35,288,990**	**100**

Governorship Election		
Party	Seats	Percentage
AC	1	2.78
ANPP	7	19.44
APGA	1	2.78
LP	1	2.78
PDP	25	69.44
PPA	1	2.78
Total	**36**	**100**

National Assembly Election The Senate		
Party	Seats	Percentage
AC	6	5.50
AP	1	0.97
ANPP	16	14.67
PDP	85	77.98
PPA	1	0.97
Total	**109**	**100**
House of Representatives		
Party	Seats	Percentage
AC	30	8.33
ANPP	63	17.5
PDP	263	73.06
PPA	3	0.83
LP	1	0.28
Total	**360**	**100**

Source: INEC 2007 (the tabulation and computation into percentage was made by the author in 2022).

maintained that the election was full of malpractice, including vote-buying, bribery, corruption, thuggery, violence, ballot snatching, ballot stuffing, ballot stealing, intimidation of the opposition and other forms of electoral irregularities. The international observers too support the positions such as NDI, IRI, Commonwealth, European Union, Human Rights Watch, USAID, UKAID and UNDP (Sule et al. 2018). The PDP became practically a one-party system in Nigeria and this terrain continued up to the 2011 general election as shown in table 3.4.

The 2011 general election took place in April with a total number of registered voters of 73,528,040 million. The total voter turnout is 39,469,484 (53.7 percent) with total valid votes of 38,209,978 million and invalid votes of 1,259,506 million votes. Several changes were observed in the election. The influx of more parties into the race affirmed the multi-party system in Nigeria in operation but the dominant PDP control of the seats indicated that the one-party practice is still ongoing. Another development is the return of ethnic and regional parties which began in the 2007 general election. The AD transformed into ACN and except for the governorship seats which the ACN continued to lament that they are being rigged by the ruling PDP, the National Assembly seats maintained a regional voting pattern where the majority of the seats in the Senate and House of Representatives were won by ACN in the 2007 and the 2011 general elections in the Southwest.

Additionally, many more parties and contestants continued to join the race since 2003 but it seemed the presidential race, specifically is reduced to contests between the ruling PDP and Muhammadu Buhari's ANPP and later CPC. He became a major opposition leader with overwhelming support and followership in the North being perceived as 'Mai Gaskiya' (man of honesty and integrity) and owing to the masses' confidence in him that he will make a difference from the political quagmire that they found themselves in. Furthermore, the election results were violently contested, particularly in the North which caused post-election violence that cost more than 2,000 lives. But the 2015 general election made a significant difference with a tremendous change where the incumbent PDP was defeated by the newly formed opposition APC after the successful merger of four major parties of ACN, ANPP, CPC and a faction of APGA when they realised that no single opposition party or leader can defeat PDP alone. The results are shown in table 3.5.

For the first time in the history of Nigeria's election, the ruling party was peacefully unseated by an opposition which many Nigerians perceived as the beginning of a new page in Nigeria's democracy, an achievement which was never attained easily. Several factors contributed to the development. Adeniyi (2017) and Abdullahi (2017) maintained that the PDP was its own enemy more than the opposition and but for the internal skirmishes among the members, it will only have itself to defeat. In essence, the PDP defeat

Table 3.4   Analysis of the 2011 general election in Nigeria

	Presidential Election		
Party	Candidate	Results	Percentage
PDP	Goodluck Jonathan	22,495,187	58.89
CPC	Muhammadu Buhari	12,214,853	31.98
CAN	Nuhu Ribadu	2,079,151	5.41
ANPP	Ibrahim Shekarau	917,012	2.40
PDC	Mahmud Waziri	82,243	0.21
PMP	Nwadike Chikezie	56,248	0.15
PPP	Lawson Aroh	54,203	0.14
ADC	Peter Nwangwu	51,682	0.14
BNPP	Iheanyichukwu Nnaji	47,272	0.12
FP	Chris Okotie	34,331	0.09
NCP	Dele Momodu	26,376	0.07
NMDP	Solomon Akpona	25,938	0.07
APS	Lawrence Adedoyin	23,740	0.06
UNPD	Ebiti Ndok	21,203	0.06
NTP	John Dara	19,744	0.04
MPPP	Rasheed Shitta Bey	16,492	0.04
ARD	Yahaya Ndu	12,264	0.03
HDP	Ambrose Owuru	12,023	0.03
SDMP	Patrick Utomi	11,544	0.03
LDPN	Christopher Nwaokobia	8,472	0.02
Total	**20 parties**	**38,209,978**	**100**

	Governorship Election	
Party	Seats	Percentage
CAN	6	16.67
ANPP	3	8.33
APGA	2	5.56
CPC	1	2.78
LP	1	2.78
PDP	23	63.89
Total	**36**	**100**

	National Assembly Election The Senate	
Party	Seats	Percentage
CAN	21	19.27
ANPP	11	10.09
APGA	1	0.92
CPC	8	7.34
DPP	1	0.92
L P	3	2.75
PDP	64	58.72
Total	**109**	**100**

(continued)

Table 3.4 (Continued)

Party	House of Representatives	
	Seats	Percentage
AC	69	19.17
ANPP	28	7.78
AP	5	1.39
APGA	7	1.94
CPC	38	10.56
DPP	1	0.28
PDP	203	56.39
LP	8	2.22
PPN	1	0.27
Total	360	100

Source: INEC 2011 (the tabulation and computation into percentage was made by the author in 2022).

itself by itself. The defeat of the PDP and the victory of the APC was orchestrated by the handiwork of PDP's internal crisis. One of them is the intra-party crisis within the PDP on the issue of zoning of the presidential seat. The northern elites insisted that it was their turn and they must finish their eight years after Obasanjo but President Jonathan placated them to allow him to run for a single term according to their narratives. When he decided to re-contest in 2015, a power tussle within the ruling party created a sharp division that witnessed the exit of five governors, ten senators and twenty-two members of the House of Representatives into the opposition APC (Sule & Yahaya, 2018b).

Other factors included the credibility and integrity of the candidate in APC who was Muhammadu Buhari with his teeming northern followers and the support of the Southwest allies, financial muscles that matched the ruling PDP and the possession of or holding of political offices by the opposition APC on the eve of the election equals or more than the ruling PDP because of party switching. Besides, the introduction of electoral reforms such as SCRs and other measures that drastically minimised rigging helped out in the victory of the opposition APC. Sule (2018) argues that sixteen reforms aided the success and credibility of the 2015 general election. This was presented in a model that the study designed as shown below.

However, the 2019 general election retrogressed from the above-examined elements on many fronts and the widely acknowledged credibility successfully witnessed in the 2015 general election declined. Violence, malpractice and campaign on sentiments instead of issues resurfaced despite the two major contenders being Muslims from the North and all of them Fulani. The election was conducted smoothly at the presidential and National Assembly levels but at the state and governorship levels, violence erupted while massive rigging, vote-buying and intimidation occurred. Unlike the previous

Table 3.5   Analysis of the 2015 general election in Nigeria

Party	Candidate	Results	Percentage
	Presidential Election		
APC	Muhammadu Buhari	15,424,921	53.96
PDP	Goodluck Ebele Jonathan	12,853,162	44.96
APA	Adebayo Ayeni	53,537	0.19
ACPN	Ganiyu Galadima	40,311	0.14
CPP	Sam Eke	36,300	0.13
AD	Rufus Salau	30,637	0.11
ADC	Mani Ahmad	29,665	0.10.
PPN	Allagoa Chinedu	24,475	0.09
NCP	Martin Onovo	24,455	0.09
AA	Tunde Anifowose Kilani	22,125	0.08
UPP	Chekwas Okorie	18,220	0.06
KP	Comfort Sonaiya	13,037	0.05
UDP	Godson Okoye	9,208	0.03
HP	Ambrose Albert Owuru	7,435	0.03
All Parties	Invalid votes	844,519	–
Total valid votes	**14 parties**	**29,432,849**	**100**
Registered voters	**All**	**67,422,005**	**100**

Party	Seats	Percentage
	Governorship Election	
APC	19	61.29
PDP	12	38.71
Total	**31**	**100**
	National Assembly Election	
	The Senate	
Party	Seats	Percentage
APC	60	55.05
PDP	49	44.95
Total	**109**	**100**
	House of Representatives	
Party	Seats	Percentage
APC	225	62.5
PDP	125	34.72
Other parties	10	2.78
Total	**360**	**100**

Source: INEC 2015 (the tabulation and computation into percentage was made by the author in 2022).

elections, about seventy-three parties presented contestants for the post of presidential candidate among the ninety-one parties that existed at the time of the election. The results displayed the voting patterns shown in table 3.6.

The 2019 general election revealed that regional and ethnic parties continued to exist with insignificant performance. The one-party system

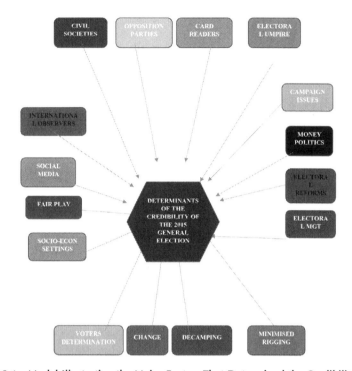

Figure 3.1   Model Illustrating the Major Factors That Determined the Credibility of the 2015 general election. *Source*: Sule (2018).

continued under the APC-led politics. Many members of the defunct ruling PDP decamped to the ruling APC and continued with their behaviour in the Nigerian political culture. Other issues of violence, rigging, manipulation, ethnic, religious and regional voting identity, excessive spending, violation of regulations, abuse of state resources in campaign financing, money politics and clientelism continued while the game of playing all strategies and options available to the players manifested and the voters voted based on some rationality of expected benefit (Sule & Sambo, 2021).

The aforementioned analysis so far displayed several characteristics of the Nigerian parties in the Fourth Republic, voting behaviour, attitude of Nigerian politicians and the changing pattern of elections and democratic transition. The incidents observed urge the need for reforms to measure up the level of integrity and credibility of the election. Both the domestic and international observers reported wide violence, massive spending, irregularities and other issues of malpractice in the general conduct of the 2019 general election. Nevertheless, the election was seen as less credible than the 2015 general election but is still far from the previous elections in terms of quality and credibility. The concern is the backwardness that was recorded. One

Table 3.6 Analysis of the 2019 general election in Nigeria

Party	Candidate	Results	Percentage
Presidential Election			
APC	Muhammadu Buhari	15,191,847	55.82
PDP	Alhaji Atiku Abubakar	11,262,978	41.39
other Parties	71 parties	759,555	2.79
Total	**73 candidates**	**29,432,849**	**100**

Party	Seats	Percentage
Governorship Election		
APC	15	51.72
PDP	14	48.28
Total	**29**	**100**

Party	Seats	Percentage
National Assembly Election		
The Senate		
APC	65	59.63
PDP	43	39.45
YPP	1	0.92
Total	**109**	**100**
House of Representatives		
AA	2	0.56
ADC	3	0.83
ADP	1	0.28
APC	217	60.28
APGA	9	2.50
APM	1	0.28
LP	1	0.28
PDP	115	31.94
PRP	2	0.56
SDP	1	0.28
Other parties	8	2.22
Total	**360**	**100**

Source: INEC 2019 (the tabulation and computation into percentage was made by the author in 2022).

fundamental feature of the 2015 and the 2019 general elections is security challenges. The two elections were conducted amid serious security threats of Boko Haram insurgency in Northeast Nigeria, farmers–herders conflict in northern Nigeria, rural banditry in Northwest Nigeria, Indigenous Peoples of Biafra (IPOB) secessionist threats and many other security challenges (Verjee et al., 2019). However, these security threats could not affect the elections tremendously since the 2015 and the 2019 general elections were handled peacefully and successfully except for violence engineered by politicians themselves.

Chapter 4

Background to the Party System and Party Politics in Nigeria's Fourth Republic

This chapter examined political parties from broader perspectives identifying their meanings, nature, types, systems, organisations, institutionalisations, variations, functions and role in democratisation in addition to some case studies. The chapter linked the background of parties with party politics in Nigeria by analysing their nature and pattern in the Fourth Republic. The chapter further delved into the background, evolution, nature, activities and character of Nigerian political parties. How parties metamorphosed and how some demised in the Fourth Republic are interesting areas that will capture attention here. Additionally, the chapter analysed the pattern of intra- and inter-party conflicts which characterise the process of party activities and candidate selection in the Nigerian Fourth Republic. This will further include the strategies of survival of parties and politicians from the perspectives of party switching and the question of ideology, principles, internal democracy and electoral process.

POLITICAL PARTIES: CONCEPTUALISATION, TYPES, SYSTEMS, FUNCTIONS, ORGANISATIONS, INSTITUTIONALISATION AND DYNAMIC CHARACTERS

Political parties and the electoral process are intertwined. Modern political parties were purposely formed to contest an election and participate in the electoral process. This may be broadened to consider that parties exist contemporarily to participate in the process of policy and decision-making, ideological promotion and advancement of group interest. A political party is regarded as the fundamental political institution necessary for democratic rule. In essence, Katz (1980) stresses that if the definition of a political party is sought, the response is simply the selection of decision-makers by major competing parties in a fair electoral process. The ability of any state to proclaim democracy as an adopted system of government relies heavily on the type and nature of political parties that operate and the fairness of the electoral process. Parties and their systems determine the quality of democracy. The difficulty is defining political parties within a universal acceptable framework (Gunther et al., 2002). This is perhaps, practically impracticable. However, presenting some convincing views and analysis will suffice in this regard. One of the simple approaches is the explanation that a political party is a group of independent citizens harbouring a goal of providing a platform for recruitment of contestants who will compete in an election purposely to capture and control government for state organisation and policymaking (White, 2006). White (2006) simply informs us that parties are the means to an end to elections and power contests in this realm. But assuming that parties aim at securing and controlling power alone will be erroneous if modern analysis of parties in advanced democracies and even developing democracies are taken into cognisance. For instance, in two-party system democracies, third parties are surfacing recently without a chance of winning elections then what are they existing for? To promote ideas, defend values and interests or provide a functioning opposition role? In the same way, parties sprang up in developing democracies like Nigeria with little or no chance of making an impact in elections, yet they continue to manifest. There may be reasons for that which shall be explained more in the later section of this chapter.

Parties are being defined or interpreted from the early modern political organisations by the philosophers and scholars in Europe. Edmund Burke (1981), for instance, defined a party 'as a body of men united for promoting by their joint endeavours the national interest, upon some particular principle in which they are all agreed'. Downs (1957) sees the party as

> a coalition of men seeking to control the governing apparatus by legal means. By coalition, we mean a group of individuals who have certain ends in common and cooperate to achieve them. By governing apparatus, we mean the physical, legal, and institutional equipment which the government uses to carry out its specialised role in the division of labour. By legal means, we mean either duly constituted or legitimate influence.

Key Jr (1964) perceives the party as a 'group of a peculiar sort within the body of voters as a whole, groups are formed of persons who regard themselves as party members'. The above few examples all point to one key issue, parties are instruments for power contests in an election by a group of people with the same ideology and interest. As summarised by White (2006), parties are organisations, groups of supporters mobilised and a group of nobles with common interests and purpose. In a similar view, Scarrow (2006) argues that there is no modern definition of parties that will not consider the ultimate purpose of competing for power in election. This view is what Mair (1997) reaffirmed that parties compete for power and make policies as the succinct purpose and interpretation of what they are and what they do. Maor (1997) prefers that parties be defined or explained by three major themes, what they do, their behaviours and how they operate instead of a normative approach which may not provide a satisfactory meaning. By distinguishing between what they can do or what they should be (normative), it will be precise to present them as what they do (real). This is a difficult task, however, it will require a comprehensive study which Maor (1997) provides in his work but which cannot be explained here because it is broad.

Parties in modern democracies evolved in different structures, systems, environments and patterns. Leadership representation through the party system was one of the outstanding innovations of nineteenth-century political development (Ziblatt, 2017). Before the nineteenth century, parties were loose formations linked with some movement or a charismatic leader. Parties were perceived as factions, dissident voices, radical left and other stereotyping of a disregard for authorities. Amid the challenges of hostilities, parties cruised their way into better organised and formal political institutions that shaped the destiny of the twenty-first-century world. In the case of Athens where democracy originated, candidates contested without a party platform (Katz, 2006). Party formation was greatly influenced by the emergence and rapid acceptance of electoral politics in Europe and America in the nineteenth century. The term 'party' was discovered and used in place of the faction which was the earlier word used. 'Party' as well derives from Latin, from the verb *partire*, which means to divide (Sartori, 1976). The interpretation from Latin perhaps was what led to the term 'faction' to refer to parties but the modern users prefer to see parties not as evil but as organised political institutions. Sartori (1976) presents parties as channels of expression in this regard. The desire for the presence of multiple, organised, competing and formal parties increased (Scarrow, 1980). As observed by Katz (1980), Scarrow (2006) emphasises that political parties created democracy. Parties did not emerge in the nineteenth century in unison or in a unilinear pattern. They took different courses and dimensions. In some cases like in European states, parties shaped and determined some political structures such as the legislature and executive type as well as policies. In the United States, franchise and representative government emerged simultaneously with parties (Crotty, 2006).

It should be understood that not all parties evolved in the same pattern described earlier. Some parties in places like Latin America transformed or converted to parties from revolutionary movements. The movement by Fidel Castro which overthrew the Batista regime in Cuba is a classic example.

The revolutionaries aim to maintain or stick to the ideologies of revolution for state policies. In this regard, the revolutionaries quickly transformed the movement into parties. In China, Mao did the same thing and succeeded in forming the state official Chinese Communist Party (CCP). Revolutionaries need to lay a solid political foundation to earn legitimacy and political prospect to control the state power and execute policies. The revolutionary parties themselves evolved in two different manifestations. The armed group movement like Cuba and China and the intellectually socially organised movement for political and socio-economic change peacefully as in the case of Salvador Allende's Chile and Eurocommunists of the 1970s. During the pre–Cold War and Cold War periods, it is difficult for armed groups to fight and survive to form legal parties recognised by states. But after the Cold War, the dynamics of changing global politics and socio-economic configuration made it possible. Revolutionary parties are also obtainable in Africa including the Frente de Libertação de Moçambique (FRELIMO), the Front for the Liberation of Mozambique, the Movimento Popular para Liberação de Angola (MPLA), the Popular Movement for the Liberation of Angola (PLMA), the Southwest Africa People's Organization (SWAPO) of Namibia and the African National Congress (ANC) from South Africa. The African examples are influenced by colonial oppression and apartheid policies, unlike the Latin American cases where it was mostly against the existing order of dictatorship (Close & Prevost, 2007). There are other parties closer to revolutionary ones but differ slightly because they are militant and they promote militant democracy. Such examples are operated in Eastern Europe, Israel, Spain, Australia and Turkey. They are formed by a radical ideology and they tend to rule with militancy unlike the revolutionary parties which may not necessarily rule militantly after assuming power.

Parties performed many functions in the democratic system. Parties provide the legal apparatus for aspiring politicians to contest an election. Parties are established for the advancement of some principles and ideologies of a group of people with a common interest (Pasarelli, 2020). Parties are also regarded as agents of political socialisation. They enlighten, inculcate, train and manifest the awareness creation of civic responsibility and political education. Parties may participate in socio-economic and cultural activities apart from political participation. They may be involved in the promotion of societal values and engagement in empowerment, social security and the promotion of skills acquisition and educational support such as scholarship endowment and entrepreneurship development (Katz, 1980). White (2006) captures that parties play key roles in democracies including enabling the citizens to participate in the process of government through selection or electing those who led them. Parties also unified the society by offering a platform for collating fragmented, conflicting and divergent groups and views toward a unique and similar purpose. Parties encourage political participation through mobilisation, holding public officers accountable, making the democratic process transparent, and parties make an opportunity for citizens or the electorates to have alternative platforms for a preferred policy choice by either allowing the satisfied parties to continue in an election or changing them if there is a dissatisfaction (White, 2006).

Parties performed more functions apart from the previously discussed ones: selecting official personnel who may not be necessarily elected but appointed is one of them, formulating and implementing public policies, criticising the government and playing the opposition role, political education, intermediation and nurturing of future leaders (Scarrow, 2006). Parties serve as mechanisms of social choices. Different social groups choose based on their social lineage or sentiments. Workers are naturally bound to lean on labour and welfare parties. Religious groups may likely identify with theocratic parties if they exist in their enclaves while capital owners may rush to liberal and free-economy parties (Hershey, 2006). Parties can mobilise for collective action and the mobilisation process is strategic, continuous and persuasive. Mobilisation is attached to recruitment by political parties of loyal members and future leaders. Norris (2006) raised an important question on who is eligible for recruitment. Candidates for recruitment into party flagbearers are determined in three stages according to Norris (2006). First is certification satisfaction. To qualify and fulfil the minimum of electoral regulations and laws for contesting is minimal. The second is nomination, which is the demand and supply of the eligible contestants and selection process. The third stage is an election, which determines who secures victory into the legislative office or any other elective office. Each of the three stages according to Norris (2006) can be likened to a 'progressive game of musical chairs', many are eligible, few are nominated and fewer succeed. The question of who nominates arises in this regard. Who nominates party candidates depends on the internal democracy and level of centralisation and laws of the party (Norris, 2006).

Hazan and Rahat (2006) extend the essence of the party's function in candidate selection which they postulate as vital for the party's success in electoral competition, a determinant of how policies are influenced and how people make choice. In the majority of world democracies except for Germany, Finland and Norway, there are no specified constitutional regulations on how candidates can be selected. They are left within the jurisdiction of the will of the parties to determine (Hazan & Rahat, 2006). Diamond and Gunther (2001) agree that recruitment, candidate nomination, societal representation, policymaking and awareness creation formed the major functions of parties. In some democracies, Nigeria for example, candidate selection may jeopardise the chance of a party winning the general election as it occurred in many cases (Sule et al., 2018a). Dalton et al. (2011) argue that parties play three roles in three different stages. The first stage is pre-election, where they recruit and nominate candidates. The second stage is the campaign and mobilisation of voters to win the election. The third stage is to secure power, initiate policies and implement them. Parties are linked inseparably with the voters in five different ways including campaign linkage, participatory linkage, ideological linkage, representative linkage and policy linkage. In essence, parties are the most influential democratic institutions because they operate democracy and run elections. They determine who competes and who wins (Dalton et al., 2011).

The type, nature and number of parties competing for electoral offices are the party systems. The term came into being by Duverger (1954) when he asserts that the interaction of parties in a state towards competition for power is the party system. One of the distinctive classifications is based on the traditional approach which identifies one-party, two-party and multi-party systems. The one-party system is the party that is a part of a whole that monopolises political power in a state often backed up by legal provisions and state powers obtainable in the communist states of Russia and China. The two-party system implies a state where two contending competing strong equal organisations in most cases, one to the left and then the other to the right or conservative and liberal groups exist as rivals of each other. It does not, however, denote that in a two-party system, only two parties exist. In America and Britain, other third parties are cropping up in recent years. In the case of a multi-party system, like in France, Germany, India and Nigeria, multiple parties compete for power. Party systems of this traditional classification are influenced by electoral systems and the nature of proportional representation (Wolinetz, 2006). The classification of parties based on number consideration was expanded by Salih (2007) to four dominant party systems in African democracies on top of the one-party, two-party and multi-party systems. The typologies of parties based on the number were overcome and expanded in the 1960s. The new classification made consists of examining relationships and interactions. One classical example is combining numbers of parties from the viewpoint of their relative size and strength (Blondel, 1968), patterns of government formations and interactions (Dahl, 1966; Siaroff, 2000) but Sartori (1976) classified parties on the consideration of configuration, internal diversities and numbers. Mair (2006) made an emphasis that change in party systems classification is not only against numbers but by the sophistication of research, dynamism and improvement in analysis in the discipline of political science.

The attempts at expanding the typology of parties continue in modern times by scholars. One useful etymology is presented by Diamond and Gunther (2001). Diamond and Gunther (2001) disliked the earlier classification because according to them, it was made based on the study and cases of European parties only without considering other parts of the world. Several criteria can be used to classify parties such as the nature of the organisation. Some are large in membership and followership with others narrow and this can make a good classification. Ideology is another premise for the classification of modern parties. Besides, orientation and character in power can also attract classification and comparison. Scholars of modern political party studies are devising various means of functionalism, comparison, organism and institutionalism to study parties and group them. This approach made the previous classification based on the number of parties existing in a state obsolete and less rigorous (Diamond & Gunther, 2001). But Hicken (2009) entirely differs from the classification and suggests a pragmatic approach. He based his study on examining the building of party systems in developing countries which he believes will offer new theoretical discourses in the arena of analysis of party politics. Hicken (2009) draws our attention to the fact that the countries he studied are battling with democracy institutionalisation. Second, he argues that there is no consensus in building a party system which leaves an open room for future efforts. Thus, party systems in developing democracies can be seen from two perspectives: nationalisation and numbers. Nationalisation means the ability of the parties to have a national outlook and recruit members in all parts of a particular country. Second, numbers mean the legal framework that indicates the parties in existence be it one, two or multiple as suggested by a constitution (Hicken, 2009).

Parties appear in variant models. Krouwel (2006) presents five different models of party based on the composition of membership, ideology and activities or policy influence. Elite parties are parties of patronage, clientelistic in nature, oligarchic and exclusively for the few privileged in the society. Mass parties are parties that mobilise and assemble the working class and poor citizens for a power contest anchored on favourable mass policies. Catch-all electoral parties are professional and multi-policy parties that strive to include all interests in the policy and governance process. Cartel parties are conglomerates of mighty parties that either merged or formed a coalition that monopolised them and threatened party competition. Business-firm parties are those established and promoted by entrepreneurs' interests and they are behind the finances of the party for business interest. Similar to Krouwel (2006), Diamond and Gunther (2001) present five types of parties but with some modifications which include the elite-based parties, mass parties, ethnic-based parties, electoralist parties and movement parties. Parties can also take the model of theocratic or religious parties formed purposely to promote religious doctrines. The German Christian Socialist Party is an example. Religious parties are found more in Islamic states because according to Islamic doctrine, governance must be conducted according to sharia guidelines

(Salih & El-Tom, 2009). Contemporarily, every state with a substantial Muslim population has at least one Islamic party or organisation that is close to that. They sometimes participate in electoral competition and oppose or play other important roles in politics such as Ikhwan (Muslim Brotherhood) in Egypt, Parti Islam se Malaysia (PAS), Turkish Islamist Parties, Ennahda in Tunisia by Rached Ghannouchi, Pakistani Islamist Parties, Islamist Parties in Algeria, Kuwait Islamic Constitutional Movement, Islamist Parties in West Africa and the Horn of Africa and other parts of Africa, Islamic Parties in Indonesia, Hizbollah in Lebanon and Palestinian Hamas (Sinno & Khanani, 2009).

Parties are witnessing expansion in their mobilisation to the extent that ethnic identity is now leveraged by some parties to win support (Ahuja, 2019). Parties take into consideration the impacts of ethnicity and pluralism in modern democracies. Some parties consciously envisage an opportunity for harmonising and embracing ethnic groups and plurality for autonomy and equity in political representation in plural societies (Luther, 2000). Lijphart (1976) made an illustrated example of such parties in Austria, Sweden, Switzerland, the Netherland and Belgium in a theory called consciosationalism or consociational democracy. Bieber (2008) analyses the efforts of political parties in providing an opportunity for political participation just like Lijphart (1976). One area which parties are performing in transition is a remarkable change in post-communist societies. The trend of post-communist change portrayed some stronghold of democratic institutionalisation among which are a transformation from personalised and authoritarian politics towards party politics; a systematic transition from the politics of symbols, identities, and hopes towards the politics of vested interests and rational choice; and an increasingly close relationship between social structures and political parties (Webb & White, 2007).

One critical aspect of party development is organisation and institutionalisation. The level of institutionalisation of parties varies from advanced democracies to semi-advanced and emerging ones, especially, after the third wave of democratisation. Some fundamentals that determine party institutionalisation include the nature of the party's root in society which in most cases is found more solid in older democracies than emerging ones. The legal process of operation of parties is another determinant of the level of institutionalisation. Some parties in some democratic climes have strong regulations that all members respect and adhere but in some democracies, personality controls the parties. Additionally, ideology matters. Parties with strong ideologies tend to maintain their roots and survival beyond the election and they can easily control aggression and subordinate individual interests to the collective interest. It is observed that one of the main issues with Nigerian political parties in the Fourth Republic is the lack of ideology which manifested in intra-party conflicts and rampant switching. Strong institutionalised parties strengthened democracy and inculcate values of civil liberty among the citizens. Weak parties have negative implications for electoral integrity and political accountability, vulnerable to anti-democratic leadership and are susceptible to political apathy and a low level of political socialisation (Mainwaring & Torcal, 2006). Where such weak parties exist, political actors activate some vulnerable joints of the electorates and capitalise on it which capitulate to electoral victory. A good example is the African political parties which kindle and rekindle ethnic politics (Mozaffar, 2006). One of the reasons advanced for the weak institutionalisation of parties in developing democracies and Africa is prolonged exacerbated authoritarian rule according to Randall (2006).

Institutionalisation is a long-term process that requires sustainability and persistence. Parties are institutionalised on two basis: internally generated and externally generated. The internally generated parties develop in three stages. First is the formation of the group of parliamentarians, the second is the formation of a local election committees in the electorate and third, a strong connection is established between the two. The externally generated parties follow the same stages but it expands to include non-political organisations such as trade unions and other ideological groups (Maor, 1997). Parties can also form and institutionalised through some critical stages including factionalisation, polarisation, expansion and finally institutionalisation (Huntington, 1965). Some parties found organisation and institutionalisation easier because a strong foundation of civil liberties was instituted before their formation as obtained in the United States (Maisel, 2007). Modern parties faced more challenges in organisation and institutionalisation according to Zulianello (2019) because of changing interaction streams and emerging modalities of integration. This process made the existing old ones fade while the newly established ones are finding it extra challenging to institutionalise. Parties in developing democracies are backed up by a legal framework. A comprehensive study by Wulff (2017) reported the various sections and legal backings in Kenya, Uganda, South Africa, Namibia, Zimbabwe, Democratic Republic of Congo, Senegal, Ghana, Nigeria and Tanzania. Parties are constitutionally in these countries legally bound to operate as institutions of political process and governance.

Parties' organisational development is undergoing structural and strategic changes in modern democracies. Structures, resources and representational strategies determine the level of organisational development of a party. Party structures can be measured in terms of the viability of leadership autonomy, centralisation and localisation, coordination and territorial concentration. In the realm of resources, parties can organise and develop if finance is strong, but if it is weak, the organisation is slowed. Resources diversification, financial autonomy from the state, volunteer strength and bureaucratic strength all determine the extent of the financial status of a party which in return facilitates party organisation. Representational strategies involved the ability of parties to establish individual linkage and group linkage (Scarrow et al., 2015). Sartori (2005) argues that parties can organise and institutionalise through a framework of pluralism, representative government, rationalisation, channelment, communication, expression, system change, continuum, discontinuities and mobilisation for competition. In some circumstances, parties are finding it difficult to organise and institutionalise because they are formed on the foundation of ethnic ideas. These are the cases in Kenya, Ghana, Namibia, Nigeria and many other states in Africa (Elischer, 2013).

Cohesion is a good attribute of parties in their survival. Lack of cooperation may lead to internal crises and factions that may divide the party and block its sustained organisation and institutionalisation. The multiplicity of interests from actors in the party if not tamed will threaten the overall interest of the party in the electioneering process (Katz, 1980). Political parties promote their interests and lobby support through campaigns. During electioneering campaigns, parties design manifestoes, make campaign allegiance and showcase their ideology, and, in some instances, ruling parties display their performance while the opposition parties narrate the failure (Farrell, 2006). Party finance is a major weapon in addressing campaign strategies. Campaign processes and mobilisation of voters require huge expenditure (Nasmacher, 2006). In some democracies, it is constitutionally private funding, in others public while in some specific places both (Alexander, 1989; Green, 2006). Party financing is often accompanied by allegations of bribery, corruption, violation of regulations and excessive spending (Walecki, 2017; Piccio & Biezen, 2018). Modern parties are constituting a problem to their legitimacy, transparency and integrity because they are gradually transforming into a platform for brokers, clientelism and distributive politics in the process of party financing. The parties indicted in this action are opening up for the highest bidders to secure their nomination or to gain heavy financial support in return for kickbacks, contracts, juicy appointment rewards and distribution of resources (Ferguson, 1956; Stokes, 2013). Mobilisation and resources required are being gradually reduced by the emergence of digital parties and cyber parties that mobilise and campaign using the internet to reach a large number of millions within a short period of time. The future of party politics, mobilisation, recruitment and activities would be transferred to the domain of cyberspace (Margetts, 2006; Gerbaudo, 2019). The concern for political corruption and violation of the campaign process necessitated an intensified legal policy framework at the national and international levels to foster accountability and transparency (Yadav, 2011; Mendilow & Phelippeau, 2018).

Once parties assume power, politics and calculations followed. If they are faced with intense competition, the first move usually is a coalition in the case of parliament where a majority could not be attained to form an absolute government. A lesser evil or less antagonistic party is wooed for a merger. Once settled, the next line of action is policy initiation, execution and evaluation (De Winter & Dumont, 2006). Such desire for a merger or majority formation led to cartelisation of political parties which is the biggest challenge facing parties leading to their decline. Competition, choice alternatives and mobilisation are becoming weak while the monopoly of political parties and leadership (Katz & Mair, 2018). More so, democracy within parties is necessary for terms of candidate selection, decentralisation, appointment into the party offices or election, participation, representation, competition and responsiveness (Hazan & Rahat, 2010) but cartelisation of parties will erode these competitive and participatory values of parties which is a form of decline. Whatever the projection, political parties in modern democracies, especially advanced industrial states, are facing changes of decline, resurgence, reshaping and transformation (Dalton & Wattenberg, 2000) and these changes will continue to affect democracy and politics in future.

An issue worthy of examining here is the politics of legislative party switching. Politicians who joined parties in modern democracies hardly hold firm to their parties if their political career is threatened. Party switching manifested in all continents and all types of democracies as well as all types of parties. The implications of party switching are the reversal of the main functions of parties of accountability, responsibility, representation and interest. A voter that voted for a candidate in a particular party but sees them later switched to another may get disconnected from them and the needed representation. The linkage function is desecrated in this regard (Heller & Mershon, 2009). A timeline for legislative switching involving some case studies of mixed democracies (advanced, emerging and communist states) reported an average of 4 percent switching from the 1980s to 2008. Party switching can be changing of affiliation, change in support and direction, adoption of candidates of other parties and decline to support (Heller & Mershon, 2009). There is a distinguishing difference between party switching in the studied democracies and African democracies particularly taking the specific case of Nigeria. A study (Sule & Yahaya, 2018a) reported at least not less than 300 high-profile cases of party switching in both the legislative and executive departments. The Nigerian case became unique because the constitution is indecisive in this aspect. While Section 8(1g) of the Nigerian 1999 Constitution as amended provides that if a lawmaker switch from a party platform upon which they were voted in into another they forfeit their seats unless there is internal rancour in the party in which their switching remains valid, no section touches on the executive. This made party switching in Nigerian politics rampant and unique to the aforementioned democracies studied by Heller and Mershon (2009). Sule and Yahaya (2018a) identified other reasons like lack of party ideology, weak institutionalisation and organisation of parties, politics of personalisation and the intensified scramble for power for primitive accumulation and a low level of political socialisation of voters.

POLITICAL PARTIES IN NIGERIA'S FOURTH REPUBLIC

Political parties emerged in Nigeria in sequence and patterns that are interesting to study. The Fourth Republic (1999–2022) has been an enduring democratic experience in Nigeria's political history. The period recorded the political parties with the longest lifetime in the country and the tenure in power. However, to understand the threshold and the vicissitudes that influenced how parties emerged in the Fourth Republic, it is germane to reflect on the background of Nigerian political parties from the inception of their emergence since the First Republic (1960–1966) succinctly. The theoretical dispositions of parties postulate that they established democracy and generate election and governance. But the circumstances and the environment differ. In the build-up to the First Republic, parties emerged with their nature, character and outlook. The vital point that influenced the formation of parties in the First Republic is the activities of the nationalists and the increased pressure for the inclusion of Africans in the process of governance. In Nigeria, the 1922 Sir Hugh Clifford Constitution provided for the permanent and non-permanent Africans to participate in the legislature in Lagos following the intensified pressure by the British-trained nationalists who felt that the natives were marginalised in the process of local governance in their territories. The British colonisers succumbed to pressure and the opportunity was offered (Agbu, 2016b).

The early First Republic parties were the Nigerian National Democratic Party (NNDP) formed by Herbert Macauley in 1922 and the National Youth Movement (later the Nigerian Youth Movement), established in 1934 by the likes of Dr Felix Vaughan. The two competed for legislative seats in Lagos and their activities were mainly limited to Lagos and Calabar only. The other parts of the colony, especially, the North, were not represented in the parties. After the Second World War (1945), the nationalists now transformed their activities from inclusion in the governance process to self-governance and freedom (Gberevbie & Oni, 2021). The radical movement by Dr Nnamdi Azikiwe through his journalism and other activities influenced positively the pressure for political self-determination and independence. By 1944, the Sir Arthur Richard Constitution introduced regionalism which was seen as the primer for the adoption and structure of Nigerian Federalism where other parties emerged (Abba & Babalola, 2017). The National Council for Nigeria and Cameroons later National Council for Nigerian Citizens (NCNC) after a plebiscite was conducted which saw the Southern Cameroon people prefer to join the Cameroon Colony was formed by Dr Nnamdi Azikiwe in 1944. The pan-Yoruba cultural group, 'Egbe Omo Oduduwa' transformed into a party known as Action Group (AG) headed by Chief Obafemi Awolowo in 1948. By 1951, some northern nationalists including Sir Ahmadu Bello and Sir Abubakar Tafawa Balewa formed the 'Jam'iyyar Mutanen Arewa' Northern People's Congress (NPC). These three major parties established after the Second World War became stronger than the previous ones and they were the pillars of the struggles toward political independence (Agbu, 2016b).

Apart from these, there are other minor opposition parties in the First Republic like the Malam Aminu Kano's Northern Elements Progressive Union (NEPU), United Middle Belt Congress (UMBC), Dynamic Party (DP) and Borno Youth Movement (BYM). Fundamentally, parties in the First Republic emerged as a reaction against colonialism and a desire to form self-governance based on autonomous representation (Jinadu, 2011). Thus, party formation in Nigeria differs from the advanced and new democracies that were inspired by the process of democratisation. Democratic values were not the major tenets but the ambition for self-rule first after the entities lost their freedom to many decades of colonial rule. Parties in the First Republic, especially AG, NCNC, NPC, NEPU, UMBC and others were characterised by ethnic outlook, regional orientation and to a certain extent, religious in nature. The parties were bedevilled with intra-party conflicts specifically the AG in the West between Awolowo and Akintola, the Western Premier, which resulted in the creation of the Mid-West in 1963, a development that Awolowo bitterly protested as an attempt to dismantle opposition by the ruling parties and to suppress the political unity of the western region (Llyod, 1965). In the same way, there was violent and intense inter-party rivalry even among the coalition parties of the NPC and NCNC that formed the parliamentary government in the 1960 independence election (Awa, 1964). Similarly, parties were accused of political corruption in the First Republic. For instance, the AG was indicted in a report for borrowing beyond the limit from African Continental Bank to finance a campaign election forbidden by law. Rigging of election results and electoral malpractice were other issues associated with the First Republic parties and elections (INEC, 2005).

There was a weak effort in party organisation and institutionalisation. Mobilisation rested well on ethnic support and regional affiliation. Parties remained fragile and undemocratic. The 1959 election could not produce a clear majority which eventually led to the formation of a coalition government between the NPC and NCNC. The NPC lost many votes to 'Purdah' (the practice of denying married women from the franchise because of religious understanding) (Akinola, 2014; Danjibo & Ashindorbe, 2018). The parties, nevertheless, ethnic and regional in outlook, displayed a greater skill in party politics, ideology and foreign policy than the parties in the Fourth Republic. One referred case was the foreign policy that created an uproar in 1961 when the Tafawa Balewa–led government suspended all forms of relationships with Israeli because of its aggression in Palestine. The coalition partner of the NCNC was not happy with the action and the same with the major opposition AG. In another case, the Tafawa Balewa Government cut diplomatic relationship with France for testing its nuclear weapon in the Sahara desert which has security and health implications for sub-Saharan countries. The opposition frowned at it (Gambari, 1970). In essence, some scholars argue that it was the sharpness of the intra- and inter-party conflicts that eventually collapsed the First Republic through a bloody coup that saw some Igbo army officers assassinating many northern leaders. The coup was quickly retaliated against with counter-coup by the northern army officers, and that set the foundation for a prolonged military rule before another effort at democratisation. It is this gap in military rule that contributed to the weak organisation and institutionalisation of political parties that are ideologically oriented in Nigerian politics (Diamond, 1995b).

After a long-term military, pressure compelled the military to surrender power in 1979. The parties and politicians that operated in the Second Republic (1979–1984) were not much different from the First Republic. New parties were formed in a replica of the First Republic ones and politicians that controlled those parties also re-emerged except for those killed by the first military coup. The conservative northern elites established the National Party of Nigeria (NPN) with Alhaji Shehu Aliyu Shagari as the flagbearer. The radical socialist Northern Malam Aminu Kano transformed NEPU into People's Redemption Party (PRP), the oldest surviving party in Nigerian political history because it still exists and participates in electoral politics in Nigeria's Fourth Republic. Chief Obafemi Awolowo formed United Nigeria People's Party (UNPP) which was seen as the new AG and he became the flagbearer of the party. Dr Nnamdi Azikiwe formed the Nigerian Peoples Party (NPP) and contested under its platform while the BYM transformed into Grand Nigerian Peoples Party (GNPP) with Waziri Ibrahim as the presidential candidate of the party. The results of the presidential election indicated Alhaji Shehu Shagari of the NPN as the winner after a controversy was thrashed out by the court of law which translated the disputed minimum of 25 percent in two-thirds of the states of the federation as the requirement for winning a presidential seat. The law was introduced in the 1979 Constitution as a remedy against ethnic and regional politics but such identity politics could not escape the Republic as displayed by the results of the election (IRI, 2020).

The Second Republic was bedevilled by ethnic politics, regional voting patterns, electoral malpractice and weak political parties that lack substantive ideologies. Although the PRP and UPN are seen more as socialist parties with socialist ideology and orientation the NPN and NPP are liberal in nature, the ideology could not play any influential role beyond the decisive role that ethnic and regional politics played. Politicians in the Second Republic were accused of bribery and corruption, embezzlement of public funds, misplacement of priorities and subversion of the electoral process, particularly in the 1983 presidential election. The weakness of the parties, their poor organisation and failed institutionalisation were attributed to the long years of military rule and the influence of the military in the formation of some of the parties themselves (Falola & Oyeniyi, 2015). After experiencing a bloody civil war that cost Nigeria an estimated 1.5 million citizens, politics and power control were decentralised through state creation. Politics or elections were decentralised from regional to the state-by-state influence but the regions maintained their ethnic semblance and regional influence despite the state demarcation in block voting for their ethnic and regional candidates. Thus, the process of the formation of the First Republic parties was heavily influenced by colonialism, and ethnic and regional factors in the same way the Second Republic parties were influenced by the military establishment and ethnic and regional factors. Additionally, the main character of Nigerian political parties in the First and Second Republics revealed a multi-party system. In essence, the Nigerian political parties developed in a multi-party system since the colonial period. The socio-economic and political factors that collapsed the First Republic manifested and led to the demise of the Second Republic (Akanji, 2021).

The third phase of the development of political parties in Nigeria and the democratic experiment is the Aborted Third Republic (popularly called so because the transition to democratic rule was scuttled by the military after the process reached its final stage of the declaration of the presidential election result on 12 June 1991). One vital factor that must be considered as a distinguishing feature of the parties in this Republic was the heavy military influence in their formation. The parties looked state-sponsored and restricted in their nature and operation. The military regime of President Ibrahim Badamasi Babangida established the National Republican Convention (NRC) to the right and Social Democratic Party (SDP) to the left. Parties' secretariats were built with state resources in each of the nearly five hundred local government councils in the federations. All politicians that were involved in the First and Second Republic politics were completely banned from participating in any electoral office in the Aborted Third Republic. A new crop of politicians, albeit, affiliates and godsons of the old generation of politicians emerged. Famous among them were Chief MKO Abiola who contested for the presidential seat under the platform of SDP and Alhaji Bashir Tofa under the NRC (Apine & Balogun, 2021).

One interesting development in the party outlook in the Aborted Third Republic was the national outlook. The 1990 gubernatorial election results displayed that both the NRC and SDP secured seats across the north and south, which was unprecedented in Nigerian party politics and elections. This record was surpassed by some Fourth Republic parties but the circumstances differed. Additionally, ethnic and regional politics were demystified because the SDP candidate, a Yoruba and a Muslim, with his deputy, a Muslim, Babagana Kingibe, won the majority of the states including many northern states where Bashir Tofa, a northern Muslim candidate of Hausa/Fulani extraction, hailed from. The politics of religion, ethnicity and regionalism were quashed down in that election which, unfortunately, could not see the light of day. The presidential election was held in June and on 12 June, the election was annulled after Chief MKO Abiola emerged as the leading candidate. The opportunity to bury regional, ethnic and religious politics in Nigeria was missed in the 12 June election as the elites reorganised themselves in the Fourth Republic and utilised these elements to their political benefit (Sule, 2019). 12th June created a political crisis in the west, the Yoruba states where they perceived it as a conspiratorial plot of blocking them from having any access to the presidential powers. The crisis which was enlivened with protests, riots, writings, assemblies and programmes pressurised the northern elites to relinquish power to the Southwest, the Yoruba zone in 1999 during the commencement of the Fourth Republic. The pressure was further extended to have capitulated to the renaming of the National Stadium as Chief MKO Abiola. Some Yorubas were still not satisfied as they want Abiola to be declared a winner and a former president, a posthumous victory. One important development that is learnt in the Aborted Third Republic is that national unity and cohesion are possible with sound leadership and good governance and parties can be ideological and national in outlook if adequate mobilisation is entrenched. The Aborted Third Republic was the only democratic period which Nigeria adopted a two-party system in the development of Nigerian political parties and electoral democracy (Abba & Babalola, 2017).

The Fourth Republic (1999–2022), currently in operation, is the longest and most enduring democratic practice in Nigeria. The Republic witnessed many breakthroughs in Nigerian political history including the emergence of parties that dominate national and local politics, strong opposition and wresting away the seat of the incumbent president unprecedented in electoral history. Parties in the Fourth Republic are multi-party systems. From 1999, the electoral body, INEC, registered over 100 political parties. In the build-up to the 1999 general election, three parties were registered (Adejumobi, 2015a). The Alliance for Democracy (AD), All People's Party (APP) and the People's Democratic Party (PDP). Initially, AD looked regional and ethnic dominated by Yorubas in the Southwest geopolitical zone. The same was observed with an APP which seemed to be northern in outlook. However, the PDP looked national, domineering and elite in nature. The 1999 presidential election saw the PDP candidate winning in a landslide victory. It was believed that the PDP candidate Olusegun Obasanjo was solidly supported by the Nigerian elites and northern cabals in response to cajole the Southwest for the annulment of the 12 June 1991 presidential election (Katsina, 2016). The AD and APP formed an alliance in which the APP declined to present a presidential candidate in solidarity with the AD candidate, another Yoruba from the Southwest. The 1999 presidential election was an all-Yoruba affair (Adejumobi, 2015b).

Parties continued to proliferate in Nigeria's Fourth Republic after the 1999 general election. The PDP continued to dominate and penetrate all parts of the country to the extent that after the 2003 general election, Nigeria became officially and practically a one-party system rule by the PDP despite the continuous registration of additional parties (Agbaje et al., 2014). The All Progressive Grand Alliance (APGA) was registered alongside several other parties that contested the post of president in the 2003 election. The PDP by Obasanjo, the APP transformed into the All Nigeria People's Party (ANPP) and was joined by the former military president general Muhammadu Buhari who contested the presidency under its platform. The Biafran (civil war) veteran Emeka Odumegwu Ojukwu contested under APGA. The parties still failed to register their national presence except for the PDP. The APGA influenced the Southeast dominated by the Igbos with Ojukwu himself being an Igbo and the ANPP secured significant votes in northern Nigeria thereby confining the APGA and ANPP as regional and ethnic parties. Thus, it can be deduced that while there is a positive development in the national outlook increasingly held by Nigerian political parties, still regional and ethnic parties persist (IRI, 2020). Other parties registered that participated in the 2003 presidential election included the UNPP with Jim Nwobodo as its flagbearer, National Conscience Party (NCP) with Gani Fawehinmi as its candidate, Progressive Action Congress (PAC) represented by Sarah Jibril, National Democratic Party (NDP) by Ike Nwachukwu and Justice Party (JP) represented by Chris Okotie, PRP with Balarabe Musa as the candidate, People's Movement Party (PMP) represented by Arthur Nwankwo, All Progressive Labour Party (APLP) represented by Emmanuel Okereke, National Nigeria People's Party (NNPP) represented by Kalu Idika Kalu, Movement for Democratic Justice (MDJ) with the candidate Muhammad Dikko Yusuf, African Redemption Party (ARP) with Yahaya Ndu as the presidential candidate, Democratic Alliance (DA) represented by Abayomi Ferreira, Blending National People's Party (BNPP) represented by Iheanyichukwu Godswill Nnaji, National Alliance Consensus (NAC) by Olapade Agoro, Labour Democratic People of Nigeria (LDPN) represented by Pere Ajunwa and Mobilisation Movement of Nigeria (MMN) represented by Mojisola Adekunle Obasanjo. Therefore, the multi-party system continued constitutionally but in practice, the PDP emerged as the only party challenged by the ANPP candidate in the election (Liebowitz & Ibrahim, 2013).

One character of Nigerian political parties in the Fourth Republic is that they are being registered to benefit from the public funding of parties until the 2011 general election, when it was abolished for private funding. Some politicians joined the race to benefit from the allocation and to block other candidates who are perceived as threats to securing the nomination and to bargain for material or position benefits in return for supporting a stronger candidate. With each election, parties increased in Nigeria's Fourth Republic. In the 2007 general election, not fewer than fifty parties were registered and most of them participated in the election at various levels. Failure of organisation and institutionalisation escalated by lack of ideology made the parties mushroom and a platform for contesting power to accumulate materialism instead of policy influence and good governance. The 2007 general election was continuously dominated by the PDP further asserting its national control and mightiness. Although eighteen candidates competed for the presidential seat, the PDP secured 69.82 percent of the total votes in the presidential election followed by 25 governorship seats out of the 36 states, 85 senators out of 109 and 263 members House of Representatives out of 360. This picture depicts domination beyond challenge by the party but the dominance will make the party arrogant enough not to consider power permutations and internal democracy as necessary which eventually culminated in the defeat of the party in the 2015 general election by the opposition All Progressives Congress (APC). Also, additional parties such as DPP, SDP, FDC, ADC, HDP, ALP, APS, CPP, BNP and NMM were registered while the AD transformed into Action Congress (AC) providing an opportunity for the Vice President Alhaji Atiku Abubakar to contest in the 2007 presidential election.

The emergence and development of political parties in Nigeria's Fourth Republic continued unabated, reaching its zenith in the 2019 general election, for which over ninety parties were registered. Earlier, the opposition parties realised that until they form a formidable front, they will never compete with the ruling PDP. In this regard, in 2013, a strong alliance was initiated which led to the formation of APC. The APC emerged from the merger of four major opposition parties. The parties included the Action Congress of Nigeria (ACN) which metamorphosed from AD to AC, the ANPP, a faction of the APGA and the Congress for Progressive Change (CPC). Later after registration in 2013 by the INEC, the party was joined by the newPDP, a faction of the ruling PDP that broke away after the 2014 Convention. The newPDP later formally joined the APC. Before the APC was registered, it encountered stumbling blocks from the perceived plot of the ruling PDP. Two APCs strove to get registered. The first African Progressives Congress and the second All Progressives Change (IRI, 2020). However, the genuine APC scaled the hurdles after the INEC determined that it was the first party to meet all the requirements with the same abbreviation (Akinola, 2014). The APC went ahead to defeat the ruling PDP in the 2015 general election in what seemed a history-making because the opposition party had never won an election in Nigeria since the First Republic (Sule et al., 2018). Perhaps, one of the reasons was the issue of longevity. The Fourth Republic lasted long for such a development to occur since the democratic experience is growing. The years spent in the Fourth Republic are more than the total years of all the previous Republics. The First Republic lasted six years, the Second Republic four years and the Aborted Third Republic two years. The three previous republics lasted for a total of twelve years less than the sixteen years when the PDP was defeated.

The parties in the Fourth Republic proliferate rampantly because of many variables. One of them is the public funding from 1999 to 2010. Most of them registered to access the fund even when they know that they don't have the chance of making any impact at all electoral levels. Second is the question of the law. The Nigerian 1999 Constitution provides for parties to be registered once they have fulfilled the criteria without specifying any number which means an unlimited multi-party system. The legal provisions made party registration easier in Nigeria. Section 225 and its sub-sections and Electoral Act 2010 provide that a party can be registered once it meets the following requirements: adopting a name, abbreviation, a logo, a non-refundable N1 million, application form, name of party chairman and secretary and their residential address and to submit fifty copies of the application. The INEC will verify and ensure that all the requirements are fulfilled and there is no clash of nomenclature or symbol with any other existing party, then register them within thirty days. If the INEC is not satisfied, it may decline but the party has the right to re-apply if it addresses the issues raised by INEC. Another factor is the court judgement. Sometimes INEC declined to register some parties but they took the case to the court and the judgement was in their favour (Sule, 2020). However, the INEC is mandated in Section 226 and its sub-sections in the Nigerian 1999 Constitution to deregister any party that failed to secure a seat in a general election at any level. Building on these powers, after the 2019 general election, the INEC deregistered seventy-four political parties that fall within the law and allow seventeen to remain. As the country is heading towards the 2023 general election, only the seventeen remaining parties are bound to contest and participate (Sule, 2022).

THE NATURE AND WORKINGS OF
NIGERIA'S FOURTH REPUBLIC PARTIES

The Nigerian political parties in the Fourth Republic have unique nature, structure, character and activities that distinguished them from the past political parties in some instances despite the existence of similarities and the continuation of the display of the same character. Taking ideology as a pretext for analysis, it will appear that while some parties examined above in the previous Republics have some semblance of ideology and the ideology had transcended into party politics and foreign policy, the Fourth Republic parties have no elements of ideology. With over 100 parties on record (now seventeen in existence), no single party can unequivocally present the doctrine it believes in or the kind of policies it stands to formulate and implement upon assuming power. Perhaps, the level of organisation and institutionalisation has been at the preliminary stage even after more than twenty years of practice. The main campaign manifesto of all parties since 1999 has been to provide infrastructure including roads, clean drinking water, electricity, quality education, and sound healthcare, eradicate poverty and generate employment and other basics of decent means of living that escaped the Nigerian state due to corruption, squander of national resources, mismanagement, massive looting and misplacement of priorities by the ruling class (Joseph, 2007).

The former ruling PDP has its campaign slogan as the power to the people which seems not to be an ideology but a slogan. Members of the former ruling PDP interviewed severally revealed that there is no clear identification to the left, right, centre or any other ideological leaning except the quest for power to control the state resources (Adejumobi, 2010). The ruling APC shares the same destiny with the PDP. They have a campaign slogan of change, which is not ideology. In essence if anything, nothing has changed from what the PDP had been doing in its years of ruling. The director of the APC Governors' Forum, Salihu Lukman, argues that most of the members of APC could not even explain the purpose and manifesto of the party including the elected under the platform of the party (Lukman, 2021a) and he also argues that the litmus test for change unveiled that the party failed to fulfil some of the promises made to change the country because the society is static and the party alone cannot do an unrealistic miracle as expected by the people (Lukman, 2021b). The lack of ideology resulted in many crises for the ruling parties in Nigeria. The incessant intra-party conflicts, party switching, weak opposition, corruption and other related crises affect tremendously both PDP and APC. Within a small period of time, the two major parties almost have the same membership emanating from party switching. This espouses the extent of the poverty of ideology in Nigerian parties in the Fourth Republic.

The Fourth Republic parties exhibit a unique character of longevity. Longevity in two dimensions, the longevity of lifespan and the time spent in power compared to the previous democratic periods. The PRP is the longest surviving party in Nigeria's political party history. Established in 1978, the party was re-registered again in 2003 and it has been participating in elections since then at various levels. Currently, the party has presented a presidential candidate for the 2023 election. The SDP is the second oldest party in Nigeria's Fourth Republic which was formed in 1990 and was reinvigorated in 2003. Since 2003, the party too like PRP has been participating in the electoral competition in Nigeria at various levels. The PDP is the third oldest party established in 1998. Other contemporaries of the PDP such as AD and APP underwent renaming of title and nomenclature, restructuring and merger that altered their faces. There were other surviving parties such as the Labour Party, APGA and many that followed the trend of longevity (Achoba, & Maren, 2021).

There is the context of longevity in the years spent in power. PDP has the highest number of years as a ruling party for a good sixteen years from 1999 to 2015 when the crisis of power shift and zoning rocked the party. In essence, many pundits (Adeniyi, 2017; Abdullahi, 2017) stress that but for the internal crisis of power shift and zoning of presidential seat between the North and the South, PDP might have ruled beyond 2015 and longer. After the two eight years of Obasanjo, he handpicked late president Yar'adua as his successor in 2007. President Yar'adua was certified sick and incapable but Obasanjo insisted that he was the most accountable and transparent governor therefore Nigerians need the one that will not be haunted by the Economic and Financial Crimes Commission (EFCC). After two years in office, President Yar'adua was overpowered by illness and died. His Deputy Dr Goodluck Ebele Jonathan ascended the throne. In the 2011 presidential election, the northern elites insisted that it was their turn to control power so President Jonathan must allow them to finish their eight years too the way the South enjoyed its own under President Obasanjo but Jonathan resisted and succeeded in placating them to allow him to serve just one term. But this so-called gentleman agreement was not written and by 2015, President Jonathan denied signing or entering into any agreement to serve one term and decided to contest. This led to a gang-up of the northern elites against him which eventually culminated in the defeat of the ruling PDP in the 2015 election, a record that never occurred in Nigerian presidential elections since 1960 as observed by Abdullahi (2017), Adeniyi (2017) and Sule et al. (2018). The ruling APC now is in its eight years of ruling and it's at the crossroads of either survival or demise just like its PDP counterparts. Several contradictions, crises, performance questions and other issues are threatening the party. The party primaries for the preparation for the 2023 general election were tumultuous, aggressive, enveloped in betrayal and the choice of the deputy in what is threatening to tear the party for a Muslim–Muslim ticket are all obstacles that the party must surmount to survive beyond the 2023 election.

The outlook of the parties in the Fourth Republic displays some semblance of national parties and the continuation of regional and ethnic parties. Specifically, the ruling APC and major opposition PDP have a national outlook and presence in all the geopolitical zones of the country. There is no zone in the six geopolitical regions that the APC and PDP have not secured gubernatorial, senatorial, representative and other elective seats. Few factors contributed to that. First, once a party assumed the status of the ruling party, other oppositions rushed to join to have access to the luxury and benefits of power. The party, to consolidate its gain and control of power, woo opposition and other perceived threats to join by incentives and the use of EFCC sometimes as a threat to the political survival of whosoever attempted to resist (Lukman, 2019). Also, the internal crisis of the parties led to party switching in which the ruling party becomes the best option for the defectors. Additionally, the elites assembled themselves in the former ruling party with the ambition of establishing a party that will dominate power for many centuries typical of the African politics where one party will continue to rule since political independence for over fifty years (Salih, 2003). The APC is perceived as a party that emerged with the sole purpose of wresting power from the PDP. By the time the party assumed power, already more than half of the former PDP members joined the APC and barely a few years into its ruling, the remaining PDP members joined. The APC and the PDP continued to switch against each other on personal political interest. One interesting case of reflection is the Edo State politics in South-South Nigeria. In the 2016 gubernatorial election, APC presented Godwin Obaseki as its flagbearer while the PDP presented Pastor Ize-Iyamu as its candidate. However, a crisis of interest and godfatherism between Governor Obaseki and the party's national chairman, Adams Aliyu Oshiomhole, who anointed the governor to succeed him after he finished his two terms, led Governor Obaseki to switch to PDP and the APC presented the former PDP candidate Pastor Ize-Iyamu to represent them. This display how the two parties joined forces in the power quest (IRI, 2020).

The other side of the outlook of parties in the Fourth Republic is the regional and ethnic outlook. Some of the parties maintain the character of the First and Second Republic parties in appearing ethnic and regional. AD is a good example formed in 1999 as a Yoruba dominant party. The party later transformed into AC, ACN and subsequently joined the APC merger just like APP which was renamed ANPP and later joined the APC merger. It can be deduced from the AD and APP experience that some parties in the Fourth Republic displayed a character beginning as regional and ethnic but later joined the mainstream national politics. Other parties maintain their regional and ethnic colouration such as APGA which is dominant in the Southeast,

PRP in the North and LP in the Southwest. But the regional and ethnic parties declined in their influence during the election because the national parties better mobilised and organised by the elites were institutionalised to exert influence and power more than the smaller regional ones (Adejumobi & Kehinde, 2010).

One notable future of Fourth Republic parties is the membership. Some of them draw their membership from across the nation, while others remain limited to some groups. There is a huge semblance in the membership of some parties through defection. Some of them draw their members through their regions and ethnic groups such as the APGA and PRP and others through national mobilisation, such as the APC and PDP. Yet others have nearly the same members such as the APC and the PDP which have over 90 percent of their members drawn from each other through switching for personal interests. One of the reasons why the membership of the parties looks the way it is may not lack relevance to the lack of recruitment and mobilisation. The voters themselves could not claim any membership. In essence, the voting pattern is always influenced by the religion, ethnic and regional affiliation of the candidate in a particular party. For instance, the entire Southwest presidential results in 2019 showcase a difference of 259,780 in favour of the APC candidate against the PDP candidate despite the region being the stronghold of the APC. This is because the candidate is a northerner. The Southwest candidate will contest the 2023 presidential election on the platform of APC and the margin of victory between the APC and the PDP candidate is projected to be around 90 percent or from 5 to 6 million if not more.

The party system in the Fourth Republic returned the party politics to multi-party after it was reversed in the Aborted Third Republic. The two-party system adopted in the Aborted Third Republic differed from even the colonial party system in Nigeria where multiple parties operated. In the Fourth Republic, parties without limit were registered. The parties can take many classifications as argued by Sartori (1976) that traditional classification based on the number of parties is no longer feasible. There are more than one hundred Fourth Republic so far even if most of them were deregistered by INEC based on performance factors. The number of parties made the electoral process expenses cumbersome and tiring (Sule, 2020). For example, the electoral expenses incurred by INEC continue to soar from N45.5 billion in 2007, N111 billion in 2011, N125 billion in 2015 and N189 billion in 2019 (Sambo & Sule, 2021). In the 2019 general election, the election materials were voluminous, bulky, longer and not legible because of the number of parties on the ballot papers and collation sheets. This made the electoral process multi-tasking for the INEC, electorates and electoral workers (Yagboyaju & Simbine, 2020).

However, the Fourth Republic parties appear multi-party in their numbers but they seem one-party or at best two-party in practice. Since 2003 when the PDP consolidated itself in power, it has been sweeping the general elections in all ranks with more than 70 percent of the total seats in all elective offices. The same feat is now repeating itself under the APC rulership. The exception is when in 2013 the APC was formed, a formidable opposition emerged and after the defeat of the PDP, it remains a strong challenger to the ruling APC. The systems of the party can also take the form of the national parties and ethnic and regional parties as analysed previously. Additionally, there are the coalition parties like APC and the lone-standing ones like the PDP but which sometimes also entered into a coalition for electoral victory (Yagboyaju & Simbinel, 2020).

The organisation and institutionalisation of political parties in the Fourth Republic in Nigeria disclosed a weak party structure and institutions. Party organisation denotes the process of the formation, mobilisation, recruitment, ideological promotion and activities. Most of the parties were formed either solely to contest power, secure power or allocate favour to the party cronies or they were formed as a form of a charade for negotiation of benefits (Adejumobi et al., 2007). This explains the reason why parties that are more than twenty years old could not devise strategies of mediation and peaceful primaries that will enable internal democracy. In the same way, a party that ruled for almost eight years or more could not institutionalise party structures at the grassroots because a few cabals (of governors specifically) hijacked the party apparatus and despotically involved their stooges in party affairs. This political parties in the Fourth Republic are finding it difficult to organise. They always face elections in disarray. The 2023 general election is closer but the two hopeful parties to clinch victory are in shambles, disorganisation and crisis of interest which may tantamount to defection and anti-party activities for those who have their personal interest ignored in the parties (Angerbrandt, 2019).

Party institutionalisation is weak in the course of party politics in Nigeria's Fourth Republic because the party-voter linkage is disconnected. Voters were not even mobilised or encouraged to register as active party members except for a few loyalists of the politicians that control the party structure. The majority of the voters are tantalised with money during elections without consideration of which party they belong to in as much as their votes will lead to victory. This explains why the parties remain fragile and vulnerable to collapse or defeat in elections while the electoral process in Nigeria is characterised by vote-buying, bribery and corruption since the parties have not recruited members and mobilised supporters for a long-term electoral victory project. Another alternative remains rigging and manipulation of the process. Once the voters display apathy, the ruling parties and opposition in their stronghold manipulate the result to emerge victorious. There is a wide chasm between parties and the electorates.

A major characteristic of the Fourth Republic parties is intra-party conflicts. The sixteen years of PDP ruling from 1999 to 2015 were marred with fierce internal schisms and volatile relationships among the members leading to crises that threatened several incidences to tear the party. One unique feature of the party's intra-conflicts is the ability to survive until the survival chance is thwarted. The PDP survived what many experts believed will tear them into pieces starting with the crisis of the party leadership itself in which more than eight party chairmen were removed in less than fifteen years (Omodia, 2018; Sambo et al., 2022). The party kicked its rule with an irreconcilable executive–legislature feud that led to the impeachment of senate presidents four times in five years. The House of Representatives also faced the crisis of the impeachment of the speakers. Besides, states' crises and national crises are the reminiscent of defection and anti-party activities (Akindele, 2010). The party ended up in a crisis that it could not surmount in 2015 which caused its defeat and its transformation into an opposition party from a ruling one. The intra-party conflicts did not stop with the PDP only. Even smaller parties such as PRP. LP, SDP, DPP and NNPP were not spared. They faced several internal wrangling to the extent that they had factions (Sule & Yahaya, 2018b).

To show how unique and similar are Nigerian ruling parties in the Fourth Republic, the APC could not spend good four years before it was hit hard by intra-party conflicts across the states, at the national level, within the party's national leadership leading to the removal of Adams Oshiomhole, the executive–legislature feud and the National Assembly leadership tussle (Sambo et al., 2022). This made a study (Sule & Yahaya, 2018b) predict that the ruling APC will have a similar destiny to the defunct ruling PDP if adequate measures are not taken to arrest the conflicts. But the party could not heed the advice and they found themselves in a crisis as threatening as that of the PDP or worse. The party primaries held by the ruling APC across all levels were enmeshed in conflicts, contradictions and crises. In many states, the imposition of governors was lamented while the presidential primaries were held with a tension that nearly tear the party away. After the primaries, the choice of the deputy is becoming a serious headache for the party flagbearer Asiwaju Bola Ahmed Tinubu. The Fourth Republic's politics was heavily polluted with religious sentiments and ethnic manipulation. Tinubu, being a Muslim from the South is in a dilemma of picking a Christian deputy from the North which is the Muslim-dominant region while picking a Muslim deputy will result in the Muslim–Muslim ticket that the Christian clerics and other national politicians had already warned strongly against. The party, just behaving like PDP, may survive this tension for now but it may not absorb it for a longer period. It will collapse and lose power due to these crises.

Party switching is another characteristic of Nigeria's Fourth Republic. While a study noted that the phenomenon of party switching, especially, in the legislature is worldwide, the Nigerian case according to Sule and Yahaya (2018b) is unique and worthy of study. From 1999 to 2018, high-profile cases of party switching were reported in the study more than 300 involving the former president, deputy president, governors, senators, members, ministers and party executive members. This is besides the daily reports of the defection of hundreds or thousands gathered in a jamboree to display the political muscle of the politicians that received the decamped. The Nigerian Fourth Republic case is believed to be peculiar because there are some politicians that changed parties more than ten times. Once they feel their ambition is at stake, they easily join another party to secure a nomination. This is the essence of the ideological deficiency and weak organisation and institutionalisation. Internal democracy is entirely lacking in the parties leading to crises that ostracise some members to other parties but the personal interest of power ambition is the major reason above anything else (Yagboyaju & Simbine, 2020).

Party switching in Nigeria's Fourth Republic succeeded in unifying the two parties of the APC and the PDP. For the close observers, APC is the past PDP while PDP is the present APC because of the same membership. About 95 percent of the APC members were former PDP members. Political office distribution can attest to that. For instance, the senate president in 2015, the speaker of the House of Representatives and major offices in the National Assembly were former PDP members. Additionally, the current federal executive cabinet has nearly ten ministers who were former PDP members. After the election of the party national executive by the ruling APC in April 2022, it was discovered that the national chairman, secretary and more than 80 percent of the party executives were former PDP members. The state governors currently in office have more than fifteen of them former PDP members (Sambo et al., 2022). Thus, party-switching unified and disentangled the APC from the PDP and the voting pattern is taking place only based on the personality of the candidates, religion, region and ethnic groups. The 2023 general election and beyond will be in this pattern.

Due to the politics of party switching, intra-party conflicts and the unification of major parties in practice, opposition politics become weak and in disarray. The opposition parties in their individual stand could not counter or challenge the ruling party and this has several implications for policymaking (Lukman et al., 2019). Ruling parties ignored people's yearnings and strive in satisfying the interest of imperial powers. The former ruling PDP was supervised by the International Monetary Fund (IMF) to sell off public assets and corporations including the telecommunications, power sector, aviation and many others which resulted in the exploitation and dissatisfaction of the consumers. The APC led-government is now being coerced by its penchant for excessive external loans to remove all subsidies. The minister of finance was reported on March 2022 to have disclosed to the IMF that we had removed electricity subsidy secretly. Imagine a federal minister reporting the subsidy removal to the IMF far away to the detriment of those who elected her government (Sule, 2022). If the government is aware of strong opposition that will challenge them squarely, they will have been cautious in their policies and activities to avoid public censure that will lead to protest votes which will oust them from power (Sule et al., 2018).

The opposition politics was weak until 2015 when the challenges of APC gave the PDP a strong fight. The opposition parties sensed that unless they form a viable platform or coalition, they will never be able to challenge the ruling PDP. The APC succeeded in challenging the PDP squarely because of many factors (Akinola, 2014). One of them is the incumbency factor because at the time of the 2015 general election the opposition APC had as equal governors, senators and members of House of Representatives with that of the ruling PDP. The second is the financial muscle. The opposition APC then had members with enough resources to challenge the ruling PDP financially. Third, is the candidate in the contest. The PDP candidate emerged through controversy and crisis with waning popularity while the APC candidate had been always supported by the majority of northern voters for more than a decade unchangeably and the candidate is perceived with a proven record of integrity. Fourth, the campaign in the 2015 general elections was executed based on issue-based such as corruption, insecurity and other socio-economic and political issues (Folarin, 2021). The ruling APC in its bid for 2023 election is faced with the same challenge that is mounted on the former ruling PDP. The ruling party is jittery about the consequences of the nomination of presidential candidates and may likely face stiff opposition in the 2023 election or it may lose if it does not strategise appropriately.

Political party financing is another characteristic activity of parties in Nigeria's Fourth Republic. Party financing was public from 1999 to 2010. The 2006 Electoral Act provides spending limit, donation limit, disclosure laws and sanctions for violators of regulations as well as the powers to INEC to monitor, audit and sanction offenders (Sule et al., 2017b). Unfortunately, party financing turned out to be a corruption bazaar premise in Nigeria in the Fourth Republic. The 2010 Electoral Act stopped public funding and grants allocated to parties by the electoral body stopped. This transferred the process of campaign funding solely to private donations and funding. The private funding allowed the politicians to violate the regulations, spent above the limit, bribe the INEC officials and other stakeholders, buy votes and engage in the abuse of public resources for personal campaign expenditure

(Onyekpere, 2015; Sule et al., 2019a). Nigeria is reported as one of the countries in Africa with the best laws of party financing well-articulated and stipulated in terms of sources of campaign financing, donation limit, legal sources and other punishable offences but the problem always is the monitoring and the sanction (Nwangwu & Ononogbu, 2016).

Party financing in Nigeria is reported as a pretext not only for violation of election regulations but also for looting of public resources and bribery and corruption. For instance, the 2015 general election saw how a sum of $2.1 billion earmarked for the procurement of weapons to fight the Boko Haram insurgency was diverted for campaign funding of the former ruling PDP. The party bribed whosoever cared to receive including INEC officials, security agencies and all stakeholders in the electoral process. Also, party financing was bedevilled with huge malpractice and vote-buying during party primaries where delegates were bribed with thousands of dollars to vote for specific candidates that have financial strength (Davies, 2021). This has been reported in the 2019 party primaries of the APC and the PDP (Sule, 2019) and it is still observed in the recently concluded party primaries of the APC and the PDP in May 2022 at all levels of electoral offices. The politicians once assume office engage in recouping their expenses and profit-making. They allocate contracts to their cronies who vie for them and receive kickbacks apart from dubious contracts, diversion of public resources and poor performance (Sule et al., 2022). Party financing in Nigeria's Fourth Republic is one of the greatest challenges of party politics, institutionalisation and democracy.

Chapter 5

Nature and Dimensions of Political Party Financing

This chapter explores one of the most critical questions of accountability and transparency in a democratic system of government. The champions and crusaders of global democratic governance always capitalise on the logic of transparency and a fair process that gives a sense of satisfaction to the government and the governed. The process of electoral conduct and governance in a democracy is made open and subject to scrutiny to the extent that not a single penny should be spent without an approved procedure under the watchdog of the electorates, the civil societies and other branches of government that are designed to checkmate the excess of the other. More importantly, the process itself that brought the leaders is questioned and cross-examined to ensure that investors have not taken the affairs of the public for private gain. Those who spent beyond the legal provisions, violate spending regulations, bribe their way and manipulate the process are accused of being selfish and can never make selfless leaders that can be held accountable in governance.

Political party financing is increasingly drawing attention and academic enquiries in recent years after a long period of neglect. It was recently in the 1990s but, especially, in the twentieth century that significant attention is given to the concept when the concern of how politicians cheat the system and circumvent regulations to secure power become inevitably annoying (Alexander, 1986). Organisations, agencies and individuals started asking questions such as if democracy is accountable and transparent, why the excessive use of money by politicians to secure power? What happened to the existing regulations on political party financing are they adequate and capable of taming the phenomenon? Why are those who aspire to lead buy their way to power what is their motive? Is there a need to re-examine the regulations and carve new laws that will be stronger in holding politicians accountable?

Why are the Electoral Management Bodies (EMBs) across the world unable to reverse the trend? Is political party financing escalating political corruption? These, and many other questions, are now being answered by scholars in individual case studies, comparative approaches and global perspectives. But not much has been done on the subject matter to satisfy researchers in the area.

Party financing takes various measures with varieties of regulations, sanctions and monitoring strategies from one country to another and from one geopolitical region to the other. Observers and electorates are increasingly becoming cynical and hesitant of the supposed democratic accountability and transparency that they are being convinced to continue to support (Yadav, 2011). Although democracy originates in Ancient Greek city-states, the great trio of Athens' Socrates, Plato and Aristotle detested democracy vehemently in their philosophical works on the perspective of a transaction that includes a replay of buyers and sellers in the market with people's votes and liberties. They, specifically, argue once leadership is thrown into the arena of election by all qualified citizens, a money-making venture is established. This is the prediction and the logical arguments more than forty centuries ago but is still manifesting in twenty-first century. It is seriously alarming (Ferguson, 1995).

The various studies (Williams, 2000; Bryan & Baer, 2005; Norris & Van Es, 2006; La Raja, 2008; Walecki, 2015; Walecki, 2017; Wulff, 2017; Piccio & Biezen, 2018; Hutagalung, 2019) conducted on party financing across the world revealed that both public and private funding exist and states forge their party financing laws based on their democratic culture and environment of politics. Take Nigeria, for example, the adoption of public funding from 1999 to 2010 led to the emergence of mushroom parties that have no desire to compete or even play a vibrant opposition politics but to grasp their share of the funding from the government-sponsored financing. This necessitated an amendment which jettisoned public funding and opened up for private funding. Laws and regulations were amended to cater for the procedure of the private funding but the maximum spending limit and other issues of disclosure and transparency become a recurring headache. This is the case in most world countries including advanced democracies of the West such as the United States, Britain, Canada, Italy, France and others. In developing democracies, the use and abuse of public funds, the crude acts of vote-buying, bribery and corruption, manipulation and influence of money politics made party financing a negation of democratic values of transparency. Victory is assured for the highest bidder with huge cash backing. In the developed democracies, corporate businesses and multibillionaires who act as godfathers truncated transparency in the financing process.

Thus, political party financing is a global political problem that must be countered. And it can best be countered using individual studies than a broader approach because of the peculiarities, political culture, political environment and elements that differentiate states in their electoral process. One cannot talk of democracy in detail without examining the election and electoral process. An electoral process is attached with its issues of party financing. This is more pronounced in new democracies where access to public office is becoming ultimate security for financial prosperity and well-being. States like Indonesia and Nigeria are good examples of political corruption in party financing. Nigeria has party financing laws in Sections 225 and 226 with their sub-sections in the 1999 Constitution as Amended and Electoral Act 2006 later amended as Electoral Act 2010 and Electoral Act 2022. One outstanding legacy that this work stands to exploit and present is that the Electoral Act 2022 provisions are yet to be analysed critically and academically. The study shoulders the task of pioneering such a breakthrough. The 2006 and 2010 Acts were scrutinised by some studies and their lapses were identified towards amendment. The study will examine whether the required amendment is made and how far they can go in fostering transparency in a corruption-ridden country where the public office holders found solace in looting public funds through the platform of election and power control (Sule & Sambo, 2021).

Party financing is associated with political corruption in Nigeria. Some studies and cases empirically expose corrupt practices in party financing. The main issue is the monitoring and compliance as well as the complicity of the officials in the process. The history of party financing in Nigeria is examined in this chapter in addition to issues attached to it in terms of corruption and accountability and transparency questions. The regulations and other related matters are discussed in chapter 7 as a sequel to what is discussed in this chapter.

POLITICAL PARTY FINANCING: A BROADER VIEW

Political party financing is the process of funding parties' campaign expenditures and fundraising of political expenses that parties and their contestants are expected to incur in the electoral process from the nomination to the final election. Parties and politicians incur expenses that accrue in the course of the budget for campaign posters, billboards, media adverts and jingles, physical contacts at wards, constituency and national levels and sometimes externally in search of support from powerful international actors and states. The charter of a plane, transportation costs, accommodation, feeding and logistics in undertaking campaign activities are either shouldered by the candidates themselves, their campaign team, parties and, in some situations, by the government through public funding (Ohman, 2014a).

Campaign funding is raised in several ways. One of them is public funding. Governments in countries that are operating the public funding provide grants through the EMB to allocate to parties based on a structured formula such as parties' performance, based on the number of contestants across elective offices and, in some instances, based on equality. The other alternative sources of funding are private in which parties are allowed by law to raise money through many legal sources. In this scenario, the electoral body regulates financing laws, legal or accepted sources to utilise, donation and contribution limit or ban and other related laws. Parties raise funds by selling forms, donations, fundraising, fines, administrative charges and other means. Private individuals can contribute or use their personal savings to sponsor their political ambition but they can also be sponsored by campaign teams and mentors (Ohman, 2018).

Democracy is regarded as a system that allows for flexibility in accountability and transparency. Taming excessive use of money by making strict laws that will limit campaign expenditure and monitor candidates is a move towards that direction. The financial strengths of candidates are parallel. Some contestants are wealthy multibillionaire business tycoons and others are having the support of these rich men in the society to win an election. Others are poor or average in financial capability. The best way to ensure fair play and equity is to set a barrier that will make the process look transparent and block the possibility of the highest-bidder syndrome. If the rich ones are allowed, they will continue to dominate and buy their way onto power with the influence of their money. This, if allowed, will ostracise credible candidates that have integrity and competency but could not compete financially from leading the society. Therefore, the need for fair play and transparency made political party financing interesting (Norris, 2018c).

In the process of party financing, a type of corruption emerges known as political corruption involving bypassing the legal norms in campaign spending. It is frightening that politicians that are promising selfless services and patriotism to the electorates can buy votes, bribe and employ other dubious illicit means to arrest electoral victory. The result is that corruption is sheltered and it breeds into a monster that crashes the moral values of the society. Leaders in this regard become looters and politicians become synonymous with liars and deceivers who manipulate the psychology of the voters to win but use the privilege of power to enjoy luxuries and opportunities at the expense of the voters (Rose-Ackerman, 1999).

To counter the phenomenon of corruption in the process of party financing, countries are initiating laws and regulations while regional areas are forging cooperation such as the Organisation for Economic Cooperation and Development (OECD) to formulate uniform basic laws on the matter. The extent to which the laws are relaxed or strict, the powers of monitoring and sanction and the ability of the agencies, organisations, civil societies and the electorates to mount effective surveillance on politicians' spending during the campaign and beyond is the issue that is not settled satisfactorily. Factors that usually cause non-enforcement are legal loopholes, ambiguous laws, ambitious laws, weak or loose penalties, lack of administrative capacity of a regulatory body, lack of transparent and neutral judicial sector, immunity clauses and unknown or excessively complex laws (United States Agency for International Development, 2005).

One of the developments that are unfolding on the issue of party financing is the increasing socialisation and interest that the citizens are showing in the process. The citizens are specifically concerned about the growing influence of party financing on political parties and the attendant corrupt practices that followed up which make politics and elections belligerent and subversive. This is critically affecting democracy and democratisation globally. The revelation of scandals across the world countries contemporarily associated with the process of party financing raises a serious concern about the integrity of elections and the democratic process. The phenomenon becomes worrisome in Europe to the point of coming together and setting a benchmark that should not be trespassed by the European Union (EU) for member countries (Van Biezen, 2003). In the proposed regulations by the EU, it was agreed that rules on party financing should consider a moderate view of the public and private funding and establish a synergy, those states with public funding policy should promote fair play in the distribution of the grants among the political parties, absolute auditing and censorship of private sources of funding and arranging strict laws and sanctions that will punish the violators and deter the innocent (Van Biezen, 2003).

Political party financing is given attention because it is recognised that a healthy and responsive democracy can flourish if the parties as institutions of democratisation are transparent and responsible. The transparency of parties can be achieved by close observation of those involved in the activities of party financing and by setting stringent laws that will compel compliance. The parties may use the window of campaign financing and expenditure to break laws and avoid the set norms if they are allowed to do so. By breaking the code of conduct of party financing and regulations, deception and unfair play sneak in because those who spend heavily can win the election meaning that those who could not match the financial muscles of the rich ones are edged out from the competition (Doublet, 2012).

In the case of the EU, Article 12 of the Council of Europe provides that all donations to political parties must be reported specifically. The specifications include the exact amount received, the type of donation, value worth and the disclosure of the identity of the donor. But the article relaxes the law and says that some minor insignificant donations may be ignored or overlooked to avoid being rigid which may result in pushing the parties to alternate strategies of circumventing the process clandestinely. Unfortunately, the problem in Europe is corporate donations which are rewarded with contracts in a form of corruption that is obvious but difficult to trace. The article suggests that corporate organisations should be banned from donations to parties in an electoral process. Political parties are required to publish their statement of income and expenditure quarterly and an independent EMB is necessary to monitor impartially the finances of all the parties. Any party or candidate that violates the agreed regulations should be sanctioned mercilessly (Doublet, 2012).

The volatile economic downtowns and increasing reports of scandals involving parties and candidates motivated the citizens to set their eyes to fix on the financing process of the political parties of their countries. The OECD (2012) reported that most citizens of Europe believed that there is corruption and violation of laws in political party financing. The survey disclosed that 87.9 percent of citizens in Greece responded that parties and politicians are corrupt, 80.8 percent in Spain and Italy, 70.9 percent in Portugal, 66.1 percent in the UK, 57.3 percent in Germany and 53.8 percent in France and 61.9 percent in Hungary. This survey informs us that most European citizens suspect corruption and nefarious scandals by politicians in their countries perpetrated in the process of party financing. In Africa, the situation is similar. It is reported (Anyadike & Eme, 2014) that about 86.7 percent of citizens in Kenya accepted that parties and politicians are corrupt and 88.6 percent in Nigeria believed the same.

Having realised the trends of corruption in parties and politicians occurring in the process of campaign financing, the OECD (2012) member countries designed some regulations including regulating private funding, increasing public grants and setting a maximum ceiling for campaign spending by office seekers. But the OECD (OECD) discovered that these measures are inadequate to tame the explosion of corruption in party financing and this encouraged them to expand the laws to improve transparency. The doctrine of disclosure was introduced and emphasised as an important measure of promoting transparency and preventing illicit financing and suspicious transactions.

A comprehensive study to examine the party financing process across the world countries is sponsored by Institute for Democracy and Electoral Assistance (IDEA). Experts on the subject matter traversed various regions and countries to uncover the scenario and the issues attached to the process and some practicable recommendations were provided. The IDEA database examined 180 countries and it reported that all countries have their unique ways and domestic laws of party financing but the most important discovery is the status of the limit ban by all countries. All countries have set limits on spending based on the nature of their political culture and socialisation, economy, democratic type and other elements (Ohman, 2014a).

The database study discovered that the main aim of spending limits and monitoring is to regulate corrupt practices and ensure transparency of the democratic system. Regulations are available in the studied countries to enforce compliance and activate sanction regimes for the violators. The IDEA database argues that the plausible means of achieving transparency in the party financing process is to have a reform worldwide that can target identified challenges and legal obstacles in the individual countries. Not forgetting the differences and peculiarities, the IDEA database study suggests that some basic regulations can be universalised and encouraged all countries to adopt them unanimously. These include donations ban and limits, public funding, spending limit and timely auditing and disclosure as well as effective monitoring and sanction (Ohman, 2014b). The level of perception of the citizens surveyed across the world indicates a worrisome situation and the need to act fast. For instance, in Africa, on average, 53 percent believed that there is political finance regulation, 28 percent in America, 5 percent in Asia, 28 percent in Eastern, Central and South Western Europe and Asia, 33 percent in Western Europe and an average of 38 percent globally (Ohman, 2014a). This reawakens the conscience of the global key players that neither the advanced democracies nor the emerging ones are transparent or doing better in avoiding political corruption disguised in party financing. It is quite alarming. The IDEA database study made a regional analysis of the situation which exposed challenges, strengths, weaknesses and divergent issues of each zone to simplify the process of remedying them.

In the African context, party financing has various regulations depending on countries but public funding is the main source. The main problems with the party financing process in Africa are inequality in access to funds for all political parties and candidates, abuse of state resources, clientelism, patrimonialism, vote-buying, illicit funding, external influence and foreign intervention in the electoral process because of external funding and excessive money politics due to cash economy. The regulations are appreciable across countries, especially, since many of the countries ratified the United Nations Conventions Against Corruption (UNCAC) among which one of the pillars of the ratification is to promote transparency in party spending and party financing of candidates. Many countries signed the agreement including Chad, Equatorial Guinea, Eritrea, Gambia, Nigeria, Somalia and South Sudan (Ohman, 2014c). Apart from the membership in the UN convention against corruption in party financing, the African Union made an effort in formulating a common regulation for all members under the auspices of the African Union Convention on Preventing and Combating Corruption.

Sources of income for parties and candidates in Africa emerged from contribution bans, contribution limits, private income, external funding, public funding and illicit funding obtained through abuse of state resources and other suspicious ways (Ohman, 2014). Regulations are poorly observed making it difficult to realise how much is at the disposal of parties and candidates or how much they spend in an election. Many countries in Africa provide public funding: the Benin Republic for the presidential and parliamentary members, Burkina Faso provides grants to cover up to 50 percent of parties' expenditure, and Cameroon makes public funding a law for all the parties to be determined by the president, the Chad Republic provides grants only to new parties, Egypt supports all parties in every election with a grant of $29,000 and in Equatorial Guinea, $30,000 is given each to the presidential candidates, a sum of $8,900 to the parties. In Gabon, each party that presents candidates for electoral contests will receive a grant of up to $34,700 while in Morocco a total of $13.6 million is allocated to public funding where all parties are given 20 percent before the election, 30 percent based on the total seats contested, 25 percent to candidates based on total votes received or performance and 25 percent to parties based on the number of seats won (Sule, 2021).

Public funding in African countries takes different modes across the countries. In Mozambique for instance, a total sum of $340,000 is earmarked lawfully as a grant to parties with ¼ to two largest parties, ¼ distributed proportionally across the presidential candidates, ¼ allocated to all the parties in the parliament and ¼ to all competing parties. Namibia provides public funding to parties that made it to the parliament only while Seychelles made funds worth $1.5 million available to parties based on performance. South Africa supports public funding with a sum of $9 million specified for parties with membership in the parliament in the same pattern as Tanzania which provides $10 million to be apportioned to parties based on membership seats in the parliament in the same way Zimbabwe is providing an undisclosed amount of grant to parties that meet the condition of securing at least, 15 percent of the seats in the parliament. In the case of Nigeria, public funding in an undisclosed amount was provided in form of a grant from 1960 to 2010 but it was abolished and the process is transformed fully to private funding with some regulations for monitoring and ensuring compliance (Sule, 2021).

Party financing in Africa is surrounded by controversies about using public treasury, clientelism, patrimonialism, vote-buying and moneybags politics as observed by many studies (Bogaards, 2007; Erdmann, 2007; Gyima-Boadi, 2007, Laakso, 2007; Nugent, 2007) while those countries with private funding and sound regulatory frameworks such as Ethiopia, Ghana, Kenya and Nigeria are observed (Sigman, 2015; February, 2016; Ohman, 2016) to have been unregulated, unmonitored with weak compliance and ineffective disclosure. Another issue with party financing in Africa is the existing donation limits are too high in many countries. For instance, in Kenya, the annual donation is limited to 5 percent of the party's spending in the previous year, which is high. In Mauritania, the law allows for only ten individuals to provide the entirety of the party's campaign expenditure. In Uganda, the limit is around N400 million shillings. In the Republic of Congo, a single donor can donate the equivalent to salaries of a minimum of 1,000 civil servants per year which is ten times higher than legally in Algeria. The annual donation limit in Morocco to candidates and parties is 100,000 Dirham. In Nigeria, the situation is unique and recommendable by the regulations which are modestly pegged at N1 million only irrespective of the office that the candidate is aspiring. Unfortunately, since the candidates are not audited by parties the regulations are unenforceable. Fundraising in 2010 by the Peoples Demcratic Party (PDP) in Nigeria received a single donation of N250 million by Alhaji Abdussamad Rabi'u basing his justification for the contribution on a ridiculous submission that it is legal since he collected the maximum limit of N1 million each from the members of his family (Ohman, 2014c).

Party financing in Asia differs from other regions studied earlier. Public funding is minimal and is regulated highly to avoid corruption and irregularities. Because private funding is encouraged, candidates with limited financial capability find it difficult to compete in electoral competition. Parties do not fund their candidates which made private donations vital in raising finance for campaign activities in Asia. Politics is commercialised in the region and giant corporations are gradually hijacking the political process through donations and sponsorship of politicians into power. This development creates concern and awareness among the stakeholders leading to increasing calls for regulations of private funding for public funding and transparency in the financing process. The national and international nongovernmental organisations (NGOs) are pivotal in the call for regulations, reforms and the fight against corruption in the party financing process and governance (Ufen, 2014).

The major issues identified with the process of party financing in Asia involved clientelism, weak regulations and ineffective implementation of enforcement, weak opposition parties impedes by lack of resources to compete and dislocation of female candidates from competing with their male counterparts due to financial constraints, abuse of state treasury and vote-buying. The financing of elections is controlled by dynasties in Asia such as in the Philippines where a few dozens of family clans are recognised as sponsors of politicians. In Thailand, the Thai Rak Thai (TRT), the ruling party before the military coup in 2006, was financed almost solely by billionaire Thaksin Shinawatra. The incumbent ruling party that was assumed after the demised of the TRT is led by Yingluk, the younger sister of the billionaire sponsor. Examples of other dynasties in South Asia are the Gandhis in India, the Bhuttos in Pakistan and the families of Sheikh Hasina and Khaleda Zia in

Bangladesh. There were collective approaches to reform the party financing process in Asia since the 1990s in the wake of the third wave of democratisation. For example, the South East Asian states initiated a framework known as ASEAN Democracy Free and Fair elections in 2009 by the Asian Network for Free Election (ANFREL) and the 2012 Bangkok Declaration on Free and Fair elections to enhance transparency and promote fair play for all parties and contestants (Ufen, 2014).

Europe has no uniform procedures for party financing due to varying degrees of democratic practice in the region. In the case of Western Europe, there is a liberal approach and more effective monitoring than in Eastern and Central Europe where some of the regimes were still authoritarian and the building of the liberal democratisation process is still slow. Like other regions examined earlier, the political financing process is beclouded by the challenges of abuse of state resources, state control of political affairs in Eastern and Central Europe, private sector sponsorship and kickbacks, vote-buying, illegal financing, violation of regulations and lack of transparency. Measures are put in place of regulating party funding in the region. The region of Europe is the most regulated, effective and efficient in adherence and monitoring of party financing compared to other regions examined previously. Countries in the region put extra effort into designing individual regulations to ensure effective regulations (Smilow, 2014).

Money politics plays a critical role in European politics because of the economic viability, political culture of rewards and kickbacks and the dominance of rich people in the control of politics. In Western Europe, regulations of spending are flexible and relaxed because of the high level of political socialisation unlike in Eastern and Central Europe where regulations are strict. Issues associated with party financing in Europe include political corruption, weak enforcement of regulations, public funding and gender inequality in accessing funding or lack of opportunity for the female gender in having privilege for accessing funds for the campaign. Regulations were introduced by OECD and are becoming effective. The regulations are adopted individually and collectively which is aiding the combating of corruption and fosters accountability and transparency (Piccio, 2014). Sources of funding in Europe are mostly from state funding in the case of some communist states like Russia, membership dues, private donations, corporate financing, contributions from party loyalists and illicit funding (Smilow, 2014).

Some European countries have no spending limits completely such as the Czech Republic, Turkey, Ukraine, Kazakhstan, Turkmenistan and Uzbekistan. In other countries, the spending limits are so high that they have no impact on political competition. In Hungary, the maximum spending limit is 386 million Hungarian forints (HUF), or HUF 1 million per candidate and while in Moldova the maximum campaign spending limit is 12 million Moldovan lei (MDL) and MDL 500,000, respectively. In Russia, the limits are 250 million roubles (RUB) for parties. In Kyrgyzstan, political parties may not spend more than 1 million monthly salaries, the exact amount is not specified. Using the country's minimum wage of 600 Kyrgyz som (KGS) per month, 65 the spending limit is very high relative to the regions considered here: 1 million minimum-wage monthly salaries equals I\$36 million. Similarly, spending limits for candidates are 500,000 times the minimum, or I\$18 million (Piccio, 2014; Smilow, 2014).

In Latin America, political party financing is enshrouded in corrupt practices amidst weak regulations and weak enforcement usually aided by the exacerbated prolonged authoritarian regimes in the region. The democratisation in the twentieth century is accompanied by increasing money politics and criminal control of politics. The regulations exist; the major issues are application and enforcement. The infiltrations of illegal funding and weak monitoring impede transparency in the process. Parties and candidates sourced their funding from contributions bans, private income, limits of contribution, the public treasury and illegal means. There are efforts individually and collectively by the states in Latin America but the level of compliance is not encouraging. Money politics bastardised the party financing process causing huge unregulated political corruption. Total campaign spending is exorbitant and it varies from one state to another. In Brazil, for example, a maximum of \$2.5 billion was spent in the 2006 election, \$301 million in Mexico in 2006, \$38.8 million in Uruguay in 2000 and \$27 million in 2010 in Costa Rica (Londono & Zobatto, 2014).

In the established Anglophone democracies in North America and Oceania, Canada, Australia, Ireland, New Zealand, the United Kingdom and the United States, party financing is similar in many aspects despite the geographical distance because they share common historical, cultural and legal semblance. Comparing their experience is easier and more so, they are all OECD members, they are also English-speaking countries, all countries were at some historical event under the British Empire, all of them are members of Commonwealth, all of them except for America are having a parliamentary system of government in political structure, they are old and advanced democracies, but they are yet to resolve the annoying issue of money politics. Most of the problems associated with party financing in these countries are enduring and they include a lack of fairness on level playing ground, overdependence on corporate bodies and trade unions for sources of funding and uncontrolled expenditure by parties, politicians, donors and godfathers. Various weaknesses in regulations of each of the countries opened a window of violation of regulations, lack of conformity and compliance and transparency (Nasmacher, 2014).

In the American state, private funding is the legal norm and it is one of the most expensive democracies in the world. Private donations are encouraged from individuals and corporations, but the law is strict on foreign donations or external sponsorship. There is flexibility in the laws which enables excessive spending. The existing laws are observed to have been weak and ineffective in enforcing compliance and efficient monitoring. Rules on party financing in America state that disclosure is mandatory on all sources of candidates and parties from personal savings to private donations (Ohman, 2014a). The 2016 presidential election in America demonstrates a high level of money politics and excessive spending. Both the candidates spent much beyond the limit as confessed by many Americans interviewed in the report (February, 2016). This was partly influenced by the 2010 Supreme Court ruling that removed many existing limitations on outside groups' spending money to influence an election (Jacob & Smith, 2016). Most Americans believed that there is a need for reform in regulations on campaign financing. Jacob and Smith (2016) conclude that the 2016 presidential election is an example of an electoral and democratic process confiscated by illicit financing, corruption and illegal activities against transparency.

It is observable that there is a considerable level of freedom of speech in the countries in Anglophone democracies but it is far from being equated with fair elections. Norms are circumvented and regulations are manoeuvered by powerful parties and politicians with better financial muscles. Abuse of state resources is a recurring phenomenon in party financing in these countries. Parties sourced their income from contribution bans, contribution limits, private funding including membership dues, individual donations, donations from corporate organisations and trade unions, fundraising, donations from elected officials, foreign funding, public funding both direct and indirect and public subsidies share of the revenue. There were individual and collective efforts in the promotion of transparency of the process. The countries initiated their own different regulations to enforce compliance, maximum spending limits and monitoring of parties' expenditure. For instance, the bodies responsible for monitoring financial reports in some of the countries are the Australian Electoral Commission (AEC), the Chief Electoral Officer in Canada (Elections Canada) and the Electoral Commission in New Zealand (ECNZ). Collectively, all the members are signatories of OECD conventions on combating corruption and the promotion of effective transparency in the political process. Reporting of income and expenditure is made mandatory by law in the countries and disclosure of donations received is also necessary. Civil society and the media are playing a great role as guardrails of democracy in these countries in monitoring party financing and campaign expenditure, which helps immensely in curbing some of the corrupt practices (Nasmacher, 2014).

Party financing is important and interesting in the Middle East and North Africa (MENA) because the states in this region are in transition to democratisation. In countries such as Libya, Tunisia and Egypt, most of the legal framework is being reformed. It is recommended that global standards for party financing regulations and transparency should prevail upon the states that are democratising in the MENA. Like its counterparts, MENA suffered from political corruption in the process of party financing, abuse of state resources, vote-buying and weak regulations coupled with excessive spending and ineffective monitoring (Ohman, 2013).

Party finance has typologies classified into two by Wiltse et al. (2019). First is the degree in regulating party income. The logic of regulating parties' income and expenditure in the electoral process is to enable a level playing ground and fair play among the strong and financially weak candidates and this can be achieved through public funding, limiting spending, monitoring and sanction. The second dimension is transparency. Disclosure is very important here in informing the public about who gives what and what it is spent for. Some of the practical ways to achieve transparency according to Santuci and Ohman (2010) is to compel the publication of campaign accounts, electoral bodies should be given the power of the supervision and auditing of parties' accounts, political parties, candidates politicians should disclose their assets, income and expenditure and liabilities to an independent body, annual financial auditing of the books of parties and the electoral body should imbibe the culture of immediate auditing after each election. Walecki (2010) argues that the practical ways to ensure spending limits successfully are to create equal conditions for all parties and candidates, reasonable limitations on campaign expenditure, the institutionalisation of parties and effective party organisation, certain types of expenditures should be prohibited by the electoral body and a severe sanction including a ban on participation and a heavy fine should be slapped on the violators. Ohman (2010) makes a case for the inclusion of political finance in the tasks of the international election observers to discourage excessive spending and violation of regulations.

Political finance regulations are important in achieving transparency and the levels varied across the countries of the world. Ohman (2012) presents some measures that world countries are regulating to achieve the desired results. These measures are bans on donations, limits on donations, provision of public funding to address accountability, bans on expenditure, limits on expenditure, financial disclosure and enforcement and sanctions. The common ban on donations is on the use of public resources, a total of 85 percent of world countries ban the receipt of donations from public resources. About 68 percent of world countries ban foreign donations but only 22 percent ban corporate donations. Globally, 55 percent of the world's countries do not limit the amount that can be donated to parties and candidates, 68 percent have provisions for direct public funding and only 29 percent limit the amount of money that parties are allowed to spend even if about 44 percent have provisions that limit candidates' expenditure. About 88 percent globally require financial reporting of parties to the regulatory bodies and in forty countries of the world, no institution is constitutionally given the mandate of monitoring and auditing parties and candidates' financial statements and where there is a mandatory requirement for presenting of financial reports of parties, they are not made public (Ohman, 2012). Rhode (2017) believed that promoting a level playing ground, ensuring transparency and accountability, fostering a culture of integrity and ensuring compliance and review will help tremendously ineffective party financing monitoring and regulations.

In an effort for reforms and devising panaceas to the perennial problems of party financing, a committee of experts converged in Prague in May 2019 under the tutelage of the United Nations Office on Drugs and Crime (UNODC) in partnership with the International Foundation for Electoral Systems (IFES) and the Office for Democratic Institutions and Human Rights (ODIHR) to brainstorm on the issue and present practical solutions that are feasible for world democracies to emulate. During the discussion, experts noted that that the Recommendation Rec (2003)4 of the Council of Europe's Committee of Ministers to the Member States on common rules against corruption in the funding of political parties and electoral campaigns is the most comprehensive soft law to date, with forty-nine states subscribing to it. It stipulates that states should provide that all donations to political parties are made public, in particular, donations exceeding a fixed ceiling (Ohman, 2021).

One vital area that most studies neglect and which is now being given attention by Ohman (2018) is the gender-targeted party financing because of the vulnerability of women in competing financially with their male counterparts in electoral contests. Ohman (2018) stresses that targeted funding globally is currently based on eligibility, allocation and public funding but to encourage women to participate in electoral competition, it is germane to introduce specifically gender-targeted public funding. Some countries including Albania, Croatia, France, Haiti and Portugal have started introducing gender-targeted funding. In the countries that provide gender-targeted public funding, the number of women in the parliament increased to 8 percent for at least ten years more than the global average increase of 6 percent in the world parliaments. The gender target funding is also instrumental in harmonising equality in future in terms of political participation and representation.

PARTY FINANCING IN NIGERIA: A
HISTORICAL BACKGROUND

Political party financing in Nigeria has its root in the pre-independence period during the battle of power supremacy among the parties that were formed during colonialism to fight for political independence. The first national election was conducted in 1959 which heralded political independence in October 1960. Before the 1959 general election, election into elective offices in Nigeria commenced in 1922 under Sir Hugh Clifford's 1922 Constitution when the Africans pressurised the British colonialists to include them in the affairs of government. The British colonial government succumbed to the pressure and introduced in the Clifford Constitution indigenous representation. During that period, no any law or regulations of party financing was introduced because even the British itself was not democratically advanced to the level of question of democratic accountability and transparency in the period. The other colonial elections that took place under the various developed colonial constitutions such as the Richard in 1944, Macpherson in 1951 and Lytetton in 1954 were all conducted in a similar manner to the earlier one. (INEC, 2005).

The electoral laws in Nigeria during the 1959 general election were derived from the British electoral laws. The British Representation of the People's Act 1948/1949 and the regulations made in it formed the basic foundation for the adoption of electoral laws in Nigeria in the period. The 1959 election was executed under the provision of the Nigeria Electoral Provisions Order-in-Council LN 117 of 1958 enacted by the British Parliament. During that period, no specific regulations on parties' financing and regulations of campaign activities including expenditure. Even the British itself have no such advanced laws at the time. However, based on what was observed, it was clear that private funding operated during the period because there was no evidence of public funding or grant but there was substantial evidence that candidates sponsored their political activities and parties catered for their expenses during the electoral process (INEC, 2005).

The lack of clearly specified regulations on sources of funding, expenditure limits, disclosure and contribution ban helped in the illicit financial activities of politicians and parties in the First Republic. Illicit funding took place and corruption manifested in the process. Two cases of corruption in the process of party financing were recorded. The Foster Sutton Tribunal of Enquiry in 1958 investigated allegations of financial misconduct of some politicians with affiliation in NCNC who have business partnerships with African Continental Bank (ACB). In 1962, a Commission of Inquiry, the Coker Commission was established to investigate some illegal political financing of some politicians involving six Western Nigerian public corporations allegedly in misconduct with some members of AG (INEC, 2005). In this case, it is not surprising that Nigerian politics is bedevilled with corruption and illicit financing because the process kick-started instantly with political independence. Smith (1961) reports an early case of the culture of corruption in Nigeria because of such allegations of political corruption. There was not much party financing in Nigeria in the First Republic because the democratic experiment lasted only for six years.

The Second Republic began in 1979 but there are no specific regulations on party financing except for the fact that both public and private funding occurred. Political parties played a greater role in the politics of the Second Republic and the country for the first time had its own indigenous electoral body, the Federal Electoral Commission (FEDECO) that handled the election in 1979 and 1983. Some regulations concerning political parties were introduced in the 1979 Presidential Constitution. The country also witnessed a giant political restructuring from parliamentarism to a presidential system of government under the 1979 Constitution. One clause that is clear in the 1979 Constitution on party financing is the provision that 'no association other than a political party (was allowed to) canvass for votes for any candidate at any election or contribute to the funds of any political party or the election expenses of any candidate at an election'. Section 205 of the 1979 Constitution enacted a law that enabled the Federal Government to provide a grant to FEDECO to disburse to political parties based on equity and fairness. In the same section, the law stated that parties and candidates can source their campaign expenditure from their personal savings or private donations while being entitled to public funding at the same time (INEC, 2005).

In the 1979 Constitution and FEDECO laws, there is no spending limit or contribution bans on parties and candidates. But the foreign donation was banned and corporate businesses and trade unions were banned from contributing to parties and candidates for campaign sponsorship. These regulations were provided in Section 201 of the 1979 Constitution. Also, there were no provisions on disclosure, auditing and monitoring of financial activities of parties and candidates. The weak regulations in the 1979 Constitution manifested in the massive corruption allegations labelled against politicians in the Fourth Republic, specifically in the use of public treasury for political financing, illicit funding and violation of regulations with impunity (INEC, 2005). Political corruption expanded from party financing to looting of public funds and squandering of public resources to the extent that when the military took over power in 1984, many politicians were sentenced to outrageous hundreds of years because of alleged misappropriation and embezzlement of public funds (Adejumobi, 2010).

Political financing in the Second Republic was exposed to godfatherism, clientelism, patrimonialism, political economy of primitive accumulation, politics of brigandage and personalisation of public resources and property. The politicians became corrupt and self-serving with the few oligarchs who were ambitious of hijacking power and providing moneybags to sponsor politicians that they can control in office for reward and rentier process. The state became a rent for a few power brokers. Money politics started gaining its roots in Nigerian politics. Politicians paid less attention to politics of ideology and principle to politics of money where they believed they can buy their way into power with their resources. Characteristics of party financing in the Second Republic revealed vote-buying, bribing electoral officials, excessive use of money and abuse of state resources and violation of regulations (INEC, 2005). One important development noticed in the party financing in the Second Republic is that politicians raised money beyond expectation and used them to buy votes. For example, a fundraising dinner by one of the parties in Lagos saw ten individuals donating N5 million and it was believed that the raised money was used in unrestricted vote-buying and bribery (Adetula, 2008).

Politicians from 1979 to 1984 had unfettered access to the use of money and expenditure during campaign elections unregulated. This excessive use of money involved both legal and illegal sources. Corporate bodies and godfathers swayed the political process to their whims and caprices. A sustained Clientelistic chain was formed with the patrons, brokers and clients' relationships fully established as examined by Post and Jenkins (1976). Reports obtained from the various tribunals established by the military to investigate financial misappropriation and the illicit conduct of politicians in the Second Republic revealed gross misconduct and abuse of office and due process. All these were directly linked in the report to parties and politicians that patronised them (INEC, 2005). Political corruption in Nigeria emerged entangled with party financing, which continues to escalate and spill over beyond the control of authorities. From corruption in the party financing process, gradually politicians graduated to massive looting of public funds and struggles of an accumulation from the public purse accentuated by holding public offices (Ogundiya, 2009).

In the Aborted Third Republic, there were no clear specific regulations of party financing introduced. In essence, it was believed that the 1979 provisions were upheld and used for guiding parties and the electoral process. The transition was incomplete and no effort was made in designing a new constitution. This perhaps may not lack relevance with the hidden intention of the military junta not to relinquish power to the civilians after the transition process started in a faulty and undemocratic process. The parties were formed by the military themselves, registered them, assigned them a marked ideology of the right and left, sponsored them and built secretariats for them and determined who contest which office. Many seasoned and veteran politicians were banned from any form of participation in electoral posts. The politicians that were allowed to run were not financially regulated. Oligarchs and wealthy individuals emerged as contestants for elective offices or sponsors. Money-spending was large and Clientelistic display determined the direction of the politics. The process was scuttled shortly after its inception when the presidential election was annulled. There are no specific laws or regulations to report in this period beyond illicit financial activities of the parties and their candidates including vote-buying, bribery, excessive spending, a free-for-all process for the wealthy and a bazaar for money politics (Sule et al., 2017a).

PARTY FINANCING IN NIGERIA'S FOURTH REPUBLIC (1999–2022)

The Fourth Republic differs from the previous democratisation attempts in Nigeria because it was the fourth wave of democratisation which saw the world advance in democratic governance with many reforms including democratic accountability and transparency in the party financing process and other regulations that will prevent corrupt practices. Nigeria started its democratic experience in the Fourth Republic (1999) without adequate and well-elaborated regulations on party financing. However, the 1999 Constitution which maintains the presidential system of government provides some sections (225 and 226) on matters that border on political parties including their registration, deregistration, composition, sources of finances, regulations, auditing, monitoring of expenses and other laws attached to them but they are not flexible and enough to curb corruption in the party financing process.

There is no demarcated boundary of contribution bans, spending limits, disclosure and sources of funding initially. From 1999 to 2010, a mixture of public and private funding existed. The government gives subvention to INEC to allocate to parties based on participation, performance and the number of seats won in the parliament. In Section 228(c) of the Nigerian 1999 Constitution, the National Assembly conferred powers to INEC to disburse annual grants to parties based on a fair and equitable basis. Based on that provision, the National Assembly allocated the N600 million grant in 2003 for disbursement to thirty registered parties on the eve of the 2003 general election. INEC allocated N180 million of the amount to all the thirty parties at the rate of N6 million each. A sum of N420 was shared by INEC to seven parties including the AD, ANPP, PDP, APGA, NDP, PRP and UNPP. The formula for the distribution was 30 percent on equality and 70 percent on equity based on the number of seats won in the election (Adetula, 2008).

However, no substantive laws were made regarding party financing until 2006 when the Electoral Act 2006 was enacted into law by the National

Assembly. In the 2006 Electoral Act, spending limits, contribution bans, disclosure, auditing and monitoring and sanction of parties and candidates that violated the regulations were provided but the main problem is the monitoring and compliance which remains a mirage. Parties spent lavishly as they wish and candidates sourced their funds from all means including legal and illicit funds such as personal savings and the public treasury. Excessive spending characterised the nature of party financing in the Fourth Republic. There were no available records of parties and candidates' expenditure. Indications of heavy and excessive spending illustrated themselves in the 2003 general election when the former president Obasanjo himself lamented that 'the parties and candidates spent together during the last election (2003) more than would have been needed to fight a successful war' (INEC, 2005).

One fundamental feature of party financing in Nigeria's Fourth Republic is the role of godfathers and oligarchs. Some framed themselves as power brokers that assumed the full control and responsibility of determining who shall govern through their organised orchestrated financial sponsorship. The first president of the Fourth Republic, Olusegun Obasanjo, was anointed, financed, sponsored and geared towards political victory by these cabals who rescued him from the penitentiary where he was incarcerated and prepared him for the task. These godfathers continued to dominate political sponsorship in Nigeria to the extent that one must have their backing to dream of vying for an elective office in Nigeria (Olarinmoye, 2008). The peak of this godfatherism is revealed (Sule et al. c) in the 2015 general election where the financiers of candidates emerged by siphoning the public treasury. The godfathers are identified to be violent and aggressive in their pursuit of power and brokerage. Some of them secured electoral victory for their anointed godsons through the use of money as in the case of Alhaji Lamidi Adedibu in Oyo State while others used both force, violence and money to cruise through electoral success for their godsons as in Anambra where Andy and Chris Uba reign supreme. The Ubas sponsored former Governor Chris Ngige, the Minister of Labour and Productivity (2015–2022) in the country to win the Governorship seat of Anambra State in the 2003 election. When Ngige went against their interest, they impeached him (Sule et al., 2018c).

Party financing in the Fourth Republic is bedevilled with vote-buying, bribery, corruption and election rigging and manipulation. Those who sponsored the process used excessive money to buy all stakeholders that stand in between them and electoral victory including INEC workers. A report indicted some of the workers who were bribed with about N34 billion by the former Minister of Petroleum, Diezani Alison Maduekwe to win the 2015 presidential election for the former ruling PDP. The $2.1 billion earmarked to procure arms to fight the Boko Haram was shared among various stakeholders involving security agencies, INEC officials, religious clerics, traditional rulers, politicians, godfathers and all categories of stakeholders involved in the electoral process (Sule et al., 2017a). Political corruption gained a deep seat in the process of party financing because the process has now surpassed the vote-buying and excessive spending witnessed before towards bribing all stakeholders, diversion of public funds and clientelism.

Party financing in the Fourth Republic is more corrupt and pervasive perhaps because the experience in the Fourth Republic is longer than in other Republics. The number of years spent revealed the pattern of the character of the Nigerian elites and the political culture of the electorates. The elites decided to win at all costs using all sorts of the matrixes of game theory whether a zero-sum game, non-zero-sum game, prisoner's dilemma and game of chicken. They devised all forms of tricks to win. Votes are traded openly and freely in the polling units. Sometimes religion is ridiculed, and a sacrilegious act is made where voters are asked to swear with their holy books and receive a token in return for voting for a particular candidate.

Most of the issues identified in party financing in Nigeria's Fourth Republic include extreme violations of regulations. Donations that are constitutionally limited to N1 million by the Electoral Act 2010 were sometimes abused to the level where a single individual donated N1 billion (1,000 times exceeded the limit) without any action or sanction against the party, or recipient candidate or the giver. Weak monitoring and enforcement are other cases. Take, for instance, the situation where the INEC staff will write and request for accounting books of parties but the response they receive is denigrating and degrading for a regulatory body of their kind. Party officials will tell them they don't have the authority to give until the state governor or the president returned from an assignment. They will never give the accounting books for auditing. In some cases where the INEC officials pay an unexpected uncourteous visit to the parties' offices to audit the books, the parties' executives dispersed and left them unattended (Sule, 2018).

Another issue is that disclosure is difficult because parties and candidates received clandestine donations that they don't reveal. In essence, this is a question of morality unless and until one is God-fearing, principled and honest, no one can detect such donations since they are given in cash or even in foreign currencies, specifically dollars which are not bulky in comparison with the Nigerian currency. Many politicians interviewed by Sule (2018) revealed that they have donated N100 million while others confessed to donating N1 billion and above. This is gross misconduct and a violation but difficult to monitor or sanction. This trajectory will continue because it is covertly carried out and the beneficiaries (the giver and the receiver) will never reveal the deal. They only came to the public limelight when there is a conflict between them that is when they will divulge their secret in some instances before the public or even in the media but nothing is being done to them which continuously motivates them to do more.

Additionally, the laws themselves that regulate party financing in the Fourth Republic are seen as inadequate and need serious reforms (Sule et al., 2022). For example, the maximum spending limit set for the presidential candidate of N1 billion is practically impossible considering the environment of the Nigerian economy and the nature of the money politics in the country. This can be seen in the report by Onyekpere (2015) when the PDP presidential candidate in the 2015 general election spent about N10 billion on a media campaign while his counterpart of the APC was around N3 billion. This is just the media campaign what about transportation, accommodation, feeding, party members' responsibilities and other logistics which are legal expenditures? But more importantly what about the bribe given to delegates and vote-buying involving individual voters in the process? In the party primaries of the PDP presidential aspirants in 2019, each of the over 2,000 delegates was allegedly bribed with $5,000. Across other elective seats, such practice is obtained (Sule, 2019). The laws should consider the economy and patterns of the polity and make a flexible and adequate provision for what is feasible and practicable by reviewing the maximum expenditure limit upward but with a strict measure of enforcing compliance, monitoring and sanction. The review was successfully made in the 2022 Electoral Act as amended which shall be examined in detail in chapter 7. There are many loopholes identified in the law which it is hoped that the 2022 Electoral Act will remedy to ensure compliance but the monitoring and sanction will continue to be a serious challenge that may not be overcome easily even in the future.

PROCESS AND MEASURES OF POLITICAL PARTY FINANCING IN NIGERIA

Many processes in Nigeria's party politics gulp huge sums of money. These processes can be measured using many variables. One of them is the corruption involved in it. The 1999, 2003, 2007, 2011, 2015 and 2019 general elections were bedevilled and involved in controversies of bribery and corruption. The political actors are interested in prosecuting electoral victory at all costs which means they are clientele, Rational and game players in the process. The politicians bribe any influential person that will be instrumental in their electoral victory. In the process, a vicious circle of corruption occurs. They bribe electoral officials, security personnel, party members, voters and other stakeholders and when they assumed power, they engaged in recouping their spent money on bribery and profit-making. Once they accumulated enough, they bulldoze their way back to power using the same trick and perpetuate themselves. This is the reason why the same faces of politicians are recycled continuously since 1999 (Lawal, 2015). Once a politician has tasted the privileges of power, he can invoke all deviant ways to continue since the objective is not to serve selflessly but selfishly.

A factor that is responsible for expensive electioneering in Nigeria is the cost of the media. Politicians spent exorbitantly on image-making and outdoor advertisements to attract voters' support. The media is gulping a huge sum of money in radio, television, billboards and other media processes which are expensive and cost-demanding. This is the reason why the maximum spending limit set by the Electoral Act 2010 failed to work. An example is given earlier where a presidential candidate that is expected to spend no more than N1 billion in all his campaign activities spent about N10 billion in just media costs alone and another spent about N3 billion in media adverts only (Onyekpere, 2015). If such expensive media costs continue in Nigerian politics, candidates will continue to spend beyond the limit even with the increase of the spending limit to N5 billion by the 2022 Electoral Act which this study feels is still far from being enough if there must be practicability and possibility of enforcing compliance based on fairness (Aghara et al., 2015).

Another dimension of party financing or why the parties and candidates spent much is the expansive geographical nature of Nigeria. As examined in the introductory aspect of this book, Nigeria is a large cluster of multi-geographical entities with evolving political structures and large geopolitical entities. For any contestants at the presidential level to cover the country, he needs to charter a plane if he has none and he must charter them for his entourage. Going around the thirty-six states in Nigeria and the FCT Abuja is a Herculean task that needs huge resources. The Nigerian political culture has not reached an advanced level of internet campaign and social media outreach despite the explosion of social media usage gradually from 2010. Candidates must tour by themselves and this is costly (Olorunmola, 2016). In the case of state elections, still, candidates need tremendous resources because some states are as big as many European smaller states or even bigger. Take Niger State, for example: one can travel as far as four hours within the state.

One process which consumes huge resources in party financing in Nigeria is the party primaries and intra-party and inter-party relationships. Some candidates compete to draw favour but not to win. To settle them, the favoured contestant must compensate them for their loss or they will switch party allegiance or engage in anti-party activities by leaking some vital strategic secrets of political tactics that the favoured candidates are designing to win. This settlement of co-contestants is followed up by the settlement of other parties' contestants who deliberately contested not to win but to create swing votes through the spoiling of some votes (Walecki, 2003). To avoid taking chances, the favoured candidates must ally with them and settle their expenses too.

Besides, delegates are another headache that the candidates must cater for. They bribe them individually to secure the party nomination. The delegates in the PDP presidential primaries in the 2019 general election were allegedly bribed with $5,000 each by one of the aspirants (Sule, 2019). In the build-up to the 2023 general election, delegates were allegedly bribed with $25,000 each by one of the contestants. Another of the contestants was speculated to have given them a sum of $15,000 each. This cuts across the two major parties of the APC and the PDP (Sule, 2022). After compensating the internal and external party members, candidates have to deal with the security, INEC officials, ad hoc staff and electorates in the polling units to buy their votes.

Chapter 6

Theorising Party Financing in Nigeria's Electoral Politics

The process of party financing in Nigeria's electoral conduct can be better situated by integrating some postulations and assumptions that can support the literature and studies on the subject matter. Theories were proposed and constructed to explain political processes either in universal practice or in isolated cases of study. This study strives to link the activities of campaign funding or party financing with electoral conduct in Nigeria in the Fourth Republic and this can best be approached through some hypothesising on the correlation between the two and by exploring how or why one influences or depends on the other. Based on this foundation, this chapter adopted and applied three main theories which are clientelism, rational choice theory and game theory. The theories are analysed in isolation and then integrated. All of them can explain issues of party financing and the corrupt tendencies associated with the process and electoral competition. In this regard, the choice of the theories followed the format of utility principles to maximise analysis.

Clientelism is usually used when a study explores how the elites, voters and intermediaries related in the process of voting or power competition. This extends to explain the anticipated outcome in terms of benefits to the parties involved and how the activities involved in it often resulted in patronage, patrimonial relationships, resources allocation based on favour and consideration of clientele relationships and the possible role of godfathers in the financial sponsorship of their loyalists to arrest political victory that tantamount to control and pursuance of mutual personal interest. In clientelism, voters are studied in a particular case study to determine what motivates them to vote for a particular candidate. It may not be necessarily money or material reward. Ethnic loyalty, religion and other emotional elements may play an important role in influencing the election outcome. An example of such a

121

study is the PhD work carried out in Nigeria by Sule (2018) which examined the party financing process and electoral activities. There are many studies carried out in other areas which are presented in the next section.

Rational choice theory is related to clientelism in assumptions and operationalisation. The rationality of choice of candidates can take any satisfactory measures including material reward and promise of project allocation or juicy appointments. Electorates are considered economic objects of consumer behaviour where any choice made is measured on the principles of maximum utility and satisfaction amid the scarcity of resources. In the electoral arena, voters are such economic actors who choose a candidate based on the satisfaction that they can derive from the competing contestants in such a way that the outcome will have a benefit or reward that will qualify as the best payoff or choice (Pincione & Teson, 2006). The expected reward can be financial, emotional, contractual, position or even promoting an interest or warding it off for a particular group.

In the case of game theory, it is a mathematical permutation that is used to analyse various issues in the field of social sciences. The theory relates in assumptions and meaning as well as applicability with clientelism and rational choice theory. In political science, game theory is used to explain electoral competition and decision-making in fierce close-substitutes contests (Hechter, 2019). In an election, party financing and the electoral process can be a fierce game because the competitors can indulge in any action possible to win and such actions can be overspending, vote-buying, reward promise and an eloquent campaign promise that will earn them voters' support. Violation of regulations in spending, excessive spending, bribing any stakeholder that cooperates, corrupt practices, abuse of state resources and any form of foul-play that will favour them, especially, if the competitors are aware that their rivals will not hesitate to do the same and if they expect to escape after the act.

CLIENTELISM

Clientelism is a framework of analysis developed by many scholars in stages over a period of time. In essence, clientelism is a work in progress because of the continuous dimensions that it is taking and the numerous case studies that are surfacing with new models and applications. Clientelism has its root in the Latin words '*cluere*' (to listen and to obey), '*clientela*' (a group of individuals who had proxies prompting for them in the public interest) and '*patronus*' (the patrons who patronised the aristocrats through some clandestine arrangements). The patrons offer jobs, material benefit, support, allocate resources and provide the favour while the clients support, promote and protect the patron's political interest (Muno, 2014). There are few works on clientelism in the 1970s and 1980s but the term was in operation and observation in the pre-industrial era even if research works or attempt at theory-building was not obtained in those days except a close observation of the scenario in the politics of Europe (Gans-Morse et al., 2010). It was erroneously expected that clientelism is a pre-industrial practice that will wither away in modern societies with the increasing liberty and demand for democratic accountability but the phenomenon persists and takes a new dimension in modern politics (Darabont, 2010).

The early efforts in researching clientelism involved case studies in the 1970s and the 1980s supported by conceptualisations and hypotheses-building mostly carried out by anthropologists and political scientists (Kobayashi, 2016). The early studies assumed that clientelism will gradually wane with the increased sophistication in democratisation and the development of modern political institutions (Roniger, 2004). The second stage in research on clientelism occurred in the 1980s and the 1990s. In this stage, historical evidence, practical cases and the workings of clientelism were presented. In this stage, clientelism was given a decisive interpretation as the 'model of social exchange and a specified strategy of political mobilisation for electoral victory and support' (Roniger, 2004). Roniger (2004) further argues that clientelism is seen as a complex societal inter-relationships of patron-broker-client activity engaged in mutual agreements with the different groups in the society, specifically affecting political parties, voters, politicians and interest groups.

The third stage or wave in research on clientelism took the period between the 1990s and the 2000s. This period is characterised by the explosion in the activities of civil societies that served as watchdogs of democracy, informal groups and the citizes–politicians linkage. This set of activities sparked a renewed interest in investigating clientelism in theory and practice. The discoveries from the investigations reported that clientelism and its practice in modern democracies are against genuine democratisation and institutionalisation of good governance. The studies suggest that there is a need to have a paradigm shift in understanding clientelism and its practical impacts on political distribution and resource allocation based on the favour that emanates from the clientele relationships. This, according to the studies, is affecting democracy, good governance, politics and the electoral process (Roniger, 2004). This study further expands the horizon of the stages of the development of clientelism beyond the third stage or wave as presented by Roniger (2004). It is identified based on a survey of the literature on modern studies on state, corruption, electoral process and governance in the world countries that research on clientelism is now in their fourth wave from the 2000s up to 2020 and beyond drawing from the case studies in different countries as examined below.

Clientelism in modern terms denotes the political economy of power competition and relationships between the politicians and the electorates on one hand and the politicians and the wider society on the other on assuming political offices. The patron-client relationships portray certain levels of interactions in the political processes where the parties involved derive their maximum benefit based on mutual principles and understanding. Clientelism demystifies the issue of accountability and transparency between the advanced democracies and the developing ones because the phenomenon is found in both in equal proportion or more than. In essence, advanced democracies instead of obliterating clientelism compelled it to evolve more vigorous dynamism and strategies of networking the legality of the act in under-estimated regulations and bypassing strictness of political relaxation (Darabont, 2010). Clientelism works in a network involving brokers to link up the poor voters with their patrons (Szwarcberg (2015). In some cases like Nigeria, for instance, religious clerics, traditional rulers and public image-makers are the networks used by the politicians to reach out to the poor voters (Sule et al., 2017c). In Italy, local mafia and brokers are used to target the rural poor (Zinn, 2019).

Clientelism in its opaque and simpler interpretation connotes a political arrangement and sublime strategies of winning an election by politicians at all costs including vote-buying, winning the opposite voters and rewarding them for switching their allegiance to a particular candidate and abuse of public resources and offices for political gain. Instead of justice, equality and equity in the distribution of public offices, appointments, resources allocation and projects, clientelism necessitated a selfish and unjust reward for the cronies and clients that supported the office-holders (Gans-Morse et al., 2010). In this regard, merit and appropriate utilisation of resources and responsibilities are sacrificed on the altar of personal gain and political ambition.

A contradictory view suggests that not in all circumstances is clientelism a rewarding mutual patron-client venture. In some cases, threats and coercion are used by the patrons against the clients to achieve their ambition. It is an act of political corruption which offers material reward for electoral support. The patrons in this perspective threaten or coerce the client through an expression of the consequences of the lack of support if victory is gained. The clients are frightened that they may not get their deserved share of political appointments, the resources allocation may not favour them and they may not get a fair share of project distribution (Stocks, 2013). Stocks et al. (2013) observed that if clientelism is not addressed properly, it will slow economic development, impair democratic growth, allows dictators to hold onto power continuously, propagates political corruption with impunity, deprives the citizens of enjoying the dividends of democracy and good governance, undermines the credibility and integrity of the electoral process and it will prevent proper political mobilisation and policy choice preferences by the citizens. Nichter (2018) laments that politicians plunder their nations for five years by buying votes for one day to show the extent of the implications of clientelism on the political economy of governance.

Clientelism is in some cases used interchangeably with 'patrimonialism' which entails the struggles to acquire political power for private advantage. In patrimonialism, the public office holders violate the laws, ignore due process, engage in suspicious transactions, double shuffle on the rule of law, favour some categories at the expense of the majority and ignore public needs and interests for their own interests (Muno, 2014). Patrimonialism is believed to have eroded democratic values, especially, in African politics. Ogundiya (2009) traced the roots of patrimonialism to the spillover effects of colonialism which truncated indigenous values and systems and handed over the remnants of fragmented fragile disorganised elites to the African states who instead of focusing on nation-building and development derailed towards primitive accumulation, ethnic and religious mobilisation for power control and control of resources based on the ethnic, religious and regional cleavages. Ogundiya (2009) limits his studies to the Nigerian context as a leading African state. Patrimonialism is synonymous with clientelism and impedes democratic development and good governance because the citizens are blocked from voting based on policy choice and performance but on the promise of benefit. The personal narrow gain annihilates the culture of holding public officers accountable and the citizens care less about the impacts of policies on them or the outcome and how it will affect them (Isaksson & Bigsten, 2013). This is in line with what Brun (2014) postulates that the quality of democracy is affected by clientelism because social policy is affected in the same way that Schweizer (2013) stresses that clientelism leads to extortion because politicians recoup what they spent on buying votes and other favours.

Muno (2014) further identifies five major assumptions of clientelism as follows: (1) the relationship is dyadic; (2) the relationship is asymmetrical; (3) the relationship is personal and enduring; (4) the relationship is reciprocal and (5) the relationship is voluntary. The relationship is dyadic because two actors are involved, the patron and the client. However, in some cases, more than two actors are involved because apart from the patron and the client, an intermediary exists known as the broker. Nevertheless, the existence of a broker does not negate that the relationship is dyadic since the broker act on behalf of both the patron and the client. The relationship is termed asymmetrical because the financial and influential status of the actors varies. The patron controls resources and the power of favour while the client offers electoral support and expects a reward. The relationship is personal because it is not a formal arrangement but a gentleman's agreement in principle to seek support for a favour. The relationship is reciprocal in the sense that each of the actors is expecting support and a reward from the other. The patron expects votes to secure electoral victory while the client expects cash, kind, appointment or contract in return and the relationship is voluntary because it is not by force in most cases (Muno, 2014) although Stocks (2013) presents a different view that the relationship can be coerced or by threats in some cases. The five assumptions of clientelism explained previously are presented in an illustrated form in figure 6.1.

As observed in the first assumption, the relationship can be dyadic with only two actors shown in figure 6.2.

In another perspective, the actors can be more than two when brokers are involved but it is still dyadic because the brokers are prompting for both the patron and the client and they are not acting on behalf of themselves as indicated in figure 6.3.

Clientelism has not limited its operation to the developing democracies as earlier observed. A study (Hagel, 2020) reports the scenario in the United States, England, France, Italy and other European states where patron and client negotiations occur during elections. Global politics has been diverted and hijacked by the world's billionaires who control the politicians and economic sectors worldwide and clientelism found its headway the world over through their influence (Hagel, 2020). Business cartels are entrenching clientelism in their support of candidates with corporate money for favour in tax cuts, tax holidays and other policies that will maximise their profits and squeeze the poor (Kuo, 2018). In some instances, as in Colombia, bureaucratic and political offices and material benefits are allocated based on the number of votes

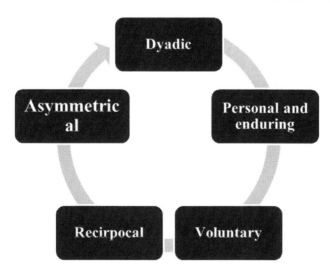

Figure 6.1   The Five Assumptions of clientelism. *Source*: Model designed by the author with data from Muno 2014.

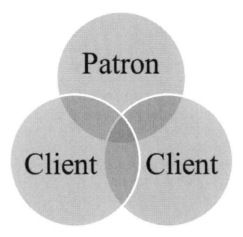

Figure 6.2 Showing the Patron-Client Relationship in a Political Process or During election. *Source*: Model designed by the author with data from Muno 2014.

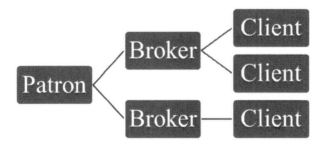

Figure 6.3 Showing a Three-way Patron-Broker-Client Relationship in a Political Process for Acquiring Power. *Source*: Model designed by the author with data from Muno 2014.

obtained in constituencies and this led to the creation of several clientelistic networks to accrue benefits (Cendales et al., 2019). This is even more tolerable than in the post-Communist Russian states of Armenia and Georgia, where the politicians buy votes to emerge victorious but after assuming offices, became voracious looters as political corruption become rampant and uncontrollable (Stefes, 2006). Nigeria has a similar character to those of the Armenian and Georgian cases (Ojo et al., 2019), and may be worse.

In Southeast Asian politics, political parties are instrumental in clientelism in countries such as Indonesia, Thailand and the Philippines. Although the parties there are weak and not taken in high esteem by the electorates, they utilised the undue advantage of poverty to supply T-shirts, caps, bikes and even food items during elections to lure voters in return for voting them into power (Tomsa & Ufen, 2013). Aspinall and Sukmajati (2019) supported the aforementioned view in the Indonesian case, where they reported that the scourge of poverty subjected the voters at the grassroots election to money politics, patronage and clientelism where politicians utilised the poor condition of the rural people to buy their votes either in cash or kind as obtained in rural China (Wang, 2014). In another study, Aspinall and Berenschot (2019) submitted that clientelism permeated the state of Indonesia during the electoral process and it is not only isolated to the grassroots poor the same phenomenon is reported in the Philippines by Hicken et al. (2019). The same scenario can be said of Nigerian politics where the deliberately orchestrated poverty of the citizens is being used as the vulnerable point for buying their votes and support during elections (Sule et al., 2018d).

A study (Muniz, 2015) reported that in the case of South America, with Brazil as the case study, clientelism is recognised as the usual business in everyday life of the Latin American countries not only during elections as observed by Hilgers (2012). In the African context, businessmen play an important role in clientelism. El Tarouty (2015), using Egypt as the premise of his analysis, argued that businessmen sponsored politicians in return for a patron-client relationship. The businessmen help them to win an election by spending lavishly on them during an electoral contests in return for juicy contracts, lucrative appointments to their cahoots and cronies and other state or official influence. In the case of Nigeria, the area of study, it is observed that godfathers are instrumental in the clientelism process (Sule et al., 2018d). They sponsor their anointed candidates with moneybags with the anticipation of favour and kickbacks in return.

In other states, the proceeds of war and insecurity hatched clientelism like in Iraq. Abdullah (2017) hypothesised that clientelism, patronage and rent-seeking became intensified after the removal of Saddam Hussein from power by the invaders' forces. The country left with a weak central authority, an oil-rich, became an avenue for the scramble towards self-enrichment through the clientele process. Other Middle East states have their own structure of clientelism where elections occur frequently. The rich oil-producing states sometimes offer the citizenry some token of free enjoyment of infrastructure which blinded them from seeing the trajectory and atrocities of mass accumulation by the ruling class (De Elvira, 2019).

There are academic efforts to link clientelism with Nigerian politics, elections and political parties since the first wave of research period in the development of the theory. One of such efforts is the one by Post and Jenkins (1973) which identified the Clientelistic structures in Western Nigeria on the eve of political independence in 1960. A patron, Adelabu, was recognised in the study in the ancient city of Ibadan who became famous for his pro-masses status. The Clientelistic activities of Adelabu involved the mobilisation of the Ibadan Muslim majority, who were marginalised in the economic and political structure that favoured the Christian and non-indigenous minority. Such fate has been the tactic of divide and rule of the British colonialist in many parts of the country. Adelabu became a patron with the popular support of the masses in any election process henceforth. Years later, from 1979 to 1983 (the Second Republic), another patron, Alhaji Adelakun, emerged again in the same Ibadan city. Alhaji Adelakun became a distributor of goods, cash and kinds as well as other favours to the clients while at the same time employing thugs and violence against his opponents. Winning an election became easier when candidates leaned on him (Post & Jenkins, 1973). Many years after in the Fourth Republic (1999–2022), Ibadan again became a hub of political clientelism with Alhaji Lamidi Adedibu as the godfather and patron that brokers with the client during any election. When his godson, Rashidi Ladoja, acted against his interest, he was impeached (Sule et al., 2018d).

The practice and operation of clientelism manifested more in Southwest Nigeria during the early process of political development in the country. This perhaps, may not lack relevance with the nature of the advancement in political activities in the region than in other parts of the country during the time. A study by Omobowale and Olutayo (2010) examined the Southwest in this regard. In their findings, Omobowale and Olutayo (2010) present the case of Mushin in Lagos where the migrants and property owners became the patron who influenced the indigenes of the surrounding villages as clients that benefited from the goods in return for political loyalty. In essence, Joseph (1991) identifies that clientelism and Prebendalism are critical determinants of the development of Nigerian politics. The socio-economic and political settings in Nigeria principally aided the emergence of patron-client relationships. The large concentration of wealth among the few urban elites and the deprivation of the majority poor in the villages created a wide gap of inequality, poverty, ignorance and other indices of a difference. The organised urban elites get access to power and national resources to the extent that during any election or political activity, they established a linkage of patronage either directly or through their brokers.

Since the birth of the Fourth Republic, clientelism become persistent and pervasive in Nigerian politics and that has affected the fundamental principles and practices of democracy in terms of accountability, transparency and deliverance of good governance and services to the represented (Osumah, 2010). Clientelism in Nigeria is operated under the politics of godfatherism (Balogun, 1997) and the state is commanded and its resources controlled by the oligarchs who conglomerated into a cartel of economic and political interests including the military, politicians, capital owners, traditional rulers and religious class who unified their energy towards unprotected access to the national commonwealth. In this perspective, the forceful imposition of elites over the state enabled for the acquisition of enough resources to exert influence over the clients and by extension, to establish patron-client linkage that will ward off opposition and threats to the political ambition of the oligarchs (Ibrahim, 1995; Diamond, 1995b; Joseph, 1995; and Olowu 1996). Clientelism flourished in the Nigerian state because of the sliding into political decay due to the inability to build and sustain strong political institutions (Diamond, 1995b). The increased militarisation of the body politic is the main cause identified by Ibrahim (1995) but Joseph (1995) linked militarisation with anti-democratisation as the cause. Joseph (1995) argues that while the Nigerian military converted the state into a rogue state, the civilian rulers set the stage for its performance.

Clientelism in Nigeria is operated in the Fourth Republic through the machinery of political parties sometimes managed and controlled by political godfathers often former military generals and their bourgeoisie business moguls. The ruling parties in Nigeria are a mere pawns of the patrons who sponsored political godsons and broker between the anointed candidates and the clients (the voters). Ethnicity, religion and regionalism are emotional tools used by the patrons while money, appointments, contracts, project allocation and other favours are the other means of reaching the clients (Silas, 2013; Oyebode, 2014). Party politics is controlled by godfathers or patrons and that is the root of entrenching clientelism in Nigerian politics. Ideology and politics of performance are discarded for those who secured the support of the patrons who in turn used money, influence, connection and ethnic and other sentiments of the clients to arrest political victory for the godsons. Unlike the European model, clientelism in Nigeria sometimes ignored the reward after the election. The cash or other goods distributed to the clients during the process is the only reward. The elected leaders concentrate on personal aggrandisement and favouring the interests of the godfathers (Zovighian, 2018).

A study (Sule et al., 2018d) differs in the examination of the application of clientelism to Nigerian politics and elections. Sule et al. (2018d) report that clientelism and godfatherism took a new dimension in the 2015 general election where the rulers converted themselves into patrons instead of relying on their godfathers. The study revealed that previously the rulers relied on the sponsorship of godfathers who were former military officers, business tycoons and other influential echelons but in the build-up to the 2015 general election, the godsons or rulers decided to amass enough by looting and diverting the public treasury to sponsor their political campaign. A sum of $2.1 billion (N1 trillion naira) was diverted by the ruling PDP to arrest their campaign finance. The relationship changed. The godfathers turned to brokers who received the goods from the ruling class and distributed them to the clients. This is an interesting development in the study of clientelism in the Nigerian state. Demarest (2021) in his findings added that the new version of clientelism in Nigeria resulted in limited effort for constituency projects and a weak legislature–voter linkage. The legislature does not pay attention to the needs of their constituents but rather engages in forging strong ties with godfathers and parties' brokers for re-election. This has been the major reason why Nigeria failed to consolidate democracy and build strong political institutions according to Oyetunde (2022).

Clientelism in Nigeria manifests in political corruption which becomes systemic, endemic, pervasive, alternated and dynamic. The political office-holders utilise all possessed arsenals at their disposal be it fair, unfair, constitutional, unconstitutional, judicial, illegal and coercive or persuasive to consolidate their control of power and their parties to continue to superintend over the established system of rents and reward. The increasing socially competitive groups in the country necessitate the expansion of clientelism and redistribution to appease the perceived upheavals. This established process can be difficult to counter or reverse soon because it is being perpetually consolidated by the rent-seekers and their masters and proxies (Ojo et al., 2019).

Hence, clientelism in Nigeria is a practically applicable theory. The studies explored previously traced its origin, changing nature and dimension from pre-independence to the present period. The pattern followed other cases examined earlier in the countries of Europe, Asia and Latin America but there is an outstanding case that differs from the others. The Nigerian case invokes both reward in material goods and emotional satisfaction where the politicians play on the sentiments of the voters including ethnicity and religion to gain support. In some cases, the electoral process has been hijacked and the clients have been rendered valueless leaving them with no option but to cooperate in the clientele process. Another unique aspect of Nigerian clientelism is that the patrons are replaced sometimes by their sponsored godsons thereby establishing a direct linkage between the brokers and the clients.

RATIONAL CHOICE THEORY

Rational choice theory is a political economy approach to explaining the rationality and behaviour of voters in an election. As consumers tend to derive maximum satisfaction from expending their scarce resources based on priority and scale of preference, the voters direct their choice in an election for the maximum utility from an expected candidate or party. The theory has its roots in 1950s and 1980s work by Anthony Downs and Kenneth Arrows. Downs (1957), in 'An Economic Theory of Democracy', postulates that the electorates choose their leaders based on some rational considerations which tantalise utility and maximum benefits to them. A typical example of how a consumer behaves when faced with several economic choices and scarcity illustrates how the voters choose from alternative parties and candidates based on those they feel can give them the maximum utility they anticipated. Arrows (1986) hypothesises that politics is a game with a decision-making and the politicians and the electorates behave like economic actors who engage in a wise choice based on satisfaction. In essence, rational choice theory believed that economic indicators including resource allocation, distribution of goods and services and other political-economic rewards are linked to political choice in an election.

Downs (1957) and Arrows (1951) assumed that if consumer behaviour principles can explain the rationale behind the choice of a commodity by users, then rationality can be used to explain political choice, particularly an election. As there is an established relationship between consumers of goods and services and competing service providers and manufacturers, there is the same correlation between voters, politicians and political parties. The logic is that since business corporations and service providers seek to maximise profit, the consumers seek to maximise utility. In the same way, it can be hypothesised that politicians and parties strive to derive maximum benefit from acquiring power in the same way the voters seek to maximise the utility of electoral gains of their choice. In politics as in economics, people often compete for scarce resources. This perception made several scholars in political science believe that the method of research and analysis in Economics can be applied in political science (Green & Shapiro, 1994). Rational choice theory faced obstacles in its accommodation as argued by Lichbach (2003) that political scientists made a strong case for housing it within the discipline but a critical examination of the features of the theory revealed that it goes beyond politics and all social sciences can claim possession of it. The rational choice theory contributes immensely to the revival of the debates on the sociology of religion. Scholars in the discipline argue that rational choice should not limit to Economics and political science disciplines. The study of why and how people choose their faith or denounce them is rational in approach and interesting to scrutinise. Rational choice theory flourishes in many disciplines of social sciences in modern times to explain various circumstances of interest choice and reason in decision-making (Archer & Tritter, 2001). Rational choice theory in modern times is expanded and studied using imprecise probabilities and utilities by many fields (Weirich, 2021).

Other scholars built on rational choice theory after Downs (1957) and Arrows (1986). For instance, Grafstein (1999) argues that rationality in choice in democratic elections involved several decisions including the provision of public goods, the relevance of ethnic identity in political mobilisation, altruism, retaliation, abstention and other retrospective behaviours, all undertaken by rational politicians and voters alike. But rationality choice was extended beyond the earlier assumptions that voters and politicians are the only parties that are involved. Olson (1965), 'The Logic of Collective

Action', emphasises that interest groups' membership and participation in politics is beyond the actions of governments and political parties. It means that groups are rational and can make a collective decision which negates the overwhelming celebratory individualism advanced by rational theorists. However, Olson (1965) discourages groups' decision-making and collective action preferring that only if the individual interests of a chooser will be satisfied that there is a logic in collective choice. Thus, we can deduce that rational choice theory consists of not only individual personal choice but it encompasses collective choice, participation and decision-making. Oppenheimer (2012) also believed that the rational choice theory has moved into sophistication from individual choice as a unit of analysis to the subordination of the individual to collective interests.

Rationality is not only limited to political choice in an election within the boundaries of the nation-states. Countries utilise rational choice in international relations and the formation of international laws according to Guzman (2008). International laws are agreed upon and signed by countries based on the expected maximum utility that a state can derive. International law is deliberately loosened to allow the strong and rogue states to escape justice by their rational thinking of the best utility for them. The nation-states, unaccustomed to foreign intervention, prefer to preserve their sovereignty free from external intrusion. There are several examples that space may not allow here. Many powerful countries abstained from signing the non-aggression treaty under the auspices of the League of Nations because they know it might affect them. Industrial countries like United States and China are found dragging in signing the international regulations against climate change. The rationale for what a state feel is better may be negative or harmful to other states but that does not prevent nation-states from taking a decision that may not augur well with the neighbourhood if that is what they perceived as the best choice (Guzman, 2008).

Rational choice theory has many strengths according to Green and Shapiro (1994). For instance, since the early propositions of the theory, many journals of political science are flooded with rational/game theory models that explained politics, reason, rationality and individual behaviours in the choice of leaders during an election. This is an explosion of knowledge in academic discourse. Rational choice theory has the empirical power of presenting values and findings which made it scientific and realistic in applicability. A small unit of analysis or even a larger one can be studied and the empirical data can point to choose based on certain rational values and reasons such as material benefit, ethnic identity, religion and geography. Also, the ambition of separating individual choice from a collective one made the study of rationality feasible and practicable beyond normative models. But Elster (1986) differs with the level of empiricism of rational choice theory. Elster (1986) argues that rational choice theory is a normative theory because it tells what we ought to do to achieve some goals instead of what we exactly do.

In the way the strength of rational choice theory is presented above by Green and Shapiro (1994), rational choice theory is criticised on its grounds of assuming that the choice for maximum benefit or utility can influence all parties involved. Ott (2006) argues that the theory is being embellished to juxtapose the bourgeois craving for societal dominance and power by deceiving the voters that all parties have economic rationality in the choice. In essence, Ott (2006) sees the rational postulation of democratic election as the extension of 'neoliberalism'. The study of rational choice theory from a religious perspective assuming that voters derive some utility from voting based on religious choice contradicts the rationale for choice based on performance and the Marxist view of the withering away of religion in the political process. The assumption that people choose reason and utilise maximum benefit at little cost contradicts humanity because the corresponding increased cost, burden, sacrifice and suffering of others are ignored in this case. It means others in the society have to bear the consequences of the individualistic selfish choices to bargain, life, reason, society and history (Ott, 2006).

The reduction of the reason, choices and decisions of human beings to individual choice is rooted in the formula of the microeconomics of the capitalist mode of production and society framing the capitalist as a rational object. Although the principle assumption of this theory pictures man as a rational being in choice in the society, in reality, this rationality is interpreted as the choice of the capitalist in the society who accrued to themselves the maximum benefit of the proceeds of production. The other classes, the working class and the poor bear the brunt of the exploitation and costs of the choice. The selfishness of the proponents of rational choice theory led to the commodification of religion where they postulate that religion is an instrument of choice of leaders in an election when the voters derive maximum utility from voting for those who share the same religious affiliation with them. This notion pushed rationality to the edge of sacrilege (Ott, 2006). Additionally, not in all democratic settings are viable options for choice or rational reason enabled. The rational chooser sometimes undergoes political frustration due to the structure of the election and party politics. In Nigeria, often voters ended up choiceless after the parties weed out the best choices for the low-key politicians. The assumption by Olson (1965) that there is no logic in collective decision-making is another serious injury to democracy and the governance process (Emily, 1996).

Rational choice theory has two major assumptions or patterns: the evaluative and the non-evaluative. Evaluative rationality depends on the voters' ability to evaluate regime performance and make choices for that reason. The non-evaluative is based on clientelistic considerations and personal benefit derived or anticipated from a specific choice such as ethnic identity, religious affiliation, geographical ties and family kinship (Coleman & Fararo, 1992). Observable behaviours are needed to be reflected in determining the rationality and choice of individuals on any given matter but particularly, in politics and elections (Kuhn, 1983). In another view, De Jonge (2012) presents three main theories that spiralled from rational choice theory: (1) Decision Making Theory, which is the theory of individual behaviour under certainty, risk and uncertainty; (2) game theory, which is the theory of rational behaviour by two or more interacting individuals and (3) Ethics, which he defined as the theory of rational value judgements. Farber (2009) stresses that individuals are aware that their choices may lead their preferred candidates to success or block their unfavoured candidates from victory. Voting in this regard is a choice to pull success or to deny success.

Rational choice theory can lead to 'swing votes', a phenomenon that denotes how the voters' choice in new democracies resulted in a certain pattern of voting behaviour. Swing voting determines whether ethnic identity, campaign strategy adopted, poverty and other Clientelistic considerations can sway votes to some candidates in an election (Lindberg & Weghorst, 2010). This is because voters in emerging democracies like Ghana and Nigeria are still influenced by the rationality of choosing their ethnic, religious and regional candidates and family ties ahead of credibility and competency. Lindberg and Morrison (2010) argue that there are some considerable levels of satisfaction that such voting patterns offer to the choosers. Apart from favour in resources allocation and project distribution to their religious and ethnic cohorts, politicians in places like Nigeria and Ghana manipulate the psychology of the voters to feel satisfied and reasonable to have their own on top of affairs to protect their identity from marginalisation or to feel the sense of belonging to the government.

It is assumed that there are three propositions of rational choice theory (Antunnes, 2010). The propositions are

- All decisions are rational. Political parties, politicians and voters always made choices that are rational to them. Self-interest and maximisation are the motivating factors that influence decisions taken;
- There is a constancy in the democratic political system supporting the predictions of decisions and the outcome of the decisions made by voters and political parties; and
- There is a gap of uncertainty in the choice process. Sometimes there is a hesitation in taking a decision or making a choice.

Rational choice theory was applied in a study by Sule (2018) on the Nigerian election with a specific case of the 2015 general election. The change experienced in the 2015 general election disclosed the pattern of rationality chosen by the voters. The PDP has been ruling for sixteen years but the leadership meted on Nigerians in those sixteen years became enshrouded in massive and pervasive corruption with impunity, insecurity, declining health sector, collapsing education sector, decaying infrastructure and misgovernance. The electoral process was bedevilled with rigging, subversion, manipulation, malpractice and ridicule of democracy where winners are imposed at all costs. The voters became desperate and determined to change the narratives. The barriers to effective political change in Nigeria in that period consisted of weak opposition, the vulnerability of voters under the spell and influence of the elite's manipulation of ethnic, religious and regional identity voting as suggested by Lindberg and Morrison (2010) and Lindberg and Weghorst (2010). However, the decay and misgovernance reached an unbearable level in 2015 and the voters decided to change the government.

It should be noted that there are several uncertainties, decisions and predictions as assumed by Antunnes (2010) that guided the determination and success of the voters' choice in the 2015 general election. The politicians themselves found their interests threatened by the former ruling PDP. Additionally, the electoral body, INEC underwent reforms such as the introduction of the Smart Card Reader (SCR) and other transparent measures. Coupled with the myriads of socio-economic and political problems, the voters made a decisive choice that they need a change and the opposition APC readily offered itself for that purpose. The voters expected to derive maximum utility of good governance, transparency and infrastructural development as their motivation for choosing the APC while the party expect to secure power and

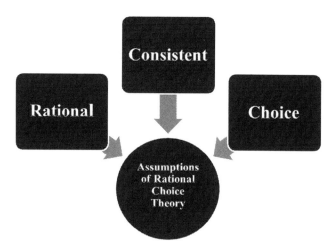

Figure 6.4   Illustration of the Major Propositions of Rational Choice Theory. *Source*: Designed by the Author 2022.

its luxury in return for the exchange. Interestingly, most of the politicians that were perceived as evil in the former PDP switched allegiance to the newly formed APC. Yet, the gullible Nigerian voters failed to distinguish between the existing politicians that collapsed the country and the phenomenon of their changed party which is not a behaviour change. The politicians here utilised the maximum benefit of a fresh new party and the gullible decision of change to secure another victory in APC but with the same attitude and motive.

The usual way of election in the 2015 general election changed tremendously and significantly. The majority of the voters rejected the ethnic and religious colouration that beclouded the Nigerian political environment on the eve of the election. However, the rationale for choosing the APC candidate in the presidential election shifted a little because he secured the permanent votes that he used to get since 2003 in his stronghold of Northern Nigeria where the rationale for voting for him was anchored around ethnic, religious, regional and the maxim of the trustworthy man of integrity reigned supreme. Unfortunately, this study postulates that the overzealously changed mantra pursued by the APC and its candidates and the voters turned out to be disappointing and resenting. The voters could not get the much-anticipated reward for the rational choice of change and this will lead us to hypothesise that there may be another rational choice in the 2023 general election. Voters may revert back to the PDP again as an alternative to the APC quagmire that failed to translate into meaningful policies and expected positive change. They may also gullibly choose APC again due to rational sentiments.

GAME THEORY

Game theory is the matrix and mathematical combinations of some sets of assumptions explaining decision-making in a complex, competitive environment of dilemma (Gibbons, 1993). The decision can be in politics, economy, management or any other related set-up (Maschler et al., 2013). John Von Neumann and Oscar Morgenstern (1953) are credited for the postulation of the game theory model. The major job that they did in contributing to the explanation of decision-making is that decision-making in a strategic situation is competitive and intense. There are many scholars (Elster, 1986; De Jonge, 2012; Oppenheimer, 2012; Frahm, 2019; Weirich, 2021) who could not establish a dividing line between rational choice theory and game theory taking them as either the same or one spilling over to the other. Most of them believed that in rational choice activity, some set of games emerged that led to decision-making in a mode of game theory and hence, the two theories traced their roots to the same philosophy since both of them are about choice or taking decision rationally for the best.

The term 'Game Theory' is interpreted as the patterns of interactions in which the payoff (outcome) is the consequence of the actions and decisions of others (Dimand & Dimand, 2002). By this assumption, games are explained here beyond what is obtainable in chess, football and other leisure play to accommodate wider principles of economic, political and social decisions and human interactions. Game theory is also perceived as the coordinated thought and predictions concerning rational strategic decision in situations of extreme close substitute competition where each player offers the same products or values and is expected to take decision based on the anticipated movement of his competitor in such a way that he maximises the outcome and minimises losses (Umbhauer, 2016). Game theory is therefore a mathematical, economic and political study of competition and decision-making using a calculative imagination and the study of the forecast of the environment of the activities. In game theory, the outcomes and strategies are correlated and the choice of a strategy for movement depends upon the decision of the other competitor. The sole aim is to rationalise the decision.

Game theory emerged in the 1950s when some social scientists began to think that game puzzles can be applied to social sciences, particularly Economics and political science. P. G. Cambray's (1932) 'The Game of Politics: A Study of the Principles of British Political Strategies' is the pioneering work on game theory followed later by Neumann and Morgenstern's (1953) 'Theory of Games and Economic Behaviour'. Game theory continues to be used, applied, expanded and critically analysed in the 1960s and is still being applied in Economics and political analysis. Game theory is used to study an infinitesimal political competition such as electoral contests in smaller and big states, political parties' policies and competition and it is being used to study a great strategic political competition and alliance including but not limited to Cold War ideological battle, international law, security and strategic studies and world system of super powers and power competition. Game theory is earlier observed to have been studied in games of pleasure such as chess, football, parlour games and poker games. In the pleasure games, there are two or more players with each of the players making a strategic decision independently but highly conscious of others' decisions when taking his own. So, decision-making in game theory is not a lone-way traffic because it involves others.

There are several assumptions of game theory. This study scrutinised them carefully and summarised them from many studies (Myerson, 1991; Ordeshook, 1995; McCarthy & Meirowitz, 2007; Watson, 2013; Prisner, 2014; Pastine et al., 2017) as follows:

- There are two or multiple players depending on the nature of the game.
- Players are decision-makers and each player is concern with arriving at a strategic decision that will earn him maximum utility at a lesser cost.

- In every game, there must be strategy and it is decided by the player of the game.
- The players of the game are rational.
- There are several alternatives to choose from.
- Choice of an alternative is being made based on a scale of preference.
- There are the consequences of decisions taken by players known as payoffs.
- The players are aware that there are loss and gains or profit and losses in the game.
- The players have a clear knowledge of the environment of the game.
- Players predict the movement of their competitors in making their own move.
- A certain amount of uncertainty is involved in the game.
- Players adopt a strategy based on the situation of the game.

There are mathematical equations that are applied to demonstrate the operation and motion of game theory including among others zero-sum game, non-zero-sum game, prisoner's dilemma game of chicken, payoff and other terminologies (Dimand & Dimand, 2002). In the case of a zero-sum game, it involves two players only and if one player wins the other loses which means that every victory gain is at the expense of the loss to the other player. A good example is an electoral contest, particularly in democracies like Nigeria where Collier (2009) argues that it is a similitude of a war. If one candidate in an electoral office secures victory, his opponent loses and since the holding of public office is akin to a good investment with a return for wealth accumulation, contestants can employ all strategies including dirty ones. This includes excessive spending and bribery to win at all costs.

The other type of game theory is a non-zero-sum game. In a non-zero-sum game, the players have a payoff that may favour one of them more but the loser may not lose totally as there are some gains that he will end up benefitting from the game too. This is found in situations of politics in plural societies like Nigeria where sometimes parties could not secure the required majority to form a government. A coalition government is formed which enabled many players to have a share of power. The parties may not have the chance to control the power solely but they are all involved in sharing the power at various levels. This has occurred in Nigeria's First Republic Westminster parliamentary model where the NPC and the NCNC formed a coalition government with the NCNC securing the seat of the president while the NPC got a seat of the prime minister. In contemporary international relations, nation-states with varying conflicting interests can decide to form an alliance or to make concessions that will look like a win-win or no victor no vanquish to allow peace to reign.

Decision-making in game theory sometimes is difficult and inimical. Take the case of prisoner's dilemma, for example. It is a situation of making a choice that is mortal to the player if he is not lucky the outcome favoured him (Holler, 2001). Prisoner's dilemma is a game developed by the American mathematician Albert W. Tucker which illustrates a situation where two suspected prisoners in a murder case were isolated in different cells and asked to confess. Prisoner A will contemplate what prisoner B will confess and vice versa. The payoff of the decision in this situation takes three consequences. If both of them confess to the crime, they go to jail. If none confess, they go to jail for a shorter term because of non-cooperation with the legal procedure. If prisoner A confesses he goes free for cooperating and if prisoner B refuses to confess he goes to jail for twenty years (Bhuiyan, 2016). The outcome of this game is shown in table 6.1.

An example of this equation obtains in several issues related to decision-making in politics. There may be more than two players in the game as in other types. For instance, several cases in Nigerian elections led to the prisoner's dilemma. The choice of a candidate in the presidential race by the APC and the PDP from 2015 became a choice of uncertainty and dilemma. Each of the two parties is anxious about the outcome of what it will present when the other made a particular choice. This game is what consumed the ruling PDP to lose the presidential seat to APC. In the build-up to the 2023 general election, an exact game of prisoner's dilemma is taking place between the ruling APC and the opposition PDP. The ruling APC nominated Asiwaju Ahmed Bola Tinubu, a Muslim from the Southwest as its presidential flagbearer. The major opposition PDP nominated Alhaji Atiku Abubakar, a Fulani man from Adamawa State of Northeast. The choice of deputy is now caged in what exactly looks like a prisoner's dilemma. The tradition of Nigerian politics in the Fourth Republic is that a presidential candidate from the majority Muslim North must adopt a Christian deputy from the majority Christian South and vice versa. But this time, the equation is altered and the choice of deputy is obnoxious and intense. Each of the two competing parties is fidgety about

Table 6.1   Game theory Decision-Making in Prisoner's Dilemma

	Prisoner B			
	Confess		*Keep Silent*	
Prisoner A				
Confess	A	B	A	B
	5 years	5 years	0 year	20 years
Remain silent	A	B	A	B
	20 years	0year	1 year	1 year

Source: Hechter 2019 (the computation of the examples using alphabets and numerical figures is initiated by the Author in 2022).

what the other might present to avoid a mistake that will cost the seat in the final election coming February 2023. The APC is contemplating picking a Muslim-Muslim ticket, a ticket that is not a sin but politicised as an absolute marginalisation and ignoring of the Christians' concern. The decision was confronted in the typical prisoner's dilemma. The APC candidate, Asiwaju Bola Ahmed Tinubu went ahead and picked Senator Kashim Shettima all the loudest protests of Christians in APC. Similarly, the PDP candidate Alhaji Atiku Abubakar proceeded to pick Delta State Governor, Ifeanyi Okowa against the much anticipated Rivers State governor Nyesom Wike. The die is cast and both are battling with serious internal dissension and crisis of choice. Definitely, the crisis will affect the chances of the two heavyweight contestants either positively or negatively or a balanced outcome.

Similarly, the prisoner's dilemma can explain decision-making in international politics. This scenario subjected the entire world to a tension of security dilemma during the Cold War armed race. The US and the Soviet blocs on several occasions took strategic decisions and movements that froze the world in awe in anticipation of the outbreak of conventional war (Niou & Ordeshook, 2015). The US bloc might have projected what decision to take in either advancement or retaliation that it thought the Soviet might take and the same with the Soviet bloc. With a distance and probably a lack of enough intelligence at hand to know the other's next strategic move, any decision is a dilemma and that had been the main tenet of the game during the era of the Cold War for many decades.

Game of chicken is another variety of game theory. It is a description of taking a decision or rational choice that is mutually collateral and the players are aware that the consequences of their choice can lead to terrible loss or a giant victory but at a scale of magnitudes of costs. The proponents of the game of chicken present an example of two drivers who drive towards each other. If one of them swerves, he is considered a chicken, and if he doesn't swerve he is considered a winner. If neither of them swerves they crash and lose (Binmore, 2007). This is the most dangerous decision-making in the matrixes of game theory because it has the potential for collateral damage. Either of the players may win, either of them may lose or both may lose.

What the game of chicken implies is the decisive ability of the players to decide while minding the consequences, keeping in mind that it is an inevitable decision irrespective of the outcome. It is gambling that pays off or affects all. It is applicable in politics within the Nigerian state and internationally. In the process of election in Nigeria, sometimes politicians resorted to the rigging which is anti-democratic and punishable by law if it is apprehended. But the players or the parties and their contestants engage in dubious malpractice to win at all costs. Player A assumed as party A or candidate A may decide that if I didn't rig my competitor may rig and he may escape with it. As such,

Table 6.2   Illustrating Decision-Making in the Game of Chicken and the Outcome

	Driver B	
	Swerve	*Straight*
Driver A		
Swerve	(0,0)	(–1, 10)
Straight	(10, –1)	(–100, –100)

Source: Nordstrom 2020 (the equation was tabulated and computed by the author in 2022).

he will devise strategies for rigging. Player B may also make the same decision. But sometimes if player A decided to rig and B decided not to rig relying on his popularity and competency, he may end up losing meaning that he is the chicken while player A is the winner. But if the two players decided to rig all or not to rig, there may be an inconclusive or rerun which means all of them to win or to lose.

In international politics, nation-states and international actors are players and they can engage in the game of chicken when they are faced with strategic decision-making for a rational choice that may result in mutual destruction or collateral damage. Such may involve the deployment of arms and the use of aggression between hostile countries. Each of the players may be contemplating the act of the first aggressor or withdrawing or waiting for retaliation. In either case, the decision is calculated and decided based on the rationality of the action (Watson, 2013). The current Russian invasion of Ukraine in 2022 is a strategic decision taken under the game of chicken because the other rival world powers of the US and the European powerful countries threatened to intervene if Russia attacked. But the Russian state under the premonition of the inability of the other world powers to engage in a direct battle proceeded to attack Ukraine knowing that the rationality has the payoff of national interest. And one of the spillover effects of the game of chicken is it will affect other spectators in some cases as in the case of the crises of food security and the financial sector in the wake of the Russia-Ukraine war (United Nations, 2022).

When it comes to the aspect of party financing and the electoral process in Nigeria, politicians who are the players played various games including the zero-sum game, non-zero-sum game, prisoner's dilemma and the game of chicken. Politicians in Nigeria strive to win elections irrespective of the price or the consequences. Many studies reported the excessive use of money (Onyekpere, 2015; Sule et al., 2017a; Sule et al., 2022) by the two major parties of the APC and the PDP. Additionally, the APC and the PDP adopted many strategies for winning the election apart from excessive spending such as rigging which was reported severally in various elections in the Fourth Republic (Human Rights Watch, 2007; Human Rights Watch, 2019). Winning at all costs is emblematic of Nigerian politicians. The game is to get access to power, enrich themselves, consolidate their tight grip on power and continue to win to enjoy the accord, luxuries and privileges of power. Policymaking neglects the basic priorities of the common man. Despite the overrated democratic accountability and transparency as the main reasons advanced for supporting democratic governance, the masses could not enjoy these basics such as clean drinking water, steady electricity, security, quality education, sound healthcare and even food security is a dilemma for the poor in the country. Hunger, disease, illiteracy, poverty, unemployment, insecurity and several other socio-economic and political crises bedevilled the Nigeria state since the resurgence of the democratic rule even with the collection of a huge revenue that is more than the total of what the country received from 1960 to 1999 according to Statista (2022).

Chapter 7

Party Financing in Nigeria
Regulations and Allied Issues

Political party financing in Nigeria is regulated by two basic laws: the Nigerian 1999 Constitution as amended and Electoral Act. The Electoral Act was developed in three sequences: The Electoral Act 2006, Electoral Act 2010 and the Electoral Act 2022. The Electoral Act 2022 is the current one in operation passed into law on 23 March 2022 by the National Assembly and assented by the president of the Federal Republic of Nigeria. The regulations make substantial provisions and laws on the registration of political parties, deregistering political parties, rules governing the operation of parties in Nigeria, legal sources of funding for the parties, disclosure, auditing and monitoring of finances of parties, maximum spending limits for all the elective offices from the presidential to the councillorship seats and sanctions on violators of the regulations.

Most or almost all the previous studies (Wakili et al., 2008; Anyadike & Eme, 2014; Lawal, 2015; Onyekpere, 2015; Nwangwu & Ononogbu, 2016; Olorunmola, 2016, Sule et al., 2017a; Sule et al., 2017b; Sule 2018; Sule et al., 2018c; Sule et al., 2018d, Sule et al., 2018e; Ayeni, 2019; Sule, 2019; Okeke & Nwali, 2020; Sule & Sambo, 2021; Sule et al., 2022) built their analysis on the previous electoral laws of the Electoral Act 2006 and Electoral Act 2010. The Electoral Act 2022 emerged a few months before the conduct of the 2023 general election. This study is the first to examine critically the laws, specifically emphasising on the strengths and weaknesses of the regulations and whether the reforms included in the 2022 Act could succeed in ensuring accountability and transparency in the process of party financing and electoral conduct in Nigeria. There were several practical recommendations presented by these studies and some of them are integrated into the new act.

However, the major issue with regulations in Nigeria, as in other parts of the world, when it comes to matters of party financing is the will to enforce regulations, sanction the violators and mount effective monitoring impartially. The cooperation of the parties, politicians and the ruling class in making available their books of income and expenditures is a worrisome aspect of the process. Disclosure is another headache that will render the regulations impracticable. Even the 2006 and 2010 Acts were not weak despite the loopholes identified in them. Mostly, studies like Sule et al. (2017b) and Sule et al. (2022) argue that the main vacuum that the 2006 and 2010 Electoral Acts left is inadequate maximum spending limits. The limits set for all the electoral offices are practically not realisable in the context of Nigerian money politics. Another issue is the contributions ban or limits which are impracticable. The provision that N1 million is the maximum donation ceiling looks like a joke in the context of Nigerian politics.

This chapter examines these regulations with specific emphasis on the 1999 Constitution provisions and the Electoral Act 2022. Although where the need arises, reference might be made to the previous regulations for comparison sake, the concentration will be on the current law to avoid duplicate references to laws and regulations. The chapter analyses the adequacy or inadequacy of the regulations and the areas that might need reform where necessary but most importantly, the emphasis, is on enforcement and strict monitoring and sanction and this is the universal concern of experts (Ohman, 2012; Ohman, 2013; Ohman, 2014; Ohman, 2016; Ohman, 2018) on global party financing regulations. Achieving accountability and transparency is only possible if the existing laws are strengthened with application and monitoring in addition to effective surveillance.

LEGAL PROVISIONS ON POLITICAL PARTY FINANCING IN NIGERIA

Political party financing in Nigeria is legally supported by two major laws: the 1999 Constitution as amended and the Electoral Act 2022. The 1999 Constitution in part I of the third schedule in paragraph 15 mentions that thereof to monitor and regulate the activities of political parties including their income and expenditures and expenses during the campaign and electoral activities. In paragraph 15(d), the INEC is empowered to initiate the annual examination and auditing of the funds and accounts of political parties and publish a report on such examination and audit for public information. Other matters of finances of political parties are provided in Section 225 and Section 226 of the Constitution as illustrated here.

This section and its sub-sections look formidable for ensuring compliance with the regulations, adherence to maximum ceiling, compelling the

Table 7.1 Sections 225 and 226 of the Nigerian 1999 Constitution on Finances of Political Parties and Annual Auditing

Sections and Sub-Sections	Regulations and Provisions
Section 225(1)	Mandates every political party to submit to INEC its published statement of assets and liabilities.
Section 225(2)	Requires every political party to submit to INEC its annual analysis of sources of funds, assets and expenditure.
Section 225(3)	Prohibits every political party from holding funds or assets outside Nigeria and retaining them sent from outside Nigeria.
Section 225(4)	Provides that the funds or assets in Section 225(3) must be forfeited to the INEC within 21 days.
Section 225(5)	Provides that INEC can give directions to political parties regarding the records of their financial transactions and their scrutiny.
Section 225(6)	Provides that INEC has powers to delegate auditors to audit political parties or members of its staff.
Section 226(1)	Makes it mandatory for every political party to prepare its annual statement of account and balance sheet and submit it to INEC.
Section 226(2)	Provides that it's the duty of INEC to ensure whether proper records of accounts of political parties are kept or not and to prepare the records and send them to the National Assembly.
Section 226(3)	Provides that every INEC official has powers to request the financial statement of political parties and must have unlimited access to them at all times in the discharge of his duties.

Source: Nigerian 1999 Constitution (compilation in a tabular form made by the author 2022).

avoidance of illicit funding and prohibited sources and accountability and transparency. However, two major weaknesses are identified here. One is the silence on the candidates assuming that parties are responsible for their candidates which is not true in the Nigerian political environment. Individual political actors tend to be more powerful than parties and people vote across parties based on the actors, not the parties themselves, particularly, the APC and the PDP. By ignoring the candidates, a big loophole is enabled for the parties to escape justice since they can present what is meagre to INEC and allow their candidates to spend excessively or possess beyond the limit. Any attempt at making the party financing process in Nigeria to be accountable should consider individual candidates. It is better if a mandatory oath of assets and liabilities are attached to the nomination forms for all the contestants and their sources of income and expenditure too should be submitted during the nomination and made public. The second weakness is the issue of compliance, monitoring and sanction. As beautiful as the laws are which if implemented appropriately will help in ensuring transparency and compel compliance, the INEC is not monitoring as it should (Sule et al., 2017b) because of a lack of cooperation by the parties and the politicians and the arm-twisting of the ruling class. INEC should be empowered with protection and extra neutrality through financial independence to pursue this gigantic task.

These provisions in Section 226 are quite good and can help immensely in assuring transparency and compliance of financial discipline of parties but again, like Section 225, two major weaknesses are impeding compliance. One of them is that all the provisions refer to parties while individual candidates are omitted. It is normal to refer to or deal with parties in other democracies since candidates do not represent themselves but the platform of their parties except for where independent candidacy is allowed, but the Nigerian political environment is unique and differs from what obtains in other climes. Individuals are stronger than their parties because of weak institutionalisation, poor organisation and lack of party ideology and personalisation of the parties. Any attempt to compel transparency through the scrutiny of the parties while neglecting individual candidates tantamount to a wasted effort. Second, INEC is battling with challenges of compliance and cooperation from parties and politicians. Sule (2018) reported that one of the senior INEC officials at the national level revealed that parties do not cooperate with them in providing their books for auditing. When they asked them to submit or to present for a glance, they will refer the INEC officials to the state governor or the president and confess that they are not allowed to give without the permission of the politicians. When asked, the party's national executives responded in an interview (Sule, 2018) that they know the rules but submitting the party's books for auditing is beyond their control they will have to obtain approval from politicians who often do not allow them to present the books.

Apart from the constitutional provisions, the other source is the Electoral Act 2022. The Electoral Act 2022 in its explanatory memorandum states:

> This Act repeals the Electoral Act No. 6, 2010 and enacts the Electoral Act 2022, to regulate the conduct of Federal, State and Area Council elections, to make provisions for the restriction of the qualification for elective office to relevant provisions of the Constitution of the Federal Republic of Nigeria 1999, use of card readers and other technological devices in elections and political party primaries, to provide a timeline for the submission of list of candidates, criteria for substitution of candidates, the limit of campaign expenses, and address the omission of names of candidates or logo of political parties. (Electoral Act, 2022)

The act was signed into law by the president of the Federal Republic of Nigeria on 25 March 2022.

The aforementioned explanatory memorandum indicates that the provisions of the Electoral Act 2022 take into cognisance the avoidance of conflict with the constitutional provisions and that new laws on the campaign expenditure limits and procedure for the conduct of the election are introduced or amended. Additionally, the Electoral Act 2022 thus, renders the Electoral Act 2010 expired. The various sections in the act would be discussed and analysed in the next sections of this chapter.

LIMITATION ON ELECTION EXPENSES AND SANCTIONS ON VIOLATION

The Electoral Act 2022 increases the limitation on election expenses of all elective offices from what was obtained in the Electoral Act 2010. This has been justified on the grounds of the reality of Nigerian money politics, the impracticability of the expenses limit and the decreasing value of the naira. The Electoral Act 2010 itself reviewed upwards the expenses limit from the Electoral Act 2006. For instance, the naira-dollar exchange rate in 2006 is $1 = N131 when the maximum limit was set in table 7.2.

The value of the naira was stable to the dollar exchange rate during the enactment of the law but it should be understood that from the inception, the expenses limit was not realisable. Nigerian politicians spent much more than

Table 7.2   Section 226 of the Nigerian 1999 Constitution on Annual Auditing of Political Parties' Finances

2006 Electoral Act	
Position	Spending Limit
Presidential Candidate	N500 million ($1,191,923.50 million)
Governorship Candidate	N100 million ($238,384.70 thousand)
Senatorial Candidate	N20 million ($47,676.94 thousand)
Member Federal House of Representatives	N10 million ($28,838.24 thousand)
State House of Assembly Members	N5 million ($11,919.24 thousand)
L G Chairmanship Candidate	N5 million ($11,919.24 thousand)
L G Councillorship Elections	N5 00,000 ($1,191.92 thousand)
2010 Electoral Act	
Presidential Candidate	N1 billion ($2,383,847.00 million)
Governorship Candidate	N200 million ($476,769.40 thousand)
Senatorial Candidate	N40 million ($95,353.88 thousand)
Member Federal House of Representatives	N20 million ($47,676.94 thousand)
State House of Assembly Members	N10 million ($23.838.47 thousand)
L G Chairmanship Candidate	N10 million ($23,838.47 thousand)
L G Councillorship Elections	N1 million ($2,383.85 thousand)

Source: Electoral Act 2006, and 2010 Electoral Act (tabulated by then author 2022. Conversion into dollar was made by the author based on the official exchange rate).

that as confessed by former president Obasanjo that the 2003 election witnessed electoral expenses that is needed to address a successful war (INEC, 2005). In the aftermath of the lamentations and reports of the inadequacy of the limits to actualise practical terms with the expenditure limit, the limit was extended by the Electoral Act 2010. Three major factors contributed to the increase. One is the naira-dollar exchange rate, which changed significantly from 2006 to 2010. The exchange rate increased to $1 = N150 in 2010, a rise of 15percent. And most of the campaign materials sometimes such as billboards and other logistics are sourced by the politicians from foreign countries using dollars. The second factor that led to the upward review was the desire to make the limit practicable and realisable to enable compliance and sanction. The third reason is the realisation of the pattern of money politics which is inevitable in the Nigerian context. The changes are shown in table 7.3.

Like the 2006 Electoral Act, a few years after the operation of the Electoral Act 2010, many experts and researchers reported that it is impracticable and if the monitoring and transparency are to be actualised, the limits need to be reviewed upwards. In one of the studies, Sule et al. (2022) recommend that the maximum spending limits for all the elective offices should be reviewed upward at least ten or twenty times if the process is to be made practical and applicable. The Electoral Act 2022 reviewed the limit upward due to many reasons. One of them is the naira-dollar exchange rate. In 2022, $1 is officially exchanged at the rate of N460 but in the parallel market, the exchange rate is $1 = N610. The decrease in the value of the naira to the dollar from 2010 to 2022 necessitated the review. The civil society, media and other watchdogs of the society kicked vehemently against the upward review but this study differs in the sense that ensuring enforcement and compliance should go hand in hand with practical reality and this cannot be achieved through a mere dream. The upward review in the 2022 Electoral Act disclosed the following.

A significant upward review takes place in the new regulations taking into consideration many factors and the bill was passed into law amidst large public outcries of the high costs of election expenditure. Civil societies, NGOs and other public commentators kicked against the increase, but many experts on the Nigerian electoral process welcomed the development on the condition that it will be supplemented with a giant effort in enforcing compliance, strict monitoring and sanction. However, this study feels that the amount is still inadequate and unrealistic if the real situation of the Nigerian election is critically examined and not an ideal situation. For example, if the presidential candidates in the 2015 presidential election can spend about N13 billion ($30,990,011.00 million), two major contenders of the APC and the PDP, for media costs alone when the exchange rate was $1 = N220, what is the average expectation of the costs of their media adverts in the 2023 general election and beyond when the exchange rate is sloping towards \$1 =N1,000. Besides, looking at the geography of Nigeria, it is not possible for a presidential candidate to spend no more than N5 billion (\$11,919,235.00 million). It is simply impracticable. Thus, reform is immediately needed and this section requires an overhaul in the future.

Section 88(8) provides punishment, sanction and a fine for those who violated the maximum spending limit set in Section 88(1–7). The fine or charges are illustrated in table 7.3. From the picture of the fine or sanction slam on violators or offenders of the law on a maximum spending limit, the law is too loose and favourable to the culprits-to-be even before they commit the offence. It is quiet, small and will not deter the violators from committing the offence. The amount slammed in the Electoral Act 2010 was insignificant and it was part of the recommendations of all the studies

Table 7.3 Election Expenses Limit on all Elective Offices and Corresponding Sanctions in the 2022 Electoral Act

Position	Section	Spending Limit
Expenses Limit		
Presidential Candidate	88(1)	N5 billion (\$11,919,235.00 million)
Governorship Candidate	88(2)	N1 billion (\$2,383,847.00 million)
Senatorial Candidate	88(3)	N100 million(\$238,384.70 thousand)
Member Federal House of Representatives	88(4)	N70 million(\$166,869.29 thousand)
State House of Assembly Members	88(5)	N30 million(\$71,515.41 thousand)
L G Chairmanship Candidate	88(6)	N30 million (\$71,515.41 thousand)
L G Councillorship Elections	88(7)	N5 million (\$11,919.24 thousand)

Position	Section	Sanction for Violation
Sanction		
Presidential Candidate	88(8)	N50 million (\$119,192.35 thousand) or 12 months in jail or both
Governorship Candidate	88(8)	N10 million (\$23,838.47 thousand) or 12 months in jail or both
Senatorial Candidate	88(8)	N1 million (\$2,383.85 thousand) or 12 months in jail or both
Member Federal House of Representatives	88(8)	N700,000 thousand (\$1,668.69 thousand) or 12 months in jail or both
State House of Assembly Members	88(8)	N300,000 thousand (\$715.15 hundred) or 12 months in jail or both
L G Chairmanship Candidate	88(8)	N300,000 thousand (\$715.15 hundred) or 12 months in jail or both
L G Councillorship Elections	88(8)	N50,000 thousand (\$119.19 hundred) or 12-month in jail or both

Source: Electoral Act 2022 (tabulated by the author 2022. Conversion into dollar was made by the author based on the official exchange rate).

consulted (Wakili et al., 2008; Anyadike & Eme, 2014; Lawal, 2015; Onyek-pere, 2015; Nwangwu & Ononogbu, 2016; Olorunmola, 2016, Sule et al., 2017a; Sule et al., 2017b; Sule 2018; Sule et al., 2018c; Sule et al., 2018d, Sule et al., 2018e; Ayeni, 2019; Sule, 2019; Okeke & Nwali, 2020; Sule & Sambo, 2021; Sule et al., 2022) on party financing in Nigeria that the amount should be high just the way some of the studies suggested that the maximum spending limit should be increased higher. Such little fine is inconsequential and will not influence a positive attitude of compliance because politicians and parties will not fear the consequences of their actions when this is the punishment.

This is often the case with the Nigerian political system. Laws tend to be soft and relaxed for those who commit serious offences including corruption scandals. Those accused of misappropriation of public funds are allowed to escape freely with no measures taken to counter the behaviour. For someone who is required by law to spend a maximum of N5 billion, he violates the regulations and possibly spent N50 billion, the commission will end up asking him to pay a paltry sum of N50 million as a sanction for such gross misconduct it is improper. The provision of twelve months in jail or fine and jail together may not be any different from the previous situation. The legal procedure in Nigeria and the judicial system lack the sophistication and the will to jail a presidential or gubernatorial candidate on account of violation of maximum spending limits when they could not jail the over 300 cases of looting, squandering, stealing, misappropriation involving political actors (Mohammed, 2013). A study (Sule & Sambo, 2021) notes that the fight against corruption in Nigeria is carried out with such a lukewarm and a lackadaisical attitude to the extent that people adopted the culture of legalising corruption.

In this aspect, this section needs a reform which will adopt strict measures and severe sanctions than what was provided in the law. In an interview, Sule (2018) asked one of the top echelons of the major parties in the country, why the laws are over-relaxed and the sanctions are too soft for the offenders when it is a matter of corruption and it affects good governance, democratic accountability and transparency. The informant responded that why should laws be made strict or indicting for the offenders? He said the National Assembly members and the executives in the country are the beneficiaries of loose laws because they are the offenders who violated the regulations how will they commit their necks into laws that will hook them? He confessed that they will never adhere to the maximum spending limit and they will continue to spend excessively and violate the law because they have pre-determined their escape route from the provision of laws. He further lamented that the judiciary could not do anything here because they are pocketed by the executive and the legislature. This is the reason why such weak laws are maintained in the act. Many analysts, researchers, media, civil society and other stakeholders thought that the 2022 Electoral Act will be harsh in punishing deliberate offenders but to their dismay, the relaxation continues.

ELECTION EXPENSES OF POLITICAL PARTIES

The Electoral Act 2022 introduced new items on election expenses of political parties which were not existing in the 2006 and 2010 Electoral Acts. Section 89(1–8) provides the following regulations.

While a glance through this section and its sub-section will give a reader a fair view of an effort to regulate parties' expenses, two major lapses weakened this section. One is the lack of specification of the amount. Section 89(2) states that the expenses to be incurred by the parties shall be determined by the INEC in collaboration with the parties. This looks like deliberate flexibility to accommodate what may not be transparent and corruption may occur in this process. In the view of this work, parties should be allowed to spend no more than N20 billion ($47,676,940.00 million) for all their campaign activities and electoral expenses at all levels in any periodic election. Fixing an amount will make the law indicting for the offenders. The second aspect is the fine or sanction which is an escapist charge that offenders can pay comfortably. A fine of N1 million ($2,383.85 thousand) in Section 89(4 and 7) for the offenders is just ridiculous and a weak sanction that will encourage a violation. Charges should be N100 million ($238,384.70 thousand) for any offence or violation in this section which will serve as a source of income for INEC in its bid for independence. It should generate income for the commission through these penalties and other charges and fines.

CONTRIBUTION LIMIT

One area that witnessed a remarkable change in the Electoral Act 2022 is the contribution limit/ban. In the Electoral Act 2010, the maximum contribution limit is N1 million ($2,383.85 thousand). But in the 2022, law the threshold is raised tremendously fifty times. This development is illustrated in table 7.4.

It is recommendable that the maximum contribution is increased significantly to a realisable and practical limit. The earlier version of the limit of N1 million ($2,383.85 thousand) seems a mirage in Nigerian politics. Multibillion business moguls and wealthy oligarchs are financiers of politics and one cannot restrict these classes from spending lavishly on their candidates. Besides, the value of the Nigerian currency is not congruent with the limit set before. A sum of fifty million ($119,192.35 thousand) is quite average which

Table 7.4 Election Expenses of Political Parties in the 2022 Electoral Act

Section and Sub-section	Regulation
89(1)	For the purposes of an election, 'election expenses' means expenses incurred by a political party within the period from the date notice is given by the commission to conduct an election up to and including, the polling day in respect of the particular election.
89(2)	Election expenses incurred by a political party for the management or the conduct of an election shall be determined by the commission in consultation with the political parties.
89(3)	Election expenses of a political party shall be submitted to the commission in a separate audited return within six months after the election and such return shall be signed by the political party's auditors and countersigned by the Chairman of the party election expenses of political parties and be supported by a sworn affidavit by the signatories as to the correctness of its contents.
89(4)	A political party which contravenes subsection (3) commits an offence and is liable on conviction to a maximum fine of N1,000,000 ($2,383.85 thousand) and in the case of failure to submit an accurate audited return within the stipulated period, the court may impose a maximum penalty of N200,000.00 thousand ($476.77 hundred) per day on any party for the period after the return was due until it is submitted to the commission.
89(5)	The return referred to in subsection (3) shall show the amount of money expended by or on behalf of the party on election expenses, the items of expenditure and commercial value of goods and services received for election purposes.
89(6)	The political party shall cause the return submitted to the commission under subsection (4) to be published in at least two national newspapers and official website of the party.
89(7)	Any political party that incurs election expenses beyond the limit set in subsection (2) commits an offence and is liable on conviction to a maximum fine of N1,000,000 million ($2,383.85 thousand) and forfeiture to the commission of the amount by which the expenses exceed the limit set by the commission.
89(8)	The commission shall make available for public inspection during regular business hours at its headquarters and state offices the audit returns of the political parties required by subsection (3) which shall include the names, addresses, occupation and amount contributed by each contributor to a party.

Source: Electoral Act 2022 (tabulated by then author 2022. Conversion into dollar was made by the author based on the official exchange rate).

is good for those intending to be law-abiding but it should be noted that the donors will not restrict themselves. Donations are often made covertly as fundraising is not often made public and where they are made public, violation appears. In most cases, the donors offer hard foreign cash, specifically dollars to evade detection by the agencies concerned. A moral question is important

Table 7.5 Contribution Limit in the 2022 Electoral Act

Section and Sub-section	Regulation
88(8)	No individual or other entity shall donate to a candidate more than N50, 000,000 million ($119,192.35 thousand).
88(10)	Any individual who knowingly acts in contravention of subsection (8) is liable on conviction to a maximum fine of N500,000 thousand ($1,191.92 thousand) or imprisonment for a term of nine months or both.
88(11)	An accountant who falsifies, or conspires or aids a candidate to forge or falsify a document relating to his expenditure at an election or receipt or donation for the election or in any way aids and abets the contravention of the provisions of this section commits an offence and is liable on conviction to a fine of N3,000,000 thousand ($7,151.54 thousand) or imprisonment for a term of three years or both.

Source: Electoral Act 2022 (tabulated by then author 2022. Conversion into dollar was made by the author based on the official exchange rate).

here because it takes a principled and honest politician to reveal the donations that they receive. They rarely do so.

Besides, setting the maximum contribution limit to N50 million ($119,192.35 thousand) is modest and will minimise violation albeit, not completely. It was established by previous studies that donors contributed over N100 million ($238,384.70 thousand) in the past elections and it should not be anticipated that they will donate less in future elections when the cost of everything is skyrocketing because of the collapsing global economy by the impacts of COVID-19 pandemic and the reckless economic management in the country. For instance, Ohman (2014) reported one of the business moguls in Nigeria who donated N250 million ($595,961.75 thousand) since 2010 fundraising by the former ruling PDP and no punishment is meted on him. The aftermath of the donation is that we have witnessed the rapid rise in business fortunes of Abdussamad Rabi'u to the level of competing with Alhaji Aliko Dangote and Alhaji Dahiru Mangal. The extent of the violation of contribution limit is displayed in the fundraising hosted during the fundraising dinner of the former president Goodluck Ebele Jonathan in his bid for the 2015 presidential election which he eventually lost. Tycoons, contractors, corporations and politicians donated outrageously beyond the limit with impunity.

The following revealed the contribution and the violation or donation above the set limit by law. Tunde Ayeni N1 billion ($2,383,847.00 million), Tunde and Group of friends N2.6 billion ($6,192,002.20 million), Jerry Gana and friends N5 billion ($11,919,235.00 million), National Automotive Council N450 million ($1,072,731.15 million), PDP Governors Forum (50 million x 21) N1.0 billion ($2,383,847.00 million), Bala Shagaya representing the oil and gas sector N5 billion ($11,919,235.00 million), Construction sector N310 million ($738,992.57 thousand), Transport and Aviation Sector represented by Didi Ndimou N1 billion ($2,383,847.00 million), The Real Estate Sector represented by Oluchi Okoye N4 billion ($9,535,388.00 million), Food and Agric Sector represented by Chief Ominife Uzeogbu N500 million ($1,191,923.50 million), Cizally Limited N250 million ($595,961.75 thousand), Power sector represented by Tunde Ayeni N500 million ($1,191,923.50 million), National association of Stevedores N2 million ($4,767.69 thousand), Mr. Sam Egwu N1 million ($2,383.85 thousand), Halima Jibril N5 million ($11,919.24 thousand) and Ajuji Best Hotel N1 million ($2,383.85 thousand) (Aluigba, 2015; Nwangwu & Ononogbu, 2016). This made a total of N22, 442 billion ($53,398,172.80 million), twenty-two times more than what was allowed in the 2010 Electoral Act as the maximum campaign spending for presidential candidates.

If individual contributors can give N1 billion ($2,383,847.00 million) as of 2015 fundraising, it should not be expected that it will decrease in 2023 and beyond. But it should be noted that Electoral Act 2022 is fair and just in putting the contribution ceiling to N50 million ($119,192.35 thousand). In a process that is fair and ethical, it should not be more than that. The logic of the contribution limit is to block clientelism, patrimonialism, kickback, rent, contracts and rewards. Corporations, business establishments and individuals that donated expect a reward in cash or kind including shoddy deals and violations of due process. The annoying aspect is the inability of the INEC to monitor effectively and sanction the violators otherwise there is nothing wrong with the set limit which is fair to the contributors (Sule et al., 2017b).

MONITORING OF POLITICAL PARTIES

Section 83(1–4) confers power on INEC to monitor parties including their activities and expenses whenever the commission decides. This is illustrated here.

This section is one of the areas expanded by the Electoral Act 2022 which is vital because parties must be monitored to enforce compliance and sanction. A study (Sule et al., 2017b) examined the monitoring of parties by INEC and discovered that there are three major problems: excessive spending, illegal funding and bribery and corruption and violation of regulations. The study concludes that INEC is unable to monitor parties' activities effectively because of the complacency of the officials and lack of cooperation of the parties and politics. The study suggests that a section is required in the future

Table 7.6   Monitoring of Political Parties in the 2022 Electoral Act

Section and Sub-section	Regulation
83(1)	The commission (INEC) shall keep records of the activities of all the registered political parties.
83(2)	The commission (INEC) may seek information or clarification from any registered political party in connection with any activities of the political party which may be contrary to the provisions of the Constitution or any other law, guidelines, rules or regulations made pursuant to an act of the National Assembly.
83(3)	The commission (INEC) may direct its enquiry under subsection (2) to the Chairman or Secretary of the political party at the national, state, local government or area council or ward level, as the case may be.
83(4)	A political party which fails to provide the required information or clarification under subsection (2) or carry out any lawful directive given by the commission in conformity with the provisions of this section is liable to a fine not more than N1,000,000 ($2,383.85 thousand).

Source: Electoral Act 2022 (tabulated by then author 2022. Conversion into dollar was made by the author based on the official exchange rate).

electoral act which will empower INEC to monitor and sanction parties. This section emerges as a welcome development and as part of the recommendations of the study by Sule et al. (2017b). However, it will be more difficult to secure the cooperation of parties and politicians in revealing and submitting to INEC as when due because the level of impunity and the effrontery that the parties are exhibiting in violating regulations even within internal party democracy is an indicator that the parties will not cooperate. For parties to comply, a proper party institutionalisation and organisation are needed which is lacking presently.

SOURCES OF POLITICAL PARTIES CAMPAIGN EXPENDITURE IN NIGERIA

The Electoral Act 2022 approves only legal sources from donations and private sources as indicated in Sections 88 and 89. Public funding is not available for the parties since 2010 when the new Electoral Act was introduced. Private sources are allowed. A study by Wakili et al. (2008) on funding parties in Nigeria reported that both the public and private funding existed from 1999 to the period of the study (2008). The study by Wakili et al. (2008) further surveyed various views of Nigerians across the six geopolitical zones on the mode of funding to be adopted as an alternative. The majority of the respondents preferred both public and private funding to continue. But a simple majority settled for private funding. The study was carried out two years before the Electoral Act 2010 was introduced which favoured full private funding. It is anticipated that the study made an impact on the policy of adopting private funding.

A bigger issue with the sources of parties' funding is the interpretation of the term 'legal' and 'illegal' in the sources. What actually constitutes legal and how could it be determined? The law states that donations can be given to parties up to N50 million ($119,192.35 thousand) and the contributions must never come from a foreign source. Apart from these two interpretations, it is vague to explain how a legal source can be determined. A study (Sule et al., 2019b) presented a comprehensive detail of the sources of parties' campaign expenditure using the 2015 general election as the case study. The study interviewed 28 informants cutting across various stakeholders in the electoral process in Nigeria. The study identifies six major sources which include grants from some people and organisations. Wakili et al. (2008) state that parties offered grants to their contestants, where a minority of 24.6percent agreed that candidates were assisted by their parties, but the majority of 86.4percent in the study believed that donation from wealthy individuals is the major source of campaign funds for political parties. The second source is godfathers and godfatherism. Most of the informants consulted in the study by Sule et al. (2019b) agreed that godfathers are the major financiers of elections in Nigeria. The study by Wakili et al. (2008) also confirmed the aforementioned statement where the respondents were reported to have agreed by a majority of 77.9percent that parties source their campaign funds from wealthy individuals and the wealthy individuals or godfathers controlled the parties and invest for a return.

The third source reported by Sule et al. (2019b) is loot from the public treasury or what most of the experts on party financing across the globe tagged as abuse of state resources. It is believed that one of the methods by which politicians have sponsored themselves or financed their election campaigns is through the use of illegal looted money. This view is supported by other studies (Wakili et al., 2008; Olarinmoye, 2008; Adetula, 2008; Kura, 2014; Anyadike & Eme, 2014, Nwangwu & Ononogbu, 2016; Sule et al., 2018c). The fourth source is a personal/private source. The major source of campaign financing in Nigeria today is private sources and personal means. The fifth source according to Sule et al. (2019b) is the selling of forms and other charges and finally, a donation is the last source and one of the biggest. The survey study conducted by Waliki et al. (2007) revealed the responses of the respondents indicating that donations are one of the major means of political party financing in Nigeria with a frequency of 22.3percent. President Muhammadu Buhari received N186 ($443,395.54 thousand) in a donation through

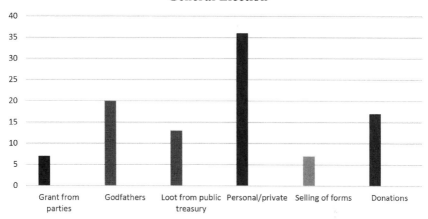

Figure 7.1 Sources of Campaign Financing during the 2015 General Election. *Source*: Field survey, 2018. *Source*: Sule (2018).

a fundraising process using recharge cards that went directly into his bank account according to Sule (2019). The findings from the study by Sule et al. (2019b) are illustrated in the following table.

DISCLOSURE BY POLITICAL PARTIES

Section 90(1-4) of the Electoral Act 2022 provides that parties shall keep proper records of their income and expenditure and all funds received must be disclosed or reported to the Commission (INEC) within a specific period and failure to do so will attract a sanction as illustrated in table 7.11.

This section replicates what the older law provides without significant changes except for the change in the amount of the contribution from N1 million ($2,383.85 thousand) previously to N50 million ($119,192.35 thousand) in the new law. However, while Section 88(8) states that the contribution limit is N50 million ($119,192.35 thousand), Section 90(3) contradicts the regulations by making the donation flexible and can be beyond the set limit provided the sources can be revealed to the commission. There should not be such legal contradiction which may result in a legal tussle in future. A party may receive more than the limit and identify the source to the commission and escape with it even if the source is not genuine. Parties can manoeuvre and make the sources look authentic. In essence, the section is good if the commission will enforce compliance.

Table 7.7 Disclosure by Political Parties in the Electoral Act 2022

Section and Sub-section	Regulation
90(1)	A political party shall not accept or keep in its possession any anonymous monetary or other contributions, gifts or property, from any source.
90(2)	A political party shall keep an account and asset book into which shall be recorded – (a) all monetary and other forms of contributions received by the party; and (b) the name and address of any person or entity that contributes any money or asset which exceeds N1,000,000 million ($2,383.85 thousand).
90(3)	A political party shall not accept any monetary or other contribution which is more than N50,000,000 ($119,192.35 thousand) unless it can identify the source of the money or other contribution to the commission.
90(4)	A political party sponsoring the election of a candidate shall, within three months after the announcement of the results of the election, file a report of the contributions made by individuals and entities to the commission.

Source: Electoral Act 2022 (tabulated by then author 2022. Conversion into dollar was made by the author based on the official exchange rate).

PERIOD TO BE COVERED BY ANNUAL STATEMENT AND THE POWERS OF THE COMMISSION TO SET LIMIT ON CONTRIBUTION TO PARTIES AND CANDIDATES

Section 86(1–4) provides regulations on the period to be covered by an annual statement of parties. This Section also has no significant changes from the previous law.

There are three issues with this section as a law or regulation. One of them is the inability of the commission (INEC) to monitor and ensure that the period stipulated is respected by parties. Second is the notion that parties do not cooperate as mentioned severally in this report. Sule (2018) reports in his study that INEC officials complained that parties do not cooperate with them in presenting annual statements and when the officials decided to visit parties' offices to examine the statements, parties do not respect or cooperate with them. In some cases, they bribe the officials as reported in the study (Sule et al., 2017b) while in other cases the politicians use the power of their office to influence the process and overpower the INEC officials to bury the matter. Another issue is that no study reports or observes the publication of parties' statements of accounts in national dailies. This might not lack relevance with the inability of the INEC to secure the reports or lack of cooperation or corruption.

The major problem with the provisions in this section is the ambiguity in the limit of the powers of the INEC to limit contribution to parties. It would

Table 7.8   Period to be Covered by Annual Statement and the Powers of the Commission to Set Limit on Contribution to Parties and Candidates

Section and Sub-section	Regulation
86(1)	Every political party shall submit to the commission a detailed annual statement of assets and liabilities and analysis of its sources of funds and other assets, together with statement of its expenditure including hard and soft copy of its list of members or in such a form as the commission may require.
86(2)	Any official of the political party who contravenes subsection (1) commits an offence and is liable to a fine of N1,000,000 ($2,383.85 thousand) or imprisonment for a term of six months or both.
86(3)	A political party shall grant to any officer authorised in writing by the commission, access to examine the records and audited accounts kept by the political party in accordance with the provisions of this act and the political party shall give to the officer all such information as may be requested in relation to all contributions received by or on behalf of the party.
86(4)	The commission shall publish the report on such examinations and audit in two national newspapers and commission's website within 30 days of receipt of the results.
87(1)	The commission shall have power to place limitation on the amount of money or other assets which an individual can contribute to a political party or candidate and to demand such information on the amount donated and source of the funds.
87(2)	Any individual, candidate or political party who exceeds the limit placed by the commission in subsection (1), commits an offence and is liable on conviction to – (a) in case of a political party, a fine not more than N10,000,000 ($23,838.47 thousand) and forfeiture of the amount donated; and (b) in case of an individual, a fine of five times the amount donated in excess of the limit placed by the commission.

Source: Electoral Act 2022 (tabulated by then author 2022. Conversion into dollar was made by the author based on the official exchange rate).

have been better if the amount had been decisively stated. But there are other reasons why the amount is not being exactly specified. Sometimes the situation may not be the same all the time and some conditions may warrant allowing the receipt of a huge sum while there are other situations that may not warrant that. Just as suggested by Ohman (2018), regulations should be flexible and rigid in some cases but the most fundamental aspect that must be emphasised is the strict and effective monitoring and sanction.

INTERNATIONAL DONOR AGENCIES AND POLITICAL PARTY FINANCING IN NIGERIA

One area that is worth mentioning in this perspective is the partnership of the international donors in the electoral process in Nigeria. Any form of foreign donation is completely banned in the Electoral Act 2022 in Section 88(6) to both the parties and the candidates. Any foreign donation receives by a party or a candidate must be forfeited to the electoral body within thirty days or face sanction. But there are other areas that the international donors are playing vital roles in some legal intervention to boost the electoral process in Nigeria and capacity building for the parties. International donors operate in Nigeria since the beginning of democratisation in 1999. They collaborate with the electoral body in capacity building, provision of logistics, training, partnership, monitoring and observation and sometimes they provide funds to the electoral body which is allowed. In the aspect of parties and politicians, international donors provide logistics, training, capacity building, intervention towards best practices and other non-material assistance. There are many of them including the International Foundation for Electoral Systems (IFES), International Republican Institute (IRI), National Democratic Institute (NDI), Thomas Carothers, Institute for Democracy and Electoral Assistance (IDEA), European Union (EU), Commonwealth, United State Agency for International Development (USAID), United Kingdom Department for International Development (UKAID), Department for International Development (DFID), Canadian Institute for Development Assistance (CIDA) and several others. They collaborate and provide funding to local civil societies in the promotion of good governance, transparent party financing monitoring and credible electoral conduct (Sule et al., 2018f).

Section 225(3) of the Nigerian 1999 Constitution is unequivocal about receiving any foreign donation from the parties and candidates. Likewise, Section 85 of the Electoral Act 2022 prohibits any party or candidate from receiving any form of donation outside Nigeria. But the INEC as a partner may receive funds from outside Nigeria from the donors to train its staff, logistics such as computers, electoral gadgets, capacity building and advice in securing election materials and global best practices can be received by the INEC from the international donors. It is also allowed for the international donors to organise workshops for parties and politicians in collaboration with civil societies and the INEC and other political groups that is not funds-based beneficial or that are not compensated with material benefit to avoid the breach of the law.

Intervention from international donors has been taking place for many decades. For instance, the US government through the agency of USAID has been assisting Nigeria in electoral conduct since 1999. For instance, USAID in partnership with the DFID provided a sum of $86.8 million (N364,117,320,000 billion) assistance to improve election performance and transparency in Nigeria. Besides the financial assistance which goes to INEC and civil societies, other interventions consist of diplomatic engagement of the Nigerian candidates and peace brokerage to shun violence and embrace a peaceful process, engagement of the party leadership towards party institutionalisation and organisation to strengthen their capacity to situate themselves for democratic consolidation, engagement with civil societies, business leaders, traditional rulers, religious clerics and prominent individuals to promote credible and peaceful elections. Also, the US government is engaging the electorates through the various programmes of awareness creation sponsored in the media, physical workshops and town hall meetings and continuous engagements through ad hoc staff all over the country (US Fact Sheet, 2015).

The United States is also providing additional assistance to aid Nigeria to execute credible elections since 1999. In 2008, the United States donated $17.2 million (N7,131,333,355.20 billion), $13.448 million (N5,621,166,000 billion) in 2009 and between 1999 to 2007, the US government had provided $74 million (N31,042,260,000 billion) to Nigeria just for electoral assistance out of which $5 million (N2,097,450,000 billion) was used for the training of poll workers in 1999, a $2 million (N838,980,000 million) was utilised for the training of 10,300 elected officials in the area of accountability and transparency. The EU too is not left behind in the intervention for electoral assistance. From 2010 to 2013, a sum of Euro 92 million (N40,529,294,823.60 billion) was disbursed to promote democratic governance in Nigeria. The money was channelled through the DFID which provided a sum of Euro 10.9 million (N4,801,840,364.97 billion) and CIDA Euro 81.1 million (N35,727,454,458.63 billion) (Bariledum et al., 2016).

The international donors mostly from the Western world are actively involved in the process of assisting Nigeria to develop and promote its capacity for conducting a fair, peaceful and credible election. The support is provided in terms of technical assistance, training of electoral officials in the areas of election management and effective deployment of election materials. Civic-voter education is another area of donors' intervention where they provide funding for the production and dissemination of materials on civic-voter education involving registration of voters' cards, participation in the electoral process, shunning of violence and unethical conduct, voting as a right, not a privilege, abstaining away from money politics and other related issues. The pamphlets are produced in major lingua francas across the zones of the country to reach wider readability. The donors also empower civil societies on youth active participation in politics and avoiding violence, and the need for peaceful voting (Bariledum et al., 2016).

One major area of intervention by the international donors is the support of both the domestic and international election observers during the process of electoral conduct in Nigeria since 1999. They participated in the observation and submit a report of what they have observed to the Nigerian Government,

INEC, security personnel and all stakeholders that are affected. They have severally raised their concern on issues of rigging, malpractice, vote-buying, violence, subversion of the process and other issues associated with the electoral conduct. An example is the report of the Human Rights Watch on the conduct of the 2003 and the 2007 general elections which they had observed as similar to war bedevilled with violence, deployment of intimidation, assassination, disenfranchisement and manipulation of the election results. The EU, Human Rights Watch, African Union (AU) and other domestic observers also reported similar incidences even in the 2011 and 2019 general elections. They made the observation and then intervene to remedy the problems. For instance, the EU supported Nigeria with the sum of Euro 7 million (N3,083,750,693.10 billion) to enhance human rights protection and democracy promotion (Sule et al., 2018f).

However, many Nigerians expressed pessimism about the activities of the donors according to Sule et al. (2018f). In the study where many stakeholders were interviewed, they eloquently expressed their reservations and premonition on the motive of the donors who have been expending huge sums of money to support Nigeria's democracy. The informants believed that the international donors and their host countries must have an interest that they are pursuing or protecting. They are not simply being charitable for the sake of humanity only. The study itself refers to Dahl's (2006) Poliarchy framework where he suggests that democracy must be controlled and this control should be executed by institutions, organisations and civil societies. The Poliarchy framework is chastised on the ground that it is just the US and other capitalist countries' agenda for the recruitment of elites in developing democracies who will collaborate with them in their quest for global governance. Many Nigerians believed that the international donors dictate the tune of the partnership instead of allowing the local communities to determine based on their culture what is to be done. Elements of truth exist according to Sule et al. (2018f) in the views of the informants because sometimes the Western political values are superimposed on local communities in the name of democratisation and that has aroused cynicism and suspicion which leads to hostile reception of the activities of the donors.

Thus, it can be summarised from the previous analysis that while the Nigerian Government has banned all forms of foreign assistance to parties and politicians, it is partnering with the international donors in democracy assistance through the electoral body and direct engagement in non-material benefit to the parties, politicians, electorates, civil societies and even the elected officials. Sometimes international donors such as USAID, Policy and Legal Advocacy Centre (PLAC) and others are involved in the process of policymaking and implementation at both the national and local levels. They provide intervention, training, logistics, equipment for operation and other emoluments. The role played by these donors cannot be over-emphasised. But it is good that Nigeria as a state ban foreign donations to parties and candidates to avoid the hijack of the polity by the foreign powers and to preserve the sanctity of the national sovereignty. It is relevant in preventing obscured and dubious sources that may corrupt the process.

Succinctly, Nigeria is recognised as one of the countries with well-articulated regulations on party financing. Two major laws provide the needed regulations which are the Nigerian 1999 Constitution and the Electoral Act 2022. Provisions are well-elaborated and adequately established to enable transparency in the party financing process. There are rules on a maximum spending limit for all elective offices, the maximum spending limit for parties, contribution limit, contribution ban, disclosure, period to be covered by the annual statement, monitoring of parties by the electoral body, private funding, auditing of parties and strict supervision of parties and candidates' expenses in addition to various sanctions for offenders and violators. This is not obtained in many countries, specifically in Africa and many developing democracies. The Nigerian case of party financing and electoral transparency is not about the regulations. This does not mean that the regulations are adequate. This chapter examines in detail and critically the regulations and the loopholes in them that should have been taken care of in the process of designing the laws. But in essence, the laws are good enough to ensure transparency but one major problem is enforcement and compliance.

The weakness of regulations in party financing in Nigeria is the enforcement and not the laws themselves. It is surprising that while Nigeria is one of the countries with well-articulated regulations but it is also one of the countries with a high prevalence of corruption and other illegal practices in the process. The excessive spending, vote-buying, bribery, violation of contribution ban, failure of disclosure and auditing as well as monitoring of the process render the regulations weak, ineffective and nominal. Politicians continue to enjoy the proceeds of illegality in the process through dubious deals and transactions in the party financing process that calls for urgent action. While most of the provisions of the regulations are sound, the area that most Nigerians frown at is the sanction. The punishment for violation is ineffective and inconsequential to detererrant behaviours. Take, for instance, a person allowed to spend up to N5 billion ($11,919,235.00 million) but spent more than the pegged amount is to be fined only N50 million ($119,192.35 thousand) or a one-year jail term or both. And in most cases, neither of the three has ever taken place since 2006 when the first regulations came into effect up to the current 2022 laws. The offender, in this case, should have been fined N500 million ($1,191,923.50 million) and he should be banned from contesting any political office in the future which will send a shock wave to the impending culprits.

Therefore, it is concluded in this section that the laws are averagely good to ensure transparency in the Nigerian party financing process but there is a big hurdle in actualising it. It is the matter of enforcement and compliance that is the most difficult aspect of the process. Politics in Nigeria is clientelism and the politicians are players that are rational in the field of playing their game. They can use any rational method including an irrational act as players in the game of competition to secure electoral victory at all costs. This means if the ruling class is the major pillar behind the enforcement with its bureaucratic subordinates, then there is a long way to go in the enforcement. In essence, the designers of the law are those who are ready to violate it, and, in some instances, they are making the laws with deliberate loopholes to enable the violation and escape with impunity. In as much as politicians can violate the laws and escape, they will continue to do it. Therefore, there must be practical and compelling strategies to enforce compliance which will involve the role of the citizens, civil societies and domestic and international observers and collaborators. There must be strict sanctions even if it is based on the loose sanction provided in the regulations to start sending signals to the community that there is a willingness and determination to implement laws as they affect others.

For now, some sections of the constitution impede the sanction of violators, especially, the executive arm of government. For instance, Section 306 of the Nigerian 1999 Constitution provides an Executive Immunity Clause for the elected president, vice president, state governors and their deputies. This section is believed to have been a serious hiccup on the neck of the Nigerian anti-corruption agencies and processes. The clause provides that both civil and criminal offences of these categories are immune from any litigation during their tenure (Lawson, 2014). This means excessive spending even if it involves abuse of state resources and other violations of the party financing process cannot be a call to account from all the categories that are included in the clause. This makes the accountability in this perspective difficult. Therefore, there is a need to harmonise some regulations to avoid overlapping of laws that can lead to ambiguity which will leave a hole for exit from the jaws of the law.

Chapter 8

Election Management Authority and Monitoring of Party Financing

The Independent National Electoral Commission (INEC) is the body that is saddled with the responsibility of conducting elections at most levels in Nigeria's Fourth Republic. Before the establishment of INEC, several electoral bodies conducted elections in Nigeria including the Electoral Commission of Nigeria (ECN) which conducted the First Republic elections, the Federal Electoral Commission (FEDECO) in the Second Republic and the National Electoral Commission (NECON) in the Aborted Third Republic. As part of the reforms initiated and advanced by international democratic assistance bodies and other agencies, new democracies were advised to make their Electoral Management Bodies (EMBs) independent and transparent. INEC was established as an independent body with constitutional powers to conduct and supervise elections in addition to several other tasks. The INEC conducts elections for presidential, National Assembly, governorship and state house of assemblies but the powers of the conduct of local council elections are on the shoulders of the State Independent Electoral Commissions (SIECs).

The INEC was established in 1998 by the military regime of General Abdulsalami Abubakar. While INEC is independent, its revenue and operating expenses are directly supplied by the executive arm of government, the presidency from the consolidated revenue. The appointment of the chairman of the commission, other principal officers and national commissioners are made by the president as approved by the national assembly. Having identified this loophole, the Justice Uwais Committee inaugurated by the late former president Yar'adua recommended that the chairman of the commission should be appointed directly by the National Judicial Council (NJC) to enhance the independence of the commission and to avoid unnecessary interference from the executive but the national assembly and other interested parties or powers in the country thwarted the implementation of this particular recommendation (Adeniyi, 2010).

INEC succeeded in conducting six general elections sequentially, and the electoral body proves its independence to a limited degree in many cases. The elections conducted by the INEC were affected by challenges that were discussed in the previous chapter questioning the credibility and the integrity of the process and the outcome but the recent elections are improving significantly. The introduction of some accountable and transparent measures such as the use of Smart Card Readers (SCRs) and accreditation of voters before the election and the use of electronic means of collating results and improved monitoring with the partnership of the international observers and domestic civil societies all improved the process (Sule et al., 2021). This chapter examined the establishment of the INEC, its organisational structures and responsibilities and the challenges encountered by INEC in discharging its responsibilities as well as the successes recorded.

THE ESTABLISHMENT OF THE INDEPENDENT NATIONAL ELECTORAL COMMISSION

The INEC establishment was the product of the transition to democracy in 1998. After the eventual death of the former later military president General Sani Abacha, who wanted to succeed himself by transforming into a civilian leader, General Abdulsalami Abubakar took over and immediately prepared a transition timetable for restoring Nigeria to the democratic path. The transition period was observed to have been the shortest in Nigeria's history of democratisation. For instance, the transition to democracy in the Second Republic took a good three years after the Murtala/Obasanjo before it was actualised. This followed the long protracted military rule of thirteen years after the bloody coup in 1966, the civil war and the crisis of governance. The leader that captured power in a reprisal coup in 1966 General Yakubu Gowon in an Aburi Accord (a small town in Ghana where ethnic and regional Nigerian leaders sat down in 1966 and agreed on a transitional timetable to democratic government), reneged on meeting the date and decided to continue in power beyond the agreed date which eventually caused civil war (1967–1970) in addition to other factors (Campbell, 2019).

The military regime of General Murtala Ramat Muhammed on assuming power in 1976 after a peaceful coup promised to return Nigeria to civilian rule in 1979 and quickly drafted a transition timetable. Unfortunately, General Murtala was assassinated in a bloody coup but General Olusegun Obasanjo, his deputy, took over and vowed to continue with the transition unfazed. In 1979, an election was successfully conducted and the country was restored to democratic rule, a regime that lasted only five years before the military struck again in 1984 (Omotola, 2010). The military rule stretched from 1984 to 1999 when the insincere and faulty transition process initiated by the Babangida military administration was aborted after the 12 June presidential election in 1991. The military annulled the election and continued to rule till 1999 when the shortest transition by the Abdulsalami Regime culminated in the longest civilian rule and democratisation in the country (United States Institute of Peace, 2019).

The Abdulsalami Abubakar Regime, however, fulfilled its promise and successfully conducted an election in 1999 and subsequently handed over power to the civilians but not before the attempt at institutionalisation of democratic pillars such as parties, constitution, electoral body and other necessary ingredients of democratic operation. The electoral body, INEC, was established before the election. The INEC was established by the Nigerian military in 1998 under Decree No 17 of 1998. On 5 August 1998, the commission was passed into law where it was stated:

> The Federal Military Government hereby decrees as follows: There should be a body known as the Independent National Electoral Commission to be referred to according to this Decree as the 'Commission'. The commission shall be a body that is corporate with perpetual succession, and may sue and be sued in its corporate name.

The decree later became famously known as the Independent National Electoral Commission Establishment Decree 1998. The formation of INEC followed the dissolving of the NECON (Sule et al., 2017b).

INEC was later given a constitutional mandate by the Nigerian 1999 Constitution where it is stated in Section 1 of the Electoral Act 2022 as Amended:

> The Independent National Electoral Commission as established by section 153 of the Constitution (in this Act referred to as 'the Commission') (a) shall be a body corporate with perpetual succession; and (b) may sue and be sued in its corporate name. (2) The National Headquarters of the Commission shall be situated in the Federal Capital Territory (FCT). 2. In addition to the functions conferred on it by the Constitution, the Commission shall have power to (a) conduct voter and civic education; (b) promote knowledge of sound democratic election processes; and (c) conduct any referendum required to be conducted under the provisions of the 1999 Constitution or an Act of the National Assembly.

The INEC went ahead and conducted the first election in 1999 and ushered a civilian rule. Many scholars (Omo-Bare, 2006; Omotola, 2010; Sule et al., 2017b; Campbell, 2019 and United States Institute of Peace) emphasise that the transition to democracy in the Fourth Republic in Nigeria is faulty and is directly imposed and supervised by the military. The supposed civil societies, independent parties and other natural processes of democratisation were not allowed to take shape and metamorphosed into a full-blown democratic system. The process was influenced and dominated by the military. In essence, Campbell (2019) argues that before the military hand over power, they strategically made a swift and scintillating arrangement that saw them usurped power control from the background and directly. The first civilian president in Nigeria's Fourth Republic was a former army General Olusegun Obasanjo. The fourth president is retired army general Muhammadu Buhari. Other strategic positions such as senate president, ministers and ambassadors were all shared with army generals in the Fourth Republic. What differentiates Nigeria's democracy in the Fourth Republic from the system of diarchy obtained in places like Thailand is an informal arrangement.

Before the military relinquished power to the civilians, an undemocratic agreement was made among the elite in the country. They agreed that power would be shared among the Northern and Southern elites after every eight years starting with the South in the Southwest. Eventually, this arrangement was interrupted by the death of the late president Yar'adua and that had caused internal schisms in the former ruling PDP resulting in its defeat in the 2015 general election (Campbell, 2019). Other issues that faulted the transition are the weak political parties, low political culture and socialisation and elite diversion of democratic operation (Omotola, 2010).

Despite several issues associated with the transition process, one of the remarkable foundations set for democratisation in the Fourth Republic is the electoral body that was independent and well-structured. The INEC delivered many elections successfully and the Commission is displaying positive progress in its years of experience with many gigantic reforms that are significantly improving the elections in recent years. The INEC engineered the establishment of the Electoral Act in 2006, initiated a reform that transformed the Act into the 2010 Electoral Act and it is currently passed into Electoral Act 2022. Other reforms introduced by INEC included the use of accreditation of voters before eligibility for election. Voters' registration exercise continued and it is been modernised into an electronic version where the permanent voters cards (PVCs) are now useful in opening bank accounts and other national assignments. The electoral process from 2015 witnessed the use of SCRs which are mini-gadgets that used or read microchip cards that are given in the form of PVCs. It is believed that the SCRs helped immensely in curbing rigging and other malpractice in the electoral process in Nigeria's Fourth Republic (Nwangwu et al., 2016; Sule et al., 2018f) in the build-up to the 2023 general election, INEC introduced additional electronic measures known as Biometric Verification Accreditation System (BVAS) which was successful in the July 2022 Osun Gubernatorial election, in addition to the declaration of the electronic collation of the 2023 election results. INEC is for the first time building a resilient partnership with domestic civil societies such as the Nigerian Civil Society Situation Room (NCSSR) which is active in monitoring elections in Nigeria from 2011 in the pre-election period, during the conduct of the election and post-election period (Sule et al., 2021). INEC is also having a good understanding of international donors and international election observers and it is expanding its process of engaging stakeholders to deliver credible elections in the future (Sule et al., 2021).

Most of the challenges faced by INEC are both endogenous and exogenous. The endogenous challenges are related to the poor preparation, logistics, funding, corruption of some officials, partisanship and poor remuneration and welfare of members. The exogenous problems are related to interference from politicians, political machinations of the intrigues of inter-play of games of winning at all costs which frustrate the electoral officials, lack of coopera-tion of parties, candidates and politicians in adhering to the regulations and disclosure and violation of laws coupled with a weak and ineffective judicial system that could not properly handle electoral offences which deny the electoral body the power of arresting offenders and sanctioning them accord-ingly (Onapajo, 2020). All these internal and external challenges have not explicitly deprived the electoral body of discharging its duties of registration of voters, delineation of constituencies, registration of political parties and deregistration, conducting elections and other major tasks even if they are not done appropriately as anticipated since elections in Africa are faulty because of the transitory democratic process that is yet to take shape and normalise (Lindberg, 2006).

THE ORGANISATIONAL STRUCTURE OF THE INDEPENDENT NATIONAL ELECTORAL COMMISSION

Sections 1 to 5 of the Electoral Act 2022 provide that the commission shall have staff. The INEC is headed by the chairman who is appointed by the pres-ident and commander-in-chief of the Federal Republic of Nigeria as approved by the National Assembly. The president will nominate a name based on qualification and meeting the minimum criteria to head the commission and forward it to the National Assembly to approve or reject and make recom-mendations. After the chairman, there are twelve national commissioners who are also nominated by the president and sent to the National Assembly to approve or reject and make recommendations. The national commissioners represent six geopolitical zones in the country. Two each are nominated from the Northeast, Northcentral, Northwest, Southeast, Southsouth and Southwest (Sule et al., 2017b). The FCT Abuja was overlooked in the equation. The national commissioners should have been thirteen with one drawn from the FCT Abuja as an independent capital territory of the country.

The INEC is divided into seven departments. The Personnel Department, Finance and Audit Department, Political Party Monitoring Department, Works and Housing Department, Information and Publicity Department, Legal Unit Department and Operations and Logistics. Each of the departments is headed by a director and assisted by many deputy directors. The departments operate independent but are interdependent on the commission. Staff who works in the various departments are recruited and are continuously recruited when the need arises or when there are vacancies through retirement, departure, dismissal or increasing workload that requires additional helping hands (Sule et al., 2017b). Vacancies are announced when they exist through national dailies. Staffing is one of the endogenous problems that INEC is facing. Nepotism, favouritism, sectionalism, religion, family background and other factors affected the recruitment process. In some cases, interviews are conducted but the applicants are short-changed and replaced with either low-performers or those who have not applied at all (information obtained from a field interview with an informant on 24 April 2017).

INEC has outstanding committees which include election Monitoring and Observation, Election Logistics and Transport, Estate and Works, Political Parties Monitoring, Information and Publicity, Legal Service and Clearance, Board of Survey and Technical, Finance and General Purposes, Senior Staff Establishment, Operations, Senior Staff Welfare and Information and Communication Technology. The standing committees are responsible for administering and taking charge of emergencies and quarterly issues that are not daily routines which are catered by the permanent staff in the commission. Their works involved internal and field work where the needs arise and they provide important inputs for policymaking and decision-making of the commission (Sule et al., 2017b).

The commission has offices in all the thirty-six states of the federation. The state offices are headed by state commissioners (Sule et al., 2017b). The commission also has offices in all the 774 local governments of the federation to ease information flow, civic voter education, collation and distribution of election materials and other important exercises such as continuous voter registration exercises and delineation of additional constituencies, transfer of polling units and other activities. The INEC conducts the periodic election according to the Nigerian Constitution which is four years interval except in cases where court litigations upturned the commencement of the tenure. In some states' governorship elections are conducted separately from the general election. The organisational structure of INEC was designed by Sule (2018) in a model illustrated in figure 8.1.

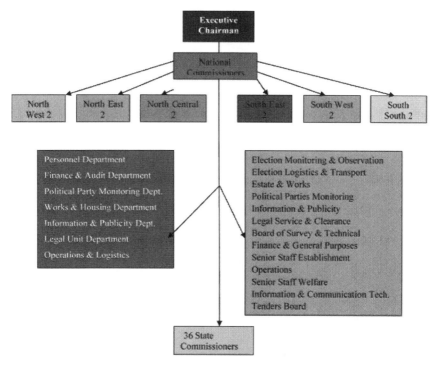

Figure 8.1 Organisational Chart of Independent National Electoral Commission.
Source: Sule (2018).

The model or chart shown in the figure by Sule (2018) neglected or omitted the local government offices. The chart makes a simple illustration that will guide in understanding the composition and operation of the commission but for the omission. Local government offices are important too because the Nigerian political system operates three structures of government which are the federal, state and local government tiers and most of the policies and programmes are structured into three levels to enable for devolution of powers and decentralisation. The local council polls are executed by SIECs based on the federal structure of the country.

Section 3 part II of the Third Schedule of the constitution provides for the establishment of SIEC which has the power to conduct local government elections (The 1999 Constitution). The SIECs have been undertaking the responsibility of election conduct since 1999. Several issues surfaced in the conduct of elections by SIECs. One of them is the contradictions and variations in the calendar. Some states delayed the elections as far as two years after the general election. In some cases, the tenure is not exactly across the country. In some states, they spent three years, in other states two years while in others less than two years (Deribe et al., 2020). Additionally, while INEC is considered to have enjoyed a certain degree of independence in its execution of elections, the SIECs become a readily available tool for control and manipulation by the state governors. The SIECs are just a pawn in the hands of the governors for their will and wish. Apart from that, the SIECs conducted elections that are believed to have been mocking Nigeria's democracy by returning a ruling party as a 100percent winner. An example is a situation where a state with 20 local governments and 300 wards will declare a ruling party in that state as a winner of all the seats without any opposition winning a single seat in that election (Deribe et al.2020).

The irony of the conduct of elections by SIECs is that all ruling parties in the country are indicted for this mishap of electoral fraud at the local government level. In several instances, the opposition boycotts the election because of perceived manipulation, injustice and lack of fairness in the process (Olaniyi, 2017). The situation of local government polls necessitates many calls by experts, policy analysts and academics for an abrogation of the SIECs to enable the INEC to conduct all elections at the same time. One of the arguments that this study observes is that the same local council polls in FCT Abuja conducted by INEC are more transparent and satisfactory and are recording fewer outcries of manipulation then why is the SIECs own too crude and manipulative always? This is perhaps because the State Joint Local Government Account is enabling the state governors to hijack the LGs' resources in return for flamboyant contractual projects than genuine rural development policies. And this justifies why SIECs should be scrapped to allow INEC to execute all the elections.

POWERS AND FUNCTIONS OF THE INDEPENDENT NATIONAL ELECTORAL COMMISSION

In June 2006, the National Assembly passed into law the Electoral Act of 2006, which spelt out the statutory functions, rights, obligations and liabilities of the INEC. Accordingly, the activities leading to the conduct in the 2011 and 2015 of general elections derived their mandates from the 1999 Constitution and the Electoral Act of 2006, updated in 2010 as the 2010 Electoral Act and Amended as Electoral Act 2022 (INEC, 2017). The constitution thereby confers on the commission powers and responsibilities to undertake the following activities:

    i. Organise, undertake and supervise all elections to the offices of the president and the vice president, the governors and deputy governors of the thirty-six States of the Federation and to the Senate, the House of Representatives and the House of Assembly of each state of the federation;

   ii. Register political parties in accordance with the provisions of the constitution and an act of the National Assembly;

  iii. Monitor the organisation and the operations of political parties including their finances;

  iv. Arrange for an annual examination and auditing of the funds and accounts of the political parties and report on such examination and audit for public information purposes;

   v. Arrange and conduct the registration of persons qualified to vote, as well as prepare, maintain and revise the register of votes for any election under the constitution;

  vi. Monitor political campaigns and provide rules and regulations which shall govern the political parties;

 vii. Ensure that all electoral commissioners and returning officers take and subscribe to the oath of office prescribed by law;

viii. Delegate any of its powers to any of the states' Resident Electoral Commissioners; and

  ix. Carry out such other functions as may be conferred upon it by an act of the National Assembly.

The Electoral Act 2022 specifies in various sections and sub-sections powers and functions of INEC which interpret the previously discussed constitutional mandate. For instance, the role of the commission in registering voters and maintaining the record of the register is provided in Section 9(1–7) as follows:

> The Commission shall compile, maintain, and update, on a continuous basis, a National Register of Voters (in this Act referred to as 'the Register of Voters') which shall include the names of all persons – (a) entitled to vote in any Federal, State, Local Government or Federal Capital Territory Area Council election; and (b) with disability status disaggregated by type of disability. (2) The Commission shall keep the Register of Voters in its National Headquarters and other locations as the Commission may determine: Provided that the Commission shall keep the Register of Voters in – (a) electronic format in its central database; and (b) manual, printed, paper-based record or hard copy format. (3) The Commission shall maintain as part of the Register of Voters, a register of voters for each State of the Federation and for the Federal Capital Territory. (4) The Commission shall maintain as part of the Register of Voters for each State and the Federal Capital Territory, a Register of Voters for each Local Government or Area Council within the State and the Federal Capital Territory. (5) The Register of Voters shall contain, in respect of each person, the particulars required in the Form prescribed by the Commission. (6) The registration of voters, updating and revision of the Register of Voters under this section shall stop not later than 90 days before any election covered by this Act. (7) The registration of voters

shall be at the registration centres designated for that purpose by the Commission and notified to the public.

Section 28(1–4) provides powers for the INEC to conduct election and give the notice of the conduct of the election time as stated:

The Commission shall, not later than 360 days before the day appointed for holding of an election under this Act, publish a notice in each State of the Federation and the Federal Capital Territory (a) stating the date of the election; and (b) appointing the place at which nomination papers are to be delivered. (2) The notice shall be published in each constituency in respect of which an election is to be held. (3) In the case of a by-election, the Commission shall, not later than 14 days before the date appointed for the election, publish a notice stating the date of the election. (4) There shall not be substitution of candidates in a by-election except where a candidate of a political party in a by-election dies, the party shall submit to the Commission the name of its substitute candidate within seven days of the death of the candidate in the Form prescribed by the Commission.

Section 75(1–6) confers INEC with the powers to register political parties and other matters related to the registration, monitoring and sanctioning as stated next:

Any political association that complies with the provisions of the Constitution and this Act for the purposes of registration shall be registered as a political party: Powers of the Commission to register political parties. Page 31 of 119 House of Reps. PROVIDED however, that such application for registration as a political party shall be duly submitted to the Commission not later than 12 months before a general election. (2) The Commission shall, on receipt of the documents in fulfillment of the conditions stipulated by the Constitution, immediately issue the applicant with a letter of acknowledgement stating that all the necessary documents had been submitted to the Commission. (3) If the association has not fulfilled all the conditions under this section, the commission shall within 90 days from the receipt of its application notify the association in writing stating the reasons for non-registration. (4) A political association that meets the conditions stipulated in the Constitution and this Act shall be registered by the Commission as a political party within 60 days from the date of receipt of the application, and if after the 60 days such association is not registered by the Commission, unless the Commission informs the association to the contrary, it shall be deemed to have been registered. (5) An association, its executive member or principal officers who gives false or misleading information, commit an offence and is liable on conviction, in the case of (a) the association to a fine of N5,000,000; and (b) each executive or principal officer of the association to a fine of N3,000,000 or imprisonment for a term of at least two years or both. (6) An application for registration as a political party shall not be processed unless there is evidence of payment of administrative fee as may be fixed by the Commission.

Other functions related to the monitoring of parties, campaign spending limits, disclosure, auditing and sanctioning were analysed in chapter 7, there is no need to repeat them here. One vital development to comprehend in the Nigerian electoral laws is they are comprehensive and eloquent enough to safeguard the process but for the weak institutionalisation and political will to apply them indiscriminately.

INDEPENDENT NATIONAL ELECTORAL COMMISSION AND THE CONDUCT OF ELECTIONS IN THE FOURTH REPUBLIC

The INEC has successfully conducted six national elections from 1999 to 2019. Funds for conducting elections in Nigeria are provided by the executive arm of government through special appropriations. Nigerian elections unlike many African countries are sponsored by the Nigerian Government. The country holds the most expensive election in Africa in the 2015 general election at the cost of N125 billion ($301, 212, 075.00 million) and in the 2019 general election N240 billion ($578,327,184.00 million). These elections are more expensive than the UK and Canada elections respectively (Abdallah, 2018). INEC will not receive any foreign donations in cash to conduct an election according to the Constitution and Electoral Act but it can partner and collaborate with international donors for capacity building and technical assistance. Oftentimes, money for conducting elections in Nigeria are not easily provided. The case of the executive-legislative feud in the 2019 general election nearly jeopardised the process when the National Assembly dragged longer before they approved the funds for the election due to squabbles between them and the presidency. Additionally, the cost of an election in Nigeria is raising dust among the electorates. Many Nigerians are cynical that the system is expensive and unsuitable for a country like Nigeria with a high poverty rate, dwindling infrastructures and collapsing economy.

Elections by INEC in the Fourth Republic are enshrouded in the controversies of malfeasance, the phenomenon of postponement which is gradually becoming acculturated aspect of election conduct in Nigeria since it keeps on recurring in 2007, 2011, 2015 and 2019, logistics problems, violence and insecurity, malpractice and irregularities, low voter turnout, bribery and corruption and several other related issues as examined thoroughly in chapter 3. The elections are progressing but the people are despairing. Despite the improvement that is being recorded in the process, especially, from 2011, people are losing hope in the process and the situation is beyond the elections themselves or INEC a bigger picture avails. The attitude of the ruling class in pervasive corruption, looting, decaying infrastructure, maladministration, mismanagement of public resources, squandering of resources, chronic hunger and the scourge of poverty, joblessness and inequality and above all, the threats of insecurity all culminated in political apathy of Nigerians which translated into voter apathy. This process is beyond INEC or the elections themselves but the voter-leaders disconnection as observed by Dalton et al. (2011) and Norris (2015).

One feature of the conduct of the election by INEC in Nigeria is that the elite or politicians have been hijacking the entire process against the will of the commission and without the active support or approval of the commission. The commission will prepare well and expresses its readiness to undertake fair and credible elections at all levels, but politicians will sponsor touts and political violence that affects the process (Sule et al., 2017b). The INEC is frustrated with the habits of politicians in sabotaging its efforts in conducting fair elections. The integrity of the elections in Nigeria is compromised by politicians who are game-players and game-changers that resolved to win no matter the costs including assassination and intimidation or threat. The security agencies are accused of complicity and complacency in the subversion and diversion of the electoral process in Nigeria because the INEC mandated them with the task of preventing electoral materials both sensitive and non-sensitive and the peacekeeping during electoral conduct (Onapajo, 2019).

One vital progress that INEC achieved and which must be applauded in the conduct of elections in Nigeria is reforms that are improving the integrity and fairness of the process. In the 2010 Electoral Act, public funding was abrogated for private funding with the support and recommendation of INEC. This change helped immensely in saving funds that are offered as a grant to parties both the functioning and passive ones. Another feat achieved is the introduction of continuous voter registration even after the period of elections which opens a window for Nigerians that reached the age of eighteen and above, travelled abroad or lost their PVCs to register or re-register again. The INEC introduced accreditation before voting in the 2011 general election which set the foundation as a pilot test for the adoption of electronic and digital elections in future.

INEC recorded tremendous success in reforming elections in Nigeria from the 2011 general election. The 2015 general election saw the introduction of SCRs which Nwangwu et al. (2016) perceived as the elixir for electoral rigging and which Sule (2018) identifies as one of the reforms that led to the credibility and success of the 2015 general election. Voters were accredited and allowed to vote only if they have PVCs and this helped greatly in drastically curbing malpractice such as multiple voting, ballot paper thumping and inflation of figures and declaration of false results. The domestic and international observers hail INEC and the Nigerian Government for achieving such a feat in electoral conduct in 2015. The election was handled amid serious security threats from Boko Haram in northern Nigeria but it was tranquil and decent.

The successes recorded in the 2015 general elections were unfortunately reversed in the 2019 general elections when violence and allegations of malpractice characterised the election at all levels. The PDP Presidential flagbearer Alhaji Atiku Abubakar alleged that he won the election but it was rigged in favour of the APC candidate Muhammadu Buhari by the INEC. He suggested that he must be allowed access to the INEC server to prove his allegations but the INEC responded that they don't have a server that collated the results of the 2019 presidential election. In the gubernatorial elections at the state level, many cases of violence, inconclusive elections and rigging and vote-buying marred the process. This was worsened with attacks in many states like Kano, Rivers, Benue and Kogi on civil societies, domestic and international observers and media both local and international. The process was characterised by irregularities (Sule & Sambo, 2021).

However, despite several challenges and issues that bedevilled the conduct of elections by INEC in the Fourth Republic, the commission displayed some degrees of independence, non-partisanship and anonymity. For instance, the contractor that supplied SCRs in the build-up to the 2015 general election was coerced to reveal the identity and the workability of the machines but he declined to reveal them. Further, the INEC was pressurised by the PDP Government in the 2015 general election to abandon the use of SCRs for accreditation and voting proper but the commission declined, insisted and went ahead to use them (Adeniyi, 2017; Abdullahi, 2017). In many cases, parties will conduct primaries that failed to meet the guidelines of INEC, and INEC cancelled or disapproved such primaries. Candidates replaced illegally were rejected by INEC and several efforts to subdue the commission into submission to the whims of the ruling parties were rejected which is recommendable and encouraging as a good future of Nigerian elections and democracy (Sule et al., 2017b).

REGULATIONS IN FINANCING OF INDEPENDENT NATIONAL ELECTORAL COMMISSION

Section 3(1) of the Electoral Act 2022 provides that there is to be established for the commission a fund to be known as the INEC fund. But, Section 3(1) of the Electoral Act 2022 suggests that the source of funding for INEC should be extracted directly from the consolidated revenue fund budgeted by the commission, presented by the executive and approved by the lawmakers. Section

3(2) of the Electoral Act 2022 identifies other sources of the commission's funds including monies allowed by the Federal Government to enable it to exercise its constitutional functions, monies accruing to it by way of interests from investments made on the fund, aids and grants made by development partners to facilitate its ability to carry out its functions. Furthermore, the commission subject to Section 3(3) of the Electoral Act 2022 is to be funded under six budgetary heads, namely

(1) Consolidated revenue fund charges (including personal emoluments of National Commissioners and Resident Electoral Commissioners).
(2) Cost comprising salaries and allowances of staff of the Commission.
(3) Overhead comprising office running costs, travels and transportation, the maintenance of equipment, utilities, bank charges etc.
(4) Special electoral capital comprising the cost of balloting instruments (i.e. ballot papers, results sheets, ballot boxes etc).
(5) Special electoral capital (including ad hoc staff training cost, allowances of ad hoc registration and poll officials, etc.) and other structural capital (comprising the construction of buildings, purchase and installation of equipment like generators etc).
(6) Purchase of vehicles etc.

There is no doubt that INEC was adequately funded in the 2011 and 2015 General elections to ensure that credible and fair elections were carried out with fewer obstacles and logistics problems that INEC faced in the 2003 and 2007 elections. Having examined the problem of underfunding which bedevilled the previous elections in Nigeria, the electoral reforms recommended increased funding of INEC and the government responded positively. The INEC was funded with the highest allocation in the history of the country in the 2015 general election in its preparation to conduct an election that will improve the process and it paid off because a significant improvement was recorded. The INEC recorded success in its conduct of the 2015 general election largely due to huge cash backup from the government and logistic support from international donors and agencies in the training of staff, provision of vital information and supply of equipment as well as observation (Sule, 2018).

The electoral body got enough funding from the government and this helped immensely in procuring equipment for the conduct of the 2015 general election such as the SCR which assisted in the easy conduct of the election. Foreign funding of the electoral body was prohibited by the Nigerian law, the government found it necessary to provide adequate funding for INEC and this helped immensely in improving electoral conduct. The 2019 general election is more expensive than the 2015 general election but the hiccups encountered in funding the 2019 election were not encountered in the 2015 election. The executive-legislative conflicts delayed the approval and release of funds for the 2019 general election and that has affected the process of reminiscing in postponement and low voter turnout (Sule et al., 2019b).

In the 2007 general election, INEC spent N45.5 billion ($108, 462, 454.10 million). The 2011 general election gulped over N111 billion ($264, 600, 712.20 million), the 2015 general election N125 billion ($297, 973, 775.00 million) and the 2019 general election cost about N240 billion ($572,109,648.00 million) (Sambo & Sule, 2021). This implies that Nigeria had spent more than Canada in the 2007 general election, more than the UK in the 2011 general election and more than Australia in the 2015 general election (Abdallah, 2018). This is the justification of the aforementioned statement by Sule (2018) that INEC is adequately funded by the Nigerian Government to conduct a good election. However, it is observed (Sule et al., 2017b and Sambo & Sule, 2021) that INEC needs to prepare all electoral materials six months before the election time to avoid continuous postponement and other logistics problems. The government should provide the required fund at least one year before the election period but this has been excellently done and included in the Electoral Act 2022. But less than eight months to the election dateline, there is no budget sent to the National Assembly to that effect and that has signified that this section in the regulations will be violated or disrespected.

INDEPENDENT NATIONAL ELECTORAL COMMISSION AND MONITORING OF CAMPAIGN FINANCES, PARTIES AND CANDIDATES

INEC is empowered by the Constitution and Electoral Act 2022 to monitor and sanction parties and their activities. Section 225 and Section 226 together with their sub-sections in the 1999 Constitution provide powers to INEC to limit parties' expenditure, audit their finances, monitor their campaign spending, inspect their books and expenditure and set a limit or guide their activities while punishing or sanctioning the defaulters or violators. The necessary powers and legal backing that INEC needs to promote accountability and transparency of the electoral process are adequately given in the 1999 Constitution. The laws are well-articulated and unambiguous when it comes to the issue of regulation and monitoring of parties and their candidates. The main obstacles as observed severally are a lack of cooperation and political will to utilise the powers as appropriate.

The Electoral Act 2022 provides INEC with additional powers apart from the 1999 Constitution to monitor parties and their activities. The processes and measures taken guarantee transparency and accountability if the laws are implemented accordingly by the INEC. For example, Section 88(1–7) of the Electoral Act set a maximum expenditure limit for parties and their candidates in campaign financing to be implemented and monitored by INEC. Section 88(8) provides powers to INEC to sanction those who violate the provisions in Section 88(1–7) with a fine of 1percent of the amount for each of the elective offices, imprisonment for one year or both. This means INEC has powers to compel compliance in campaign expenditure, especially, considering that the maximum spending limit has been reviewed upward in the Electoral Act 2022 by 400percent to allow for reality to manifest.

In Section 89(1–3), INEC is mandated to set a limit for election expenses of political parties in collaboration with the parties based on what the commission feels is appropriate and in consideration of other factors at the time of the decision. Section 89(3) specifically empowers INEC to receive the books of parties indicating their income and expenditure as audited and to inspect the books within a stipulated time. Section 89(4) provides a sanction of N1 million if it contravenes any provision in Section 89(1–3). Section 89(7) provides that any party that spent beyond the set limit will be fined a sum of N1 million and is liable to forfeit the amount of the expenditure to the commission. This section as analysed in chapter 5 is weak in the provision of the sanction which is believed to be encouraging for the offence because it is negligible but the prime purpose of the provisions is deterrence if INEC can develop the zeal to operate them which is the most important aspect of monitoring. INEC can also generate revenue from fines and other charges of the offenders thereby reducing cash over-reliance on the consolidated revenue.

Section 88(8–11) empowers INEC to set a maximum limit for contribution from individuals and corporate bodies pegged at N50 million, a fair amount that is in tandem with the political reality in the country in comparison with the N1 million in the Electoral Act 2010. Other sections which may not be mentioned here as they were analysed in chapter 7 empower INEC to monitor and sanction offences while enforcing disclosure and auditing. The purpose of presenting some sections here is to demonstrate the powers and the legal backing that INEC has in enforcing compliance and sanctioning of the defaulters to understand that INEC has the legal backing to monitor campaign finances and not only to monitor but to sanction where the laws are violated.

The question now that is being asked is how well did INEC monitored campaign financing in Nigeria and to what extent has the monitoring deterred or prevented violations? Parties are involved in fundraising sometimes during election campaigns and they received donations from individuals and groups as well. One example of the violation of campaign financing is the fundraising made by the former ruling PDP in the build-up to the 2015 presidential election.

The fundraising as reported by Nwangwu and Ononogbu (2016) showcased a massive violation of the contribution ban where some individuals that are not expected to contribute more than a maximum of N1 million donated N1 billion, 1,000 times more than the limit, an unimaginable violation. The INEC never call them to account or sanction the parties that are involved in the violation.

On the open violation, Aluigba (2015) quoted Professor Jonah Onuoha in an interview with the *Punch* newspaper on 4 January 2015, making a critical assessment of the PDP fundraising as follows:

> But if you look at the recent fundraiser for President Goodluck Jonathan's 2015 re-election bid, it's all too easy to see there is a problem. The electoral act stipulates that a presidential candidate cannot raise more than N1bn for his or her campaign. Therefore, what we are contending with here is not the fundraiser but the amount generated the amount cannot be justified. The law is very clear on the amount of money to be donated. What we have seen in that fundraiser is a clear violation of the electoral law. Other issues like whether those who donated money for the president are corrupt people or not do not arise here. I will admit that they have a right to raise money for campaigns but the People's Democratic Party will have some explanations to do about the amount donated to it.

The violators sometimes even tried to justify their actions shamelessly. Such an example was given by Ohman (2014) when a business tycoon, Alhaji Abdussamad Rabi'u, donated a sum of N250 million to the Goodluck Jonathan campaign fundraising and when his attention was drawn he responded that since the maximum limit is N1 million for each individual, there was no violation here because he received a donation of N1 million each from his family members, 250 of them making the total to be N250, a laughable scenario. Another cause of an open violation is the excessive campaign spending in the 2015 general election by the two major parties of the APC and the PDP. The parties are required by the old law of the Electoral Act 2010 to spend a maximum of N1 billion. But their media campaign finances alone illustrate the following.

The media spending of two major political parties (APC and PDP) in the 2015 general elections in billions of Nigerian naira revealed the following: campaigns and rallies for PDP N280,374,870.00 million and for APC N671,062,200.00 million, expenses on billboards for PDP N473,160,000.00 million and N190,380,000.00 million for APC, electronic media campaign for PDP N532,100,000.00 million and N410,050,000.00 million for APC, electronic media advert for PDP N3,988,822,125.00 billion and N1,064,706,805.00 billion for APC and print media campaign for PDP N2,475,228,301.00 billion and N579,647,687.00 million for APC. The accumulated media expenditure alone for PDP totalled N8,749,685,296.00 billion and for APC N2,915,846,737.00 billion (Onyekpere, 2015).

Other studies (Sule et al., 2017b; Sule et al., 2018c; Sule, 2019; Sule & Sambo, 2021; Sule et al., 2022) reported the cases of open violation and failure of the INEC to take decisive action. For example, in the party primaries of the APC and PDP at the National Assembly and governorship elections, reports of vote-buying and bribery were presented by observers and the media. In the PDP Presidential primaries, it was reported that some candidates bribed the delegates with as much as $5,000 to secure the nomination. Despite several reports and evidence to justify the allegations, no action is taken by INEC. The INEC itself indicted the parties of the failure to comply with the process when in the 2011 audit report of political parties that was published, the INEC indicted all the then-existing fifty-five parties for their inability to properly keep their books of accounts as enshrined in Section 93(2) of the Electoral Act 2010 (Aluigba, 2015). This means that the INEC is willing and ready to monitor and sanction the violators if it had the capacity and the support it needed to do so as against some perceptions that INEC willingly overlooked the violation.

There are several factors why INEC is not effectively monitoring parties and their campaign expenditure or finances. Money politics and the difficulty in checking and detecting sources of funds for parties are one of them (Sule et al., 2019b). Another obstacle is the lack of capacity of the INEC to effectively monitor the finances of many parties because INEC has offices in the 36 states of the federation and offices in the 774 local governments with inadequate staff to operate (Aluigba, 2015). Lack of cooperation as reported by Sule (2018) is another barrier to the effective monitoring of parties' finances in Nigeria. In most cases, the INEC officials will write to the parties' secretariats requesting audited books or to audit the books but the response is discouraging. The party officials will ask the INEC officials to wait till the 'oga' (a common pidgin word used to show a superior officer) returned from his travel or till I get clearance from the higher authorities in Abuja or the Government House. Hence, the issue is not the regulations that by themselves have their loopholes as identified and discussed elsewhere, the bigger problem is the implementation of the laws to enforce compliance and sanction accordingly. This will require a reform that will involve all stakeholders, particularly, the civil societies and the electorates who can do better in pressurising the politicians and watching them than INEC.

Chapter 9

Party Financing and Money Politics

Money politics is a universal problem and not a unique incidence in the Nigerian state alone. Democracy in the twenty-first century become competitive and the scramble for votes by politicians is an activity that requires massive financial support. The lobby for votes, persuasion to support and the presentation of parties' nominees are all activities that require cash backing. The resources required to attain the democratic project are huge and the states cannot cater for this phenomenon even in the case of areas or states where public funding is operated. The competition for power control has its own price and the corresponding sacrifices that involved energy, time, resources and other valuable possessions. Democracy is the most expensive form of government because power contest is consuming resources through multi-level processes including reaching out to the electorates through the media and other channels such as direct contact and social media. To secure the nomination of parties today, candidates must spend resources and all these are required to be carried out using money.

Money politics dominated the democratic scene across the globe. The advanced democracies are never absolved of the effects of money politics. Nichols and McChesney (2013) lamented that because of the huge use of money in the American elections and politics, democracy is dollarised to the biggest investors. Ohman (2016) argues that European democracies are bedevilled with the menace of money politics and gradually the freedom of choice in the custom of democracy is being relegated to a choiceless strategy by the moneybags where the plutocrats hijacked politics systematically with their resources. Piccio and Van Biezen (2018) stress that the influx of money in global democracies is threatening the accountability and the transparency that democracy promises as to its main principle of governance and it is eroding the integrity of elections as argued by Norris (2018a). Money politics has several impacts including the side-lining of credible candidates that could not compete financially with the oligarchs, politicians prioritise their personal goals and interests ahead of representation and the public common good, malpractice and deceit occur on the part of the politicians and apathy and low political culture prevailed.

In the Nigerian context, money politics is identified as one of the biggest problems that are affecting elections and democratisation in the Fourth Republic. Many studies (Walecki, 2003; Walecki et al., 2006; Adetula, 2008; Adeyi, 2008; Aiyede, 2008; Ayoade, 2008; Best, 2008; Ojo, 2008; Smah, 2008; Walecki, 2008; Ologbenla & Adisa, 2012; Lucky, 2014; Onah & Nwali, 2018; Sule et al., 2018e; Babatunde et al., 2019; Nelson & Saka-Olokungboye, 2019; Omoyele et al., 2019; Okeke & Nwali, 2020; Nwozor et al., 2021; Davies, 2021) explored the nature, causes, manifestations and consequences of money politics in Nigeria's Fourth Republic, specifically on the integrity and the quality of elections. One irony of money politics in Nigeria is the pattern in which politicians spend lavishly and exorbitantly in a country where poverty and squalor are throwing a significant percentage of the population into deprivation and impoverished life. The level of Nigerian poverty is falsified by the extravagant spending of politicians in their bid to actualise their political ambition. For instance, a country where poverty affects more than 50percent of the population according to the National Bureau of Statistics (2022) is witnessing twenty-five aspirants buying a nomination form for the presidential position in the ruling All Progressives Congress (APC) at the cost of N100 million in the APC primaries in May 2022. This will discredit the claim of insufficient funds by the Nigerian Government to cater for the basic needs of the poor (Ogbeifun, 2022).

Systematically, money politics is threatening to bastardise the Nigerian democratisation into a plutocrat's aristocratic version of ruling witnessed in the medieval era when the rulers feed fat on the treasury of the state and became wealthier than the state itself. Politics has become a lucrative investment and a business venture that pays dividends instantly to investors. Gradually, the poor and the average are screened out from contesting any position while bribery and corruption have escalated political corruption unabated and with impunity. The menace of money politics is urging the stakeholders who are keenly following the trajectories of the unfolding events to call for reforms and actions immediately. Money politics takes place in the process of party financing. The process of campaign expenditure is tantalising the excessive use of money to secure victory for the oligarchs' politicians in Nigeria. Thus, this chapter examines the relationship between money politics and party financing and how they are affecting the electoral process in the country.

THE POLITICAL CULTURE AND POLITICAL ECONOMY OF MONEY POLITICS

Party financing and its corresponding political corruption are universal to all democracies in the world. However, the Nigerian party financing process is influenced by two major factors: political culture and political economy. Nigeria has a history of the existence of various political systems with different political structures during the pre-colonial period. Some political organisations were centralised such as the Hausa states, the Oyo Empire, Kanem Bornu Empire, Tiv Kingdom and the Jukun Kingdom with others decentralised consisting of Igbo and Niger Delta societies (Audu & Oshewolo, 2021). During colonialism, all those entities with different roots, political structures, history and other dynamic institutions were compelled into a marriage of convenience for British easy access to resources of Nigerian territory. The new institutions, structures and systems introduced in the Nigerian colony were alien and not compatible with the indigenous culture and political economy of pre-colonialism. After political independence, the country found it difficult to settle within the framework of foreign structures that it was installed (Akanji, 2021).

Thus, the foundation of Nigerian political culture began with regional parties, ethnic elites, religious leaders and regional affiliation. The electorates voted in colonial elections according to their ethnic, regional and religious identities. During that period, the influence of money was minimal because of stronger elements that meant more than money or any material value to the voters (Sule et al., 2017). Electorates were mobilised and socialised based on the trio elements identified previously. The elites were not exceptionally obsessed with money or seeking power to accumulate. Instead, some were ideological like Awolowo's AG and Malam Aminu Kano's NEPU which were socialist in orientation. Other party leaders are interested in capturing power to the advantage and development of their regions and ethnic groups. Money was less influential (Sule et al., 2017c).

The intrusion of the military into Nigerian politics radically altered the political system. The military set Nigeria on the dangerous trend of authoritarian states with repressive politics. The clamp down on media and civil societies enabled the military to rule as they wish leading to looting and accumulation. The politicians, eagerly and covertly watching the scenario in military rule, in some instances, co-ruling together as civil administrative subordinates, developed the culture of accumulation and personalisation of politics. The civilians with active support from external forces and domestic civil societies pressed the military for democratisation to which the military succumbed in 1979 (Adedire & Olanrewaju, 2021). Unfortunately, a few years into the over-celebrated and much sought-after democracy, Nigerians were not satisfied with the direction of the ship. Meanwhile, unlike the previous experience, politicians, in addition to the exploitation of regional, ethnic and religious sentiments, exposed Nigerian voters to the intricacies and vagaries of money politics. Clientelism and patrimonialism emerged. Vote-buying, bribery, money for political support, contract awards to cronies and other abuses of state resources and corrupt practices emerged (Olayode, 2015).

The Nigerian political culture continues in the pattern of Second Republic politics. The military returned boldly and escalated political corruption. The euphoria that heralded the resurgence of civilian rule in the Fourth Republic in 1999 was unprecedented. Nigerians were framed and situated in expectation of accountable and transparent management of state resources and responsive representative government. Unfortunately, the military covertly sneaked into the political arena and dominate major party decisions and politics, particularly, in the former ruling People's Democratic Party (PDP) and the current ruling APC. Moneybags and godfathers became decisive factors in the political victory. Electorates were bought and electoral officials (Adedire & Olanrewaju, 2021).

In the process, a lethal political culture is innovated by Nigerian politicians. The politics of winning elections at all costs orchestrate political violence, manipulation of the electoral process, excessive use of money and other influential means to secure electoral victory. Thus, Nigerian elections were reported aggressive, violent bedevilled with malpractice, irregularities, characterised by massive riggings and worse of all, looting and raping of the national treasury by a few ruling elites who constitute themselves as power brokers, monopolised politics and control national resources (Adams & Agomor, 2015). A fresh pattern of electoral politics known in the Nigerian language as do-or-die emanates from politics of violence. Politicians hire thugs, bribe electoral officials, collaborate with security agencies, buy the media, silence civil societies, suppress opposition and intimidate voters (Sule et al., 2017c). All these are efficacious in drawing electoral victory to the Nigerian elites because of abject penury, high rate of unemployment, deprivation, dysfunctional infrastructures, collapsing educational system and other indicators of social backwardness that overshadow reasoning and active responses of the citizenry. Voters become easily manipulated and deceived by politicians using a token during the voting process. Once these politicians acquire power, they engage in massive looting to recoup their investments, enrich themselves and accumulate enough to arrest comfortably the next election and beyond (Bogaards, 2010).

The culture of money politics is propelled by the Nigerian political economy. To understand the Nigerian political economy and its impacts on the party financing process and electoral and political corruption, reflection is germane on the historical inter-play that shaped the state itself and the political economy. Before the advent of colonial exploiters, the various kingdoms, chiefdoms and societies mentioned earlier that eventually formed the present-day Nigerian territory were engaged in subsistence farming, commercial agriculture, commerce, merchandise and craftsmanship as well as other occupations both traditional and non-traditional (Adewara, 2021). Taxes were paid based on personal income, trade goods and services. In Northern Nigeria, poll tax (Jizyah in Arabic) and Jangali (cattle taxes) were collected. People respected and obeyed their rulers and they paid their tributes willingly in most cases. Trade in agricultural commodities, mining, products and other occupations formed the major sources of revenue for the rulers (Akhaine, 2020).

Colonialism altered the evolutionary destiny of the Nigerian political economy by replacing the political systems of absolute monarchy in some kingdoms and chiefdoms with a loose decentralised system while reversibly, introducing a flexible centralised system in non-centralised societies (Sule-Kano, 2020). Superior power and administrative decision-making were usurped by the British colonisers gradually. The economy was redirected from the production of food crops to cash crops and heavy taxes were introduced on both products and personal heads (Aderemi et al., 2020). Due to the harsh effects of the taxation system, many attempts were reported of protests and violence, especially in South Nigerian territory including the Aba Women Riot of 1925 and many others (Siollun, 2021). A modern money system was introduced and wage labour was introduced.

During colonialism, the Nigerian political economy was dominated by agricultural products, trades, craftsmanship and taxes. After political independence, destiny was disrupted and suddenly Nigeria became a commercial oil producer in the 1960s (Olaoye et al., 2020). This discovery harmed the Nigerian political economy and consolidated its structural overdependence and economic laziness on the monoeconomy. The ruling class relaxed and relied solely on oil exportation as the mainstay of foreign earnings. The seemingly cheap oil money crippled the drive toward policies of diversification, industrialisation, mechanisation of agriculture and exploration of the bountiful Nigerian resources both human and material (Ayobade, 2020). The scramble for controlling power by elites intensified. A fierce rivalry emanated between the military and civilians in the control of power and the Nigerian economy (Le Van, 2015). The Nigerian economy was handicapped by the mercies, brutalities and fluctuations of global oil prices and eventualities that influenced fixing the price. If any influential global war or economic volatility emerges, oil shocks and oil boom enrich Nigeria and its peers as in the case of the Gulf War in the 1990s but if the reverse occurs like the COVID-19 outbreak, the oil glut paralyses the Nigerian economy. The other oil-producing states converted the excess proceeds for diversification into tourism, industrialisation and commercial agriculture thereby cushioning the effects of future oil shocks. Sadly, Nigeria refused to prepare for the rainy day and continues to be at the mercy of the forces of demand and supply deliberately (Akinsola, 2020).

The Nigerian oil economy converted the ruling class into rapacious and chronic accumulators of wealth. Power struggles are wealth-driven while primitive accumulation dominates the scene. Politics become synonymous with access to wealth. In the process, the military and political class successfully created a master-slave relationship between the rulers and the citizens. In between, a middle or intermediary class was created that is responsible for brokering a political bargain between the patrons and clients (Le Van, 2015). Thus, when democracy resumed in the Fourth Republic in 1999, the system met on the ground a well-organised elite that is characterised by selfish motives, a desire for accumulation and a penchant for insatiable power control. Equally, democratic rule in the Fourth Republic encountered a poorly organised citizenry, devastated by poverty, deprived of inadequate infrastructures, pummelled by unemployment, hunger, malnourishment, diseases, illiteracy and divided by ethnic, regional and religious manipulation of the elites, the political class finds it easy to use money excessively to buy power (Onuoha, 2020).

The oil politics and competition over national resources established a culture of money politics and the political economy of neoliberal policies that are vehemently pursued by elites who are often misled by global neoliberal institutions and agencies to withdraw all forms of government support to the populace thereby further crippling the economy and impoverish millions who are edge out from a decent means of living to the poverty line and destitution (Ovadia, 2020). The ruling class is comfortable with the teeming ignorant and restive population who see an election period as a bazaar for leasing votes to the highest bidder due to the scourge of poverty. The ruling class having accumulated much from oil contracts, shoddy deals and looting set aside some percentage to buy their way into power again and perpetuate their hold on power control. Thus, excessive spending, vote-buying, bribery and electoral corruption in the process of party financing cascade into political corruption and broader corruption in Nigeria (Le Van, 2015).

NATURE OF MONEY POLITICS IN NIGERIA

Money politics in Nigeria historically predates the country's independence. The foundation of money politics in Nigeria was set by the colonial rulers in the 1922 Clifford Constitution which introduced the Elective Principle and created four elective seats: three for Lagos and one for Calabar. The Clifford's Elective Principle enabled suffrage for the first time in Nigeria, an income-based franchise. The provision of the Elective Principle set a pre-requisite for the exercise of a franchise on financial qualification. The elector-ates are qualified if they have an annual income of £100 or more to participate in the election. This pre-requisite was set at a period when the annual salary of most Nigerians was less than £100. The consequence was that many Nige-rians were disenfranchised since they could not contest or even vote in elec-tions. Therefore, between 1923 and 1946, only four Nigerians were elected as members of the Legislative Council by electorates composed of the wealthier members of the communities (Onah & Nwali, 2018).

Money politics determine who secures electoral victory and power in Nigeria. This is because some oligarchs and plutocrats, a group of small members known as godfathers have hijacked and taken over the control of the electoral process in Nigeria. These godfathers are multinational business tycoons, retired army generals, retired paramilitary echelons, technocrats and bureaucrats and corporate establishments that are controlling the Nige-rian economy (Olarinmoye, 2008). The godfathers financed their anointed candidates to control national power and the economy by proxy because the anointed godsons pursue their interests and succumb to their biddings for political offices (Ayoade, 2008). Once the godfathers installed their godsons in power, they devise means of recouping the money spent to secure victory for the godsons. These mechanisms used include inflated contracts for kick-backs, offering them lucrative appointments to plant their stooges which is another method of kickback and accumulation, nepotism and patrimonialism (Sule et al., 2018c).

Nigeria has a long history of godfatherism in its politics which is syn-onymous with money politics because the godfathers are the moneybags that sponsored politicians. Post and Jenkins (1976) traced the root of godfatherism to Southwest Nigeria, particularly in the city of Ibadan where one Adelabu emerged as the sponsor of politicians and this culture was maintained in the city of Ibadan and beyond when in the Fourth Republic, Alhaji Lamidi Ade-dibu became the tenant of the Oyo politics determining who wins what and how using his moneybags (Omobowale & Olutayo, 2010). The same scenario persists in the southeast city of Anambra, where the Ubas family is notorious for godfatherism. They went to the shrine and swore an oath of allegiance with the former Anambra state governor Chris Ngige on certain conditions. When Ngige failed to satisfy their interest, they engineered his impeachment (Human Rights Watch, 2007).

Money politics takes the nature of vote-buying which involved a clien-tele transaction among the politicians, electorates, parties, party officials, electoral officials and other stakeholders. In some instances where direct vote-buying will not yield the anticipated result, politicians and their god-fathers sponsored thuggery and allied with security personnel to ostracise the voters from the polling units to give them the needed breathing space to perpetrate their crimes of altering polling results. Vote-buying are being reported in all the Nigerian elections increasingly since 1999. Money politics has gradually taken the centre stage of Nigerian democratisation to the extent that the strength of one's pocket influences his chance of securing the party's nomination and winning the final elections (Sule et al., 2018c). The phenomenon of vote-buying is escalating and is accentuated by the desperation of politicians to win by hook or by crook. From buying votes at the cost of N100, N200 and N500, politicians bought votes in the 2019 general election per voter at the cost of N15,000 (Sule, 2019; Sule et al., 2019b). The phenomenon of vote-buying portends a dilemma for the Nigerian election and democracy because leadership is completely converted into business.

It is of course noticeable that money is an important ingredient of election and democracy worldwide and without money, politics will be inapproachable by many ambitious politicians and the inalienable rights of the parties to contest for political positions rest on the ability to mobilise resources to garner influence and sale ideas to sail through. Political party financing involves money and modern democracies are increasingly detaching public funds from private political ambition. Public funding is being de-emphasised for full private funding to foster accountability and transparency. Unfortunately, political party financing is an avenue that enables scandalous use of money such as excessive spending, illicit sourcing of campaign funds, abuse of state resources, violation of maximum spending limit, evading disclosure and other dubious ways of avoiding transparency (Nelson & Saka-Olokungboye, 2019). In essence, money politics and party financing lubricates corrupt practices in environments like Nigeria where enforcement is weak and ineffective.

Political finance is influenced by money politics and the process of party funding influences relations between parties, politicians, party membership and the electorates. Political party financing is centrally dominating the debates on political corruption across the globe. The clandestine donations by the plutocrats and the breaking of rules in contribution ban are tantamount to illegal financing. The link between party financing, money politics and corruption has been established to the extent that any reform in fighting corruption in Nigeria that neglects this aspect will backfire unsuccessfully. Vote-buying has deprived Nigerians of enjoying the luxury of electoral choice and democratic participation (Adeyi, 2008). Many voters believed that elections are about to give and take in negotiation of cash and carry where the highest bidder is elected. A particular political culture of money politics is now embedded in Nigerian democracy.

The campaign process in Nigeria is affected tremendously by money politics. Politicians do not care to display their performances, legacies and goodwill to get elected. Once one gathered enough resources (in many cases from the public treasury), he feels himself fit to contest for any elective position. The cost of the campaign is shot up astronomically by the use of money politics (Walecki, 2008). Visibly, electorates are wooed with money to vote for candidates with financial muscles but the nature of money politics in Nigeria is beyond what mere eyes can see. Those intending to aspire for political offices must covertly settle traditional rulers, religious clerics, the media, opinion moulders, security personnel and electoral officials in addition to other relevant stakeholders. These influential figures are settled with money in some instances as in the case of the 2015 and 2019 general elections, in foreign currencies, specifically, the dollar and British sterling pound (Sule et al., 2018d). Without enough money, one cannot venture into politics in Nigeria. This is an explanation of why gender and unprivileged classes in Nigeria hardly compete for any electoral office (Best, 2008).

The annoying aspect of money politics is that sometimes the money spent to arrest campaign expenditure is looted from the public treasury. The scarce resource that is meant to provide basic services and infrastructures to the populace are diverted by the ruling class to fill their purse to have more than enough to pursue the future political ambition. As observed by Ohman (2014) in a cross-country study of political finance, African countries and indeed, other world countries, are guilty of abuse of state resources in campaign funding. The Nigerian case manifested in many instances. Politicians that passed through an electoral process poor emerged super wealthy with enough money to compete favourably for more offices. This is justified in a study by Sule et al. (2019a) in investigating the sources of parties' campaign expenditure that about 27percent of the sources of campaign financing in Nigeria are from the loot of the public treasury by the ruling class.

Money politics takes the shape of a bargain to settle the parties to secure the nomination and then to buy the parties' delegates to score votes that will earn the richest a victory in the party primaries. This is a Herculean task, because millions or billions of naira are spent by the contestants depending on the position that one is aspiring for. After the nomination is dusted, another difficulty is competing for votes which are marketed by the voters because they were negatively inculcated with a misperceived idea that elections are a money-making period and they must seize the opportunity to enrich themselves or get their share of booty before the election season pass (Ologbenla & Adisa, 2012). While all these activities are taking place, politicians compounded the process with the eloquent promise of making life better for Nigerians. Attempts by the media and the civil societies as well as other concerned citizens to enlighten the voters could not yield the required result because of culture, perception, poverty and ignorance (Babatunde et al., 2019).

Money politics is theoretically given attention by many scholars. Clientelism is one of them. Scholars (Roniger, 2004; Darabont, 2010; Doublet; 2010; Lindberg & Morrison, 2010; Aspinall & Berenschot, 2019) described how money politics and vote-buying lead to a series of negotiation and renegotiations by clients, brokers and patrons in promising rewards and benefit to the two sides of the bargain which involves political corruption in it. In another theoretical postulation, Downs (1957), Arrows (1951), Arrows (1968), Olson (1961) and Kuhn (2018) emphasised that election and power contests are a similitude of rational choice in economic equilibrium. As consumers strive to have the best choice and maximum satisfaction from the purchase of a commodity with scarce resources on a scale of preference, so the voters are determined to derive maximum benefits from their votes or choice of leaders in the same way that the leaders or politicians are ever ready to maximise profits just like investors or entrepreneurs in the market. On another dimension, Morgenstern and Von Neumann (1957) and Smith (2015) support that elections are game-playing like soccer and other plays. As players and teams strategise and take risky decisions in intense competition to outwit their competitors and win that is how politicians play games in the election including money politics, vote-buying, rigging and other strategies that anchor victory to them.

CAUSES OF MONEY POLITICS IN NIGERIA

A major cause of money politics in Nigeria is political desperation to win power at all costs. Politicians in Nigeria are intolerant of losing power and are so desperate that they can adopt any measure to win. They know quite the benefits and the luxuries that are attached to their office away from the public scrutiny and this gingered them to seek victory at all costs including vote-buying and money politics. A former senate president, Adolphus Wabara, confessed that politics is a business in Nigeria. He was quoted saying

> You invest huge sums of money so as to reap bountifully, by way of fat pay packages, spurious allowances and inflated contracts. With all these firmly in place can that intelligent, patriotic but poor citizen ever get to the pedestal of political power? And will our type of democracy ever favour those on the lowest rung of the societal ladder? I have my doubts. (Baje, 2022)

These privileges mentioned by the former senate president are what forced the Nigerian politicians to seek electoral victory by spending huge resources.

Political parties devoid of ideologies are causing money politics in Nigeria. In party politics with a well-established ideology and institutionalisation and organisation, voters are lured with the promise of ideological pay-off, and their enthusiasm is anchored on the ideological leaning to support parties and candidates. In Nigerian politics, parties are not ideological and they do not have any principle upon which they built their action plan. Their purchasing and bargaining power is the use of money excessively to buy power, buy votes, bribe electoral officials, bribe the security personnel and buy who-soever cares to cooperate. This process is a cycle because once a party or a politician used the money to get power, they will recoup their investment, make profits and then accumulate it for a future campaign expenditure. This scenario led to massive stealing and exportation of Nigeria's resources for investment in a tax havens and other islands with security such as Panama and Dubai (Sule & Sambo, 2020).

The Nigerian political structure and its heterogeneous nature contributed to money politics. Nigeria operates strong federalism constitutionally where a huge resource allocation formula favours the centrifugal unit against the centripetal components. To access these huge resources at the centre, politi-cians used not only religion, ethnicity and regionalism but money to earn a representation at the national level which reward them with material accu-mulation. At the state level, the nature of ethnic composition and plurality made holding state powers accessible to state resources and distributing them to the cronies and clans and kins. Politicians used money excessively to win to have control over local resources and to distribute favours to their families and friends. The prime aim is to enrich self by the politicians themselves through inflated contracts, kickbacks, diversion of resources and looting.

The low level of political culture and socialisation is a contributory factor to money politics in Nigeria. Ignorance and low civic-voter education turned the Nigerian voters into a conglomerate of electoral retailers who exhibit their products during a trade fair or in a bazaar. Most Nigerians according to Adet-ula (2008) perceived that money is necessary to arrest any electoral ambition and they could not vote until they are given a token because they believed that politicians will never fulfil their campaign promises and they will never look back to their constituencies until the next election (Onah & Nwali, 2018). This negative perception is also reported by Sule (2018) in fieldwork where some of the informants narrated that they believed that money must be given to them before they elect any candidate because they don't have confidence in the promises of politicians after power. Since the electorates are yet to understand the linkage between voting and policymaking, voting and repre-sentation, voting and political change, voting and influence of public decision and voting and political participation, they will never value elections as the process that can touch their lives positively or negatively depending on their actions to it.

Poverty and socio-economic crises in Nigeria aided money politics. Nigerian poverty is a paradox of deprivation in affluence. The country is not poor in nature but the inactions and character of its voracious rapacious scavenging elite pushed many into unwanted penury (Yahaya et al., 2021). From 1960 to 2017, the African Union reported that over $500 billion (N207,500,000,000,000.00 trillion) was stolen from the Nigerian treasury. The World Poverty Clock (2020) reported Nigeria as the world poverty headquarters in 2020 taking over from India and China respectively. About 95.1 million (50percent) of Nigerians are in poverty. The scourge of poverty obfuscates the right-thinking faculty of the poor and when election time comes, they are given a negligible token and they will eagerly collect and vote for the highest bidder. This scenario is further pushing Nigerians into poverty because those who utilised the opportunity of their poverty to win elections will never improve their standard of living but will prefer to keep them perpetually in a vulnerable situation that will enable them for buying their votes and support in future.

Money politics is enhanced in Nigeria by weak laws and regulations. The sections on party monitoring and campaign monitoring are good as provided in the Nigerian 1999 Constitution in Sections 225 and 226 and their sub-sections and several sections of Electoral Act 2022 but the sections on sanctioning are flexible and weak to deter errant behaviours on violation of regulations and compliance. Weak monitoring by INEC motivates politicians to buy votes which is an offence in the Electoral Act 2022. But because politicians are not apprehended and are not sanctioned even where compelling evidence appeared, they continued to buy their way through money politics by violating regulations and engaging in illegality. The challenge is not the rules themselves. They have their weak points. Implementation and effective monitoring to compel compliance is the problem. One of the many examples occurred in one of the states in the presidential election where the weakness and ineffectiveness of the sanctions were exposed when a local government councillor was caught handing out N295,000 thousand ($710.50 hundred) to voters. The Economic and Financial Crimes Commission (EFCC) arrested and charged him in court on three counts bordering on vote-buying. But on conviction, the trial judge sentenced him to one month in prison on each count but with an option of fines totalling N170,000 thousand ($409.50 hundred) only which is negligible considering the enormity of the offence (Okeke & Nwali, 2020).

MANIFESTATIONS OF MONEY POLITICS IN NIGERIA

Money politics manifested in Nigeria in different stages of the electoral cycles. Money plays vital roles in the pre-election period, during the election and post-election periods. In the first category, many steps and financial activities take place including the purchase of nomination forms, party primaries and consensus with competing party members. To secure the nomination form in Nigeria is an expensive task financially. Parties pegged their cost of expression of interest and buying of nomination forms exorbitantly. For example, the cost of nomination for various elective offices of the former ruling PDP in the 2007 party primaries was N5 million ($12,044.13 thousand) for the presidential aspirants, N3 million ($7,226.48 thousand) for gubernatorial aspirants, N2 million ($4,817.65 thousand) for Senatorial and House of Representatives and N500,000 ($1,204.41 thousand) for members State House of Assemblies (Onah & Nwali, 2018). Onah and Nwali (2018) added that the former president Obasanjo used his presidential influence and powers to install Yar'adua in the 2007 general election by the monetary inducement of party delegates, voters and electoral officers and security agents to rig the 2007 election.

The parties skyrocketed the cost of nomination in future elections after the 2007 general election to the extent that only the super-rich could afford it. In the 2019 general election, the cost of party nomination shoots off comparatively with that of 2007 as shown in the table 9.1.

Thus, by their deliberate action in soaring the cost of nomination, the poor candidates irrespective of their qualities and competency are strategically eliminated from vying for elective offices in Nigeria. This is just one strategy of using money politics to corner the hard-earned democracy to all-elite affairs and the exclusion of the average and poor from the equation. The scenario is becoming more interesting as democracy is gaining root in the country the elite are continuously introducing strategic money politics that screened out the low earners and level the playing ground for the wealthy only. The cost of expression of interest and nomination in the build-up to the 2023 general election terrified many observers of the Nigerian election and democracy.

The cost of nomination forms in the ruling APC for president is fixed at N100 million ($240,884), governorship at N50 million ($85,470), Senate

Table 9.1 Comparative Cost of Tickets for Party Primaries in APC and PDP in the 2019 Party Primaries

Position	APC	PDP
Presidential	N45 million ($108,397.17)	N12 million ($28,905.91)
Gubernatorial	N22.5 million($54,198.58)	N6 million ($14,452.96)
Senatorial	N7 million ($16,861.78)	N4 million ($9,635.30)
House of Representatives	N3.85 million ($9,273.98)	N1.5 millionb($3,613.24)
State House of Assemblies	N850,000 ($2,047.50)	N600,000 ($1,445.30)

Source: Lawal (2018). The conversion into dollars is made by the author using the official exchange rate of 2022.

at N20 million ($34,188), House of Representatives at N10 million ($17,094) and State Assembly at N2 million ($3,418). The leading opposition party the PDP pegged N40 million ($68,376) as the cost for presidential nomination forms, N21 million ($35,897) for governorship, N3.5 million ($5,982) for Senate, N2.5 million ($4,273) for House of Representatives and N1.5 million ($2,564) for State House of Assembly (Itodo, 2022). This orchestrated conspiracy of the rising cost of party nomination is targetted at eliminating all potential contenders to clear the field for the incumbent office holders who can easily afford already having access to the public treasury, the use and abuse of state resources and those with strong godfathers that can sponsor their financial needs to win the election. About twenty-five aspirants in the ruling APC purchased the forms at the cost of N100 million ($240,884) each which raised the sum of N25 billion ($103,755,000,000,00.00 million) (Othman, 2022). The disgusting aspect of this show of financial muscle is that some of the aspirants that purchased a form at the cost of N100 were asked to resign from their ministerial position but instead of complying, they forfeited the nomination form and clung to their seats. Others went to the party primaries and secured zero votes for a form purchased at the cost of N100 million. This unfolding event has a terrible disaster for the Nigerian economy because these aspirants are political office holders and it is believed that they are using the public treasury for the purchase of the forms (Ogunbiyi, 2022).

The second step in the party primaries is another hurdle of money politics in Nigeria. As observed by Onah and Nwali (2018), incumbents used public money and their power to install their anointed candidates and rig them into power after buying delegates to secure the nomination for them. The party primaries of the ruling APC and the major opposition PDP in the build-up for the 2019 general election displayed money politics nakedly. Some candidates at the presidential contests were allegedly reported to have bribed the delegates with a sum of $5,000 each. In other elective offices in both APC and the PDP, aspirants bought delegates' votes and the highest bidders in most of the cases won (Sule, 2019a). The recent party primaries in the build-up for the 2023 general election saw the price for bribing the delegates to gain their votes rose astronomically. In the PDP presidential primaries, allegations surfaced of the buying of delegates' votes by some aspirants at the cost of $10,000 (N4,150,200.00 million), $15,000 (N6,225,300.00 million) and $25,000 (N10,375,500.00 million). The APC presidential primaries too were allegedly enmeshed in the same clandestine vote-buying of delegates and bribing the state governors that controlled the APC states. In other elective offices party primaries, wide reports of vote-buying of delegates and bribery were reported (Baje, 2022; Ogbeifun, 2022; Ogunbiyi, 2022; Othman, 2022).

Apart from the cost of nomination and party primaries, the pre-election has another form of money politics in disguise. The contenders that lost the election must be compensated for stepping down, aligning or covert support of the winner of the nomination. In some instances, even the losers that gave a hard fight must be compensated or they will switch to another party, obtain nomination and scatter the votes to prevent the other candidate from winning. In this game, the winner set aside a humongous sum of money to settle the grievances and to block strategic and swing votes (Walecki et al., 2006). This might be a good explanation of why some aspirants will buy a nomination form at the cost of N100 million in a collapsing economy like that of Nigeria and then forfeit the form or score a zero vote. They might have anticipated a bargain for rewards before the contests.

Money politics manifests in the electoral process once the campaign ban is lifted. The cost of advertisements, media expenditure, mobility, accommodation and feeding are all incurred expenses during the electoral process. Besides, other groups must be wooed to have their influence and support including the traditional rulers, religious clerics, the media, opinion leaders, electoral officials and security agents (Sule et al., 2018c). These categories are bribed as unveiled by a study (Sule et al., 2017a) after the Dasuki scandal was exposed involving a sum of $2.1 billion in armed money allocated for the procurement of arms to fight the Boko Haram insurgency. The study (Sule et al., 2017a) reported all the above-mentioned groups. One funny aspect of it is that a sum of N400 million ($963,530.36 thousand) was given to the former Sokoto state governor Attahiru Bafarawa for distribution to clerics for prayers according to the revealed source, an illicit diverted money offered for prayers of success. All these must be transacted before the election.

During the election conduct or on the election day, votes are openly bought and sold between the patrons and their clients through the brokers who are the party agents. Many studies (Onah & Nwali, 2018; Sule et al., 2018d and Okeke & Nwali, 2020) reported several incidences of vote-buying on election day. For instance, the elections conducted in Ekiti in 2014 saw votes bought at the cost of N5,000 ($12.04) and in the Osun election in 2018, votes were bought up to N10,000 ($24.08). In the 2019 Gubernatorial elections across many states, votes were bought at the cost of N15,000 ($36.12) and N20,000 ($48.16) in Sokoto, Plateau, Benue and many states (Sule & Sambo, 2021b). In the post-election period, politicians still have to use the money to settle the judiciary due to the retinue of litigations that accompanied the aftermath of the contentious elections in several places. They will have to bribe the judges to avert a fair judicial process that may truncate their victory in court. Additionally, the numerous donations received and support physically and in cash or kind by power brokers must now be compensated (Nwozor et al., 2021). They are being compensated with contracts, inflated projects, kickbacks, appointments, dubious transactions and other favours (Davies, 2021; Folarin, 2021). In all these tragedies, the category on the receiving end is the voters or the populace who have their liberty usurped by money politics and delivery of the common goods elude them because the political officeholders serve themselves while in the office instead of representation.

VOTE-BUYING, BRIBERY AND ELECTORAL PROCESS IN NIGERIA: IMPACT OF MONEY POLITICS

Vote-buying and bribery are believed to have been obstacles that money politics heralded in Nigeria. Money politics is aided by the intervention of business tycoons, corporations, godfathers and other wealthy groups. Adetula (2008) quoted General TY Danjuma saying 'I raised $7 million. Slightly more than half of it came from my business associates.' General Danjuma also added, 'Not once did he (Obasanjo) find out from me where this money came from. Was it from me, from my business associates, whether l stole it or whatever he didn't ask me!' Adetula (2008) added that there were such cases too numerous to mention in Nigerian elections and money politics. This is an admission of illegal funding by one of the influential former army generals and a multinational business mogul. Thus, vote-buying emanates from the actions of the godfathers and the sponsors who provide illicit money to their godsons.

Rational choice Theory postulates that vote-buying in elections is perceived by politicians as a rational choice and decision-making that involves a profitable outcome. Voters perceived the selling of votes as a marketable venture that yield maximum satisfaction for casting a vote to the buyer (Downs, 1957; Arrows, 1968). Together, the politicians and the electorates are likened by the rational choice theorists to negotiators of a commodity in a market between buyers and sellers where the buyer targets maximum utility while the seller opts for maximum profit. This, as criticised by Ott (2006), is a capitalist persuasion to justify an amoral attitude in politics including illegal means of acquiring power. However, no matter how sentimental the theory looks, the truth is voters and politicians acted in the way postulated and predicted by rational choice theory and they will continue to act in the same way.

The term vote-buying is identified as the exchange of material benefits for political support through voting. Vote-buying is a contract or an auction typical of an environment of a bazaar where the voters sell their votes to the highest bidder. Vote-buying can be in form of any financial, material or promising incentives by a party, candidate, patron, broker, client or party supporters to influence the electoral decision of a voter to cast his vote for a particular candidate to win an election. It may take the form of abstaining away from voting where it is perceived that if a group of voters voted for a particular candidate he may win, the voters can be persuaded or influenced to abstain away which will jeopardise his chance of winning to enable the opposition win. It can be perpetrated through the use of violence sometimes if it is understood that the voters will not play to the game some political thugs are armed and sponsored financially to chase away voters from casting their votes. Thus, any promise of an immediate reward or later benefit that influenced a voter to elect a candidate or party or to abstain from voting is considered vote-buying (Onuoha & Ojo, 2018).

Vote-buying is not unique or limited to Nigeria only. It is recognised as one of the attributes of African politics and global democracies. About 80percent of voters from African countries surveyed believed that voters are bribed and about 16percent of the respondents responded that they were induced with money during elections in Africa (Onuoha & Ojo, 2018). Schaffer and Schedler (2005) designed a model explaining the conceptual illustration of vote-buying in the electoral process. In their view, Schaffer and Schedler (2005) argue that vote-buying is a market exchange due to problematic enforcement, problematic monitoring, countervailing norms and countervailing laws. Vote-buying according to Schaffer and Schedler (2005) is personalised normative inducements in the clientelistic exchange of material rewards against political support, the established social networks and personal relationships and the cooperation addressed by parties and candidates through instilling the fear of informal sanctions on the voters. The means of rewards include an advance payment, a wage, a gift, a reparation, an affront, a threat, a sign of virtue, a sign of vice and a sign of strength.

Vote-buying is prohibited and criminalised in the Nigerian Electoral Act 2022. Section 22(a-c) of the Electoral Act 2022 provides that

> any person who (a) is in unlawful possession of any voter's card whether issued in the name of any voter or not; or (b) sells or attempts to sell or offers to sell any voter's card whether issued in the name of any voter or not; or (c) buys or offers to buy any voters' card whether on his own behalf or on behalf of any other person, commits an offence and is liable on conviction to a fine not more than ₦500,000 or imprisonment not more than two years or both.

This is a prohibition in respect of voters' cards since elections can only be conducted legally and accepted in Nigeria with effect from 2022 using voters' cards mandatorily.

Section 121 and its sub-sections frown at conspiracy and attempts by politicians to lure any influence to favour a candidate to win through vote-buying and other related acts. The Section states:

> 121. (1) Any person who does any of the following – (a) directly or indirectly, by his or herself or by any other person on his or her behalf, corruptly makes any gift, loan, offer, promise, procurement or agreement to or for any person, in order to induce such person to procure or to endeavour to procure the return of any person as a member of a legislative house or to an elective office or the vote

of any voter at any election; (b) upon or in consequence of any gift, loan, offer, promise, procurement or agreement corruptly procures, or engages or promises or endeavours to procure, the return of any person as a member of a legislative house or to an elective office or the vote of any voter at any election; (c) advances or pays or causes to be paid any money to or for the use of any other person, with the intent that such money or any part thereof shall be expended in bribery at any election, or who knowingly pays or causes to be paid any money to any person in discharge or repayment of any money wholly or in part expended in bribery at any election; (d) after any election directly, or indirectly, by his or herself, or by any other person on his or her behalf receives any money or valuable consideration on account of any person having voted or refrained from voting, or having induced any other person to vote or refrain from voting or having induced any candidate to refrain from canvassing for votes for his or herself at any such election, commits an offence and is liable on conviction to a maximum fine of ₦500,000 or imprisonment for a term of 12 months or both.

Additionally, Section 121(2–6) suggests that a voter is guilty of vote-selling if

(2) A voter commits an offence of bribery where before or during an election directly or indirectly by his or herself or by any other person on his or her behalf, receives, agrees or contracts for any money, gift, loan, or valuable consideration, office, place or employment, for his or herself, or for any other person, for voting or agreeing to vote or for refraining or agreeing to refrain from voting at any such election. (3) Nothing in this section shall extend or apply to money paid or agreed to be paid for or on account of any lawful expenses bona fide incurred at or concerning any election. (4) Any person who commits the offence of bribery is liable on conviction to a maximum fine of ₦500,000 or imprisonment for a term of 12 months or both. (5) Any person who conspires, aids or abets any other person to commit any of the offences under this Part of this Act commits the same offence and is liable to the same punishment. (6) For the purpose of this Act, a candidate shall be deemed to have committed an offence if it was committed with his or her knowledge and consent.

It should be noted that these sections and their sub-sections existed in the Electoral Act 2010 before the amendment but that has not deterred or minimise vote-buying in Nigerian elections in the Fourth Republic. Adetula (2008) and Ojo (2008) stressed that the 2003 and 2007 general elections were heavily influenced by vote-buying worth some few hundred naira and bribing election officials, security agents and other stakeholders to rig the election. Similarly, Sule et al., (2018e) and Nwagwu et al. (2022) reported vote-buying in the 2015 and the 2019 general elections. Factors attributed to the continuous and escalating vote-buying by the studies mentioned earlioer included poor monitoring and lack of proper sanction, money politics, poverty and political culture.

Money politics has many implications for the Nigerian democratisation process. Vote-buying impedes credible elections and slows the democratisation process in Nigeria (Adetula, 2008). Walecki (2008) suggests that vote-buying and money politics is causing political corruption in Nigeria which requires a giant reform to remedy. Vote-buying draws the attention of the electorates away from performance and credibility to the promise of rewards which impedes good choice of leadership and representation (Ojo, 2008). Vote-buying leads to rent-seeking and flawed elections in Nigeria that affects democratisation (Olog-benla & Adisa, 2012) as presented by Lucky (2014) that vote-buying is the bane of good governance in Nigeria. Sule et al., (2018) concluded that vote-buying leads to the rigging of elections, violence, malpractice and irregularities, poor service delivery, misrepresentation, subversion of the genuine democratisation process and poor socio-economic and political development. Babatunde et al., (2019) argue that vote-buying has national security implications of misgovernance which resulted in ethno-religious crises, herdsmen and militants activities, Boko Haram insurgency, separatist agitations, IPOB secessionist threat and dethronement of the fair and credible democratic process in the country.

Other scholars (Onah & Nwali, 2018; Ajagba et al., 2019; Okeke & Nwali, 2020; Davies, 2021; Nwozor et al., 2021; Nwagwu et al., 2022; Sule et al., 2022) agreed that vote-buying and money politics weakens INEC and its capacity to deliver sound elections as expected despite reforms, the electoral process is subverted and the public choice option is blocked, the liberty of choice by the electorates is curtailed, delivery of campaign manifestoes and democratic good governance, accountability and transparency are all lost out to merchants and entrepreneurs of electoral investors. In essence, the INEC chairman himself, Professor Mahmood Yakubu lamented the influx of vote-buying and excessive money politics in Nigeria ahead of the conduct of the 2023 general election, complaining that

> there are three critical challenges to overcome in the conduct of the 2023 elections namely; insecurity, fake news and money politics. My third area of concern is the influence of money on politics which is becoming more present and the risk is that ours may soon become a plutocracy for the rich rather than a democracy for the people. The way money is exchanging hands is a source of concern. Yes, we have collaboration with ICPC and the EFCC and only recently we renewed our collaboration with the EFCC . . . we are going to do something together. However, there are two dimensions to it: when you have willing connectors it becomes a bit more difficult to contain the situation. (Ogbeifun, 2022)

This statement is annoying if the INEC Chairman will express worry about the incessant use of money in Nigerian politics ahead of a national election. This also demonstrates the willingness and the readiness of the INEC to do the needful if a suitable cooperating environment is enabled.

Chapter 10

Party Financing and Corruption in the Electoral Process

Corruption is a cancer that is preventing transparency in governance and it is listed among the causes of misgovernance, misrepresentation and deprivation of many sections of the population in a state. Corruption if it is allowed in society permeates all governmental structures and systems. All societies are affected by the corruption of one kind or the other and in one form or the other as noted by Rose-Ackerman (2000). Interestingly, democracy is supposed to mitigate and minimise corruption because of the mechanism put in place to checkmate abuse, excesses and illegal transactions but modern democracies are unable to address the problem. Therefore, it is egocentric and chauvinistic to assert that democracy is responsible for abetting corruption contemporarily (Rose-Ackerman, 1999). Of course, advanced democratic settings exhibit intolerance to corruption because the citizens are better informed and are keenly following the financial activities of their governments and policies, but dubious and illegal transactions continue in all forms of governments around the world (Rose-Ackerman, 2000).

Corruption takes different forms, nature, dimensions and practice. The degree and the practice vary from one state to another and the level of sanctions and policy responses differ. Some states made headway in displaying sanctions and deterring corrupt practices by setting good examples of handling corruption allegations impartially and decisively. Other states are battling with the influence of the ruling class whose crass obsession with primitive accumulation evades all logic and the power of a jury to submit to the law. Yet, corruption remains a global headache and the international community is devising policies, programmes and conventions as well as agreements to reduce corruption incidences and increase transparency. Corruption has different types and levels such as grand corruption, petty corruption and political corruption.

This chapter investigates political corruption in Nigeria vis-à-vis party financing, which is one of the branches of the phenomenon. The process of party financing is often associated with illicit funding, vote-buying, bribery, clientelism, abuse of public resources, violation and stepping beyond the limit of the law. All of these are linked to political corruption because it is a kind of a cycle that begins somewhere and continues in an iterative style. The politicians that are engaged in these illegal practices may emerge as winners in elections and they will not relent in softening corruption practices and charges to allow for an escape route when it is confirmed. The rulers are found to have been deeply involved in several corruption scandals but they are well-equipped with resources and holes in the law to exit unscathed from the allegations (Sambo & Sule, 2021b). On many occasions, the law in the country is accused of enabling a safe landing for the offenders. For instance, the Economic and Financial Crimes Commission (EFCC), established in 2001 as an anti-corruption crusader is weak in approaching its duty because the laws of establishing the commission could not charge them with effective powers to arrest and handle cases. They could only receive petitions, charge to court and follow up the litigations. The culprits found it easy to escape by prolonging the legal process and other ways.

Electoral corruption is the major theme in this section. Electoral corruption is a branch of political corruption which involves several offences involving financial illegality in the process of electoral conduct including vote-buying, bribery, clientelism, excessive spending, violation of laws and other financial inducements not allowed by law which politicians and parties employ to win elections at all costs in Nigeria. Electoral corruption is affecting the integrity, credibility and acceptability of elections in Nigeria. A study (Sule et al., 2018d) argues that despite the overwhelming reports by civil societies, agencies, donors and domestic and international observers on the credibility of the 2015 general election in Nigeria, an important aspect omitted undermined the integrity and credibility of the election and that is the process of party financing. The study (Sule et al., 2018d) concludes that because of the excessive use of money, violation of the process, spending above the limit and electoral corruption, the integrity of the election is drastically minimised in the findings of the study. Electoral corruption impedes the elections from being a choice of liberty by the voters, leaders that have no business whatsoever in politics are controlling power and the economy including those who could not appropriately account for even their school certificates. This causes disastrous leadership that is throwing the national values and sovereignty into the jungle of doom.

Thus, this chapter examines electoral corruption and its practice in Nigeria's Fourth Republic and how it affects the integrity of elections. In doing that, the broader view of corruption is succinctly explored from the global perspective since corruption is a universal problem that affects all world countries. No single state is immune from the practices even though the degrees and incidences vary sharply. Transparency international in its annual analysis of the Corruption Perception Index (CPI) informs us that corruption is everywhere but in countries where democracies are deeply rooted, the phenomenon is less observed than in authoritarian regimes and new democracies where institutions are still weak and unable to check the excesses of the ruling class. This view is what Rose-Ackerman (1999) disputed in her discourse because she believed corruption exists practically in advanced democracies. A view that an African scholar, Ake (1996), justified in his thesis on democracy and development in Africa is that democracy is not necessarily a form of government that can enhance good governance, transparency, fight corruption and other malaise of underdevelopment in Africa because the feasibility of practising democracy in Africa is bleak (Ake, 2000).

CONCEPT OF CORRUPTION

Corruption is a virus that beleaguered world countries due to its tendency for blocking transparency and progress and development (Rose-Ackerman & Palifka, 2016). Corruption deprives the progress and well-being of societal members by disconnecting them from the benefits of the scarce resources and the anticipated provision of public goods and essential services and that is recently fuelling public uproar and protests (Rose & Peiffer, 2018). Corruption is greased by misgovernance, weak institutions, authoritarian control of the state and ineffective sanction regimes (Maddow, 2019). Corruption is pervasive and prevalent all over the world and there are varieties of corruption with different causes and implications (Holmes, 2015). Corruption has negative implications for society including sabotage of the economy, increasing deprivation and impoverishment of the populace by a few ruling class and it causes an infrastructure deficit (Rose-Ackerman, 2013). To study corruption, it is germane to take a look at a case study that will guide a sound understanding of how it operates and varies from one society to the other (Miller, 2016). If corruption is that destructive, a fundamental question that begs an answer is why corruption exists and continues amid its evil consequences? The answer to this vital question is necessary through a survey of the term and its meaning in addition to its forms and dimension.

Corruption is an old phenomenon difficult to trace its beginning. In essence, corruption is as old as mankind and its existence (Uslaner, 2017). From the scriptures, we are spiritually informed that corruption among man began with Adam and his children themselves. When the two sons of Adam, Abel and

Cain, were asked by their Creator to sacrifice before their Lord, one of them presented a good one while the other presented a corrupted one. The one from a good source was accepted as a sacrifice and that triggered jealousy which disappointingly led to the murder of the good one by the bad one (Q.5:27-32 and Genesis.4:1-5). Islam and Christianity believed that this is the root of corruption among mankind on earth. In modern times, society changed with new and sophisticated governmental structures, societal structures and other related developments. Corruption takes a new form and approach.

Corruption is given various meanings, interpretations and analyses by academics, agencies, international organisations and public policy analysts. The word corruption originates from the Latin word 'corrumpere' meaning something that fails to meet the desired standard (Rose et al., 2019). The Transparency International defines corruption as 'the abuse of entrusted power for private gain' (The World Bank, 2020). Transparency International from the this definition classifies corruption as grand and petty. Grand corruption is annoying and challenging because it involves politicians, civil servants and bureaucrats in dubious and undue process transactions such as inflating contracts, kickbacks and rewarding cronies for political gains using the platform of the public resources. Petty corruption is bribery by public officials or the offer of a bribe by individuals to the public officials for a favour or breaking the standard norm and practice of engagement (The World Bank, 2020).

Corruption is seen as a cultural haemorrhage where values and etiquettes are bypassed and ignored for unethical conduct involving bribery, inducements, prizes, tips, patronage and kleptocracy by politicians perpetuated by bi-lateral monopolies and dominated states (Rose-Ackerman, 1999). Rose-Ackerman (1999) added that the electoral process in democracies is accompanied by practices that encourage buying political influence and vote-buying all of which can only be remedied through domestic and global collective reforms. The study of corruption is perceived (Rose-Ackerman, 2013; Standing, 2016) from the perspective of the political economy of the democratic system where a designed pattern of wealth distribution is legalised and that does not translate into equality of voting because, strategically, the process is empowering one section of the society against another by the virtue of the privilege of holding lucrative offices. Girling (1997) believed in the above view that democracy fosters corruption through vote-buying, kickbacks, pay-offs and clientelism.

Theoretically, corruption is illustrated by the broken windows theory postulated by George Kenneth and James K. Wilson in 1982. Broken windows are unattended holes of community control breakdown enabling lethal crimes to exist and continue in society and this gradually makes societies tolerant of deviant behaviours such as corruption. Practicalised in an example of a house with unrepaired broken windows, other systems of the house such as doors, roofing and walls will crack and allow foreign undesired fellows to intrude. Some social progress is needed to reverse corrupt practices including good governance, improved performance in CPI, civil liberties and transparency (Alford, 2012). Once minor corrupt practices such as bribes, petty breaking of law and order and favour are allowed to occur, corruption will gain roots and uprooting it will require a huge effort in good governance and civil liberty of the governed.

Corruption takes the forms of crimes and violence, bribery, extortion, graft, embezzlement, various forms of fraud, patronage, influence, favouritism, abuse of office by the public office holders and violation of due process (Sambo & Sule, 2021b). White-collar corruption is another form of corruption, which is the bribery and breaking of standard rules and norms by corporations in the process of winning contracts awards and execution. State corporate corruption motivates the globalisation of corruption (Kratcoski, 2018). Corruption is aided by many drivers in society central among which is misgovernance which translates into a lack of accountability and transparency tolerated by ignorant and non-responsive citizens (Bakar & Ghosh, 2014). Poverty and the squandering of public resources germinate corruption because the money meant for the provision of basic needs such as roads, education, health, and electricity is now pocketed into private accumulation leaving the majority impoverished and complacent of the illegal practices due to abject penury (Fisman & Golden, 2017). Anthropologically speaking, Muir and Gupta (2018) identify the causes of corruption as the breaking of the rules of engagement, how the public reacted to the crimes and violations and how the perpetrators act or play their game to negotiate their rescue from the claws of law. The practices continue in these societies where the culprits escaped and the public tolerates or portrays a nonchalant attitude to the offences (Smith, 2014).

The anti-corruption agencies which are expected to be at the forefront of crusaders against the menace of corruption are often politicised and crippled by politicians in many societies. Hough (2013) tagged such anti-corruption agencies as 'a dog that could barely raise a whimper'. Elites sometimes disguise under the umbrella of democracy to infiltrate the corridors of power and penetrate societal resources in a conspiracy of private accumulation through organised crimes and international collaborative financing, criminalisation of the international finance system and operations and corrupting democratic transitions and regimes with kleptocracy, clientelism, patrimonialism, patronage and prebendel politics (Jordan, 1999; Katzarova, 2019). In some developing countries such as Nigeria, Ghana and Kenya, weak institutions, ineffective legal enforcement and a largely dominated uninformed and indifferent crowds allowed the ruling class to perpetrate, perpetuate and practised corruption scandals with an escapist guarantee and impunity (Smith, 2008; Oluyitan, 2016; Hope Sr, 2017).

Corruption is manifesting across the globe based on annual or quarterly reports from international organisations, agencies and research bodies examining practices such as official theft across world countries, cybercrime, money laundering and results of a survey based on the CPI by Transparency International. The CPI is the most popular and reliable data on corruption incidences worldwide. The CPI ranked world countries based on performance from 1 to 180 or beyond depending on the number of countries selected and surveyed. The CPI is not without its politics and prejudices because sometimes some countries debunk the ranking and reject their position in the report. Nigeria rejected the 2020 CPI ranking citing it as inconsiderate and out of touch with the reality of the achievement of the government in anti-corruption crusades (Sambo & Sule, 2021b). Nevertheless, the CPI is the most comprehensive data and coverage of the globe obtained in a singular report. The CPI uses a scale of 0 to 100, where 0 is highly corrupt while 100 very clean to measure the CPI of world countries. In the 2021 CPI, the report indicates that the global average is 43, unchanged for 10 years, meaning that 131 countries have made no significant progress in the fight against corruption in the last decade. The report indicates that two-thirds of the countries scored below 50, interpreted as a high level of corruption globally while twenty-seven countries scored their lowest in the history of their ranking (Transparency International, 2022).

In essence, the 2021 CPI report expresses worry that even the top performers are showing a slight sign of backsliding with corruption rocking them increasingly and no country is untouched by corruption scandals. Some top performers are Denmark and Finland jointly sharing the first position with a score of 88, followed by New Zealand with 88, Norway and Sweden with 85, Switzerland with 84, Netherlands with 82, Luxembourg with 81 and Germany with 80. The least performers include South Sudan with 11, Syria with 13, Somalia with 13, Venezuela with 14, Yemen with 16, North Korea with 16, Afghanistan with 16, Libya with 17 and Equatorial Guinea with 17. The average performers include Cyprus with 53, Rwanda with 53, Saudi Arabia with 53, Oman with 52, Slovakia with 52 and Armenia with 49, Greece with 49 and Jordan with 49 (Transparency International, 2022). The highest score or performance by region is Western Europe and Scandinavia with an average score of 66 while the lowest score or performance is in sub-Saharan Africa with an average score of 26. The report identified political corruption as the biggest cause and threat to combating corruption globally as observed by the Chair of Transparency International in the following words: 'Governments must urgently address the corrupting role of big money in political party financing and the undue influence it exerts on our political systems'

(Transparency International, 2022). Philip (2015) holds this view when he opines that political corruption is a big question and it has no answer in the near future. The Global Financial Integrity (2020) emphasises that the menace of corruption is escalating as observed after a twenty-year assessment from 1998 to 2018. The GFI added that CPI of the countries studied revealed that 10 percent worsened their scores; 59 percent remained relatively unchanged; and only about one-third (32 percent) improved their scores over the period. This is stressed by Rowden and Wang (2020) when they suggest that corruption is fast increasing and spreading globally.

Similarly, in a special report prepared during the period of the intense effects of the COVID-19 pandemic, Transparency International (2021) observed that corruption is being exported from some countries to others. The summary of the report reads:

> Bribery of foreign public officials has huge costs and consequences for countries across the globe and those costs have become more severe during the COVID-19 pandemic. With so many cases of foreign bribery occurring in health care, we cannot afford for corruption to cost any additional lives. (Transparency International, 2020)

The report analysed the performance of forty-seven leading global exporters, including forty-three countries that are signatories to the Organisation for Economic Cooperation and Development (OECD) Anti-Bribery Convention, in cracking down on bribery of foreign public officials by companies operating abroad. The sharp effects of COVID-19 created intense competition among the corporate bodies in search of contracts and the desperation to secure the contracts pulled the corporations into bribing officials of the recipient states.

Corruption manifested in the level of money laundering estimated at around $800 billion to $2 trillion equivalent to 2–5 percent of global GDP (Cheek, 2020). Africa has the highest record of money laundering $88.6 billion annually and Nigeria has the top value of 47 percent of the total world money laundering crime (Kuhlmann, 2020). Cybercrime is a manifesto of global corruption and the net worth of what is being lost to hackers and fraudsters reached 1 percent of global GDP at the toll of $600 billion each year since 2014. The total value of projected loss to the crime is $10.5 trillion annually by 2025 if adequate measures of cybersecurity and digital safety are not taken. The corrupt nature of national elites denied many states from designing secure cyberspace which is an associated factor that leads to crime (Lewis, 2020).

Corruption has several implications globally. The growth, development and well-being of any society that is dominated by corruption are negatively affected. Money meant to supply basic common goods for the populace is cornered by a few privileged individuals either through looting or short-changing the state with dubious contracts and kickbacks thereby impoverishing the majority and depriving them of their blessed national resources throwing them into poverty, unemployment, disease, hunger, malnutrition, insecurity and a huge infrastructure gap (Rose-Ackerman & Palifka, 2016). Corruption slows economic growth and development (Ivanyna et al., 2018) and this manifested in Africa South of the Sahara (Blundo et al., 2013). Official corruption and short-changing of the society through dubious transactions and the illegal process is not limited to Africa or emerging democracies. Schweizer (2018) and Schweizer (2020) dig numerous corruption scandals affecting the US leaders in his mention that 'anyone who does not see the connection between the Clintons' official government power and their ability to raise money overseas is clearly not paying attention'. Corruption compromises global peace and security (Rotberg, 2009b) because when the majority of the population is denied access to decent living by the selfish aggrandisement of the few ruling class, they turned violent and take weapons against the state and the citizens (Chayes, 2015; Rose-Ackerman & Palifka, 2016). Even global terrorism and its war are perceived to have been engineered by the corrupt and shoddy deals of the ruling elites (Rotberg, 2009a & Teets & Chenoweth, 2009).

Some efforts were made nationally and collectively to combat corruption by organisations, agencies and states. States including America, Britain, France, Germany, Canada, Italy, Hong Kong, Singapore and several other world countries are making efforts to reform towards countering corruption and corrupt practices (Dixit, 2018). In Africa, Asia, Europe and America, anti-corruption agencies are being established to address the problem of corruption (Édes, 2016). An agreement was made by the OECD member countries to tackle corruption and all countries in the membership have signed the agreement (Rothstein, 2011). Regional bodies such as the European Union (EU), African Union (AU), Association of South-East Asian Nations (ASEAN), Economic Community of West African States (ECOWAS) and many others designed models and conventions to combat corruption, money laundering, illicit financial flows, cybercrimes and agreement on repatriation of illegal money to their source or original destination (Lambsdorff, 2007). The United Nations and World Bank are carrying out annual global research on reforms for curbing corrupt practices through grants to scholars and Transparency International and other agencies for policy implications (Yadav & Mukherjee, 2016). Domestic commitment and strong local institutions with political will and the desire to sanction are discovered more effective in combating corruption than global institutions (Rotberg, 2019). Sambo and Sule (2021b) suggest a spiritual approach from the Islamic perspective where deterrence or abstention from the practice can be achieved through a radical reduction of power contests and obsession for power and wealth accumulation.

ELECTORAL CORRUPTION IN NIGERIA

Corruption is a big problem in the Nigerian socioeconomic and political systems. Political corruption is the main challenge in countering corruption scandals in Nigeria. Scholars like Jain (2001), Hope Sr. (1999), Ogundiya (2010) and Mohammed (2013) are of the view that official corruption is the major obstacle to good governance and national development in Nigeria. The doggedness of corruption and its rampant spread across all sectors of the economy and politics in Nigeria earned it the following description 'corruption in Nigeria is complex, multifaceted and polyvalent' by Pierce (2016). Public service has been criminalised by corruption in Nigeria in the scenario that graft fuelled political and electoral violence while basic needs are denied to the majority of the populace by a few rich ruling class that personalised public treasury into private gain against all the promised human rights of decency to the electorates (Human Rights Watch, 2019). Corruption blocks transparency, good governance, accountability and political and socioeconomic development (Bailey, 2006; Balboa & Medalla, 2006). Tanzi (2009) argues that states with huge resource endowments such as Nigeria are finding it difficult to move forward economically, politically and socially because of the evil of corruption.

The political system breeds corruption that is appearing in the demand of electoral politics, the extensive use of patronage in political appointments, and the use of dubious transactions. The public sector is rotten with corruption where access to employment and public procurement are obtained through corrupt procedures (Smith, 1961). The systemic corruption in the Nigerian political system leads to a particularistic political culture. This, in essence, is a system in which the government's treatment of citizens depends on their status or position in society (Asobie, 2012). Corruption is correlated with politics and political leadership in Nigeria (Ogbeidi, 2012). Ogundiya (2009) describes Nigerian political corruption and corrupt practices in Nigeria as 'Clientelism, Prebendalism and Patrimonialism'. Corruption has different types as observed earlier but the most interesting one in this area of study is electoral corruption which involves all the illegal and criminal activities that take place in the electoral process from the process of registration of voters to campaign financing and campaign activities as well as the election conduct proper (Sule, 2018).

Electoral corruption takes different forms and patterns in Nigeria. Electoral corruption is perceived by scholars (Hoffman, 2002; Bailey, 2006; Nield, 2006; Balboa & Medalla, 2006) as a process of subverting the legal and ethical procedures of the conduct of an election. Multiple registers of voters, underage voting, vote-buying, bribing of electoral officials and other stakeholders in the electoral process, refusal to use card readers for accreditation of voters and voting proper, cancellation of results in some places unnecessarily, manufacturing of election results in some areas, excessive use of money in the campaign process, godfatherism, patron-client relationship and violation of electoral acts on many instances during electioneering campaign (Sule et al., 2018c). Many electoral body officials were bribed including religious clerics, royal fathers, opposition political parties and security agencies (Sule et al., 2017a) and it was regarded as corruption because in the process the money itself was sourced through the looting of the public treasury and was redistributed to the different groups of public opinion makers and other important players (Sule et al., 2019a).

Electoral corruption and other forms of corruption are caused by many factors in Nigeria. Poverty and poor condition of living is one of them (Asobie, 2012). Economic bargain and the influence of multinational corporations in the contracts awarding process is another cause of corrupt practices and scandals in Nigeria (Knuckles, 2006; Rose-Ackerman & Palifka, 2016), rent and rent-seekers (Mauro, 1998), weak political institutions and lack of political will to address the phenomenon honestly (Eguae-Obazee, 2014; Mbaku, 2010), socioeconomic and political factors (Dike, 2001), prolonged military rule and authoritarian culture (Shehu, 2004) and godfatherism and party financing process are all considered as the fuel for corruption in Nigeria (Olarinmoye, 2008; Sule et al., 2018b).

The amount of money and continuous discoveries of looting and diversion of public resources can conclude that Nigeria is rendered poor by corruption majorly. For instance, Achebe (2012) and Ribadu (2013) estimated the figure of money stolen from the Nigerian treasury by the ruling class to be $400 billion (N166,040,000,000,000 trillion), an amount that is enough to settle all infrastructure deficits in the country squarely. The amount reported by the AU (2018) is higher than what Achebe (2012) and Ribadu (2013) mentioned. The AU estimated the amount to be $600 billion (N249,060,000,000,000 trillion). A report by the Civil Society Legislative Advocacy Centre (CISLAC) and Transparency International UK in 2017 revealed that the former Nigerian army chiefs stole as much as $15 billion (N6,226,500,000,000 trillion) through fraudulent armed procurement deals between 2011 and 2016. In a Conference in State House Abuja, the Chairman of the Presidential Advisory Committee Against Corruption Itse Sagay disclosed that fifty top government officials and private businessmen allegedly diverted about $7.5 billion (N3,113,250,000,000 trillion) to themselves between 2006 and 2013 at the expense of ordinary Nigerians (Sagay, 2017). All these scandals are political corruption directly linked to electoral corruption because these corrupt leaders emerged through a corrupt electoral process of vote-buying and bribery and they are accumulating to arrest future elections.

The Nigerian CPI in 2021 shows a ranking of 154 out of 183 countries with a low score of 24 out of 100. Another survey by the National Bureau of Statistics in collaboration with the United Nations on Drugs and Crimes (UNODC) carried out in 2019 which surveyed 33,000 Nigerians across the 36 states and the FCT Abuja through designing a questionnaire revealed that 30.2 percent of Nigerians are involved in the proceeds of corruption either by giving bribe or collecting and a total sum of N400 billion ($963,632,200 million) was paid as bribe in just 2019 alone. Imagine the magnitude of the economic sabotage that Nigerians are doing through corruption at the detriment of national development and patriotism. The report further emphasises that direct bribery requests by public officials accounted for 60 percent of all bribery transactions in Nigeria, and around two-thirds of bribes (67 percent) are paid before a service is provided by a public official, according to the survey. More than 93 percent of all bribes paid in 2019 were paid in cash and the prevalence of institutions involved in collecting bribery is Police with 44 percent, prosecutors at 33 percent, judiciary with 31 percent and Customs and Immigration with 31 percent. Men likely pay more bribes than women and the citizens respond that bribes are paid not necessarily but to speed up or facilitate a process of services. Vote-buying in the electoral process and nepotism in the recruitment process and promotion in the public sector took a large share of bribery according to the survey (NBS & UNODC, 2019).

Page (2018) stresses that electoral and political corruption are the gateway to corruption scandals and incidences in Nigeria. Page (2018) decries that 'electoral corruption and kleptocratic capture of political party structures unlock corruption opportunities across a range of other sectors and that corruption is ripe across the country's economic sector'. Corruption by sector according to Page's (2018) taxonomy shows that political corruption and political parties are big key players in polluting the Nigerian environment with bribery. This is followed by media corruption, electoral corruption, legislative corruption, bureaucratic corruption, petro corruption, trade-related corruption, industrial corruption, agricultural corruption, infrastructure corruption, power sector corruption, financial sector corruption, environmental corruption, security sector corruption, judicial corruption, anti-corruption corruption, education sector corruption, health sector corruption and humanitarian sector corruption. This indicates that no sector in Nigeria has not been penetrated by corruption. The Nigerian CPI based on the annual reports of Transparency International is illustrated in the table 10.1 to indicate how the performance is dwindling.

Electoral corruption has several implications for Nigeria's overall development. The entire democratic process is diverted to elite servitude by the Nigerian state. Institutions remain weak and ineffective despite more than twenty years of the democratic experiment. Political parties, legislature, civil

Table 10.1   Corruption Perception Index of Nigeria 1996–2021

Year	CPI	Countries Selected	Rating
1996	1.2	54	54
1997	1.3	52	52
1998	1.9	85	81
1999	1.9	99	98
2000	1.9	90	90
2001	1.6	102	100
2002	1.7	91	90
2003	1.4	133	132
2004	1.6	145	144
2005	1.9	158	154
2006	2.2	160	142
2007	2.2	183	127
2008	2.2	183	127
2009	2.2	180	130
2010	2.7	174	134
2011	2.7	183	143
2012	2.4	174	139
2013	2.7	175	144
2014	2.5	176	136
2015	2.7	167	136
2016	2.6	176	136
2017	2.1	180	136
2018	2.7	180	148
2019	2.6	180	144
2020	2.6	183	146
2021	2.4	183	156

Source: Transparency International (compiled and tabulated by the author 2022).

servants, bureaucrats and other sectors of policymaking become unproductive and stagnated. The supposed democratic values and dividends that Nigerians anxiously await with the inception of civilian rule elude them subterraneously because they sold their liberty and freedom of choice to vote-buying and corruption (Aiyede, 2008). The moribund and inadequate infrastructure in the country continues to collapse and dilapidate because it could not be attained sincerely. A country that is the tenth-largest oil producer in the world is importing fuel and other petroleum products with intermittent scarcity that is often complemented by illegal byroads hawkers known as 'black markets' (Page, 2018).

Good governance remains elusive and representation is not channelled towards serving people's interests but rather the vote-buyers who feel that their money earned them the seats and not a fair process based on their merit and track records. The health and education sector collapsed to the level of being avoided by Nigerians that could afford it. Annually, Nigerians are paying around $5 billion (N2.1 trillion) in paying medical and tuition fees abroad to America, Europe and Asian countries. The government-owned health and educational institutions are deserted by the ruling class and the rich. These collapsed institutions are only attended by the poor who are unprivileged and helpless. Roads are described by Nigerians as death holes or traps. Epileptic power supply perpetually keeps the majority of the population in darkness while security has become a prerogative of the ruling class only (Page, 2018).

As observed by Rotberg (2009a), political and electoral corruption caused massive global insecurity. Nigeria is now ranked fourth on the Global Terrorism Index in 2021 after Afghanistan, Syria and Iraq. The phenomenon of Boko Haram insurgency in Northeast Nigeria, rural banditry in Northwest, farmers–herders conflict in Northcentral, IPOB secessionists' threat in Southeast, Niger Delta militants and sea pirates in the Southsouth and separatist agitations and human rituals and killings in Southwest Nigeria all tantamount to the politics of regional security threats that Nigeria is facing fuelled by money politics and corruption as well as scrounging aggrandisement of the ruling elites (Sule et al., 2022).

Electoral corruption affected the electoral process and its credibility as observed in the previous chapter. The integrity and credibility of the process and the leaders that emerged through the process are questioned. Violence, rigging, thuggery, malpractice, vote-buying and violation of procedures all conglomerate into myriads of electoral challenges that are making electoral conduct difficult in Nigeria. The relationship between the elected and the electorates becomes that of the lords and servants once they assume power. They blocked the represented from having access to them to demand their rights or to lay their complaints on issues affecting them. The representatives from time to time distribute vehicles and other material benefits to a few selected individuals in their constituencies and televised it in the mainstream and on social media to earn applause because that is what Nigerians applauded or perceived as a performance by representatives. In the election period, they will distribute money and engage their brokers to buy votes for them to win again. This cycle continues enriching the ruling class who represented themselves and accumulate wealth while leaving their constituencies in deplorable conditions.

VIOLATION OF POLITICAL PARTY FINANCING REGULATIONS

Several studies (Ohman, 2014; Nwangwu & Ononogbu, 2016; Sule et al., 2017a; Sule et al., 2017b; Okeke & Nwali, 2020; Sule et al., 2022) uncovered how party financing regulations are violated and trespassed by parties and their candidates and that has raised more questions than answers. Are the provisions of the regulations adequate and thoroughly prepared in congruent with the Nigerian political environment? Is the mechanism for monitoring and enforcement for compliance effective? What role for citizens and civil societies and what measures are needed for a reform? A study (Sule, 2021) examined African democratic accountability and transparency and revealed that Nigerian party financing regulations are one of the best in the continent with adequate provisions in the constitution and the Electoral Act 2010 then (Electoral Act 2022 as amended) for contribution ban, expenditure limit, powers to monitor parties' campaign expenditure and financial status by INEC, disclosure, power to audit parties' financial status quarterly or annually and sanctions for violators.

Several issues were raised by some studies (Anyadike & Eme, 2014; Kura, 2014; Lucky, 2014; Ohman, 2014; Lawal, 2015; Nwangwu & Onon-ogbu; 2016; Olorunmola, 2016, Onah & Nwali, 2018; Nwozor et al., 2021; Nwagwu et al., 2022) that the Nigerian party financing is expensive and the expenditure limit is high but a study (Sule et al., 2022) differs from this point because it suggests that future reforms should consider an upward review of the maximum expenditure limit to meet the current reality of the Nigerian money politics and the rising cost of living in the country. The Electoral Act 2022 reviewed the maximum expenditure limit five times for each of the elective offices. Civil societies and analysts kicked against this increase as an attempt at monetising Nigerian politics and legalising exorbitant campaign expenditure that will open a window for huge spending. However, the reports from the above-mentioned studies suggested that if the violation experienced in 2011, 2015 and 2019 general elections are considered, the trend will continue until measures are adequately and strictly taken.

In another dimension, it is understood that the issue is not about the laws themselves but the mechanism of implementing them. The debates that accompanied the passing of the Electoral Act 2022 looked at the contribution limit and expenditure limit as the function of practicability and not a responsibility of figures. Even if the amount is going to be fixed at a trillion naira or more, politicians and parties will continue to spend what they have and what can earn them victory no matter what it will cost. The 2015 general election expenditure of the PDP headed towards a trillion naira, unprecedented spending that was reported to have been sourced from the public treasury, another problematic aspect of the matter (Sule et al., 2017a). Wherever politicians have access to money they will not consider its legality and illegality and they will readily deploy it for their electoral ambition. No matter how much is pegged it will be violated. If the amount is too high to be surmounted, disclosure, auditing and contribution are other aspects of violation that will continue.

The most important action in this regard is the capability to enforce compliance and sanction the violators which are lacking for now. INEC is perceived to be annoyed and willing to address the problem but parties and politicians are saboteurs that refused to cooperate with the commission in tackling the problem. Aluigba (2015) observed that INEC was annoyed with the level of money politics, violations and corruption in the campaign process and electoral conduct and it has revealed that as of 2015, none of the existing parties submit its audited books as required by law despite many efforts to access them. Another version (Sule et al., 2017b) reported that INEC is monitoring campaign financing based on its feasibility but the slippery nature of politicians and their games continues to evade all efforts at enforcing them to comply. Besides, Aluigba (2015) stresses that INEC lacks the capacity to monitor all parties and politicians' expenditure before an election, during the election or after. This occurred due to inadequate manpower, lack of technical skills and compromise by some of the officials and lack of cooperation by politicians. Sule (2018) mentions that on several occasions the INEC will write asking for audited books or will visit frequently parties' offices and demand to scrutinise the financial books but the party officials refused to cooperate with them.

The main problem, however, is the violation is committed openly and with alarming impunity. An offence that is perpetrated covertly means there is the fear of the consequences and apprehending it may have its aftermath. But in the case of the donation, it was openly bastardised and some of the contributors tried to justify their law-breaking act by citing some flimsy reasons that will not stand the test of the law (Ohman, 2014). Offences committed secretly may be overlooked as part of flexibility and benefit of the doubt to the culprits but the ones that are brazenly done overtly should be handled decisively and bravely. The commission should have mustered the courage to deal with the open ones and monitor closely the closed ones. The INEC chairman himself was reported to have lamented money politics may systematically block the poor and average Nigerians and open a window for the plutocrats to have the field to themselves (Ogbeifun, 2022). This is a stern warning from the monitors themselves which means the commission is worried.

Violation of party financing regulations will continue if measures are not taken and if reforms are not initiated. The reforms should be practical and proactive in such ways that the fear of the repercussions will compel open compliance and reduce clandestine deals. Any other measure of reviewing the amount and lamentations will never yield the desired results. This is, particularly, because the issue of opaque party financing is not unique to any state or Nigeria and Africa. It is a universal phenomenon that the entire globe is battling. The over-celebrated democracy and its principles of accountability and transparency are being ridiculed by the political corruption involved in the party financing process. The political corruption of clientelism, patronage, vote-buying and other related electoral corruption is identified as the biggest trouble of corruption globally (Rose-Ackerman & Palifka, 2016; Transparency International, 2022). The global institutions too are designing agreements and processes for mitigating the problem but it is better approached through domestic resolutions than global institutions.

EXCESSIVE SPENDING ABOVE LIMIT

A major problem with party financing in Nigeria and electoral corruption is spending above the limit. This has been propelled by the inability of the regulations to fix a reasonable amount or expenditure limit that will tally with the visible needs of parties and candidates in their financial responsibilities. The 2006 Electoral Act provides that a presidential candidate can spend only a maximum of N500, an amount that the electoral body and the legislature found incapable of meeting the financial obligations of candidates that aspire for the presidential post. This necessitated a review in the Electoral Act 2010 up to N1 billion, an increase of 100 percent to curtail illegal spending and excessive spending beyond the limit. The provision in the 2010 law is also found inadequate and out of touch with the reality of the financial tasks of presidential candidates in Nigeria (Sule et al., 2022). This led to an upward review of 500 percent from N1 billion in the Electoral Act 2010 to N5 billion in the Electoral Act 2022. Even the recent provisions in 2022 are believed to have been unrealistic and inadequate if the maximum spending is to be just to the aspirants according to practical terms and not an ideal view. The maximum limit set by the Electoral Act 2022 for the presidential contestants had been stampeded upon since 2010 how could it be considered workable in 2022 and beyond?

Similarly, the Electoral Act 2022 raised the maximum spending limit for all the elective offices from the presidential to the councillorship by 500 percent to enable a fair process that will guarantee adherence to the laws according to the lawmakers and the electoral body. Here, issues affect the limit. One of them is the designing of laws for the chairman and councillor of maximum spending where the INEC is not conducting the elections except for FCT Abuja only. The SIECs or the state electoral bodies have their independent and varied laws of electoral conduct at the local government level. The law may not be uniformly applied unless other legal interpretations are made. Setting laws by one body and implementing it by another is not a character of institutions of developing democracy like that of Nigeria. It has been mentioned that the INEC itself is battling with the process of enforcement, compliance and monitoring what can the SIECs do when they are pocketed by the state governors?

In the same way, the presidential aspirants and candidates spent above the limit, the other elective ranks including Senatorial, Houser of Representatives, Governorship and State House of Assemblies spent above the limit excessively. The irony is that while the INEC is making a good effort in monitoring and reporting the presidential cases, the other elective ranks are ignored virtually. Nigerian politics is anchored in the centre because of the way the federal state was converted into unitarism by practice. The centrifugal powers overwhelmed the centripetal components and this deviates the attention of the citizens from local governance to national politics. The SIECs have obscured laws or rather are not drawing the interest of academic research because the researchers gave up on them knowing well that the state governors manipulated and took over the total control of the local governments. Nobody knows how and when they monitor excess spending. However, not all the time that excessive spending is recorded, especially at the local level. A study (Sule, 2018) interviewed some contestants at the levels of State House of Assembly, Chairmanship and Councillorship and the outcome of the interviews revealed a surprising result from some of the informants that confessed to spending less than the maximum limit. This was unexpected.

As observed always, excessive spending is fuelled by the nature of Nigerian politics. Money politics permeates Nigerian political culture and the contenders are quite aware of the process. The amount that politicians spent on campaign expenditure is huge and excessive above the constitutional limit according to Sule et al., (2019b) because the money spent on media adverts, posters, billboards, transportation, accommodation, logistics and settlement of stakeholders to buy their support are much in a populated large geographical area with clusters like Nigeria. Owing to the economic sabotage and the cultural imperialism that Nigeria faces, most of these materials for the campaign are often procured from abroad in America and Europe. The cost of obtaining them skyrocketed campaign funding. Other studies (Nwangwu et al., 2016, Sule et al., 2017b and Sule et al., 2022) believed that the inability of INEC to sanction and monitor effectively the income and expenditure of parties and candidates hatched an environment of excessive spending and violation. If adequate measures are taken and parties are monitored effectively and sanctioned accordingly, the excessive spending would have been curbed.

Excessive spending could not be divorced from electoral corruption because a large part of the money according to Adetula (2008), Walecki (2008) and Aluigba (2015) are spent on bribery and corruption where party officials, the electoral officials, security agents, voters and other influential categories in elections are bought through clientelism and patrimonialism. In essence, excessive spending is associated with electoral corruption. This is what Rose-Ackerman (1999) cautions the champions of democracy to be wary of because according to her, the over-rated democratic accountability and transparency are being compromised and undermined by political corruption that manifested in vote-buying, contracts to the cronies for kickbacks, corporate bribery in winning contracts, clientelism and favouritism. The spending above the set limit itself is electoral corruption and that alone is used to justify the low performance and credibility of the 2015 general election (Sule et al., 2018e) even when the election was given a high score in terms of credibility but the integrity is questioned by the study owing to the violation in spending after presenting several cases in the 2015 election to establish the compromised integrity.

Thus, excessive spending is a branch of electoral corruption identified by this study and it must be countered instantly. Excessive spending implies that financially disadvantaged candidates and parties are side-lined in the electoral competition which is expected to promote democracy and good governance. Excessive spending ridiculed democratic accountability and make the task of monitoring and compliance difficult for the electoral body. The voters are the most affected because their political liberty and freedom of choice are strangulated unconsciously without allowing them to know the dangers of their actions. The citizens that are expected to engage in direct voting through the public choice of policy agenda as noted by Norris (2015) are voting based on who pays the best. And those who pay the highest price will have more package of neoliberal policies to the masses by surrendering the country's economy and political decision to the external forces who financed their ambition or support them covertly to pursue their interests. Thus, it is not only the domestic godfathers that hijack elections in Nigeria but foreign powers are active collaborators through corporations as stressed by Rose-Ackerman (2000). The process of reverting excessive spending will need a radical reform that will compel compliance but not definitely in the current form and manner that the monitoring and the sanctions are approached. A better mechanism must be adopted.

PARTY FINANCING AND ELECTORAL
INTEGRITY IN NIGERIA

It is not only the violent aspect of elections that discredits the process. It is one aspect of them. Several measures are considered by scholars as components of electoral integrity, Norris (2015, 2018a & 2023) is regarded as the most outstanding scholar who dedicated significant works of his literature to explain the process and measures of electoral integrity. In his view, Norris (2015) argues that the entire electoral cycle has pre-requisite characteristics that a minimum of them must be existing to establish electoral integrity. Electoral integrity is ascertained in the preparation to conduct the election where parties and candidates are expected to have a level fair playing ground, equal access to media, freedom of campaign and movement to sell manifesto to the voters, devoid of intimidation and threats and where the electoral body takes its tasks of electoral preparation seriously. The voter registration, display of voter data and attending to the complaints of the voters and other relevant matters are a part of electoral integrity. In addition, the freedom and independence of the electoral body determine its readiness the efficiency in delivering credible elections. Besides, the ability to conduct the election peacefully and the eligibility of the voters to vote and have their votes counted and resulted in a choice of leadership all determine the integrity of elections. But most importantly, fair play in spending and adherence to regulations and effective monitoring and compliance are all considered by Norris (2015) as parts of electoral integrity.

In Nigeria, party financing is identified as a phenomenon that undermined the integrity of elections in the Fourth Republic. Most of the criteria mentioned by Norris (2015) are not enjoyed in the Nigerian electoral conduct. Politicians established the rules of the game according to their favoured anticipated decisions and results. Party financing in Nigeria has regulations that are considered the best in Africa (Sule, 2021) after a thorough study of the process among many African countries. The laws are well-articulated better than in many African states and a promising reform is constantly being made periodically by the global best practices and norms. Civil societies and public analysts in addition to academics are increasingly becoming interested in democratic accountability and transparency in Nigeria and much attention is now dedicated to the course.

However, while INEC is happy and the policymakers boastfully present improved elections as achievements in Nigeria's democratic journey, an important omission is the question of party financing as part of the integrity of the elections. The money politics and excessive spending and violation of regulations in party financing are becoming unbecoming and the phenomenon is threatening to monetise political offices in the country. Delivering credible elections should not be limited to a violence-free process. Other integrated approaches must be considered. Of course, conducting a violence-free election in democracies like Nigeria that is likened to war with guns (Collier, 2009) is a great achievement and a remarkable improvement. African democracies are in transition to democratisation and institutionalisation of democratic structures (Lindberg, 2006) and therefore it should not be expected that all the values and well-institutionalised structures in the West must be obtained in Africa suddenly. The process is tedious, cumbersome and gradual. Elections that were marred by rigging, malpractice, violence and other problems but graduated to violence-free and minimised rigging are a success (Lindberg, 2006).

However, the reason why party financing is vital in African democracies and Nigerian politics is that the process is being converted into a gateway for political corruption that is eroding some fundamental democratic principles such as participation, representation, accountability, transparency and healthy elections. The pervasive nature of electoral and political corruption perpetuated in disguise through the process of party financing is threatening to collapse the democratic practice in Nigeria because the freedom of the choice and the liberty to change leaders or allow them to continue based on policy performance and reactions are prevented. If the party financing is allowed to continue to evade transparency and provides an opportunity for the highest bidders, democracy is sold out and the much pandemonium about global democratisation will decline. The prominent scholars of democracy (Norris, 2018a; Dahl, 2019; Diamond, 2019) are expressing disappointment and fear about the future of democracy because of subverted processes and unethical practices that are declining the operation and the system worldwide and the assertions by scholars (Chomsky, 2000; Blum, 2013) that democracy is being unnecessarily forced unto developing countries without commensurating positive impacts will gain a strong backing. Ake (1996) expressed his cynicism about the democratic operations in Africa (Ake, 2000) in his view because there is no direct correlation between democracy and development in Africa (Ake, 1996) except for a condition of misgovernance and leadership failure. Other systems may yield the same desired result of development with sound leadership.

Therefore, electoral integrity can be pursued by addressing all the challenges and minimising them to the barest minimum level, particularly, political corruption. Excessive spending, violation of regulations, vote-buying and clientelism can be reversed through strong and sound reforms in the case of Nigeria going beyond policymakers and their imaginative loose laws. A formidable third force such as civil societies (Cohen & Felson, 1979; Bottom & Wiles, 1997) should be vibrant and proactive in countering this nemesis. Nigeria cannot boast of electoral integrity with the shameless exhibition of the political bazaar during primaries and the open vote-buying that transpired in the previous elections in the Fourth Republic and the preparation for the 2023 general election. A particular new political culture is being introduced which is psychologically sending messages to the electorates that democracy and electoral contests are completely a business affair of the wealthy and the powerful godfathers and the ruling class. The desperation and the impatience portrayed by some aspirants and contestants in buying and bulldozing their way is triggering questions on the authentic intention of the ambition and the outcome of the success of those desperadoes. Thus, until the party financing process is monitored and compliance to the best ability of all the stakeholders is enforced and assured, the Nigerian electoral process and democracy are far from integrity and transparency.

Chapter 11

Conclusion

The book concludes that there is an established correlation between party financing, electoral politics and political corruption in Nigeria. This democratic challenge is a universal problem that all world democracies are facing. Parties are examined as motivating factors of democratisation worldwide. In essence, parties organise democracy and compete for democratic influence and control. Democracy is a system of government that operates with financing. The process of selling ideologies, policies, programmes and manifestoes involved financial implications. Yet, democracy is a form of government that is strict in fostering accountability and transparency. Where money is involved, justifying accountability and transparency is difficult, particularly if clandestine affairs are part of the process.

To ensure transparency and eschew corrupt practices in the party financing process in Nigeria, regulations were enacted in 2006, modified in 2010 and amended in 2022. The various loopholes and omitted areas that will consolidate the laws and enhance transparency were identified and integrated. Major issues of party financing including maximum parties' expenditure, maximum campaign spending for all elective offices, donations ban, maximum contribution limit, disclosure, auditing and monitoring in addition to sanctions were revisited and strengthened in 2010 and 2022. The lawmakers and the policymakers put their heads together to give the Nigerian party financing a credible process that will promote integrity.

Nigerian party financing is guided by two major laws as espoused in the study. The 1999 Constitution as Amended in Section 225 and its sub-sections and Section 226 and its sub-sections. In the constitutional provisions, legal sources of parties' income and expenditure and types of donations and contributions were spelt out and sanctions are recommended for violations accordingly. The other legal source of regulations for party financing in Nigeria is the Electoral Act 2006, Electoral Act 2010 and Electoral Act 2022. The acts were amended twice, particularly, sections that specify maximum spending limits which are reviewed upward in consideration of inflationary trends and the pervasive Nigerian political culture and the political economy of money politics. These regulations were perceived as inadequate and weak by previous studies, specifically, the 2006 and 2010 Electoral Acts because the 2022 Electoral Act came into effect in May 2022 and only the Osun State Gubernatorial election was conducted in July 2022 using the new regulations. This motivates this work to ascertain the extent of the weakness and strengths of the regulations and how to strengthen them.

The study observes that the new law, 2022 Electoral Act, is progressing in achieving accountability and transparency in party financing in Nigeria but a critical analysis of the various provisions and sections such as maximum spending limit, sanctions, donations bans, contributions limit, auditing and monitoring are not consolidated as anticipated by experts in the field of study. Most of the recommendations of previous studies on improving the 2006 and 2010 Electoral Acts were not captured accordingly. This leaves a vacuum in which this study revisited, analysed and suggested further reforms to satisfy the minimum standard of accountability and transparency in party financing. The maximum campaign expenditure and sanctions for erring parties and politicians are reported in this study as inadequate and weak to open a medium for violation. The full application of the 2022 Electoral Act will be in the 2023 general election but on the issue of financing, little or no change is expected based on the projection and observation of the laws critically.

Nigeria is one of the democracies that adopted private funding. Party financing takes three dimensions: public funding, private funding and a mixture of public and private funding. The funding pattern dominates debates and policies by global key players. The funding process is left open to the discretion of states but a harmonised stand is recommended for a reform that will enhance accountability and transparency. Nigeria is recommended as one of the best in Africa in terms of the provision of comprehensive rules of party financing. Nigeria itself practised public funding in the Fourth Republic from 1999 to 2010 but it was abolished and private funding was favoured and adopted. However, the regulations on party financing provide and specify the interpretations of private sources, legal funding, prohibited sources and other related laws. Parties and politicians sponsored their campaigns using private sources.

The party financing in Nigeria is alarming concerning the malpractice and violations that are surfacing. An informal relationship emerges from the process of clientelism and patrimonialism. Money politics and electoral corruption dominate the scene. Parties and their candidates spent beyond the maximum limit while violating regulations of party funding. Vote-buying, bribery of electoral officials, patron-client relations, godfatherism, a promise of reward and coercion become dominant in the Nigerian electoral process. The politicians found the party financing process an avenue for game-playing spending heavily to secure electoral victory at all costs because politics is converted into investment in Nigeria where contestants spend excessively to win and recoup their money to make an extra profit through accumulation, looting of public treasury and prebendel politics. Thus, political corruption emerges which challenges the Nigerian electoral conduct.

The illegal practices and corrupt actions of politicians influence the electoral process in Nigeria. Money becomes a decisive factor in determining who secures a party nomination, who contests an election and who wins. Electoral corruption and fraud affect the credibility and integrity of Nigeria's elections in the Fourth Republic. Votes are traded like market commodities while the laws are violated with impunity. Several established cases of violations by politicians, voters, officials of the electoral body, allies of parties and politicians' frontmen were discovered in this study some from previous studies while many from fieldwork. With all the confirmed cases, it is expected that measures are to be taken in sanctioning the offenders but the body that is saddled with the responsibility of monitoring and sanction, INEC, failed to discharge its duties.

It is observed in the study that INEC is not monitoring party financing in Nigeria appropriately because of several factors. Apart from the dubious character of politicians who are not willing to cooperate, the inadequate manpower by INEC, the indifference of the voters, weak regulations and inaction in sanctioning violators and other political actors blocked investigation and monitoring. It is revealed that INEC is willing and ready to monitor and sanction the offenders if the necessary environment for doing so is provided. However, it seems Nigerian politicians have successfully turned Nigerian elections into games and clientele affairs and they will never accede to any process that will prevent them from using their financial leverage to buy their way into power. Hence, it is better to look beyond the regulations and the sanctioning body, the INEC, in countering the menace of money politics and electoral and political corruption. This can be done if all stakeholders are involved in the process actively in monitoring and blocking the process of vote-buying, bribery and corrupt practices in the party financing process. It will be more difficult but not impossible if feasible strategies are identified.

THE IMPERATIVE FOR REFORM AND MONITORING

The purpose of the study is not to explore the problems and leave matters on the way. The desire is to present and proffer plausible and feasible remedies that can be applied minimally to counter the menace of money politics and political corruption in the party financing process. All over the world, experts on party financing are continuously and constantly calling for reforms. These reforms can be approached at a multi-level pattern because of weak institutions at the domestic level. When the old democracies like the United States, Italy, Britain and several other advanced ones are still battling with the question of integrity and transparency of the electoral process and party financing it is not surprising that new democracies like Nigeria will face more issues with the phenomenon. But this does not entail that policymakers and academics will despair and wait for the West to make a breakthrough before they fix their problem. The issue is affecting the developing democracies more than the advanced ones because it is threatening to entirely wipe out democratic liberty and freedom of choice by reducing democracy and elections in places like Nigeria to heavy investment involving huge sums of money and that is mocking democracy in the country.

The stakeholders including the academics, media, civil societies and international monitors must step up to pressurise the National Assembly to look into the sections on sanctions and make them strict and severe to enable deterrence when the monitoring becomes effective. For a presidential candidate that is allowed to spend N5 billion in the Electoral Act 2022 and if he violates by spending above the ceiling or receives donations from anonymous sources beyond the contribution ban or foreign sources or buying votes or other offences, the provisions are not discouraging to deter future violation. If the presidential candidate spent for example N50 billion or above, the sanction simply means to pay a fine of N50 million or one-year imprisonment or both. In all the cases identified in this study so far, none is subjected to these sanctions even when the sanctions are being weak and flexible to allow the culprits to escape. A more severe punishment that will prevent many out of the fear of the consequences is needed. This cannot be achieved easily. The lawmakers are beneficiaries of the weak laws and the violation with impunity. To design laws that will hang them will be difficult. Until internal and external pressure is mounted on them incessantly, they will never do the needful.

It is suggested that violations of financial regulations by candidates should be sanctioned through a reasonable amount that will discourage the actions. Thus, 50 percent of the total maximum spending limit is recommended in the proposed amendment with a proposed twelve-year jail term or both. In addition, the candidate in question should be banned from contesting any elective office in Nigeria permanently. This will scare the impending actions in future even if it will not stop them completely. In addition, the INEC should be empowered to recommend the culprits to the Economic and Financial Crimes Commission (EFCC) for the blacklist to the international community for a possible travel ban to the favoured tourism destination of the Nigerian ruling class. If the violation is from a party, the party should stand a chance to lose its seats in that particular case to the immediate runner-up and the party should be suspended for two election periods of eight years in that specific seat irrespective of the level that the crime is committed. This will help immensely in frightening other fellow parties into committing the same offence in the future.

Therefore, any reform in Nigerian party financing should start with the laws themselves. All areas that are observed to have been weak should be reviewed and strengthened accordingly. Likewise, where it is sensed that the provisions are inadequate may be tantamount to violation they should be reviewed upward to give enough chance for the candidates and the parties to operate within legality to avoid the violation and the sanction. The aim is not to punish but to prevent the offences from occurring. Any amount required that the politicians and parties feel is fair to them as a maximum donation or spending limit should be debated and a modest view should be adopted. This study disagrees with the new maximum spending limit as inadequate but it has agreed with the contribution limit. To avoid unjust sanction of the contestants for violation, the amount should be reviewed upward at least, by doubling them at all the elective offices.

A reform that is limited to domestic laws will not yield the required results in Nigeria because of weak institutions and political will. The international monitors and other organisations such as OECD, the United States, UN and other powerful countries and agencies should slam a travel ban and other privileges to the reported violators. This is not to exonerate leaders in the above-said countries from the same offences but since they claimed ownership of democracy and shouldered the task of its global promotion, they should help strengthen the developing ones at least, to their level of transparency. If the violators in Nigeria learn that a travel sanction awaits them to America, Europe and other countries that they have turned into medical and educational tourism for themselves and their families, they would be afraid and it will be a terrific dilemma for them. Some elections were believed to have been improved because of a similar approach. The United States made it clear to the Nigerian leaders in the 2015 general election that it will not tolerate any attempt at truncating democracy in the country and any leader found to involve in the act will be punished severely. This is believed to have been a contributing factor to the improved election. In the 2019 general election, a similar feat repeated itself and the actors involved were declared among those to be banned from travelling to the United States and other exotic European countries.

The powerful world countries and the international organisations can help the emerging democracies to institutionalise by being bold in introducing measures that will compel compliance for transparent measures. Another way that they will help the Nigerian party financing is to help in surveillance of the movement of funds from within and outside the countries targeted at the specific accounts of the contestants. A special money laundering unit should be established purposely for this role. Many reports like Panama Papers and Dubai Reports (Sule & Sambo, 2020) indicated that most Nigerian ruling class have properties there and other destinations such as the United States, United Kingdom, Dubai and European states. The countries should be honest and committed to watching the movement of funds during elections from the accounts of these classes and report any suspected violations. The countries should confiscate the properties as a sanction, slam a travel ban and disconnect diplomacy with them.

Domestic civil societies have a great role to play in enforcing transparency and compliance in the party financing process in Nigeria. The civil societies are lucky that INEC is willing to work with them in cooperation and collaboration. They should be a watchdog of the process of party primaries and final elections and reveal their findings. Some of them such as the Centre for Democracy and Development (CDD), Civil Society Legislative Advocacy Centre (CISLAC) and the Nigerian Civil Society Situation Room (NCSSR) have been doing so. Most of the information that is made public on the violation and excessive spending was divulged by these civil societies and their counterparts. The civil societies should collaborate more with INEC and expand the cooperation with the international monitors and powerful world countries in giving them data and evidence of violation of the suggested sanction discussed earlier. Civil societies are a strong force in the democratic process. The role played by civil societies in the transition to democracy in Nigeria's Fourth Republic is outstanding (Sule et al., 2021b). They should not relent in sustaining and improving the democratic process as they played a role in the emergence of the process.

Civil societies should intensify their role in civic-voter education. They should come closer and simpler to the voters, especially, at the grassroots through the medium of the media and direct physical contact. The level of engagement of civil societies with the Nigerian populace is inadequate. They should work hard to earn grants from sponsors to take the responsibility of radio and television and other media outlets in enlightening the voters on the need not only to shun vote-selling or bribery but also to pay closer attention to excessive spending and violation. The populace should be awakened to understand that watching and pressurising the ruling class is their responsibility. It should be understood that citizens in advanced democracies of the West are having their liberty and freedom respected by their leaders because they watch them closely and react when they are not satisfied sometimes through protests and other means such as social media. The Nigerian citizens should know that until they live up to their expectations, this unconscious destruction of the hard-earned democracy by the ruling elite will continue.

The media is an important instrument that will help the reform work successfully. No agency or platform has the power to manipulate and influence people's perceptions in a short period of time like the media. The media should reach out to the citizens in their local languages and entertain them with a basic understanding of democracy, laws, elections and processes and the process of governance. The services of experts can be engaged such as academics, INEC officials, anti-corruption agencies, security operatives and experts in various matters of election, democracy, governance and other related matters. If the media is interested, people will sit up from their slumber and do what is expected of them.

Besides, social media can be used by both media itself and the civil societies which are penetrating and accessible in all nooks and crannies of the country. Programmes that are meant to enlighten the citizenry should be designed and sponsored. Many of the media houses are doing that but they should double the efforts. Some jingles, plays and other comedies that will entertain but educate are needed to deliver the messages as expected. The media should also use the investigative journalism perspective and report dubious and suspicious illegal transactions that will impede transparency in the electoral process. Some shocking revelations will awaken the conscience of the citizens to act accordingly. The media should also use a comparative approach by showcasing some examples from the neighbourhood and other peer countries.

The INEC has a herculean task in monitoring and sanctioning. The independence of INEC is not doubted but the meddlesomeness of politicians is also possible and obtainable. INEC should be reformed. The procedure for the appointment of the chairman should change. As suggested by Justice Uwais Committee formed by the late Yar'adua Administration, the National Judicial Council should appoint the chairman of the commission independent of the executive or any other arm of government. The INEC has the task of inviting and receiving suggestions for reforms from the concerned citizens and other stakeholders. The review of the Electoral Act and some sections on sanctions suggested earlier in this chapter is only possible if INEC is willing and determined to do it. INEC also has the task of cooperating with civil societies in giving vital non-classified information and data that will help in enforcing compliance and exposing violations. The INEC has the task of displaying neutrality and determination to deliver credible elections with integrity including effective monitoring and enforcement of laws.

Effective monitoring is only possible if INEC is empowered. The commission should be given extra financial strength to employ additional staff and to employ the leverage of its collaboration with civil societies and the media in the monitoring. INEC should open a room for collating observations and other data on the violation and excessive spending and illegal financial flow to the parties and candidates. The data received should be put to effect. All confirmed cases should be handled with utmost sincerity and the zeal to address the cases by sanctioning. Even the perceived weak and flexible sanctions need to start operating before the strict ones suggested come into effect. If the INEC is sanctioning the confirmed cases of violation it will discourage the parties and candidates from committing the offences because they will anticipate that if the stronger sanctions are included, they will fall victims.

The academics have a great role to play. Of course, they have been doing it, but they need to do more. They should study laws, regulations of party financing and the changing patterns of Nigerian elections and money politics and vote-buying, disseminate the findings globally and make strong suggestions and recommendations on possible ways that are succinct but comprehensive with the detail of applicability practically. The academics can collaborate with INEC, secure grants and go to the field to uncover many issues of violation that INEC and other bodies may not find easier. There are such efforts recently but more are needed. The academics can orient their students and societal members on the projected dangers of money politics and the ways to shun it and the evil of selling their votes. They can attend media programmes, public lectures, seminars, workshops and round table discussions in addition to local community engagements face-to-face to convey their messages.

The voters or the citizens have a greater task in the reform. They should demand for fair process and monitor the process. No actor can do more than them. Instead of sponsoring politically motivated national security-threatening protests such as EndSARS and others, such protests should be directed to demanding reform for transparency in the electoral process. The way the ruling class became terrified and the protest was backed by the Western media and their leaders, if demand for transparency is the motive, it will generate more support and the Nigerian Government will succumb to making some concessions that they will not do under normal circumstances. Additionally, following the electoral process, budgetary process, campaign activities of contestants and other related events will help in exposing the suspicious transactions that the citizens will now take up against the culprits in social media and other platforms to pressurise for investigations and actions. In the process of reform, the country can study other models and adopt them. It is discovered in the African case studies that the institutions in countries like Botswana, Rwanda and South Africa are more assertive in taking measures against corrupt politicians. Such measures can be taken and implemented in the Nigerian context.

References

Abba, S.A., & Babalola, D. (2017). Contending Issues in Political Parties in Nigeria: The Candidate Selection Process. *Africology: The Journal of Pan African Studies.* 11(1), 118–134.

Abbink, J. (2000). "Introduction: Rethinking Democratisation and Election Observation". In Abbink, J., & Hesseling, G. (Eds.), *Election Observation and Democratisation*, pp. 1–20. London: Macmillan Press.

Abdallah, N.M. (2018). "2019 Elections Set to be Nigeria's Most Expensive". In *Daily Trust Newspaper Online*. Retrieved from https://www.dailytrust.com .ng/2019-elections-set-to-be-nigeria-s-most-expensive-263938.html on 25th June 2022 at 11:40 pm.

Abdullahi, B. (2017). *On a Platter of Gold: How Jonathan Won and Lost Nigeria.* Ibadan: Booksellers Limited.

Abdallah, S.M. (2017). *Clientelism, Rent-Seeking and Protection: A Study of Corruption in Iraq after 2003.* A Thesis submitted for the Degree of Doctor of Philosophy, School of Geography, Politics and Sociology. Newcastle University.

Achebe, C. (2012). *There Was a Country: A Memoir.* London: Penguin.

Achen, C.H., & Bartels, L.M. (2016). *Democracy for Realists: Why Elections Do Not Produce Responsive Government.* Princeton: Princeton University Press.

Achoba, F., & Maren, B.A. (2021). "Postcolonial Party Politics and Some Aspects of Intergroup Relation in Nigeria up to 2019". In Ajayi, R., & Fashagba, J.Y. (Eds.), *Nigerian Politics*, pp. 289–304. Switzerland: Springer.

Adams, S., & Agomor, K.S. (2015). Democratic Politics and Voting Behaviour. *International Area Studies Review.* 18(4), 365–381.

Adedire, S.A., & Olanrewaju, J.S. (2021). "Military Intervention in Nigerian Politics". In Ajayi, R., & Fashagba, J.Y. (Eds.), *Nigerian Politics*, pp. 395–406. Geneva: Springer.

Adejumobi, S. (2010). "Democracy and Governance in Nigeria: Between Consolidation and Reversal". In Adejumobi, S. (Ed.), *Governance and Politics in Post-Military Nigeria*, pp. 1–22. New York: Palgrave Macmillan.

Adejumobi, S. (2015a). "Introduction". In Adejumobi, S. (Ed.), *Democratic Renewal in Africa: Trends and Discourses*, pp. 1–10. New York: Palgrave Macmillan.

Adejumobi, S. (2015b). "Introduction". In Adejumobi, S. (Ed.), *National Democratic Reforms in Africa: Changes and Challenges*, pp. 1–11. New York: Palgrave Macmillan.

Adejumobi, S., Hamdok, A., Nordlund, P., Rukambe, J., & Dowetin, T. (2007). *Political Parties in West Africa: the Challenges of Democratisation in Fragile States*. Stockholm: International Institute for Democracy and Electoral Assistance.

Adejumobi, S., & Kehinde, M. (2010). Building Democracy Without Democrats? Political Parties and Threats of Political Reversal in Nigeria. *Journal of African Election*. 6(2), 95–113.

Adeniyi, O. (2010). *Power, Politics and Death: The Last 100 Days of Yar'adua*. London: Prestige Publishers.

Adeniyi, S. (2017). *Against the Run of Play: How an Incumbent President was Defeated in Nigeria*. Lagos: Book Baby.

Aderemi, A., Oshodi, T., & Oyefulu, S. (2020). "The Political Economy of the African Crisis Through the Lenses of Bade Onimode". In Oloruntoba, S.O., & Falola, T. (Eds.), *The Palgrave Handbook of African Political Economy*, pp. 315–326. New York: Palgrave Macmillan.

Adetula, V.O.A. (2008). "Money and Politics in Nigeria: An Overview". In Adetula, V.O.A. (Ed.), *Money and Politics in Nigeria,* pp. 1–18. Abuja: DFID.

Adewara, S.O. (2021). "Nigerian Economy During Colonial Era: An Overview". In Ajayi, R., & Fashagba, J.Y. (Eds.), *Nigerian Politics*, pp. 245–258. Geneva: Springer.

Adeyi, E.M. (2008) "Funding of Political Parties and Candidates in Nigeria: Analysis of the Past and Present". In Adetula, V.O.A. (Ed,), *Money and Politics in Nigeria,* pp. 29–38. Abuja: DFID.

African Union. (2018). *Fighting Against Corruption in Africa*. Addis Ababa: African Union.

Agbaje, A. (2010). "Whose Catalyst? Party Politics and Democracy in the Fourth Republic: From Theory to Denial". In Adejumobi, S. (Ed.), *Governance and Politics in Post-Military Nigeria*, pp. 61–88. New York: Palgrave Macmillan.

Agbaje, A., Akande, A., & Ojo, J. (2014). Nigeria's Ruling Party: A Complex Web of Power and Money. *South African Journal of International Affairs*. 14(1), 79–97.

Agbu, O. (2016a). "The Nigerian State and Politics in the Fourth Republic". In Agbu, O. (Ed.), *Elections and Governance in Nigeria's Fourth Republic*, pp. 9–26. Dakar: Council for the Development of Social Science Research in Africa.

Agbu, O. (2016b). "An Overview of Party Formation in Nigeria". In Agbu, O. (Ed.), *Elections and Governance in Nigeria's Fourth Republic*, pp. 9–27. Dakar: Council for the Development of Social Science Research in Africa (CODESRIA).

Aghara, V., Nwaizgbo, I., Chukwuemeka, E., & Onyeizugbe, C. (2015). "Changing Perspectives in Politics Marketing in Nigeria". *Review of Business and Finance Studies*. 6(2), 105–115.

Ahuja, A. (2019). *Mobilising the Marginalised: Ethnic Parties Without Ethnic Movements*. New York: Oxford University Press.

Ajagba, C.O., Gberevbie, D.E., & Agbu, O. (2019). Rebranding the Electoral Process in Nigeria's Fourth Republic (1999–2019): Constraints and Prospects of the Independent National Electoral Commission. *Academic Journal of Interdisciplinary Studies*. 9(1), 56–69.

Akanji, O.O. (2021). "Nigeria Between 1914 and 1960: Political-Constitutional Changes and Crises in an Era of Colonialism". In Ajayi, R., & Fashagba, J.Y. (Eds.), *Nigerian Politics*, pp. 37–54. Switzerland: Springer.

Ake, C. (1981). *A Political Economy of Africa*. London: Longman.

Ake, C. (1996). *Democracy and Development in Africa*. Washington: Brookings Institutions.

Ake, C. (2000). *The Feasibility of Democracy in Africa*. Ibadan: IFRA Nigeria.

Akhaine, S.O. (2020). "The Political Economy of Claude Ake". In Oloruntoba, S.O., & Falola, T. (Eds.), *The Palgrave Handbook of African Political Economy*, pp. 209–220. New York: Palgrave Macmillan.

Akindele, S.T. (2010). Intra and Inter Party Post-Election Crisis/Feud Management in a Pluralistic Democracy: An x-ray of the Nigerian Political Landscape. *African Journal of Political Science and International Relations*. 5(6), 287–330.

Akinola, A. (2014). *Party Coalitions in Nigeria: History, Trends and Prospects*. Ibadan: Safari Books Limited.

Akinsola, F. (2020). "The Global Financial Crisis and the African Economy". In Oloruntoba, S.O., & Falola, T. (Eds.), *The Palgrave Handbook of African Political Economy*, pp. 519–534. New York: Palgrave Macmillan.

Aldrich, J.H., Blais, A., & Stephenson, L.B. (2018). "Strategic Voting and Political Institutions". In Aldrich, J.H., Blais, A., & Stephenson, L.B. (Eds.), *The Many Faces of Strategic Voting: Tactical Behaviour in Electoral Systems Around the World*, pp. 1–27. Ann Arbor: University of Michigan Press.

Alexander, H.E. (1989). *Comparative Political Finance in the 1980s*. New York: Cambridge University Press.

Alford, R.P. (2012). A Broken Windows Theory of International Corruption. *Ohio State Law Journal*. 73, 1253. Retrieved from https://scholarship.law.nd.edu/law_faculty_scholarship/572 on 29th June 2022 at 06:14 pm.

Ali, Y.A. (2015). *The Glorious Quran: Transliteration and Translation*. Beirut: Darul Fikr.

Aluigba, M.T. (2015). *Taming a Lion: Monitoring Campaign Finances of Political Parties Prior to the 2015 Elections in Nigeria*. A Paper Presented at a Two-Day National Conference on The 2015 General Elections in Nigeria: The Real Issues Organized by The Electoral Institute, Abuja Held at The Electoral Institute Complex, INEC Annex, Opposite Diplomatic Zone, Central Business District, Abuja on July 27 to 28, 2015.

Alvarez, R.M., & Hall, T.E. (2008). *Electronic Elections: the Perils and Promises of Digital Democracy*. Princeton: Princeton University Press.

Angerbrandt, H. (2019). Party System Institutionalization and the 2019 State Elections in Nigeria. *Regional and Federal Studies*. 30(3), 415–440.

Antunnes R (2010). *Theoretical Models of Voting Behaviour*. Escola Superior De Educacao- Instituto Politecnico de Coimbra.

Anyadike, N., & Eme, I.O. (2014). Political Financing in Africa: A Comparative Study for Kenya and Nigeria: Proposal for Reform. *Mediterranean Journal of Social Sciences MCSER*. 5(27), 22–34.

Apine, M., & Balogun, S. (2021). "Party Politics and Political Parties Under Presidential and Parliamentary Democracy in Nigeria". In Ajayi, R., & Fashagba, J.Y. (Eds.), *Nigerian Politics*, pp. 233–245. Switzerland: Springer.

Aral, S. (2020). *The Hype Machine: How Social Media Disrupts Our Elections, Our Economy and Our Health, and How We Must Adapt*. New York: Penguin Random House LLC.

Arceneaux, C., & Leithner, A. (2017). "International Monitors". ". In Norris, P., & Nai, A. (Eds.), *Election Watchdog: Transparency, Accountability and Integrity*, pp. 31–53. New York: Oxford University Press.

Archer, M.S., & Tritter, J.Q. (2001). "Introduction". In Archer, M.S., & Tritter, J.Q. (Eds.), *Rational Choice Theory: Resisting Colonisation*, pp. 1–16. London: Routledge, Taylor & Francis.

Aristotle (2015). *Politics*. Chicago: University of Chicago Press.

Arrows, K. (1951). *Social Values and Individual Values*. New York: John Wiley & Sons.

Arrows, K. (1986). Rationality of Self and others in Economic System. *The Journal of Business*. 59(4), 385–399.

Asobie, H.A. (2012). Conceptual, Theoretical and Empirical Issues on the Interface between Corruption, Governance and Development". In Mohammed, H., Aluaigba, T., & Kabir, A. (Eds.), *Corruption, Governance and Development in Nigeria: Perspectives and Remedies*, pp. 24–43. Washington: UNDP Publication.

Aspinall, E. & Berenschot, W. (2019). *Democracy for Sale: Elections, Clientelism and the State in Indonesia*. Ithaca: Cornell University Press.

Aspinall, E., & Sukmajati, M. (2019). *Electoral Dynamics in Indonesia: Money Politics, Patronage and Clientelism at Grassroots Indonesia*. Singapore: NUS Press.

Audu, M., & Oshewolo, R. (2021). "Nigeria up to 1914: Some Emerging Political and Economic Issues". In Ajayi, R., & Fashagba, J.Y. (Eds.), *Nigerian Politics*, pp. 25–36. Geneva: Springer.

Awa, E.O. (1964). *Federal Government in Nigeria*. California: University of California Press.

Ayeni, O.O. (2019). Commodification of Politics: Party Funding and Electoral Contest in Nigeria. *Sage Open*. April-June 2019, 1–8. doi: 10.1177/2158244019855.

Aylott, N., & Bolin, N. (2021). "Conflicts and Coronations: Analysing Leader Selection in European Political Parties". In Aylott, N., & Bolin, N. (Eds.), *Managing Leader Selection in European Political Parties*, pp. 1–18. New York: Palgrave Macmillan.

Ayoade, J.A.A. (2008) "Godfather Politics in Nigeria". In Adetula, V.O.A. (Ed.) *Money and Politics in Nigeria,* pp. 85–96. Abuja: DFID.

Ayobade, A. (2020). "Deindustrialization and Entrepreneur Dynamism: An Assessment of the Replacement of Industrial Clusters with Event Centres in Lagos, Nigeria". In Oloruntoba, S.O., & Falola, T. (Eds.), *The Palgrave Handbook of African Political Economy*, pp. 467–486. New York: Palgrave Macmillan.

Babatunde, H.O., Iwu, H.N., & Osuji, A.O. (2019). Money Politics and Vote Buying in Nigeria's Fourth Republic: Implications for National Security. *SocialScientia: Journal of the Social Sciences and Humanities*. 4(2), 40–55.

Babatunde, H.O., Shaibu, M.T., & Olawale, A.O. (2019). Money Politics in Nigeria's Fourth Republic: Implications for Electoral Process and Democratic Consolidation. *Journal of Research in Humanities and Social Science*. 7(2), 34–42.

Bailey, J. (2006). *Corruption and Democratic Governability in Latin America: Issues of Types, Arenas, Perceptions, and Linkages*. Unpublished Paper Delivered at the 2006 Meeting of the Latin American Studies Association, San Juan, Puerto Rico, 15–18.

Baje, A. (2022). "Money Politics and its Implications for Nigeria". *The Guardian*. Retrieved from https://guardian.ng/opinion/money-politics-and-its-implications -for-nigeria/ on 29th June 2022 at 02:02 am.

Bakar, S.M.A., & Ghosh, R.N. (2014). "Introduction". In Bakar, S.M.A., & Ghosh, R.N. *Corruption, Good Governance and Economic Development: Contemporary Analysis and Case Studies*, pp. 3–8. (Vol. 28). Singapore: World Scientific.

Balboa, J., & Medalla, E.M. (2006). Anti-Corruption and Governance: The Philippine Experience. *APEC Study Centre Consortium Conference*, 1–28. Ho Chi Minh City, Viet Nam.

Baldini, G., & Pappalardo, A. (2009). *Elections, Electoral Systems and Volatile Voters*. New York: Palgrave Macmillan.

Bale, T., Webb, P., & Poletti, M. (2020). *Footsoldiers: Political Party Membership in the 21st Century*. London: Routledge, Taylor & Francis.

Balogun, M.J. (1997). Enduring Clientelism, Governance Reform and Leadership Capacity: A Review of the Democratisation Process in Nigeria. *Journal of Contemporary African Studies*. 15(2), 237–260.

Barberà, O., Sandri, G., Correa, P., & Rodríguez-Teruel, J. (2021). "Political Parties Transition into the Digital Era". In Barberà, O., Sandri, G., Correa, P., & Rodríguez-Teruel, J. (Eds.), *Digital Parties: The Challenges of Online Organisation and Participation*, pp. 1–22. Geneva: Springer.

Bariledum, K., Abang, O.P., & Nwigbo, T.S. (2016). The Political Ecology in Nigeria and the Fragility of Democratic Sustainability. *Global Journal of Political Science and Administration*. 4(3), 9–19.

Bariledum, K., Godpower, N.B., & Tambari, N.S. (2016). Foreign Democratic Assistance to Nigeria (1999-201): The Nexus Between Strategy and Elections Results. *Global Journal of Political Science and Administration*. 14(1), 29–37.

Basile, L. (2019). *The Party Politics of Decentralisation: The Territorial Dimension in Italian Party Agenda*. New York: Palgrave Macmillan.

Bendor, J., Diermeier, D., Siegel, D.A., & Ting, M.M. (2011). *A Behavioural Theory of Election*. Princeton: Princeton University Press.

Best, K.C. (2008). "Gender, Money and Politics in Nigeria". In Adetula, V.O.A. (Ed.), *Money and Politics in Nigeria,* pp. 53–64. Abuja: IFES.

Bhuiyan, B.A. (2016). An Overview of Game Theory and Some Applications. *Philosophy and Progress*. LIX(LX), 112–128.

Bieber, F. (2008). "Introduction". In Skopje (Ed.), *Political Parties and Minority Participation*, pp. 5–30. Macedonia: Friedrich Ebert Stiftung.

Bigman, D. (2011). *Poverty, Hunger and Democracy in Africa: Potential and Limitations of Democracy in Cementing Multi-ethnic Societies.* New York: Palgrave Macmillan.

Binmore, K. (2007). *Game Theory: A Very Short Introduction.* New York: Oxford University Press.

Birch, S. (2020). *Electoral Violence, Corruption and Political Order.* Princeton: Princeton University Press.

Birch, S., Daxecker, U., & Hoglund, K. (2020). Electoral Violence: An Introduction. *Journal of Peace Research.* 57(1), 3–14.

Blais, A. (2011). *To Vote or Not to Vote: The Merits and Limits of Rational Choice Theory.* Pittsburgh: University of Pittsburgh Press.

Blondel, J. (1968). *An Introduction to Comparative Government.* London: Routledge.

Blum, W. (2002). *Rogue States: A Guide to the World's Only Superpower.* London: Zed Books.

Blum, W. (2013). *America's Deadliest Export Democracy: The Truth about US Foreign Policy and Everything Else.* London: Zed Books.

Blundo, G., De-Sardan, J.-P.O., Arifari, N.B., & Alou, M.T. (2013). *Everyday Corruption and the State: Citizens and Public Officials in Africa.* London: Zed Books Ltd.

Bogaards, M. (2007). "Electoral Systems, Party Systems and Ethnicity in Africa". In Basedau, M., Erdman, G., & Mehler, A. (Eds.), *Votes, Money and Violence: Political Parties and Elections in Sub-Saharan Africa*, pp. 168–187. Scottsville: University of KwaZulu-Natal.

Bogaards, M. (2010). Ethnic Party Bans and Institutional Engineering in Nigeria. *Journal of Democratisation.* 17(4), 730–749.

Bogdan, R.C., & Biklen, S.K. (2007). *Qualitative Research for Education: An Introduction to Theories and Methods.* Boston: Pearson Education.

Bolger, G. (2019). "The Uses and Challenges of Survey Research in Elections] Campaigns". In Nelson, C.J., & Thurber, J.E. (Eds.), *Campaigns and Elections American Style: The Changing Landscape of Political Campaigns*, pp. 94–122. London: Routledge, Taylor & Francis.

Bottoms, A.E., & Wiles, P. (1997). "Environmental Criminology". In Maguire, M., Moran, R., & Reiner, R. (Eds.), *The Oxford Handbook of Criminology*, pp. 620–656. Oxford: Clarendon Press.

Bratton, M. (2008). Vote buying and Violence in Nigerian Election Campaigns. *Electoral Studies.* 27(4), 621–632.

Braun, C., & Clarke, P. (2013). *Qualitative Research Method for Social Science.* New Delhi: Pearson Education Inc.

Brennan, J. (2016). *Against Democracy.* Princeton: Princeton University Press.

Brewer, M.D., & Maisel, L.S. (2021). *Parties and Elections in America: The Electoral Process.* Lanham: Rowman & Littlefield.

Brun, D.A. (2014). "Introduction: Evaluating Political Clientelism". In Brun, D.A., & Diamond, L. (Eds.), *Clientelism, Social Policy and the Quality of Democracy*, pp. 1–16. Baltimore: Johns Hopkins University Press.

Bryan, S., & Baer, D. (2005). *Money in Politics: A Study of Party Financing Practices in 22 Countries*. Washington, USA: National Democratic Institute for International Affairs.

Burchard, S.M., & Simati, M. (2019). The Role of the Courts in Mitigating Election Violence in Nigeria. *Review of African Studies*. 38(1), 123–144.

Burke, E. (1981). *Thoughts on the Cause of the Present Discontents: the Writings and Speeches of Edmund Burke*. Oxford: Clarendon Press.

Burlacu, D., & Toka, G. (2014). "Policy-Based Voting and the Type of Democracy". In Thomassen, J. (Ed.), *Elections and Democracy: Representation and Accountability*, pp. 60–78. New York: Oxford University Press.

Buttorff, G.J. (2019). *Authoritarian Elections and Opposition Groups in the Arab World*. New York: Palgrave Macmillan.

Campbell, J. (2019). *The Legacy of Nigeria's 1999 Transition to Democracy*. Washington, USA: Council on Foreign Relations.

Campbell, J., & Page, M. (2018). *Nigeria: What Everyone Needs to Know*. New York: Oxford University Press.

Casimir, A., Omeh, E., & Ike, C. (2013). Electoral Fraud in Nigeria: A Philosophical Evaluation of the Framework of Electoral Violence. *Open Journal of Political Science*. 3(4), 167–174.

Cendales, A., Guerrero, H., Wilches, J., & Pinto, A. (2019). "Introduction: The Paradox of a Formally Open and Materially Exclusive Democracies". In Cendales, A., Pinto, A., Mora, J.J., & Guerrero, H. (Eds.), *Analytical Narratives on Sub-National Politics in Colombia: Clientelism, Government and Public Policy in the Pacific Region*, pp. 1–8. Geneva: Springer.

Ceron, A. (2019). *Leaders, Factions and the Game of Intra-Party Politics*. London: Routledge, Taylor & Francis.

Cesari, J. (2020). "Religion, State and Nation: Islamic Parties Between Ideology and Religion". In Haynes, J. (Ed.), *The Routledge Handbook to Religion and Political Parties*, pp. 20–30. London: Routledge, Taylor & Francis.

Chambray, P.G. (1932). *The Game of Politics: A Study of the British Principles of Political Strategy*. California: The University of California.

Chasman, D., & Cohen, J. (2020). *The Right to be Elected: 100 Years after Women's Suffrage*. Massachusetts: MIT Press.

Chayes, S. (2015). *Thieves of State: Why Corruption Threatens Global Security*. New Jersey, USA: WW Norton & Company.

Cheek, M. (2020). "Money Laundering Around the World". *Smart Search. Smartsearch*. Retrieved from https://www.smartsearch.com/resources/blog/money-laundering-around-the-world on 29th June 2022 at 04:52 pm.

Cheeseman, N., & Klaas, B. (2018). *How to Rig an Election*. New Haven: Yale University Press.

Cheeseman, N., Lynch, G., & Willis, J. (2020). *The Moral Economy of Elections in Africa: Democracy, Voting and Virtue*. New York: Cambridge University Press.

Chomsky, N. (2000). *Rogue States: The Rule of Force in World Affairs*. London: Pluto Press.

Close, D., & Prevost, G. (2007). "Introduction: Transitioning from Revolutionary Movements to Political Parties and Making the Revolution "Stick"". In Deodandan, K., Close, D., & Prevost, G. (Eds.), *From Revolutionary Movements to Political Parties Cases from Latin America and Africa*, pp. 1–16. New York: Palgrave Macmillan.

Cohen, L.E., & Felson, M. (1979). Social Change and Crime Rate Trends: A Routine Activity Approach. *American Sociological Review*. 44(4), 588–608.

Coleman, J.S. & Fararo, T.J. (1992). *Rational Choice Theory: Advocacy and Critique*. London: Sage.

Coleman, S., & Brogden, J. (2020). *Capturing the Mood of Democracy: The British General Election 2019*. New York: Palgrave Macmillan.

Collier, D. (1993). "The Comparative Method". In Ada, W.F. (Ed.), *Political Science: The State Of the Discipline II*. Washington, DC: American Political Science Association.

Collier, P. (2009). *Wars, Guns and Votes: Democracy in Dangerous Places*. New York: Harper Collins E-Book.

Coma, F.M.I. (2017). "Electoral Reform". In Norris, P., & Nai, A. (Eds.), *Election Watchdog: Transparency, Accountability and Integrity*, pp. 72–91. New York: Oxford University Press.

Creswell, J.W. (2014). *Research design: Qualitative, Quantitative & Mixed Methods Approaches*. California: Sage Publication.

Creswell, J.W. (2015). *Educational Research: Planning, Conducting, and Evaluating Quantitative and Qualitative Research*. New Delhi: Pearson.

Cross, W., Kenig, O., Pruysers, S., & Rahat, G. (2016). *The Promise and Challenge of Party Primary Elections A Comparative Perspective*. Montreal: McGill-Queen's University Press.

Crotty, W. (2006). "Party Origins and Evolutions in the United States". In Katz, R.S., & Crotty, W. (Eds.), *Handbook of Party Politics,* pp. 25–33. London: Sage.

Dada, J.O. (2021). A Holistic Appraisal of Electoral Fraud and other Electoral Irregularities in Nigeria: Way Forward. *Global Journal of Politics and Law Research*. 9(4), 21–31.

Dahl, R.A. (1966). *Polyarchy: Participation and Opposition*. Yale: Yale University Press.

Dahl, R.A. (2006). *A Preface to Democratic Theory*. Chicago: University of Chicago Press.

Dahl, R.A. (2019). *Dilemmas of Democracy: Autonomy versus Control*. New Haven: Yale University Press.

Dalton, R.J., & Anderson, C.J. (2011). "Citizens, Contexts and Choice". In Dalton, R.J., & Anderson, C.J. (Eds.), *Citizens, Context, and Choice: How Context Shapes Citizens' Electoral Choices*, pp. 3–32. New York: Oxford University Press.

Dalton, R.J., Farrell, D.M., & McAllister, I. (2011). *Political Parties and Democratic Linkage: How Parties Organise Democracy*. New York: Oxford University Press.

Dalton, R.J., & Wattenberg, M.P. (2000). "Unthinkable Democracy: Political Change in Advanced Industrial Democracies". In Dalton, R.J., & Wattenberg, M.P. (Eds.),

Parties Without Partisans: Political Change in Advanced Industrial Democracies, pp. 3–18. New York: Oxford University Press.

Danjibo, N., & Ashindorbe, K. (2018). The Evolution and Pattern of Political Party Formation and the Search for National Integration in Nigeria. *Brazilian Journal of African Studies.* 3(5), 85–100.

Darabont, C.A. (2010). The Entrenchment of Clientelistic Practices: Methodological and Conceptual Issues of Transferability. *European Journal of Interdisciplinary Studies.* 2(1), 21–34.

Davies, A.A. (2021). "Money Politics in the Nigerian Electoral Process". In Ajayi, R., & Fashagba, J.Y. (Eds.), *Nigerian Politics,* pp. 341–352. Switzerland: Springer.

Daxecker, U., Jessica Di Salvatore, J., & Ruggeri, A. (2019). Fraud Is What People Make of It: Election Fraud, Perceived Fraud, and Protesting in Nigeria. *Journal of Conflict Resolution.* 63(9), 2098–2127.

De Elvira, L.R., Schwarz, C.H., & Irene Weipert-Fenne, I. (2019). "Introduction: Networks of Dependency, a Research Perspective". In De Elvira, L.R., Schwarz, C.H., & Irene Weipert-Fenne, I. (Eds.), *Clientelism and Patronage in the Middle East and North Africa: Networks of Dependency,* pp. 1–16. London: Routledge, Taylor & Francis.

De Jonge, J. (2012). *Rethinking Rational Choice Theory: A Companion on Rational and Moral Action.* New York: Palgrave Macmillan.

Delay, J. (2019). *Nigeria: Widespread Violence Ushers in President's New Term Investigate Attacks, Ensure Justice.* Abuja: Human Rights Watch.

Dele-Adedeji, I. (2019). "Nigeria has a History of Doggy Elections: Will it be Different this Time?" *The Conversation.* Retrieved from https://theconversation.com /nigeria-has-a-history-of-dodgy-elections-will-it-be-different-this-time-111093 on 25th June 2022 at 11:30 pm.

Demarest, L. (2021). Elite Clientelism in Nigeria: The Role of Parties in Weakening Legislator-Voter Ties. *Party Politics.* 8(1), 1–12.

Demarest, L. (2021). Men of the people? Democracy and Prebendalism in Nigeria's Fourth Republic National Assembly. *Democratisation.* 28(4), 684–702.

Demarest, L., & Langer, A. (2019). Reporting on Electoral Violence in Nigerian News Media: "Saying it as it is"? *African Studies Review.* 62(4), 83–109.

Deribe, A.U., Sambo, U., Sule, B., & Salihu, I. (2020). Unmasking the Tape of Electoral Fraud at Grassroots Nigeria: Evidence from the Management of the Local Council Elections by the State Independent Electoral Commissions (SIECS). *Kashere Journal of Humanities Management and Social Sciences.* 4(1), 19–42.

Dervin, F., & Simpson, A. (2021). *Interculturality and the Political within Education.* London: Routledge, Taylor & Francis.

De Winter, L., & Dumont, P. (2006). "Parties into Government: Still Many Puzzles". In Katz, R.S., & Crotty, W. (Eds.), *Handbook of Party Politics,* pp. 5–15. London: Sage.

Diamond, L. (1995a). *Class, Ethnicity and Democracy in Nigeria: The Failure of the First Republic.* London: Macmillan Press.

Diamond, L. (1995b). "Nigeria: The Uncivic Society and the Descent into Praetorianism". In Diamond, L., Linz, J., & Lipset, S. (Eds.), *Politics in Developing*

Countries: Comparing Experiences with Democracy, pp. 19–36. Boulder: Lynne Rienner Publishers.

Diamond, L. (2019). "Facing up the Democratic Recession". In Diamond, L., & Plattner, M.C. (Eds.), *Democracy in Decline?* pp. 98–118. Baltimore: Johns Hopkins University Press.

Diamond, L., & Gunther, R. (2001). *Political Parties and Democracy*. Baltimore: Johns Hopkins University Press.

Dickson, B.J. (2021). *The Party and the People: Chinese Politics in the 21st Century*. New Jersey: Princeton University Press.

Dike, V.E. (2001). *Democracy and Political Life in Nigeria*. Zaria: Ahmadu Bello University Press.

Dimand, M.A., & Dimand, R.W. (2002). *The History of Game Theory Volume I: From the Beginnings to 1941*. New York: Routledge, Taylor & Francis.

Dimova, G. (2020). *Democracy Beyond Elections Government Accountability in the Media Age*. New York: Palgrave Macmillan.

Dixit, A. (2018). "Anti-Corruption Institutions: Some History and Theory". In Basu, K., & Cordella, T. (Eds.), *Institutions, Governance and the Control of Corruption*, pp. 15–49. New York: Palgrave Macmillan.

Donno, D. (2017). "International Enforcement". ". In Norris, P., & Nai, A. (Eds.), *Election Watchdog: Transparency, Accountability and Integrity*, pp. 54–71. New York: Oxford University Press.

Doublet, M.Y.M. (2010). *Fighting Corruption: Political Funding*. Paris: GRECO's Third Evaluation Round.

Downs, A. (1957). *An Economic Theory of Democracy*. New York: Harper & Row.

Duverger, M. (1954). *The Study of Politics*. Netherlands: Springer.

Eddy, B. (2019). *Why We Elect Narcissits and Sociopaths and How We Can Stop It*. Oakland: Berrett–Koehler Publishers, Inc.

Edes, B.W. (2016). "Regional Anti-Corruption Initiatives in Asia". In Gong, T., & Scott, I. (Eds.), *Routledge Handbook of Corruption in Asia*, pp. 487–502. London: Routledge, Taylor & Francis.

Eguae-Obazee, G.A. (2014). *The Effects of Corruption on the Inflow of Foreign Direct Investment into Ten Sub-Saharan African Countries: Using Ghana and Nigeria as Discussion Points*. PhD Thesis Submitted to the Wilmington University (Delaware).

Elischer, S. (2013). *Political Parties in Africa Ethnicity and Party Formation*. New York: Cambridge University Press.

Elster, J. (1986). "Introduction". In Elster, J. (Ed.), *Rational Choice*, pp. 1–33. New York: New York University Press.

El Tarouty, S. (2015). *Businessmen, Clientelism and Authoritarianism in Egypt*. New York: Palgrave Macmillan.

Emerson, P. (2012). *Defining Democracy: Voting Procedures in Decision-Making, Elections and Governance*. Geneva: Springer.

Emily, H. (1996). *Putting Choice Before Democracy: A Critique of Rational Choice Theory*. New York: State University of New York Press.

Erdmann, G., Basedau, M., & Mehler, A. (2007). "Introduction: Research on Electoral Systems, Parties and Party Systems in Africa". In Erdmann, G., Basedau,

M., & Mehler, A. (Eds.), *Votes, Money and Violence: Political Parties and Elections in Sub-Saharan Africa*, pp. 1–7. Scottsville: University of KwaZulu-Natal Press.

European Union (2018). *Good Practice Handbook on Political Parties Financing*. Brussels: European Union.

Evans, M. (2020). "Coalitions through a Comparative Politics Lens: Parties and Political Culture". In Evans, M. (Ed.), *Coalition Government as a Reflection of a Nation's Politics and Society: A Comparative Study of Parliamentary Parties and Cabinets in 12 Countries*, pp. 1–4. London: Routledge, Taylor & Francis.

Ezeh, U. (2023). "Contested Elections in Africa: The Roles of Courts in Electoral Processes". In Schultz, D., & Toplak, J. (Eds.), *Routledge Handbook of Election Law*, pp. 269–287. London: Routledge, Taylor & Francis.

Falguera, E., Jones, S., & Ohman, M. (2014). *Funding of Political Parties and Election Campaigns: A Handbook on Political Finance*. Stockholm: Institute for Democracy and Electoral Assistance.

Falola, T., & Genova, A. (2009). *Historical Dictionary of Nigeria*. Lanham: the Scarecrow Press Inc.

Falola, T., & Oyeniyi, B.A. (2015). *Nigeria*. Santa Barbara: ABC-CLIO.

Farber, H.S. (2009). Rational Choice and Voter Turnout: Evidence from Union Representation Elections. CEPS Working Paper No. 196 October 2009.

Farrell, D.M. (2006). "Political Parties in a Changing Campaign Environment". In Katz, R.S., & Crotty, W. (Eds.), *Handbook of Party Politics,* pp. 122–133. London: Sage.

February, J. (2016). *Elections for Sale? Political Party Funding: A Necessary Evil?* Paper Presented as part of the Project Exploring New Approaches and Strategic Entry Points for Anti-Corruption Efforts, financed by the Swedish International Development Cooperation Agency (Sida).

Federal Government of Nigeria (1999). *Nigerian 1999 Constitution as Amended*. Abuja, Nigeria: Federal Government Publication.

Federal Government of Nigeria and Independent National Electoral Commission (2006). *Electoral Act 2006*. Abuja, Nigeria: INEC.

Federal Government of Nigeria and Independent National Electoral Commission (2010). *Electoral Act 2010*. Abuja, Nigeria: INEC.

Federal Government of Nigeria and Independent National Electoral Commission (2022). *Electoral Act as Amended 2022*. Abuja, Nigeria: INEC. Federal Government of Nigeria.

Ferguson, M. (1995). *Golden Rule: The Investment Theory of Party Competition and the Logic of Money-Driven Political Systems*. Chicago: The University of Chicago Press.

Fiorelli, C. (2021). *Political Party Funding and Private Donations in Italy*. New York: Palgrave Macmillan.

Fisman, R., & Golden, M.A. (2017). *Corruption: What Everyone Needs to Know*. New York: Oxford University Press.

Fjelde, H., & Hoglund, K. (2014). Electoral Institutions and Electoral Violence in Sub-Saharan Africa. *British Journal of Political Science*. 46(1), 297–320.

Foblets, M., Reintein, A., & Graziadai, M. (2019). *Personal Autonomy in Plural Societies: A Principle and its Paradoxes*. London: Routledge, Taylor & Francis.

Folarin, S. (2021). "Corruption, Politics and Governance in Nigeria". In Ajayi, R., & Fashagba, J.Y. (Eds.), *Nigerian Politics*, pp. 377–394. Switzerland: Springer.

Foley, E.B. (2020). *Presidential Elections and Majority Rule: The Rise, Demise, and Potential Restoration of the Jeffersonian Electoral College*. New York: Oxford University Press.

Fombad, C.H., & Steytler, N. (2021). "Introduction Democracy, Elections, and Constitutionalism in Africa". In Fombad, C.H., & Steytler, N. (Eds.), *Democracy, Elections, and Constitutionalism in Africa*, pp. 1–16. New York: Oxford University Press.

Forsberg, O.J. (2021). *Understanding Elections through Statistics Polling, Prediction, and Testing*. Boca Raton: Routledge, Taylor & Francis.

Fowler, J.H., & Smirnov, O. (2007). *Mandates, Parties and Voters: How Elections Shape the Future*. Philadelphia: Temple University Press.

Frahm, G. (2019). *Rational Choice and Strategic Conflict: The Subjectivistic Approach to Game and Decision Theory*. Boston: Walter De Gruyter.

Fredrickson, C. (2019). *The Democracy Fix: How to Win the Fight for Fair Rules: Fair Courts and Fair Elections*. New York: The New Press.

Freeman, P. (2012). *How to Win an Election: An Ancient Guide for Modern Politicians*. New Jersey: Princeton University Press.

Gallagher, M., & Mitchell, P. (2018). "Dimensions of Variations in Electoral Systems". In Herron, E.S., Pekkanen, R.J., & Shugart, M.S. (Eds.), *The Oxford Handbook of Electoral Systems*, pp. 23–40. New York: Oxford University Press.

Gambari, I.A. (1970). *Party Politics and Foreign Policy in Nigeria's First Republic*. Zaria: Ahmadu Bello University Zaria Press.

Gans Morse, J., Mazzuca, S., & Nichter, S. (2014). Varieties of Clientelism: Machine Politics during Elections. *American Journal of Political Science*. 58(2), 415–432.

Gardasevic, D., & Toplak, J. (2023). "Voting Rights and Limitations". In Schultz, D., & Toplak, J. (Eds.), *Routledge Handbook of Election Law*, pp. 32–45. London: Routledge, Taylor & Francis.

Gberevbie, D.E., & Oni, S. (2021). "4 Postcolonial Nigeria: Power and Politics in the First Republic, 1960–1966". In Ajayi, R., & Fashagba, J.Y. (Eds.), *Nigerian Politics*, pp. 55–76. Switzerland: Springer.

George, A.L., & Bennett, A. (2005). *Case Studies and Theory Development in Social Sciences*. Cambridge, MA: Cambridge University Press.

Gerbaudo, P. (2019). *The Digital Party: Political Organisation and Online Democracy*. London: Pluto Press.

Gerken, H.K. (2009). *The Democracy Index: Why our Election System Is Failing and How to Fix It*. New Jersey: Princeton University Press.

Gerring, J. (2007). *Case Study Research: Principles and Practices*. Cambridge, MA: Cambridge University Press.

Gibbons, R. (1993). *A Primer in Game Theory*. London: Prentice Hall.

Girling, J. (1997). Corruption, Capitalism and Democracy. *Psychology Press*. 4(1), 1–12.

Global Financial Integrity (2020). "Anonymous Companies, Money Laundering and Transnational Crimes". *Global Financial Integrity*. Retrieved from https://gfintegrity.org/ on 29ᵗʰ June 2022 at 06:48 pm.

Global Legal Research Centre. (2011). Nigeria: Election Law. The Law Library of Congress. Law.GOV. www.law.gov.

Golosov, G.B. (2022). *Authoritarian Party Systems: Party Politics in Autocratic Regimes 1945–2019*. New Jersey: World Scientific.

Gomez, E.D. (1996). Electoral Funding of General, State and Party Elections in Malaysia. *Journal of Contemporary Asia*. 26(1), 81–96.

Grafstein, R. (1999). *Choice Free Rationality: A Positive Theory of Political Behaviour*. Michigan, USA: University of Michigan Press.

Green, D.P., & Shapiro, I. (1994). *Pathologies of Rational Choice Theory: A Critique of Applications in Political Science*. New Haven: Yale University Press.

Green, J. (2006). "On the Cusp of Change: Party Finance in the United States". In Katz, R.S., & Crotty, W. (Eds.), *Handbook of Party Politics,* pp. 134–145. London: Sage.

Gunther, R., Montero, J.R., & Linz, J.J. (2002). "Introduction". In Gunther, R., Montero, J.R., & Linz, J.J. (Eds.), *Political Parties: Old Concepts New Challenges*, pp. 1–11. New York: Oxford University Press.

Guzman, A.T. (2008). *How International Law Works: A Rational Choice Theory*. New York: Oxford University Press.

Gyima-Boadi, E. (2007). "Political Parties, Elections and Patronage': Random Thoughts on Neo-Patrimonialism and African Democratisation". In Erdmann, G., Basedau, M., & Mehler, A. (Eds.), *Votes, Money and Violence: Political Parties and Elections in Sub-Saharan Africa,* pp. 21–33. Scottsville: University of KwaZulu-Natal Press.

Hagel, P. (2020). *Billionaires in World Politics*. New York: Oxford University Press.

Haider, K., & Wauters, B. (2019). "Party Membership as Linkage". In Haider, K., Wauters, B. (Eds.), *Do Parties Still Represent? An Analysis of the Representativeness of Political Parties in Western Democracies*, pp. 1–14. London: Routledge, Taylor & Francis.

Hakeem, O., & Okeke, U.U. (2014). Rigging through the Court: The Judiciary and Electoral Fraud in Nigeria. *Journal of African Election*. 13(2), 137–168.

Hale, K., Montjoy, R., & Brown, M. (2015). *Administering Elections: How American Election Works*. New York: Palgrave Macmillan.

Hamalai, M., Egwu, S., & Omotola, S.J. (2017). *Nigeria's 2015 General Elections Continuity and Change in Electoral Democracy*. New York: Palgrave Macmillan.

Harmel, R., Svåsand, L.G., & Mjelde, H. (2019). "Party Institutionalisation: Concepts and Indicators". In Harmel, R., Svåsand, L.G. (Eds.), *Institutionalisation of Political Parties Comparative Cases,* 9–24. London: Rowman & Littlefield.

Harrop, M., & Miller, W.L. (1987). *Election and Voters: A Comparative Introduction*. London: Macmillan Press.

Haynes, J. (2020). "Introduction". In Haynes, J. (Ed.), *The Routledge Handbook to Religion and Political Parties*, pp. 1–6. London: Routledge, Taylor & Francis.

Hazan, R.Y., & Rahat, G. (2006). "Candidates Selection: Methods and Consequences". In Katz, R.S., & Crotty, W. (Eds.), *Handbook of Party Politics,* pp. 109–121. London: Sage.

Hazan, R.Y., & Rahat, G. (2010). *Democracy Within Parties: Candidates Selection Methods and their Political Consequences.* New York: Oxford University Press.

Hechter, M. (2019). *Rational Choice Theory and Large Scale Data Analysis.* London: Routledge, Taylor & Francis.

Heller, W.B., & Mershon, C. (2009). "Introduction: Legislative Party Switching, Parties, and Party Systems". In Heller, W.B., & Mershon, C. (Eds.), *Political Parties and Legislative Party Switching*, pp. 3–28. New York: Palgrave Macmillan.

Hemmingway, M. (2021). *Rigged: How the Media, Big Tech and the Democrats Seize our Elections.* Washington: Regnery Publishing.

Herron, E.S., Pekkanen, R.J., & Shugart, M.S. (2018). "Terminology and Basic Rules of Electoral Systems". In Herron, E.S., Pekkanen, R.J., & Shugart, M.S. (Eds.), *The Oxford Handbook of Electoral Systems*, pp. 1–22. New York: Oxford University Press.

Hershey, M.R. (2006). "Political Parties as Mechanisms of Social Choice". In Katz, R.S., & Crotty, W. (Eds.), *Handbook of Party Politics,* pp. 75–88. London: Sage.

Hesseling, G. (2000). "Preface". In Abbink, J., & Hesseling, G. (Eds.), *Election Observation and Democratisation*, pp. xi–xiv. London: Macmillan Press.

Hicken, A. (2009). *Building Party Systems in Developing Democracies.* New York: Cambridge University Press.

Hicken, A., Aspinall, E., & Weiss, M. (2019). "Introduction: the Local Dynamics of the National Elections in the Philippines". In Hicken, A., Aspinall, E., & Weiss, M. (Eds.), *Electoral Dynamics in the Philippines: Money Politics, Patronage and Clientelism at the Grassroots*, pp. 1–42. Singapore: National University of Singapore Press.

Higashijima, M. (2015). "Do Contentious Elections Overthrow Leaders?" In Norris, P., Frank, R.W., & Coma, F.M.I. (Eds.), *Contentious Elections: From Ballots to Barricades,* pp. 64–86. London: Routledge, Taylor & Francis.

Hilgers, T. (2012). "Democratic Processes, Clientelistic Relationships, and the Material Goods Problem". In Hilgers, T. (Ed.), *Clientelism in Everyday Latin American Politics*, pp. 3–24. New York: Palgrave Macmillan.

Hinnebusch, R., Cavatorta, F., & Storm, L. (2021). "Political Parties in MENA: An Introduction". In Hinnebusch, R., Cavatorta, F., & Storm, L. (Eds.), *Routledge Handbook on Political Parties in the Middle East and North Africa,* pp. 1–14. London: Routledge, Taylor & Francis.

Hiskey, J.T., & Moseley, M.W. (2020). *Life in the Political Machine: Dominant-Party Enclaves and the Citizens They Produce.* New York: Oxford University Press.

Hodge, J.K., & Klima, R.E. (2005). *The Mathematics of Voting and Elections: A Hands-on Approach.* Massachusetts, USA: American Mathematical Society.

Hoffman, D.E. (2002). *The Oligarchs: Wealth and Power in the New Russia.* New York: Public.

Holler, M.J. (2001). *Classical, Modern and New Game Theory.* Retrieved from https://law.yale.edu/sites/default/files/documents/pdf/holler.pdf on 15th June, 2022 at 11:13 pm.

Holmes, L. (2015). *Corruption: A Very Short Introduction.* New York: Oxford University Press.

Holy Bible: *King James Version.*

Hope, Sr, K.R. (2017). *Corruption and Governance in Africa: Swaziland, Kenya, Nigeria.* Geneva: Springer.

Hope, Sr, K.R., & Chikulo, B. (1999). *Corruption and Development in Africa: Lessons from Country Case Studies.* Geneva: Springer.

Hough, D. (2013). *Corruption, Anti-Corruption and Governance.* Geneva: Springer.

Howell, S. (2017). "Trump: Political Financing Not Yet Transparent". *The Guardian Online.* Accessed December 26, 2021. https://www.theguardian.com/politics.

Hudson, A. (2021). *The Veil of Participation: Citizens and Political Parties in Constitution-Making Processes.* New York: Cambridge University Press.

Human Rights Watch (2007). *Report on 2007 General Election in Nigeria.* Abuja: Human Rights Watch Publication.

Human Rights Watch (2019). *Nigeria: Widespread Violence Ushers in President's New Term.* Abuja: Human Rights Watch Publication.

Huntington, S.P. (1965). *Political Order in Changing Societies.* New York: Yale University Press.

Hutagalung, D. (2019). Demokrasi dan Sisi Gelapnya: Pengalaman dari Eropa, Afrika, Asia dan Amerika Latin. *Siasat, Journal of Religion, Social, Cultural and Political Sciences.* 4(4), 40–45.

Ibrahim, J. (1995). *Obstacles to Democratisation in Nigeria.* Paper presented at the University of Wisconsin's Conference on Dilemmas of Democracy in Nigeria (otherwise referred to as the Wisconsin Conference), Madison, 10–12 November 1995.

Igiebor, G.O. (2019). Political Corruption in Nigeria: Implications for Economic Development in the Fourth Republic. *Journal of Developing Societies.* 35(4), 493–513.

Igwe, P.I., & Amadi, L. (2021). Democracy and Political Violence in Nigeria Since Multi Party Politics in 1999: A Critical Appraisal. *De Gruyter, Open Political Science.* 4(1), 101–119.

Imukudo, S. (2021). Nigerian Professor Jailed for Election Fraud. *Premium Times Newspaper.* Retrieved from https://www.premiumtimesng.com/news/headlines /451132-nigerian-professor-jailed-for-election-fraud.html on 25th June 2022 at 4:08 pm.

Independent National Electoral Commission (2000). *The 1999 General Election Results.* Abuja: INEC. Retrieved from www.inec.gov.ng.

Independent National Electoral Commission (2003). *The 2003 General Election Results.* Abuja: INEC. Retrieved from www.inec.gov.ng.

Independent National Electoral Commission. (2005). *Political Party Finance Handbook.* Abuja, Nigeria: INEC Publication.

Independent National Electoral Commission (2007). *The 2007 General Election Results.* Abuja: INEC. Retrieved from www.inec.gov.ng.

Independent National Electoral Commission (2011). *The 2011 General Election Results*. Abuja: INEC. Retrieved from www.inec.gov.ng.

Independent National Electoral Commission (2015). *The 2015 General Election Results*. Abuja: INEC. Retrieved from www.inec.gov.ng.

Independent National Electoral Commission (2017). *Reforms and Regulations in Electoral Laws*. Abuja: INEC. Retrieved from www.inec.gov.ng.

Independent National Electoral Commission (2019). *The 2019 General Election Results*. Abuja: INEC. Retrieved from www.inec.gov.ng.

International Republican Institute (2020). *The Role of Political Parties in Nigeria's Fledgling Democracy*. Washington: IRI.

Isaksson, A.S. & Bigsten, A. (2013). *Clientelism and Ethnic Division*. Working Papers in Economics No. 598, University of Gothenburg, Department of Economics.

Isma'ila, Y., & Othman, Z. (2016). Challenges of Electoral Malpractices on Democratic Consolidation in Nigeria's Fourth Republic. *International Review of Management and Marketing*. 6(S8), 103–107.

Itodo, S. (2022). *Political Party Nomination and the Shrinking Political Space*. Abuja: Institute for Democracy and Electoral Assistance. Retrieved from https://www.idea.int/news-media/news/political-party-nomination-fees-and-shrinking-political-space on 26th June 2022 at 11: 41 am.

Ivanyna, M., Mourmouras, A., & Rangazas, P. (2018). *The Macroeconomics of Corruption*. Geneva: Springer Texts in Business and Economics.

Jacob, B., & Smith, D. (2016). "How Far is Transparent the America's Democracy? 2016 Election Too Expensive". *The Guardian Online*. Retrieved from www.guardianonline. on 19th June, 2022 at 12:31 am.

Jain, A.K. (2001). Corruption: A review. *Journal of Economic Surveys*. 15(1), 71–121.

James, T.S., & Garnett, H.A. (2023). "Electoral Management". In Schultz, D., & Toplak, J.(Eds.), *Routledge Handbook of Election Law*, pp. 46–59. London: Routledge, Taylor & Francis.

Jinadu, L.A. (2011). *Inter-Party Dialogue in Nigeria: Examining the Past, Present and Future*. Lead paper at the inaugural DGD Political Parties Dialogue Series, held on October 4, 2011 at Bolingo Hotel, Abuja.

Johnson, D.W. (2020). *Campaigns and Elections: What Everyone Needs to Know*. New York: Cambridge University Press.

Johnston, R., & Pattie, C. (2014). *Money and Electoral Politics: Local Parties and Funding at General Elections*. Bristol: Policy Press.

Jones, L.E. (2020). *The German Right, 1918–1930: Political Parties, Organized Interests, and Patriotic Associations in the Struggle against Weimar Democracy*. New York: Cambridge University Press.

Jordan, D.C. (1999). *Drug Politics: Dirty Money and Democracies*. Oklahoma: University of Oklahoma Press.

Joseph, R. (1991). *Democracy and Prebendel Politics in Nigeria: The Rise and Fall of the Second Republic*. Ibadan: Spectrum Books Limited.

Joseph, R. (1995). The Dismal Tunnel: From Prebendel State to Rogue State in Nigeria. Paper presented at the University of Wisconsin's Conference on Dilemmas of

Democracy in Nigeria (otherwise referred to as the Wisconsin Conference), Madison, 10–12 November 1995.

Joseph, R. (2007). Political Parties and Ideologies in Nigeria. *Review of African Political Economy*. 5(13), 78–90.

Kam, C., & Newson, A. (2020). *The Economic Origins of Political Parties*. New York: Cambridge University Press.

Kane, B.R. (2019). *Pitchfork Populism: Ten Political Forces that Shaped an Election and Continue to Change America*. Connecticut: Prometheus Book.

Katsina, A.M. (2016). Peoples Democratic Party in the Fourth Republic of Nigeria: Nature, Structure, and Ideology. *Sage Open*. April–June 2016, 1–11. doi: 10.1177/2158244016651910.

Katz, R.A. (1980). *A Theory of Parties and Electoral Systems*. Baltimore: Johns Hopkins University Press.

Katz, R.A. (2006). "Party in Democratic Theory". In Katz, R.S., & Crotty, W. (Eds.), *Handbook of Party Politics*, pp. 34–46. London: Sage.

Katz, R.A., & Mair, P. (2018). *Democracy and the Cartelisation of Political Parties*. New York: Oxford University Press.

Katzarova, E. (2019). *Global Anti-Corruption Talks in the 1970s and 1990s: The Story of Two Utopias. In The Social Construction of Global Corruption*. Geneva: Springer.

Kelly, C.L. (2020). *Party Proliferation and Political Contestation in Africa: Senegal in Comparative Perspective*. New York: Palgrave Macmillan.

Kenneth J.A., Patrick, S., & Samuel, K. (1982). *Mathematical Models in the Social Sciences, 1959: Proceedings of the first Stanford symposium*. Stanford, CA: Stanford University Press.

Kernalegenn, T., & Van Haute, E. (2020). "Introduction: Why Study Political Parties Abroad? Diasporas as New Arenas for Party Politics". In Kernalegenn, T., & Van Haute, E. (Eds.), *Political Parties Abroad: A New Arena for Party Politics*, pp. 1–18. London: Routledge, Taylor & Francis.

Key, Jr., V.O. (1964). *Politics, Parties, and Pressure Groups*. New York: Crowell.

Khan, F.B. (2019). *The Game of Votes: Visual Media Politics and Elections in the Digital Era*. London: Sage.

King, B.A., Brown, M., & Hale, K. (2020). "Introduction". In Brown, M., Hale, K., & King, B.A. (Eds.), *The Future of Election Administration*, pp. 1–16. New York: Palgrave Macmillan.

Knuckles, J. (2006). *A Study of Corruption's Causes in Botswana and Nigeria*. Unpublished work. Retrieved from https://unpublishedworks.files.wordpress.com /2013/03/a-study-of-corruptions-causes-inbotswana-and-nigeria.pdf on 29th June 2022 at 05:00 pm.

Kobayashi, M. (2016). "Political Clientelism and Corruption: Neostructuralism and Republicanism". In Kawata, J. (Ed.), *Comparing Political Corruption and Clientelism*, London: Routledge, Taylor & Francis.

Kovalik, D. (2018). *Plot to Control the World: How the US Spent Billions to Change the Outcome of Elections Around the World*. New York: Hot Books.

Kratcoski, P.C. (2018). "Introduction: Overview of Major Types of Fraud and Corruption. Fraud and Corruption". In Kratcoski, M., & Edelbacher, M. (Eds.),

Fraud and Corruption Major Types, Prevention, and Control, pp. 3–21. Geneva: Springer.

Krimmer, R., & Esteve, J.B.I. (2023). "Electronic Voting". In Schultz, D., & Toplak, J. (Eds.), *Routledge Handbook of Election Law*, pp. 60–72. London: Routledge, Taylor & Francis.

Krouwel, A. (2006). "Party Models". In Katz, R.S., & Crotty, W. (Eds.), *Handbook of Party Politics,* pp. 249–269. London: Sage.

Kuhlmann, M. (2020). *Africa Could Gain $89 Billion Annually by Curbing Illicit Financial Flows.* United Nations: UNCTAD.

Kuhn, P.M. (2015). "Do Contentious Elections Trigger Violence?" In Norris, P., Frank, R.W., & Coma, F.M.I. (Eds.), *Contentious Elections: From Ballots to Barricades,* pp. 89–110. London: Routledge, Taylor & Francis.

Kuhn, T.S. (1983). Rationality and Theory Choice. *The Journal of Philosophy.* 80(10), 563–570.

Kuo, D. (2018). *Clientelism, Capitalism and Democracy: The Rise of Programmatic Politics in the United States and Britain.* New York: Cambridge University Press.

Kura, B.Y. (2014). Clientele Democracy: Political Party Funding and Candidate Selection in Nigeria. *African Journal of Political Science and International Relations.* 8(5), 124–137.

Kwarkye, S. (2019). *Roots of Nigeria's Election Violence.* Retrieved 5 August 2020 from https://issafrica.org/iss-today/roots-of-nigerias-election-violence on 25th June, 2022 at 3:35 pm.

Laakso, L. (2007). "Insight into Electoral Violence in Africa". In Erdmann, G., Basedau, M., & Mehler, A. (Eds.), *Votes, Money and Violence: Political Parties and Elections in Sub-Saharan Africa,* pp. 224–252. Scottsville: University of KwaZulu-Natal Press.

Lambsdorff, J.G. (2007). *The Institutional Economics of Corruption and Reform: Theory, Evidence and Policy.* New York: Cambridge university press.

Langguth, J. (2019). *The Green Factor in German Politics: from Protest Movement to Political Party.* London: Routledge, Taylor & Francis.

La Raja, R. (2008). *Small Change: Money, Political Parties, and Campaign Finance Reform.* Michigan: Michigan University Press.

Lawal, S.M. (2015). An Appraisal of Corruption in the Nigeria Electoral System. *European Scientific Journal.* 11(25), 1–18.

Lawson, P.S. (2014). Immunity Clause in Nigeria's 1999 Constitution: Its Implications on Executive Capacity. *American Journal of Social Sciences.* 2(6), 130–136.

Le Van, C.A. (2015). *Dictators and Democracy in Nigeria: The Political Economy of Good Governance in Nigeria.* New York: Cambridge University Press.

Levitsky, S., & Way, L. (2019). "The Myth of Democratic Recession". In Diamond, L., & Plattner, M.C. (Eds.), *Democracy in Decline?* pp. 58–76. Baltimore: Johns Hopkins University Press.

Levitsky, S., & Ziblatt, D. (2018). *How Democracies Die.* New York: Crown.

Lewis, J. (2020). *Economic Impact of Cybercrime: At $600 Billion and Counting No Slowing Down.* Centre for Strategic and International Studies. Retrieved from

https://csis-website-prod.s3.amazonaws.com/s3fs-public/publication/economic
-impact-cybercrime.pdf on 29th June 2022 at 06:28.

Lichbah, M.I. (2003). *Is Rational Choice Theory All of Social Science?* Ann Arbor: the University of Michigan Press.

Liebowitz, J., & Ibrahim, J. (2013). *A Capacity Assessment of Nigerian Political Parties.* Nigeria: UNDP.

Lijphart, A. (1979). *Democracy in Plural Societies: A Comparative Exploration.* New Haven: Yale University Press.

Lijphart, A. (1994). *Electoral Systems and Party Systems.* New York: Oxford University Press.

Lindberg, S.I. & Morrison, M. (2010). Are African Voters Really Ethnic or Clientelistic? Survey Evidence from Ghana. *Political Science Quarterly.* 123(1), 95–122.

Lindberg, S.I. & Weghorst, K.R. (2010). Are Swing Voters Instruments of Democracy or Farmers of Clientelism. Evidence from Ghana. The QOG Institute Quality of Government.

Litt, D. (2020). *Democracy in One Book or Less: How It Works, Why It Doesn't, and Why Fixing It Is Easier Than You Think.* New York: Harper Collins.

Lloyd, P.C. (1965). The Development of Political Parties in Western Nigeria. *The American Political Science Review.* 693–707.

Londono, J.F., & Zovatto, G. (2014). "Regional Studies on Political Finance: Regulatory Framework and Political Realities, Latin America". In Falguera, E., Samuel, J., & Ohman, M. (Eds.), *Funding of Political Parties and Election Campaign: A Handbook of Political Finance*, 38–75. Stockholm, Sweden: International Institute for Democracy and Electoral Assistance.

Lu, J., & Chu, H. (2022). *Understandings of Democracy: Origins and Consequences Beyond Western Democracy.* New York: Oxford University Press.

Lucky, O.O. (2014). Money Politics and Vote Buying in Nigeria: The Bane of Good Governance. *Mediterranean Journal of Social Sciences.* 5(7), 99–106.

Lukman, S., Oluwashina, O.M., & Rafi'u, B.A. (2019). Political Parties and Opposition Politics in Nigeria's Fourth Republic. *Journal of Management and Social Sciences.* 8(1), 536–549.

Lukman, S.M. (2019). *Power of Possibility and Politics of Change in Nigeria.* Abuja: Treokreation.

Lukman, S.M. (2021a). *APC and Progressive Politics in Nigeria.* Abuja: Treokreation.

Lukman, S.M. (2021b). *APC's Litmus Tests: Nigerian Democracy and Politics of Change.* Abuja: Treokreations Limited.

Lune, H. & Berg, L. (2017). *Qualitative Research Methods for the Social Sciences.* Edinburgh: Pearson Education Limited.

Luther, K.R. (2000). "A Framework for the Comparative Analysis of Political Parties and Party Systems in Consociational Democracy". In Luther, K.R., & Deschouwer, K. (Eds.), *Party Elites in Divided Societies Political Parties in Consociational Democracy*, pp. 2–18. London: Routledge, Taylor & Francis.

Maddow, R. (2019). *Blowout: Corrupted Democracy, Rogue State Russia, and the Richest, most Destructive Industry on Earth.* New York: Crown.

Madsen, J.K. (2019). *The Psychology of Micro-Targeted Election Campaigns*. New York: Palgrave Macmillan.

Mainwaring, S., & Torcal, M. (2006). "Party System Institutionalisation and Party System Theory after the Third Wave of Democratisation". In Katz, R.S., & Crotty, W. (Eds.), *Handbook of Party Politics,* pp. 204–227. London: Sage.

Mair, P. (1997). *Party System Change: Approaches and Interpretations*. New York: Oxford University Press.

Mair, P. (2006). "Party System Change". In Katz, R.S., & Crotty, W. (Eds.), *Handbook of Party Politics,* pp. 63–74. London: Sage.

Maisel, L.S. (2007). *American Political Parties and Elections: A Very Short Introduction*. New York: Oxford University Press.

Maisel, L.S. (2022). *American Political Parties: A Very Short Introduction*. New York: Oxford University Press (New Ed.).

Mantilla, L.F. (2021). *How Political Parties Mobilise Religion: Lessons from Mexico and Turkey*. Philadelphia: Temple University Press.

Maor, M. (1997). *Political Parties and Party Systems: Comparative Approaches and the British Experience*. London: Routledge.

Maoz, Z., & Henderson, E.A. (2020). *Scriptures, Shrines, Scapegoats, and World Politics: Religious Sources of Conflict and Cooperation in the Modern Era*. Ann Arbour: University of Michigan Press.

Margetts, H. (2006). "Cyber Parties". In Katz, R.S., & Crotty, W. (Eds.), *Handbook of Party Politics,* pp. 528–535. London: Sage.

Maschler, M., Solan, E., & Zamir, S. (2013). *Game Theory*. New York: Cambridge University Press.

Mauro, P. (1998). Corruption: Causes, Consequences, and Agenda for Research. *Journal of Finance and Development*. 35(1), 11–14.

Mbah, P.O., Nwangwu, C., & Ugwu, S.C. (2019). Contentious Elections, Political Exclusion, and Challenges of National Integration in Nigeria. *Cogent Social Sciences*. 5(15), 1–21.

Mbaku, J.M. (2010). *Corruption in Africa: Causes, Consequences, and Clean-ups*. Lanham: Lexington Books, Rowman & Littlefield. .

McAllister, I. (2018). "Democratic Theory and Electoral Behaviour". In Fisher, J., Fieldhouse,E., Franklin, M.N., Gibson, R., Cantijoch, M., & Wlezien, C. (Eds.), *The Routledge Handbook of Elections, Voting Behaviour and Public Opinion*. London: Routledge, Taylor & Francis.

McCarthy, M., & Meirowitz, A. (2006). *Political Game Theory: An Introduction*. New York: Cambridge University Press.

McLean, I. (2018). "Electoral Systems". In Fisher, J., Fieldhouse, E., Franklin, M.N., Gibson, R., Cantijoch, M., & Wlezien, C. (Eds.), *The Routledge Handbook of Elections, Voting Behaviour and Public Opinion*. London: Routledge, Taylor & Francis.

Mcmenamin, I. (2013). *If Money Talks, What Does it Say? Corruption and Business Financing of Political Parties*. New York: Oxford University Press.

Mehta, N. (2022). *The New BJP: Modi and the Making of the World's Largest Party*. Chennai: Westland Non-Fiction.

Mendilow, J., & Phelippeau, E. (2018). *Handbook of Political Party Funding*. Cheltelham: Edward Elgar Publishing Limited.

Miezah, H.A.A. (2018). *Elections in African Developing Democracies*. New York: Palgrave Macmillan.

Miller, M.K. (2021). *Shock to the System Coups, Elections, and War on the Road to Democratisation*. Princeton: Princeton University Press.

Miller, S. (2016). *Corruption and Anti-corruption in Policing--Philosophical and Ethical Issues*. Geneva: Springer.

Min, B. (2015). *Elections and Electricity in the Developing World*. New York: Cambridge University Press.

Mohammed, H. & Aluigba, M.T. (2013). Election Rigging and Political Instability in Nigeria: The Case of 2007 General Elections. *Journal of Democratic Studies Mambayya House*. 4(2), 1–13.

Mohammed, U. (2013). Corruption in Nigeria: A Challenge to Sustainable Development in the Fourth Republic. *European Scientific Journal*. 9(4), 118–137.

Moody, T. (2022). *Breaking the Impasse: Electoral Politics, Mass Action, and the New Socialist Movement in the United States*. Chicago: Haymarket Books.

Mozaffar, S. (2006). "Party, Ethnicity and Democratisation in Africa". In Katz, R.S., & Crotty, W. (Eds.), *Handbook of Party Politics,* pp. 239–248. London: Sage.

Muir, S., & Gupta, A. (2018). Rethinking the Anthropology of Corruption: An Introduction to Supplement 18. *Current Anthropology*. 59(S18), S4–S15.

Mulroy, S.J. (2023). "Election Law in Advanced Countries". In Schultz, D., & Toplak, J. (Eds.), *Routledge Handbook of Election Law*, pp. 73–86. London: Routledge, Taylor & Francis.

Muniz, C.S. (2015). *Ideology Versus Clientelism: Modernisation and Electoral Competition in Brazil*. A Dissertation submitted in partial fulfillment of the requirement for the Degree of Doctor of Philosophy. University of Wisconsin, Milwaukee.

Muno, W. (2014). *Conceptualising and Measuring Clientelism*. Hamburg, Germany: German Institute for Global and Area Studies.

Myerson, R.B. (1991). *Game Theory: Analysis of Conflict*. Cambridge: Harvard University Press.

Nasmacher, K. (2006). "Regulation of Party Finance". In Katz, R.S., & Crotty, W. (Eds.), *Handbook of Party Politics,* pp. 446–455. London: Sage.

Nasmacher, K. (2014). "The Established Anglophone Democracies". In Falguera, E., Jones, S., & Ohman, M. (Eds.), *Funding of Political Parties and Election Campaign: A Handbook of Political Finance*, pp. 255–298. Stockholm: International IDEA.

National Bureau of Statistics (2022). *Nigerian Poverty Profile*. Retrieved from https://nigerianstat.gov.ng/elibrary?queries[search]=poverty on 29th June 2022 at 02:21 am.

National Bureau of Statistics/United Nations Office on Drugs and Crimes. (2019). *Corruption in Nigeria: Patterns and Trends. Second Survey on Corruption as Experienced by the Population*. Abuja: NBS and UNODC.

National Democratic Institute (NDI) (1999). *The Nigerian 1999 General Election*. Abuja: NDI.

Nelson, A., & Saka-Olokungboye, N. (2019). Money Politics, Vote Buying and Selling in Nigeria: An Emerging Threats to Good Governance. *International Journal of Advanced Academic Studies.* 1(2), 146–152.

Neumann, J.V., & Morgenstern, O. (1953). *Theory of Games and Economic Behaviour.* Princeton: Princeton University Press.

Nichols, J., & McChesney, R.W. (2013). *Dollacracy: How the Money-and-Media Election Complex Is Destroying America.* New York: Nation Books.

Nichter, S. (2018). *Votes for Survival Relational Clientelism in Latin America.* New York: Cambridge University Press.

Nield, R. (2000). *Public Corruption: The Dark Side of Social Evolution.* London: Anthem Press.

Nikolayenko, O. (2015). "Do Contentious Elections Depress Turnout?" In Norris, P., Frank, R.W., & Coma, F.M.I. (Eds.), *Contentious Elections: From Ballots to Barricades,* pp. 25–44. London: Routledge, Taylor & Francis.

Niou, E.M.S., & Ordeshook, P.C. (2015). *Strategy and Politics: An Introduction to Game Theory.* London: Routledge, Taylor & Francis.

Nnoli, O. (1988). *Ethnic Politics in Nigeria.* Onitsha: Fourth Dimension Publishers.

Nohlen, D., Krennerich, M., & Thibaut, B. (1999). "Elections and Electoral Systems in Africa". In Nohlen, D., Krennerich, M., Thibaut, B. (Eds.), *Elections in Africa Data Handbook,* pp. 1–40. New York: Oxford University Press.

Nordstrom, J.F. (2020). *Introduction to Game Theory: A Discovery Approach.* Retrieved from https://digitalcommons.linfield.edu/linfauth/83/ on 15th June 2022 at 11:25 pm.

Norris, P. (2004). *Electoral Engineering: Voting Rules and Political Behaviour.* New York: Cambridge University Press.

Norris, P. (2006). "Recruitment". In Katz, R.S., & Crotty, W. (Eds.), *Handbook of Party Politics,* pp. 89–108. London: Sage.

Norris, P. (2017). "Transparency in Electoral Governance". In Norris, P., & Nai, A. (Eds.), *Election Watchdog: Transparency, Accountability and Integrity,* pp. 3–30. New York: Oxford University Press.

Norris, P. (2018). "Electoral Integrity". In Fisher, J., Fieldhouse, E., Franklin, M.N., Gibson, R., Cantijoch, M., & Wlezien, C. (Eds.), *The Routledge Handbook of Elections, Voting Behaviour and Public Opinion.* London: Routledge, Taylor & Francis.

Norris, P. (2018). "Electoral Systems and Electoral Integrity". In Herron, E.S., Pekkanen, R.J., & Shugart, M.S. (Eds.), *The Oxford Handbook of Electoral Systems,* pp. 491–512. New York: Oxford University Press.

Norris, P. (2023). "Challenges in Electoral Integrity". In Schultz, D., & Toplak, J. (Eds.), *Routledge Handbook of Election Law,* pp. 87–100. London: Routledge, Taylor & Francis.

Norris, P., Frank, R.W., & Coma, F.M.I. (2015a). "Contentious Elections: from Voters to Violence". In Norris, P., Frank, R.W., & Coma, F.M.I. (Eds.), *Contentious Elections: From Ballots to Barricades,* pp. 1–22. London: Routledge, Taylor & Francis.

Norris, P., Frank, R.W., & Coma, F.M.I. (2015b). "The Risks of Contentious Elections". In Norris, P., Frank, R.W., & Coma, F.M.I. (Eds.), *Contentious Elections: From Ballots to Barricades,* pp. 133–151. London: Routledge, Taylor & Francis.

Norris, P., van Es, A.A., & Fennis, L. (2006). *Checkbook Elections?: Political Finance in Comparative Perspective*. Sydney: University of Sydney.

Nugent, P. (2007). "Banknotes and Symbolic Capital: Ghana's Election under the Fourth Republic". In Erdmann, G., Basedau, M., & Mehler, A. (Eds.), *Votes, Money and Violence: Political Parties and Elections in Sub-Saharan Africa*, pp. 253–275. Scottsville: University of KwaZulu-Natal Press.

Nwangwu, C., Onah, V.C., & Otu, O.K. (2018). Elixir of Electoral Fraud: The Impact of Digital Technology on the 2015 General Elections in Nigeria. *Politics and International Relations*. 4, 1549007. doi: 10.1080/23311886.2018.1549007.

Nwangwu, C., & Ononogbu, O.A. (2016). Electoral Laws and Monitoring of Campaign Financing During the 2015 Presidential Election in Nigeria. *Japanese Journal of Political Science*. 17(4), 614–634.

Nwagwu, E.J., Uwaechia, O.G., Udegbunam, K.C., & Nnamani, R. (2022). Vote Buying During 2015 And 2019 General Elections: Manifestation and Implications on Democratic Development in Nigeria. *Cogent Social Sciences*. 8(1), 1995237. doi: 10.1080/23311886.2021.1995237.

Nwankwo, C.F. (2019). Religion and Voter Choice Homogeneity in the Nigerian Presidential Elections of the Fourth Republic. *Stat Polit Pol*. 10(1), 1–25.

Nwankwo, C.F. (2020). Rurality and Party System Fragmentation in the Nigerian Presidential Elections of the Fourth Republic. *Statistics, Politics and Policy*. 11(1), 59–85.

Nwozor, A., Oshewolo, S., Ifejika, S.I., Olanrewaju, J.S., & Ake, M. (2021). Has Anything Changed with Illegitimate Electoral Financing and Political Power Contestation in Nigeria? *Cogent Social Sciences*. 7(1), 1961396. doi: 10.1080/23311886.2021.1961396.

Ogbeidi, M.M. (2012). Political Leadership and Corruption in Nigeria Since 1960: A Socio-Economic Analysis. *Journal of Nigeria Studies*. 1(2), 22–42.

Ogbeifun, S. (2022). *2023 Polls: Money Politics: Nigeria Inching Toward Plutocracy, Government of the Rich and for the Rich — INEC Chairman*. Abuja: Open Society Initiative for West Africa. Retrieved from https://www.osiwa.org/news-room/2023-polls-money-politics-nigeria-inching-toward-plutocracy-government-of-the-rich-and-for-the-rich-inec-chairman/ on 29th June 2022 at 02:00 am.

Ogunbiyi, T. (2022). "Money Politics and the Nigerian Economy". *Business Day*. Retrieved from https://businessday.ng/opinion/article/money-politics-and-the-nigerian-economy/ on 29th June 2022 at 02:04 am.

Ogundiya, I.S. (2009). Political Corruption in Nigeria: Theoretical Perspectives and Some Explanations. *The Anthropologists*. 11(4), 281–292.

Ogundiya, I.S. (2010). Corruption: The Bane of Democratic Stability in Nigeria. *Current Research Journal of Social Sciences*. 2(4), 233–241.

Ohlin, J.D. (2021). "Election Interference: A Unique Harm Requiring Unique Solution". In Hollis, D.B., & Ohlin, J.D. (Eds.), *Defending Democracy: Combating Foreign Elections Interference in a Digital Age*, pp. 239–264. New York: Oxford University Press.

Ohman, M. (2010). "Practical Solutions for the Public Funding of Political Parties and Election Campaigns". In Ohman, M., & Zainulbhai, H. (Eds.), *Political Finance Regulation: The Global Experience*, pp. 57–81. Washington, USA: IFES.

Ohman, M. (2012). *Political Finance Regulations Around the World: An Overview of the International IDEA Database*. Stockholm: IDEA.

Ohman, M. (2013). *Controlling Money in Politics: An Introduction*. Washington: International Foundation for Electoral System.

Ohman, M. (2014a). "Getting the Political Finance System Right". In Falguera, E., Jones, S., & Ohman, M. (Eds.), *Funding of Political Parties and Election Campaign: A Handbook of Political Finance*, pp. 1–13. Stockholm: International IDEA, 2014.

Ohman, M. (2014b). "Regional Studies on Political Finance': Regulatory Framework and Political Realities, Africa". In Falguera, E., Jones, S., & Ohman, M. (Eds.), *Funding of Political Parties and Election Campaign: A Handbook of Political Finance*, pp. 14–39. Stockholm: International IDEA, 2014.

Ohman, M. (2014c). "Africa". In Falguera, E., Jones, S., & Ohman, M. (Eds.), *Funding of Political Parties and Election Campaign: A Handbook of Political Finance*, pp. 39–75. Stockholm: International IDEA, 2014.

Ohman, M. (2016). *The State of Political Finance Regulations in Africa*. Stockholm: Institute for Democracy and Electoral Assistance.

Ohman, M. (2018). *Gender-targeted Public Funding for Political Parties: A Comparative Analysis*. Stockholm: IDEA.

Ojo, E.O., Prusa, V., & Amundsen, I. (2019). "Congenitally Conjoined and Inseparable: Politics and Corruption in Nigeria". In Amundsen, I. (Ed.), *Political Corruption in Africa: Extraction and Power Preservation,* pp. 27–48. Cheltenham, UK and Northampton, MA: Edward Elgar Publishers Ltd.

Okeke, G.S.M., & Nwali, U. (2020). Campaign Funding Laws and the Political Economy of Money Politics in Nigeria. *Review of African Political Economy*. 47(164), 238–255.

Okolie, A., Nnamani, K.E., Ezirim, G.E., Enyiazu, C., & Ozor, A.C. (2021). Does Liberal Democracy Promote Economic Development? Interrogating Electoral Cost and Development Trade-off in Nigeria's Fourth Republic. *Cogent Social Sciences*. 7(1), 1–22.

Olaniyi, J.O. (2017). State Independent Electoral Commissions and Local Government Elections in Nigeria. *African Online Scientific Information Centre*. Retrieved from https://apsdpr.org/index.php/apsdpr/article/view/133/246 on 27th June 2022 at 4:24 pm.

Olaoye, I.J., Ayinde, O.E., Adewumi, M.O., Alani, E.A., & Babatunde, R.O. (2020). "Fertilizer Policy, Governance, and Agricultural Transformation in Nigeria: A Review of Political Economy from Historical Perspectives". In Oloruntoba, S.O., & Falola, T. (Eds.), *The Palgrave Handbook of African Political Economy*, pp. 449–446. New York: Palgrave Macmillan.

Olarinmoye, O.O. (2008). Godfathers, Political Parties and Electoral Corruption in Nigeria. *African Journal of Political Science and International Relations*. 2(4), 066–073.

Olayode, K.A. (2015). *Ethno-Regional Cleavages and Voting Behaviour in the 2015 General Elections: Issues and Challenges for Democratisation and Nation Building*. National Conference on 2015 Elections in Nigeria. The Electoral Institute (TEI) Abuja, pp. 1–23.

Ologbenla, D., & Adisa, W.B. (2012). Money-Bag Politics, Rent-Seeking and Flawed Elections in Nigeria: A Theoretical Statement. *Journal of Public Administration and Governance*. 2(1), 188–211.

Olorunmola, A. (2016). *Cost of Politics in Nigeria*. Abuja, Nigeria: Westminster Foundation for Democracy.

Olowu, C. (1996). *Bureaucracy and the People: The Nigerian Experience*. Obafemi Awolowo University, Inaugural Lecture Series III. Ile-Ife: Obafemi Awolowo University Press.

Olson, M. (1965). *The Logic of Collective Action: Public Goods and the Theory of Groups*. Cambridge: Harvard University Press.

Oluyitan, F.E. (2016). *Combatting Corruption at the Grassroots Level in Nigeria*. Geneva: Springer.

Omo-Bare, I. (2006). The Democratic Transition in Nigeria. *AP Central*. Retrieved from https://apcentral.collegeboard.org/courses/ap-comparative-government-and -politics/classroom-resources/democratic-transition-nigeria on 27th June 2022 at 04:52 pm.

Omobowale, A.O., & Olutayo, A.O. (2010). Political Clientelism and Rural Development in Southwest Nigeria. *Africa: Journal of the International Africa Institute*. 80(3), 453–472.

Omodia, S.M. (2018). Political Parties and National Integration in Emerging Democracies: A Focus on the Nigerian State. *Mediterranean Journal of Social Sciences*. 9(6), 69–74.

Omotola, S.J. (2010). Elections and Democratic Transition in Nigeria under the Fourth Republic. *African Affairs*. 109(437), 535–553. doi: 10.1093/afraf/adq040.

Onah, E.I., & Nwali, U. (2018). Monetisation of Electoral Politics and the Challenge of Political Exclusion in Nigeria. *Commonwealth & Comparative Politics*. 56(3), 318–339. doi: 10.1080/14662043.2017.1368157.

Onapajo, H. (2014). Violence and Votes in Nigeria: The Dominance of Incumbents in the Use of Violence to Rig Elections. *Africa Spectrum*. 49(2), 27–59.

Onapajo, H. (2020). The Tragedy of the Umpire: the Electoral Management Body and Nigeria's 2019 General Elections. *The Round Table: The Commonwealth Journal of International Affairs*. 109(4), 368–376.

Onapajo, H., & Babalola, D. (2020). Nigeria's 2019 General Elections – a shattered hope? *The Round Table: The Commonwealth Journal of International Affairs*. 109(4), 363–367.

Önnudóttir, E.H., Helgason, A.F., Hardarson, O.T., & Thórisdóttir, H. (2022). *Electoral Politics in Crisis after the Great Recession: Change, Fluctuations and Stability in Iceland*. London: Routledge, Taylor & Francis.

Onuoha, F., & Ojo, J. (2018). *Practice and Perils of Vote Buying in Nigeria's Recent Elections*. Accord. Retrieved from https://www.accord.org.za/conflict-trends/ practice-and-perils-of-vote-buying-in-nigerias-recent-elections/ on 29th June 2022 at 02:19 am.

Onuoha, G. (2020). "The State, Resources and Developmental Prospects in Sub-Saharan Africa". In Oloruntoba, S.O., & Falola, T. (Eds.), *The Palgrave Handbook of African Political Economy*, pp. 621–643. New York: Palgrave Macmillan.

Onuoha, F.C., Okafor, J.C., Ojewale, O., & Okoro, C. (2020). Militarisation of the 2019 General Elections and Electoral Integrity in Nigeria. *The Round Table: The Commonwealth Journal of International Affairs*. 109(4), 406–418.

Onyekpere, E. (2015). *Still Above the Ceiling: A Report on Campaign Finance and Use of State Administrative Resources in the 2015 Presidential Election*. Washington: Centre for Social Justice, USAID & UKAID.

Oppenheimer, J. (2012). *Principles of Politics: A Rational Choice Theory Guide to Politics and Social Justice*. New York: Cambridge University Press.

Ordeshook, P.C. (1995). *Game Theory and Political Theory: An Introduction*. New York: Cambridge University Press.

Organisation for Economic Cooperation and Development (2013). *Background Paper. Money in Politics: Sound Political Competition in Government*. Paris: OECD.

Organisation of Economic Development Countries (OECD) (2012). *Financing Democracy*. Paris: OECD.

Orr, G. (2023). "Elections as Rituals". In Schultz, D., & Toplak, J. (Eds.), *Routledge Handbook of Election Law*, pp. 101–111. London: Routledge, Taylor & Francis.

Osumah, A. (2010). Patron-Client Politics, Democracy and Governance in Nigeria, 1999–2007. *LWATI: A Journal of Contemporary Research*. 7(2), 276–289.

Othman, M.K. (2022). "Nigeria 2023: Money Politics and its Catastrophic Consequences". *Blueprint Newspaper*. Retrieved from https://www.blueprint.ng/nigeria-2023-money-politics-and-its-catastrophic-consequences/ on 29th June 2022 at 02:06 am.

Ott, M.R. (2006). "The Notion of the Totally "Other" and its Consequence in the Critical Theory of Religion and the Rational Choice Theory of Religion". In Goldstein, W.S. (Ed.), *Marx, Critical Theory, and Religion*, pp. 121–150. London: Brill.

Ovadia, J.S. (2020). "Natural Resources and African Economies: Asset or Liability?". In Oloruntoba, S.O., & Falola, T. (Eds.), *The Palgrave Handbook of African Political Economy*, pp. 667–678. New York: Palgrave Macmillan.

Oyebode, M.O. (2014). Rethinking Deification, Gerontocracy and Clientelism in Nigerian Political Space. *International Journal of Development and Sustainability*. 3(1), 135–149.

Oyetunde, O. (2022). Neopatrimonialism and Democratic Consolidation in Nigeria. *E-International Relations*. 1(1), 1–6.

Ozoemena, A.M., & Evangeline, D.E. (2019). Electoral Frauds and Challenges of Good Governance in Nigeria. *International Journal of Contemporary Applied Research*. 6(11), 15–27.

Page, M.T. (2018). *New Taxonomy for Corruption in Nigeria*. Washington, USA: Carnegie Endowment for International Peace.

Pasarelli, G. (2020). *Preferential Voting Systems: Influence on Intra-Party Competition and Voting Behaviour*. New York: Palgrave Macmillan.

Pastine, I., Pastine, T., & Humberstone, T. (2017). *Introducing Game Theory: A Graphic Guide*. London: Icon Books Ltd.

Payton, T. (2020). *Manipulated: Inside the Cyberwar to Hijack Elections and Distort the Truth*. Lanham: Rowman & Littlefield.

Pettitt, R.T. (2020). *Recruiting and Retaining Party Activists: Political Management at the Grassroots*. New York: Palgrave Macmillan.

Philip, M. (2015). The definition of political corruption. In Heywood, P.M. (Ed.), *Routledge Handbook on Political Corruption*, 17–29. London: Routledge, Taylor & Francis.

Piccio, D.R., & Ohman, M. (2014). "Regional Studies on Political Finance: Regulatory Framework and Political Realities, Northern, Western and Southern Europe". In Falguera, E., Samuel, J., & Ohman, M. (Eds.), *Funding of Political Parties and Election Campaign: A Handbook of Political Finance*, 179–208. Stockholm, Sweden: International Institute for Democracy and Electoral Assistance.

Piccio, D.R., & Van Biezen, I. (2018). Political Finance and the Cartel Party Thesis. In Mendilow, J & Phelippeau, E. (Eds.), *Political Party Funding*, pp. 68–83. Cheltelham: Edward Elgar Publishing Limited.

Pierce, S. (2016). *Moral Economies of Corruption: State Formation and Political Culture in Nigeria*. Manchester: Duke University Press Books.

Pincione, G., & Teson, F.R. (2006). *Rational Choice and Democratic Deliberation: A Theory of Discourse Failure*. New York: Cambridge University Press.

Plato (2005). *Republic*. New York: Cambridge University Press.

Policy and Legal Advocacy Centre. (2019). *Laws Governing Elections in Nigeria*. Abuja: PLAC.

Post, K.W.J., & Jenkins, G.D. (1973). *The Price of Liberty: Personality and Politics in Colonial Nigeria*. Cambridge: Cambridge University Press.

Power, S. (2018). *Party Funding and Corruption in Great Britain and Denmark: Contexts and Considerations*. Presented at the 12th Annual California Graduate Student Conference, UC Irvine.

Prabhu, N. (2020). *Middle Class, Media and Modi: The Making of a New Electoral Politics*. London: Sage.

Prisner, E. (2014). *Game Theory Through Examples*. Massachusetts, USA: The Mathematical Association of America.

Przeworski, A. (2018). *Why Bother with Elections?* Cambridge: Polity Press.

Randall, V. (2006). "Political Parties and Social Structure in the Developing World". In Katz, R.S., & Crotty, W. (Eds.), *Handbook of Party Politics,* pp. 387–395. London: Sage.

Reed, Q., Jouan-Stonestreet, B., Devrim, D., Zew, T.K., Kubekova, B., Blomeyer, R., & Zew, F.H. (2021). *Financing of Political Structures in EU Member States*. Brussels: European Parliament.

Rhode, C. (2017). *An OECD Framework for Financing Democracy*. Ifo DICE Report 2 / 2017 June Volume 15. IFO Institute.

Ribadu, M. (2013). *Corruption and National Development in Nigeria*. National Conference. Lecture delivered on 24th June 2014 in International Conference Centre Abuja.

Richard, K.S., & Peter, M. (2018). *Democracy and the Cartelisation of Political Parties*. New York: Oxford University Press.

Richey, S., & Taylor, J.B. (2021). *Political Advocacy and American Politics Why People Fight: so often about Politics*. London: Routledge, Taylor & Francis.

Roberts, H. (2023). "Election Observation: Using Law and International Standards-A Practitioner's Perspective". In Schultz, D., & Toplak, J. (Eds.), *Routledge Handbook of Election Law*, pp. 124–136. London: Routledge, Taylor & Francis.

Rodney, W. (1972). *How Europe Underdeveloped Africa*. London: Panaf Books.

Roniger, L. (2004). Political Clientelism, Democracy, and Market Economy. *Comparative Politics*. 36(3), 353–375.

Rosanvallon, P. (2018). *Good Government: Democracy Beyond Elections*. Cambridge: Harvard University Press.

Rose, R., & Peiffer, C. (2018). *Bad Governance and Corruption*. Geneva: Springer.

Rose-Ackerman, S. (1999). Political Corruption and Democracy. *Quarterly Journal of Economics*. 1(114), 707–738.

Rose-Ackerman, S. (2013). *Corruption: A Study in Political Economy*. Amsterdam: Elsevier Science.

Rose-Ackerman, S., & Palifka, B.J. (2016). *Corruption and Government: Causes, Consequences, and Reform*. New York: Cambridge University Press.

Rotberg, R.I. (2009a). *Corruption, Global Security, and World Order*. Washington: Brookings Institution Press.

Rotberg, R.I. (2009b). "How corruption compromises world peace and stability. Corruption, Global Security, and World Order". In Rotberg, R.I. (Ed.), *Corruption, Global Security and World Order,* pp. 1–28. Cambridge: World Peace Foundation and American Academy of Arts & Sciences.

Rotberg, R.I. (2019). *The Corruption Cure: How Citizens and Leaders can Combat Graft*. Princeton: Princeton University Press.

Rothstein, B. (2011). *The Quality of Government: Corruption, Social Trust, and Inequality in International Perspective*. Chicago: University of Chicago Press.

Rowden, R., & Wang, J. (2020). The Global Crisis of Corruption. *Global Financial Integrity*. Retrieved from https://gfintegrity.org/global-crisis-of-corruption/ on 29th June 2022 at 06:46 pm.

Runciman, D. (2018). *How Democracy Ends*. London: Profile Books.

Rush, M.E. (2023). "Representative Government and Elections". In Schultz, D., & Toplak, J. (Eds.), *Routledge Handbook of Election Law*, pp. 18–31. London: Routledge, Taylor & Francis.

Sagay, I. (2017). Achieving Transparency and Anti-Corruption Initiatives. *Sahara Reporters Online* (16th June, 2017). Speech Delivered at the State House on Conference on The War Against Corruption.

Sakyi, E.K., Agomor, K.S., & Appiah, D. (2015). *Funding Political Parties in Ghana Nature, Challenges and Implications*. International Growth Centre: United Kingdom Agency for International Development.

Salih, M.A.M. (2009). "Introduction". In Salih, M.A.M., & El-Tom, O. (Eds.), *Interpreting Islamic Political Parties*, pp. 1–28. New York: Palgrave Macmillan.

Salih, M.J. (2003). *African Political Parties*. London: Pluto Press.

Sambo, U., Deribe, U., Sule, B., Adamu, U., & Musa, A. (2022). The Implications of Party Leadership Crises on Nigerian Democracy: A Comparative Analysis of the People's Democratic Party (PDP) and All Progressives Congress (APC). *Randwick International of Social Sciences*. 3(3), 513–528.

Sambo, U., & Sule, B. (2021a). Independent National Electoral Commission (INEC) and the Process of Electoral Conduct in Nigeria: The Phenomenon of Election Postponement and its Effects on the Outcome and Performance of the 2019 General Election. *Wilberforce Journal of the Social Sciences (WJSS)*. 6(1), 226–258.

Sambo, U., & Sule, B. (2021b). Strategies of Combating Corruption in Nigeria: the Islamic Perspective. *International Journal of Islamic Khazanah*. 11(1), 12–28.

Samples, J. (2005). "Introduction Taxpayer Financing of Campaign". In Samples, J. (Ed.), *Welfare or Politicians? Taxpayer Financing of Campaigns*, pp. 1–22. Washington: CATO Institute.

Sandri, G., & Seddone, A. (2021). "Intra-Party Selection Methods and Political Elites: New Trends and Consequence". In Sandri, G., & Seddone, A. (Eds.), *New Paths for Selecting Political Elites: Investigating the Impact of Inclusive Candidate and Party Leader Selection Methods*, pp. 1–19. London: Routledge, Taylor & Francis.

Santucci, J., & Ohman, M. (2010). "Practical Solutions for the Disclosure of Campaign and Political Party Finance". In Ohman, M., & Zainulbhai, H. (Eds.), *Political Finance Regulation: The Global Experience*, pp. 25–42. Washington, USA: IFES.

Sartori, G. (1976). *Parties and Party System: A Framework for Analysis*. Cambridge, MA: Harvard University Press,

Sartori, G. (2005). *Parties and Party Systems: A Framework for Analysis*. London, UK: European Consortium for Political Research Press.

Sautter, C. (2019). "US Elections on the Brink". In Nelson, C.J., & Thurber, J.E. (Eds.), *Campaigns and Elections American Style: The Changing Landscape of Political Campaigns*, pp. 136–159. London: Routledge, Taylor & Francis.

Scarrow, H.A. (1980). *Parties, Elections, and Representation in the State of New York*. New York: New York University Press.

Scarrow, S.E. (2006). "The Nineteenth-Century Origins of Modern Political Parties: The Unwanted Emergence of Party Based Politics". In Katz, R.S., & Crotty, W. (Eds.), *Handbook of Party Politics,* pp. 16–24. London: Sage.

Scarrow, S.E., & Webb, P.D. (2017). "Investigating Party Organisations: Resources and Representatives Strategies". In Scarrow, S.E., Webb, P.D., & Poguntke, T. (Eds.), *Organising Political Parties: Representation, Participation and Power*, pp. 1–30. New York: Oxford University Press.

Schaffer, F.C., & Schedler, A. (2005). *What Is Vote Buying? The Limits of the Market Model*. Paper delivered at the conference "Poverty, Democracy, and Clientelism: The Political Economy of Vote Buying," Stanford University, Department of Political Science, Bellagio Centre, Rockefeller Foundation, 28 November – 2 December 2005.

Schnurr, E. (2023). "Role of Money in Campaigns and Elections". In Schultz, D., & Toplak, J. (Eds.), *Routledge Handbook of Election Law*, pp. 147–159. London: Routledge, Taylor & Francis.

Schofield, M., & Callabero, G. (2015). "Introduction". In Schofield, M., & Callabero, G. (Eds.), *The Political Economy of Governance Institutions, Political Performance and Elections*, pp. 1–6. Geneva: Springer.

Schultz, D., & Toplak, J. (2023). "Introduction". In Schultz, D., & Toplak, J. (Eds.), *Routledge Handbook of Election Law*, pp. 1–4. London: Routledge, Taylor & Francis.

Schweizer, P. (2013). *Extortion: How Politicians Extract Your Money, Buy Votes, and Line their Own Pockets*. Boston: Houghton Mifflin Harcourt.

Schweizer, P. (2018). *Secret Empires: How the American Political Class Hides Corruption and Enriches Family and Friends*. New York: Harper Collins.

Schweizer, P. (2020). *Profiles in Corruption: Abuse of Power by America's Progressive Elite*. New York: Harper Collins.

Schwörer, J. (2021). *The Growth of Populism in the Political Mainstream: The Contagion Effect of Populist Messages on Mainstream Parties' Communication*. Geneva: Springer.

Scott, J. (2006). "Social Research and Documentary Sources". In Scott, J. (Ed.), *Documentary Research*, Vol. 1, pp. 23–79. London: Sage Publication.

Sedziaka, A., & Rose, R. (2015). "Do Contentious Elections Catalyse Mass Protests?" In Norris, P., Frank, R.W., & Coma, F.M.I. (Eds.), *Contentious Elections: From Ballots to Barricades,* pp. 45–63. London: Routledge, Taylor & Francis.

Sharan, M.P. (2009). *Qualitative Research Method*. San Francisco: John Wiley & Sons.

Shaw, C. (2018). *The Campaign Manager: Running and Winning Local Elections*. London: Routledge, Taylor & Francis.

Shehu, A.Y. (2004). Combating corruption in Nigeria—bliss or bluster? *Journal of Financial Crime*. 12(1), 69–87.

Shenga, C., & Pereira, C. (2019). The Effects of Electoral Violence on Electoral Participation in Africa. *Cadernos de Estudos Africanos*. 10(1), 145–165.

Shugart, M.S., & Taagepera, R. (2018). "Electoral Systems Effects on Party Systems". In Herron, E.S., Pekkanen, R.J., & Shugart, M.S. (Eds.), *The Oxford Handbook of Electoral Systems*, pp. 491–512. New York: Oxford University Press.

Siaroff, A. (2000). Women's Representation in Legislatures and Cabinets in Industrial Societies. *International Political Science Review*. 21(2), 197–215.

Sigman, R. (2015). *Which Jobs for Which Boys? Party Financing, Patronage and State Capacity in African Democracy*. Dissertations-ALL. Paper 325.

Sigman, R., & Lindberg, S.I. (2020). "Neopatrimonialism and Democracy". In Lynch, G., & Von Doepp, P. (Eds.), *Routledge Handbook of Democratisation in Africa*, pp. 17–37. London: Routledge, Taylor & Francis.

Silas, A.S. (2013). Political Clientelism and the Independence of Political Office Holders in Nigeria and National Development. *Humanities and Social Sciences Review*. 2(2), 425–441.

Simons, H. (2014). "Case Study Research: In-depth Understanding in Context". In Leavy, P. (Ed.), *The Oxford Handbook of Qualitative Research*, pp. 455–470. New York: Oxford University Press.

Singh, S.P. (2021). *Beyond Turnout: How Compulsory Voting Shapes Citizens and Political Parties*. New York: Oxford University Press.

Sinno, A.H., & Khanani, A. (2009). "Of Opportunities and Organization: When Do Islamist Parties Choose to Compete Electorally? In Salih, M.A.M., & El-Tom,

O. (Eds.), *Interpreting Islamic Political Parties*, pp. 29–50. New York: Palgrave Macmillan.

Siollun, M. (2021). *What Britain Did to Nigeria: A Brief History of Conquest and Rule*. London: Hurst Publisher.

Smah, S.O. (2008) "Money Politics and Electoral Violence Nigeria". In Adetula, V.O.A. (Ed), *Money and Politics in Nigeria,* pp. 65–84. Abuja: DFID.

Smilow, D. (2014). "Regional Studies on Political Finance: Regulatory Framework and Political Realities, Eastern, Central and Southeastern Europe". In Falguera, E., Samuel, J., & Ohman, M. (Eds.), *Funding of Political Parties and Election Campaign: A Handbook of Political Finance*, pp. 82–123. Stockholm, Sweden: International Institute for Democracy and Electoral Assistance.

Smith, A.F. (2020). *Political Party Membership in New Democracies: Electoral Rules in Central and East Europe*. New York: Palgrave Macmillan.

Smith, D.J. (1961). *A Culture of Corruption: Everyday Deception and Popular Discontent in Nigeria*. Princeton: Princeton University Press.

Smith, D.J. (2014). Corruption complaints, inequality and ethnic grievances in post-Biafra Nigeria. *Third World Quarterly*, 35(5), 787–802.

Smith, D.M. (2018). "Electoral Systems and Voter Turnout". In Herron, E.S., Pekkanen, R.J., & Shugart, M.S. (Eds.), *The Oxford Handbook of Electoral Systems*, pp. 193–212. New York: Oxford University Press.

Smith, J.F.H. (2021). *Minority Party Misery: Political Powerlessness and Electoral Disengagement*. Ann Arbour: University of Michigan Press.

Smith, S.B. (2015). *Chance, Strategy, and Choice: An Introduction to the Mathematics of Games and Elections*. New York: Cambridge University Press.

Spengler, O. (2016). *Decline of the West: Volume I&II*. London: Random Shack.

Standing, G. (2016). *The Corruption of Capitalism: Why Rentiers Thrive and Work Does Not Pay*. London: Biteback Publishing.

Statista (2022). *Nigeria: Country Outlook*. Accessed June 03, 2021 from https://www .statista.com/outlook/co/economy/nigeria at 11:48 pm.

Stefes, C.H. (2006). *Understanding Post-Soviet Transitions Corruption, Collusion and Clientelism*. New York: Palgrave Macmillan.

Stocks, S.C. (2013). "Political Clientelism". In Goodin, R.E. (Ed.), *The Oxford Handbook of Political Science,* pp. 1–27. New York: Oxford University Press.

Stocks, S.C., Dunning, T., Nazareno, M., & Brusco, V. (2013). *Brokers, Voters and Clientelism: the Puzzle of Distributive Politics*. New York: Cambridge University Press.

Stonestreet, B.J. (2023). "Political Finance". In Schultz, D., & Toplak, J. (Eds.), *Routledge Handbook of Election Law*, pp. 160–173. London: Routledge, Taylor & Francis.

Sule, B. (2018). *Political Party Financing and Election Reformations in Nigeria's 2015 General Election: Issues and Impacts*. A Thesis Submitted to Ghazali Shafie Graduate School of Government, in Fulfillment of the Requirement for the Degree of Doctor of Philosophy Universiti Utara Malaysia.

Sule, B. (2019a). "Money Politics and Party Primaries in Nigeria's Preparation for the 2019 General Election: the All Progressives Congress (APC) and Peoples

Democratic Party (PDP) in Focus". 7ᵗʰ Annual International Conference on Social Injustice. Sociology and Criminal Justice Department, Virginia State University.

Sule, B. (2019b). The 2019 Presidential Election in Nigeria: An Analysis of the Voting Pattern, Issues and Impact. *Geografia: Malaysian Journal of Society and Space.* 15(2), 129–140.

Sule, B. (2020). Multiplicity of Political Parties and Its Implications on the Conduct of the 2019 General Election and Parties' Performance. *Studies in Politics and Society.* 9(1), 386–404.

Sule, B. (2021). How Accountable and Transparent is the African Democracy: Reviewing Political Party Financing and Regulations. *African Social Science and Humanities Journal (ASSHJ).* 2(3), 168–184.

Sule, B. (2022). Effects of Money Politics on Party Primaries in Nigerian 2019 General Election: Reflections on All Progressives Congress (APC) and People's Democratic Party (PDP). *POLITICON: Jurnal Ilmu Politik.* 4(20), 261–293.

Sule, B., Azizuddin, M.S.M., & Mat, B. (2017a). Political Party Financing and Corruption in Nigeria's Fourth Republic: The Case of 2015 General Election. *Arts and Social Sciences Journal.* 8(4), 2–8.

Sule, B., Azizuddin, M.S.M, & Mat, B. (2017b). "Independent National Electoral Commission (INEC) and Campaign Financing Monitoring in Nigeria: The 2015 General Election". *Journal of International Studies.* 13(1), 15–31.

Sule, B., Azizuddin, M.S.M., & Mat, B. (2017c). Political Behaviour and Voting Pattern in Nigeria's Fourth Republic: The Case of 2015 Presidential Election in *Asia Pacific Journal of Education Arts and Sciences.* 4(4), 1–13.

Sule, B., Azizuddin, M.S.M., & Mat, B. (2018a). Corruption and Electoral Process in Nigeria: Examining the 2015 General Elections. *Journal of Techno-Social.* 10(1), 1–16.

Sule, B., Azizuddin, M.S.M., & Mat, B. (2018b). Opposition Political Parties and Democratic Consolidation in Nigeria: Examining All Progressive Congress (APC) in the 2015 General Elections. *Tamkang Journal of International Affairs.* 21(4), 81–112.

Sule, B., Azizuddin, M.S.M., & Mat, B. (2018c). Godfatherism and Political Party Financing in Nigeria: Analysing the 2015 General Election in *Geografia Malaysian Journal of Space and Society.* 14(1), 1–14.

Sule, B., Azizuddin, M.S.M., & Mat, B. (2018d). Impact of Political Party Financing on Integrity of 2015 General Election in Nigeria. *Tamkang Journal of International Affairs.* 22(2), 165–218.

Sule, B., Wurobokki, H.S., & Sambo, U. (2018e). International Donor Agencies and Electoral Support in Nigeria's Fourth Republic: The Missing Link. *International Journal of Social Science Research Macrothink Institute.* 6(1), 76–92.

Sule, B., Azizuddin, M.S.M., & Mat, B. (2018f). Nigerian 2015 General Election: The Successes, Challenges, and Implications for Future General Elections. *Journal of Social and Political Sciences.* 1(2), 183–204.

Sule, B., Mat, B., Azizuddin, M.S.M., & Ibrahim, S.Y. (2019a). Sources of Political Parties' Campaign Expenditure in Nigeria's Fourth Republic: Examining the 2015 General Election. *International Area Studies Review.* 22(4), 369–389.

Sule, B., Adamu, U., & Sambo, U. (2019b). The 2019 General Election in Nigeria: Examining the Issues, Challenges, Successes and Lessons for Future General Elections. *International Journal of Social Sciences Perspectives.* 6(2), 100–113.

Sule, B., & Sambo, U. (2020). Dubai Properties: An Oasis for Nigeria's Corrupt Elite: A Review. *United International Journal for Research & Technology.* 2(2), 55–58.

Sule, B., & Sambo, U. (2021a). The 2019 General Election and the Transparency Question in Nigeria: Political Party Financing As the Bane of Youth Participation. *Britain International of Humanities and Social Sciences.* 3(1), 37–49.

Sule, B., & Sambo, U. (2021b). Strategies of Combating Corruption in Nigeria. *International Journal of Islamic Khazanah (IJIK).* 11(1), 12–28.

Sule, B., Sambo, U., Ahmed, A., & Yusuf, M. (2021a). Nigerian Civil Society Situation Room (NCSSR) and Electioneering Process in Nigeria (2015–2019). *Sage Open.* April-June 2021, 1–15. doi: 10.1177/215824402110067.

Sule, B., Sambo, U., & Saragih, Y. (2021b). The 2019 General Election and the Transparency Question in Nigeria: Political Party Financing as the Bane of Youth Participation. *Britain International of Humanities and Social Sciences Journal.* 3(1), 37–49.

Sule, B., Sambo, U., Mat, B., Azizuddin, M.S.M., & Yahaya, M.A. (2022): Issues and Regulations in Party Financing and Electoral Expenses in Nigeria (1999–2020), *Journal of Contemporary African Studies.* 40(2), 253–269.

Sule, B., & Yahaya, M.A. (2018a). The Politics of Decamping and the Future of Democracy in Nigeria. *Proceedings of International Conference on Poverty and Sustainable Society (ICOPSS'18),* pp. 220–232. University Malaysia Kelantan.

Sule, B., & Yahaya, M.A. (2018b). Internal Democracy and Nigerian Political Parties: the Case of All Progressives Congress (APC). *Qualitative and Quantitative Research Review.* 4(1), 113–142.

Sule-Kano, A. (2020). "African Political Economy and Its Transformation into Capitalism". In Oloruntoba, S.O., & Falola, T. (Eds.), *The Palgrave Handbook of African Political Economy,* pp. 83 92. New York: Palgrave Macmillan.

Szakonyi, D. (2020). *Politics for Profit Business, Elections, and Policymaking in Russia.* New York: Cambridge University Press.

Szwarcberg, M. (2015). *Mobilizing Poor Voters: Machine Politics, Clientelism, and Social Networks in Argentina.* New York: Cambridge University Press.

Tar, U.A., & Zak-William, A.B. (2007). Nigeria: Contested Elections and an Unstable Democracy. *Review of African Political Economy.* 34(113), 540–548.

Teets, J.C., & Chenoweth, E. (2009). To Bribe or to Bomb: Do Corruption and Terrorism Go Together? In Rotberg, R.I. (Ed.), *Corruption, Global Security and World Order,* pp. 167–193. Cambridge: World Peace Foundation and American Academy of Arts & Sciences.

Themner, A. (2017). "Introduction: Warlord Democrats: Wartime Investments, Democratic Returns?" In Themner, A. (Ed.), *Warlord democrats in Africa Ex-military Leaders and Electoral Politics,* pp. 11–57. London: Zed Books.

Thurston, A. (2018). The Politics of Technocracy in Fourth Republic Nigeria. *African Studies Review.* 61(1), 215–238.

Timmerman, K.R. (2020). *The Election Heist.* New York: Post Hill Press.

Tomsa, D., & Ufen, A. (2013). "Introduction: Political Parties and Clientelism in Southeast Asia". In Tomsa, D., & Ufen, A. (Eds.), *Party Politics in Southeast Asia: Clientelism and Electoral Competition in Indonesia, Thailand and Philippines*, pp. 1–19. New York: Routledge, Taylor & Francis.

Torres-Van Antwerp, A.C. (2022). *Legacies of Repression in Egypt and Tunisia: Authoritarianism, Political Mobilization, and Founding Elections.* New York: Cambridge University Press.

Transparency International. (2020). *Exporting Corruption Progress Report 2020: Assessing Enforcement of the OECD Anti-Bribery Convention.* Washington: Transparency International.

Transparency International. (2022). *Corruption Perception Index. Transparency.* Retrieved from https://www.transparency.org/en/cpi/2022 on 29th June 2022 at 06:05 pm.

Uberoi, E. (2016). *Political Party Funding: Sources and Regulations.* London, UK: House of Common Library. Briefing Paper: Number 7137, 8 January 2016.

Ufen, A. (2014). "Asia". In Falguera, E., Jones, S., & Ohman, M. (Eds.), *Funding of Political Parties and Election Campaign: A Handbook of Political Finance*, pp. 83–127. Stockholm: International IDEA.

Umbhauer, G. (2016). *Game Theory and Exercises.* London: Routledge, Taylor & Francis.

United Nations (2022). *Global Impact of War in Ukraine on Food, Energy and Finance Systems.* Washington: The United Nations.

United Nations Office on Drugs and Crimes (2019). *Expert Group Meeting Transparency in Political Finance 21 May 2019, Prague, Czechia REPORT.* Prague: UNODC.

United States Agency for International Development (2005). *Enforcing Political Finance Laws Training Handbook.* Washington: USAID.

United States Institute of Peace (2019). *Exploring Nigeria's Democracy in the "4th Republic" Movie Screening: New Film Looks at the Reality of Nigeria's Elections.* Washington: USIP.

US Factsheet (2015). *Nigeria Elections Factsheet.* Abuja: USAID.

US International Centre for Electoral Support (2018). *Preventing Election Violence in Nigeria 2018.* Retrieved from https://www. US+International+Centre+for+Electoral+Support+%282018%29+Preventing+Election+Violence+in+Nigeria+2018 on 25th June, 2022 at 03:47 pm.

Uslaner, E.M. (2017). *The Historical Roots of Corruption: Mass Education, Economic Inequality, and State Capacity.* New York: Cambridge University Press.

Usuanlele, U., & Ibhawoh, B. (2017). *Minority Rights and the National Question in Nigeria.* New York: Palgrave Macmillan.

Van Biezen, I. (2003). *Financing Political Parties and Election Campaigns Guidelines.* Germany: Council of Europe Publishing.

Van Biezen, I., Bertoa, F.C., Genckaya, O.F., Jouan-Stonestreet, S., Katz, R., Kelin, L., & Thomas, A. (2017). *Opinion on Laws Regulating the Funding of Political Parties in Spain.* Spain: OSCE Office for Democratic Institutions and Human Rights.

Varrella, S. (2021). *Prevalence of Vote Buying in Nigeria in 2019, by Gender and Area*. Statista. Retrieved from https://www.statista.com/statistics/1198751/prevalence-of-electoral-fraud-in-nigeria-by-area/ on 25th June 2022 at 3:55 pm.

Verjee, A., Kwaja, C., & Onubogu, O. (2018). *Nigeria's 2019 Elections: Change, Continuity, and the Risks to Peace*. Washington: United States Institute of Peace.

Wagner, W. (2020). *The Democratic Politics of Military Interventions Political Parties, Contestation, and Decisions to Use Force Abroad*. New York: Oxford University Press.

Wakili, H., Zango, I., & Mohammed, H. (2008). *Research Report on Financing Political Parties in Nigeria, 1999–2007*. Kano: Centre for Democratic Research and Training Mambayya House, Bayero University Kano

Walecki, D.M. (2003). *Political Money and Political Corruption: Considerations for Nigeria INEC Civil Society Forum*. Abuja, Nigeria: USAID Publication.

Walecki, J.M., Jeffrey, M., & Carlson, G. (2006). *Money in Politics Handbook: A guide to Increasing Transparency in Emerging Democracy*. Washington: USAID Publication.

Walecki, M. (2010). "Practical Solutions for Spending Limits". In Ohman, M., & Zainulbhai, H. (Eds.), *Political Finance Regulation: The Global Experience*, pp. 43–54. Washington, USA: IFES.

Walecki, M. (2015). Public Funding in Established and Transitional Democracies. In Walecki, M., Casas-Zamora, K., Genckaya, O., Ammar, D., Sarkis-Hanna, C., Ekmekji-Boladian, K. & Elobaid, E.A. (Eds.), *Public Funding Solutions for Political Parties in Muslim Majority Parties,* pp. 25–38. Washington: International Foundation for Electoral System.

Walecki, M. (2017). *Political Parties and Political Corruption*. Stockholm: Organisation for Cooperation in Europe.

Walecki, M.C. (2008). "Political Money and Corruption: Limiting Corruption in Political Finance". In Adetula, V.O.A. (Ed), *Money and Politics in Nigeria,* pp. 1–12. Abuja. DFID.

Wallis, W.D. (2014). *The Mathematics of Elections and Voting*. Geneva: Springer.

Walter, A.S. (2021). "Introduction: the Study of Political Incivility and its Challenges". In Walter, A.S. (Ed.), *Political Incivility in the Parliamentary, Electoral and Media Arena: Crossing Boundaries*, pp. 1–16. London: Routledge, Taylor & Francis.

Wang, G. (2014). *Tamed Village: "Democracy" Elections, Governance and Clientelism in a Contemporary Chinese Village*. Geneva: Springer.

Watson, J. (2013). *Strategy: An Introduction to Game Theory*. New York: WW Norton & Company.

Waxman, W., & McCullough, A. (2022). *The Democracy Manifesto: A Dialogue on Why Elections Need to be Replaced with Sortition*. Lanham: Lexington Books.

Webb, P. & White, S. (2007) Party Politics in New Democracies. In Webb, P & White, S. (Eds.), *Conceptualising the Institutionalisation and Performance of Political Parties in New Democracies*, pp. 1–11. London: Oxford University Press.

Weirich, P. (2021). *Rational Choice Using Imprecise Probabilities and Utilities*. New York: Cambridge University Press.

White, J.K. (2006). "What is a Political Party?" In Katz, R.S., & Crotty, W. (Eds.), *Handbook of Party Politics,* pp. 5–15. London: Sage.

Williams, R. (2000). "Aspects of Party Finance and Political Corruption". In William, R. (Ed.), *Party Finance and Political Corruption*, pp. 1–14. New York: Palgrave Macmillan.

Wiltse, D.L. (2019). Typologies of Party Finance Systems: A Comparative Study of How Countries Regulate Party Finance and Their Institutional Foundations. *Election Law Journal.* 1(1), 1–19.

Wolinetz, S. (2006). "Party Systems and Party Systems Types". In Katz, R.S., & Crotty, W. (Eds.), *Handbook of Party Politics,* pp. 51–62. London: Sage.

Woolley, S.C., & Howard, P.N. (2018). *Computational Propaganda: Political Parties, Politicians and Political Manipulation on Social Media.* New York: Oxford University Press.

World Bank. (2020). *The Fight Against Corruption: Taming Tigers and Swatting Flies.* Washington: The World Bank Group.

World Poverty Clock (2020). *The Percentage of Nigerians Living in Extreme Poverty Could Increase by 2030.* Retrieved from https://worldpoverty.io/blog/index.php?r =12 on 29th June 2022 at 02:24 am.

Wulff, D.A. (2017). *Legal Framework for Political Parties in Selected Countries of Sub-Saharan Africa.* Nairobi: Konrad-Adenauer-Stiftung.

Yadav, V. (2011). *Political Parties, Business Groups, and Corruption in Developing Countries.* New York: Oxford University Press.

Yadav, V., & Mukherjee, B. (2016). *The Politics of Corruption in Dictatorships.* New York: Cambridge University Press

Yagboyaju, D.A., & Simbine, A.T. (2020). Politics, Political Parties, and the Party System in Nigeria: Whose Interest? *International Letters of Social and Humanistic Sciences.* 89(1), 33–50.

Yahaya, M.A., Sule, B., Sambo, U., Tal, M.K., & Muhammad, M.I. (2021). The Paradox of Deprivation in Affluence: the Technique of Profiling Nigerian Poverty (1999–2017). *Journal of Development Economics and Finance.* 2(2), 355–385.

Yin, R.K. (2018). *Case Study Research and Applications: Design and Methods.* London: Sage.

Yli-Viikari, T., & Krokfors, K. (2018). *National Audit Office's Report on the Monitoring of the Funding of Political Parties in 2017.* Helsinki: National Audit Office of Finland.

Ziblatt, D. (2017). *Conservative Party and the Birth of Democracy.* New York: Cambridge University Press.

Zinn, D.L. (2019). *Raccomandazione: Clientelism and Connections in Italy.* New York: Berghahn.

Zovighian, D.M.A. (2018). *Clientelism and Party Politics: Evidence from Nigeria.* A Dissertation submitted to the Faculty of the Graduate School of Arts and Sciences of Georgetown University in partial fulfillment of the requirements for the degree of Doctor of Philosophy in Government.

Zulianello, M. (2019). *Anti-Systems Parties: From Parliamentary Breakthrough to Government.* New York: Routledge, Taylor & Francis.

Index

About the Author

Babayo Sule (PhD) is senior lecturer in the Department of Political Science, Federal University of Kashere, Gombe State, Nigeria. He obtained a Bachelor of Science in Political Science from the University of Maiduguri, Nigeria, Masters of Science in Political Science from Bayero University Kano, Nigeria, and a Doctor of Philosophy in Political Science from Universiti Utara Malaysia. He has interest in research in election and political parties, security, corruption and African politics. He has published numerous research articles in local and international journals and he has attended several local and international conferences. He has supervised numerous undergraduate and postgraduate theses. Currently, he is engaged in teaching of undergraduates and postgraduates, research and community services.